THE BLOB THAT ATE OAXACA & OTHER TRAVEL TALES

BY
CARLOS A. AMANTEA

Mho & Mho Works 1992 San Diego, California

This book is published by Mho & Mho Works.
Manufactured in the United States of America

Most of these essays first appeared in *The Fessenden Review*. Sections of "The Blob That Ate Oaxaca" also appeared in *Margin, The Sun*, the *Washington Post*, the *90's Newsletter*, and *Mainstream*.

For a complete catalog of other books offered by Mho & Mho Works send a stupid, undressed elephant to *Mho & Mho Works, Post Office Box 33135, San Diego, California 92103.*

Library of Congress Cataloging-in-Publication Data

Amantea, Carlos.
The blob that ate Oaxaca & other travel tales / by Carlos A. Amantea
p. cm.

ISBN 0-917320-32-8 (softcover): $12.95
1. Amantea, Carlos—Journeys. 2. Voyages and travels—1991 _
I. Title. II. Title: Blob that ate Oaxaca and other travel tales.
G465.A49 1992
910.4—dc20 91-19828
CIP

1 2 3 4 5 6 7 8 9 10 J Q K A

TABLE OF CONTENTS

THE BLOB THAT ATE OAXACA & OTHER TRAVEL TALES

What gives value to travel is fear. It is the fact that, at a certain moment, when we are so far from our own country we are seized by a vague fear, and an instinctive desire to go back to the protection of old habits. This is the most obvious benefit of travel. At that moment we are feverish but also porous, so that the slightest touch makes us quiver to the depths of our being. We come across a cascade of light, and there is eternity. This is why we should not say that we travel for pleasure.

— CAMUS

I SAY IT'S INDIA AND I SAY THE HELL WITH IT

DECEMBER 6, 1984 [CALIFORNIA]

It all begins when I call the Indian Tourist Bureau in San Francisco, and ask when the South Indian Music Festival is scheduled to start. "There is no music festival in Madras in December," the voice tells me. "How about January?" I ask. "No — the only music festival is in May, a Beethoven festival." I call Adela and ask her what the hell is going on, and she says that it is a perfect introduction to India. She's already bought the tickets to the Carnatic music festival which will start on the 10th of December. "You never know in India," she says: "You can never be sure what the truth is." She and her husband Alexander Nevski will meet me in Singapore.

DECEMBER 7 [EN ROUTE]

As we fly over the clouds, I catch myself thinking how they resemble the human brain. Are we not flying over the brain of the earth? And is it not true that the sun is alive — a living creature flinging itself (burning with life) through the sky each day, over our naked earth-brain. Isn't the sun a living distant cousin of ours, thinking, seeing, talking — but in a language we don't understand, with words we have to feel rather than hear: a live entity, with which we haven't had the sense or ability to communicate. We should be aiming some strong hydrogen-based simple word-thought transmissions at its surface each day, asking for a response. "Hello, come in. Come in, sun. Hello. Can you hear me? *CAN YOU HEAR ME?*" And this eerie answer, in a swirling voice: "Can I hear you? Hell — I *AM* you."

Adela tells me that she doesn't like Singapore. When she and Alex were travelling here a decade ago, they saw a sign in a restaurant that said "People with long hair will be served last." The Singaporeans have the reputation of being the Germans of the Far East. The airport is so slick and efficient we might as well be in Milwaukee.

The ozone of India is creeping into our plans. Our flight, it turns out, either goes to Bombay first, or to Madras, or perhaps both, or perhaps neither. I want to buy rupees so I won't get stranded at the Madras airport — but they cannot be bought or sold outside of India. And the time differential from Singapore is not two hours, nor three — but rather, two-and-a-half.

The Air India flight is something called an "airbus" which means that we sit cheek-by-jowl, in uncomfortable intimacy with strangers. The man next to me is from Bombay, and tells me he's "in oil." Every fifteen minutes, he makes himself what he calls a "dee-jes-TEEF," which is a fresh green betel leaf, smeared with pinkish calcium, sprinkled with betel nuts, and dunked in sweet tobacco. He puts it into his mouth telling me all the while that the tobacco is very bad for him. In our four hour trip, he consumed an even dozen of them, complaining all the while about how they are ruining his health.

There are ragas coming over the airplane music system, and Adela sends me up a note "Via Air Mail" telling me that the passengers all around her are eating these green leaves, smeared with pink stuff and nuts, and tobacco.

We arrive in Madras, and I get helped down a veritable mountain of stairs. We get to customs, and stand around for an hour or so, and then they see my word processor (big, grey, electronic looking) and say "no." Nothing else, just "No." I've dealt with truculent customs before — Moroccan customs, for instance — and know the trick is to just stand there, looking bewildered, saying "Isn't there anything we can do?" Customs man sends for his superior, who sends for his superior. He has an idea: they'll keep my return ticket as hostage, and let me keep the computer (this is to assure them that I will not sell the Kaypro and make an enormous profit on it.) It takes another forty-five minutes to fill out all the forms, the long grey forms, on soft moist paper, each one to be filled out in detail, checked by a superior, signed by all.

By the time we get out of there, it is eleven at night, or six-thirty in the morning (in California — or is it three p.m.?) I get in a taxi that is so tiny that I have to slump down on the seat and put my body at a sixty degree angle, with my head on the driver's shoulder. I am doubled up in the fetal position, and we are on a road with no lights, with trucks, monster trucks, and busses, monster busses, coming straight at us. There are bicycles, and pedestrians, and clouds of dust, and I am about to witness, first-hand, a head-on, between a two hundred passenger bus and an innocent and sweet American and his wretched taxi-driver. My back hurts enough from my stance that I find myself not caring about the head-on, in fact, wishing it would come and relieve me of this accordion syndrome. Bicycles, horns, blinking lights, dust, and me wondering why I came all this distance for this lumbago.

DECEMBER 8 [MADRAS]

I stop up the hotel toilet. The way it gets fixed is this: I tell the maid that it isn't working, and he goes in there and flushes it to see that it's not working, so it overflows. He goes out and in fifteen minutes, a mechanic comes up. He takes the top off the flushbox, flushes the toilet, and it overflows. He goes away with his pliers (that don't work), and sends up the flush man. He flushes the toilet, and it overflows, so he goes away. After another hour, the plunger man comes in, flushes the toilet, and it overflows. The baggage man, and a waiter, come in to supervise, and the plunger man plunges, then talks, then plunges again, then the baggage man tells him he's doing it all wrong, and the plunger man flushes the toilet and it overflows. Then the waiter tells him to try it again, so he flushes it and it overflows and I look through my suitcase for my water-wings. Then Alex comes in, grabs the plunger, gives a couple of swift hard plunges, flushes the toilet and it works. When plunge man, flush man, baggage man and waiter leave, Alex says that they do it all on purpose. "You ask for something, they understand, but they pretend not to. They are just encouraging confusion. They don't want to act," he says.

Later the baggage man comes back and says:

"Are you married?"

"No. I was, but I'm not now."

"You don't have a wife?"

"I did, but I don't now."

"How many children do you have?"

"I have a girl."

"You don't have any boys?"

"No."

He looks sympathetic.

"Do you want to be my friend?"

I roll my eyes.

"Tomorrow, I will bring you my address, so you can come over and meet my family."

[EXEUNT]

I report this conversation to Alex and Adela. Adela says that once in Bombay they left the door open to their hotel room while they were putting in their contact lenses, and some neighbors came in and sat down (on Alex's bed) to watch them. Just sat down to watch them put in their contacts, till finally Alex shooed them out the door. Adela then tells a story about her friend Meg who was supposed to leave on an airplane from Delhi, and there was something wrong with the plane, so Air India stuffed her and her friend in a car with a driver and two shoe salesmen. The driver got lost, the monsoon started, they were out in this road to nowheresville turning to mud, and the rain was so bad the driver couldn't see so he just stopped the car, said he wasn't going to drive any further. So they just sat there, Meg, her friend, and the driver, and a couple of shoe salesmen, in some backwater in India, sat there for two days, looking out the window at the rain. "Can you imagine being in a car, as small as the taxi you came here in, for two days, with three strangers, including a pair of shoe salesmen?" she says.

DECEMBER 10

Adela rang me up this morning, asking me if I could hear the naraswaram music (a naraswaram is a long, double-reeded instrument with a low, piercing sound). I told her that I heard nothing. I advised her that she had died, and gone to Indian Heaven, having bled to death (she's feeling sick today). "It's a divine experience we had planned for you," I tell her: "You will now spend eternity, in a hotel in Madras, listing to nothing but naraswaram music." Music is the reason for our visit. We are here to attend the Carnatic Music Festival which — contrary to the San Francisco Indian Travel Bureau — starts today and runs until January 1. It's the delicate and beautiful South Indian music that brought the three of us 12,000 miles.

Before we set out, we have lunch at the hotel. We order Thali. We get pappadum and chapati — both breads, one crispy, one fried. You dip the chapati into the dahl (mashed lentils) and into the various condiments. There's chutney, and "Water Buffalo" brand yoghurt, and chopped-up vegetables. Then, when you are through with the chapati and pappadum — they bring the rice, dumped into the middle of the platter, eaten with the fingers (right hand only).

Across from us, a family of twelve Indians, solemnly eating Thali. Mother, Father, various Aunts and Uncles and Children. Silently sitting, silently eating — twenty-five hundred years of Indian Patience and Peace before us. The thinness! Some of the aunts and grannies look so thin I think they might blow away in a stray breeze. Their dark skins, their eyes shining, their arms and legs under their saris no bigger than the bones of a wren. Wire-thin bony hands, thin lips, sunken cheeks.

Then, as they eat, the mother starts speaking. She so straight, sitting so straight, speaking with that upper class Indian accent and song, turning English into a lilting song. And her words? Sentences filled with "should" and "ought to" and "must." She is speaking English Nanny Style. That high, sing-song voice of shoulds and oughts.

"What a curse," I think. "For India, for America, for the world. The Queen Victorian Nanny — with all those directives on what people should and shouldn't do, what they should and shouldn't think." The disease of the English Upper Class, transmitted to all the rest of us. Inner Responsibility — the same discipline and must and ought that drove the East India Company for four hundred years, riding atop the 'heathens' as master, as moral arbiter for the world.

The disease: Control, Aplomb, Right-and-Wrong. This Sickness called Should — infecting the straight-from-the-soul Indians, the hearty Africans, the rough-hewn Americans. The Sickness of Should, the Infestation of Ought, the Disease of Must. A curse on the whole world — the "civilizing" of the world, giving ulcers to the passionate, migraines to the romantics, stiff upper lips to the dolts, aching backs to the lusty. The infection that still has us. A system born of Puritan England, germs taken to the far world by carriers called Raffles, and Stanley, and Livingston, Rhodes and Captain Pigot. Emissaries of infection from the hot-house overstuffed living rooms occupied by black-dress, corseted and overstuffed, nostril-flaring women, the ramrod back man. A tightness wrapped like an iron band about the ease of Malaysia, the music of Bermuda, the passion of Nigeria, the gentleness of Madras, the lust of the Americas.

Our driver takes us along the Bay of Bengal, so we can see the beaches, and the wondrous cupolas and Arabic architecture of the old Raj buildings. The streets are filled with barefooted pedestrians, and bicycles, and pedicabs, and three-wheeled passenger scooters, and trucks, busses, and a few cars. There is a sign saying "City Clean Is City Beautiful," in a square filled with cows (and cow-flop). As we reach the city center, there is the press of people dodging the press of wheels. Everyone shows red teeth from the betel nuts. Thin, bony Indians walk past fat cows. Pedicabs — the three-wheeled taxicabs run on foot-power by black, hollow-eyed men and boys — and they seem scarcely able to make the next plunge. Our driver attempts to point out the sights to us as he is aiming, at high speed, directly for some leper to maim even further. "Keeking lerandi," he'll say. "Tuawara mateeri, al roroMONgrow. Karali forteenfg, caTARee," he'll say, trilling his r's in perfect sing-song. Alex claims later to understand him perfectly, but I notice when the driver points to some red-bricked building, with arched doorways of the Arabic Mode, and says "Keering duthari, PEE-lung..." Alex will say "I didn't understand you" or "WHAT?" about fourteen times.

We stop in the midst of a sea of people. I become the center of attention for two or three thousand Madrasians. I pretend to be thinking of something else, anything else except those eyes on me, some two inches away from my averted face. "The Medievalists were right when they believed that love, or hate, or sickness could be conveyed through the eye-beams," I think: "Indian wins the Burning Coals Contest, hands down," I think. A beggar baby, four years old, stands near the window, on the street side, looking at me with his burning grey-fire simmering eyes, burning into my own eyes, piercing the darkness inside of me, a gaze that is no child's gaze, for children, at least children as I know them, look with joy or interest or cheer or curiosity. But there is no mildness in this coalburning look, a fierceness right out of Shiva, asking not "Who are you?" but saying "I know who you are."

Shiva is alive and well on the streets of Madras, in the guise of a four-year-old laughing beggar. Later, as I am talking to Adela about this, I'm looking out the hotel window, and there on the balcony railing is a crow, a big one, with a huge beak and burning black eyes. "I think he came back," I say.

Later, she tells me she had the following dialogue with the chambermaid.

"Married?"

"Yes," she says.

"How long?"

"Fifteen years."

"Any children?"

"No."

"Not even a girl?"

"No."

DECEMBER 20 [MORNING]

Room-service waiter, bringing me thali:

"Do you like India?"

"I love it; that's why I'm here."

"Do you like meat?"

"What?"

"I said: do you like me?"

{PAUSE.} "Why... sure. I like you fine. {PAUSE.} Do you like me?"

"Yes. {PAUSE.} Is there anything else?"

"No. That'll take care of me."

For those of us who are Indian Music nuts, All India Radio Madras has a rich selection of classical music, starting about seven in the morning — with veena, or violin, voice, and tamboora. They go until about ten in the morning, and then abruptly give up and go off the air. Then, at four in the afternoon, they resume until ten or so at night. For all of Madras, there are two radio stations — and for much of the late morning and early afternoon, there are none.

At four this morning, I wake up, as a mosquito, by the name of Sri Baba, dive-bombs my left ear. "Malaria!" I think, and pop out of bed, find my insect repellant, cover up my face, hands, nose, forehead, hair, ears, buttocks, knees and other private parts — and vow to sleep with the porch-door open no more. At seven-thirty, my maid rings the bell and without waiting for a reply, comes in to deliver a cup with two roses and a piece of fern. I am wondering if it is my breakfast — wondering if we are reduced to flower-power food in this strange country.

Adela calls me from their room on the second floor. I was telling her about being woken up by Sri Baba Skeeter, and she said that that was nothing. "Last time we were here, we were staying in the "travelers" hotel. We'd wake up to The Morning Puke, at 5:30," she says.

"The Morning What?" I say, hoping I hadn't heard what I had heard.

"The Morning Puke. It's better than an alarm clock." Since Hindus think that mucus is unclean, they spend the first few minutes of each day expunging the fluids of the nasal passage. In their old hotel in downtown Madras, the walls were very thin, so Alex and Adela would hear the neighbors as if they were sitting on their laps.

"What did you do?" I ask.

"We put our hands over our ears," she says. She tells me to come down to hear the naraswaram playing since it doesn't reach my 10th floor room. I think she's getting delusional, but I get dressed and go down. The music is pouring in from the building next door. Since saliva is unclean, only the lower castes can play the naraswaram, which means the barbers are the only ones allowed to do so. The sun comes in so brightly into the room, and the sounds of the street, and the crows in the trees outside, and these musicians; out the window I can see the green clad yard men sweeping the walkway with a broom with about two bristles, and I know, now, I am in India. Nowhere else would there be this combination of music and vision and light.

The Music Academy, where the bulk of the festival is to be held, is about 100 yards from our hotel. There is only one step down, and so I can come and go as I please in my new Quickie blue-steel colored wheelchair. ("It's the Mercedes 250 SL of wheelchairs," I tell people.) When I go out on Edward Elliot's Road, I am at one with the pedicabs, the tricars, the bicycles, and the water buffalo wagons. I got my "wheels," too and people don't seem to pay attention to bizarre me, 6'4" in my bright new chair. The traffic gets a little thick at the intersection of Mylapore Bazaar Road. I might be an unwilling participant in the first head-on of a Quickie and a Morris Minor cab. The only other dangers to me are the cows and the cow-flop, both of which fill the streets. The cattle are bony and hairless, usually guided along the road by an eighty pound woman with bare feet, sari, and a quick stick on the rump to guide Bossy to the left or to the right, right into me...

[EVENING]

In Buddhism, there is a phrase that one is invited to say over and over again. It is said that if the phrase is repeated, on the inhale and the exhale, for long enough, then one will achieve some sort of mental transformation, a realization. One has just to repeat over and over again:

Who Am I?

That's it. Over and over again...

Who Am I?

With the repetition, maybe 30,000 times, maybe 3,000,000, maybe more — one will, one day, come to the ultimate understanding. All falsity and make-believe will fall away. One will understand, truly, for the first time,

Who I Am!

Who am I? Why have I travelled, 12,000 miles from home, from the environment that makes me comfortable, to be here in this strange environment, with 5,000,000 strangers. How do I dare to presume to come here, and what do I hope to gain?

Our first concert consisted of "Bharathanatyam," classical Indian dance. Music for the nagaswaram (the reed instruments from earlier today) and thavil (drum). The dance, ah, the dance! Srinidhi Rangarajan dancing, the accompaniment of two male vocalists, tabla, violin, flute, mridangam, and finger cymbals. She dances for two hours. Highly stylized, dancing with hands, fingers, arms, body, legs, feet, toes, eyes, head, and mouth. Each stance, held for a split second, is a statue: the thousand sacred statues of India. Her smiles are not for the audience, but part of a highly structured series of kept emotions playing over her face. Her frowns, pouts, her sensual invitation, her depiction of her love for Krishna, her depiction of the passage of time, her triangular stance (feet and knees turned outwards), her movements back and forth, from side to side. And her eyes! From thirty-five feet away, I can see her eyes moving as precisely as her arms and legs and body. She wears a red costume, with trim of silver and black. Eyes are painted scarlet on her palms. She is able to arch her fingers back, beyond a right angle. She moves with the music, the music moves with her, like the sail of a bark. She is at one with the eight musicians. I can't take my eyes off of her.

I also couldn't take my mind off of thoughts of the raj, colonialism. "Backwards," they say of those they have conquered. "Dirty," "The Turd World" (that's the phrase Paul Theroux uses.) And yet while the English were still painting themselves blue, the South Indians were playing music, dancing the dance of artistry like this. While the Americans were busy inventing Stephen Foster and the English Sir Edward Elgar and Michael Tippett and Benjamin Britten — the Indians were perfecting music for mridingam, and tabla, and veena, and shenai — calling it, as it was, art.

While the Indian musicians get such high marks, the Indian audience gets a double zero. During the Bharathanatyam, the audience is moving about, talking to friends, chastising (or feeding) their children, banging through the entryway door, bobbing about in their seats, seeking out friends, walking, constantly, in front of me in my back row seat. The American reverence for classical music is reprehensible; but the opposite — where Indians wander about and gossip and jiggle their babies during the performance — is inexcusable.

Adela says that wherever you go in India, there is always someone, someone. "You can never be alone," she says: "If you fall down, there'll always be someone there to pick you up."

"One time in Calcutta, I was taking a pee, in this large room," she says, "And I looked up, and there, at the top of the wall, through the chicken wire, at the twelve foot level, was a man, watching me. I don't think he was a voyeur; he was just watching me, to be sure that everything was OK. Last night when I was sleeping, I heard the door bang, and I thought it was Alex, but when I called out, I realized it wasn't him. Just some Indian, come in, to watch me sleep. Not to hurt me: just to watch."

DECEMBER 21

"It is said that there are some 300,000,000 Indians who have never heard of the United States of America."

— *I SEEM TO BE A VERB*
BUCKMINSTER FULLER

"The deliberations of OPEC take on the semblance of pettifogging."

— *THE HINDU*

Last night when we were on our way to the Music Academy, I guided the wheelchair over the hump in the road. Alex was supposed to be there behind me, but he wasn't — so I lost balance and went over backwards and bonked the back of my head (on his foot!) I was so pissed, but Alex was so very nervous and apologetic that I couldn't stay mad. "That's all right," I said. "You know the last time I fell over and hit my head, it detached one of my retinas. For a week, there was a black curtain over everything. Don't fret if I can't see the dancer tonight..."

We were talking about words. I told Adela that my friend David can't get over the word "ointment." He thinks it sounds strange and beautiful. Groucho Marx always said that the most beautiful phrase in the English language was "cellar door," and I myself favor the one that Yeats used: "lapis lazuli." Adela likes the word "seersucker," and I told her that in The Hindu this morning they were talking about a flower called "Misskiss."

At the Music Academy last night, shortly into the first selection (vocal, mridingam, tambura, violin), the fan system was turned one. There are some fifty of sixty huge white fans on the walls and ceiling, and as they revved up, I though the whole auditorium would be helicoptered into the stratosphere. The second singer, one Muthu Subramaniam, gesticulates a great deal with his singing, and there was one point where he and the mridingam were in perfect counterpoint with each other, and I was sure that we were all going to just take off into outer space. I wrote in my notebook:

"There are three Americans, dressed in lungis, with leather satchels — out Indianing the Indians. They came to the vocal concert, stayed all of ten minutes before bailing out. Good thing too. If they had stayed longer, they might have heard something they liked."

I myself sat in on four hours of nagaswaram and singing, and an hour of dancing in the evening. Despite my prodigious neckache, I was ravished by the dancer's hands, which moved like butterflies. I know that because earlier in the day, while Adela and I were sitting in the hotel lobby, a black butterfly, with bead-chain of white pearls across the lower wings, drifted in and perched on the ledge of the window overlooking the courtyard. "Where are you, now that we need you, Vladimir Nabokov?" said Adela. Also saw lizard in the courtyard; strictly prehistoric. He chowed down on a dusty brown moth as I watched, and hightailed it out of there (literally — they raise their tails when they make their lizard run) chomping down on those tasty wings, that tasty carapace.

❧ ❧ ❧

Adela and I are talking about why we do the things we do. She claims that "we always respond to anticipated response." That is, we don't react to facts; we react to what we think people's reactions will be. We second-guess; and often, second-guess wrong. I tell her about Alice Miller's theory of our growing up. When we're young, we're just tiny creatures around these monsters with huge haunches and arms and nostrils. These are called parents. In our awe of them, we subvert ourselves: we cancel out our own wants in anticipation of their wants. After all, what is there at that age (and size) but survival? The cutting edge is that when we grow up, we still seek to satisfy these parents that no longer exist — at least, not in the form that we knew them.

"One of the theories is that we either marry our mothers, our fathers, or ourselves," I tell Adela.

"Which did you marry?" she asks.

"I probably married myself," I say. "My wife was so beautiful. I wanted the love and envy of men, men saying 'How did that guy end up with such a beautiful woman?' What a foolish basis for a marriage." For me, it was exactly the wrong way to get me. For her — it was a perpetuation of the agony of being beautiful. "Beautiful men and women are potty anyway," I tell her: "Everyone wants something from them. They are subject to endless projections. Beautiful handsome people become distorted because others are always laying their desires on them. Look at the Kennedys. Have you ever seen a more screwed up family?" Beauty and power: a poisonous combination.

Adela and I always take what others say and turn it around a bit. I do it on her like this:

"You should try some lassi," she says.

"Some what?"

"Some lassi."

"What's that?"

"Yoghurt and water, with a little cube in it."

"A little Cuban in it?" I say, knowing very well that isn't what she said. "Who is it — Fidel Castro? Fulgencio Batista? Do you know I went to school with Fulgencio Batista's son? His name was 'Fulgencio Batista.'" Rather than battle me over this whopper — she changes the subject.

Adela: "Remember that grade school joke?"

Me: "Which one?"

Adela: "The one about the girl with three tits."

Me: "I can't say as I remember it."

Adela: "She had two tits in front, and one behind. She wasn't much to dance with, but she was a great feel."

[LATER]

Adela and Alex and I go next door to the New Woodlands Hotel for some thali, with eggplant curry and sliced up okra and split pea dahl and huge pillows of fried bread, and the thin chappati crunchy bread. Someone in San Diego told me I wouldn't eat well in India — but they must have been looking for Col. Sanders or McDonalds. Alex and Adela and I are members of what she calls "The Clean Plate Club." They eat in the Indian mode — with the right hand. Me — I cheat: I use the tiny spoon they bring for the water-buffalo yoghurt. At the end of the meal, the waiter gives us pan which is the betel nut concoction we saw on the airplane. Alex and I insist on trying it, but we spit it out quickly enough. Faugh! Very bitter. Supposed to be a digestive, but it's more like an emetic.

We go to the big temple in Madras, the one with 800 or so statues of Vishnu on the roof. Of course, one doesn't go to visit temples in India. One tries to visit temples, and spends most of the time fending off beggars. Alex claims that he used to tickle the girl beggars in Delhi, causing Adela to say "Have you tickled a leper today?" We're trying to figure out how to handle them — the stick-and-bones man on foot, pushing the lady in the old railway baggage cart, with her leg and arm stumps wrapped in white cloth. Her eyes have the universal beggar kick-me-if-you-wish-but-spare-me-a-few-piastres look. I keep thinking that because I am a crip they won't bother me — that I have certain brotherhood rights which permit me to pass by. And Alex is so naturally in Outer Space he doesn't even notice them. It's Adela who is the softie, and a good beggar recognizes that in a moment. She claims that they do have an ethic. If you give them something, no matter how small, they'll leave you alone. It's just if you try to ignore them they'll follow you everywhere, even back to your hotel (waking up in the morning, you find them scratching at your window).

As we are driving back, Adela tells me that in India, nothing, absolutely nothing is thrown away. When they'd buy fruit in Calcutta, it would be wrapped in whatever paper they had — school exercise books, newspapers, even in one case, coroner's lab reports from the Calcutta Hospital. "You'd be eating a kumquat, reading, drooling kumquat juice of Mr. Foo-Foo's liver section analysis and brain cell dissection report." I don't pay much attention to her story because I am more intent on trying to help the taxi driver with his navigation. He plays chicken with anything that moves, anything, including, but not limited to, bicycles, pedicabs, pedestrians, children, jitneys, lorries, chickens and at one point, the derrière of a large and bony cow, said orifice of which passes about one inch from my wide-open window.

"Did you see that?" I say indignantly. "That cow just mooned me," I say.

The driver navigates with his horn, in lieu of slowing down, to the point that I take off my glasses and concentrate on fixing the screws in them rather than having any inkling of the vast, overcrowded road flashing by us. "Be still my heart," intones Adela, sotto voce. To distract Alex and Adela, I visit on them my People-Are-All-The-Same Theory. Adela was talking about how there seemed to be an especial malevolence in the people of western Iran, and Eastern Turkey. She claimed that there was a vicious hatred of foreigners (this was in 1973 when they were journeying by Jeep from Yugoslavia to India by way of Iran, Turkey, Afghanistan). I explain that the only reason they, the natives, acted that way, those Iranians and Turks, was because they didn't get enough love as kids, that all the hate and violence in the world comes from someone who didn't get enough of the right kind of love.

"That Turk," I explained: "When he spat on the ground in front of you just saw the reflection of what he didn't get when he was two years old, when he needed love. Maybe their culture says that you have to beat your two-year old child with a stick. You are just the shadow reflection of his parents." Adela said that she would take my theory under advisement, but that she is more inclined to think that Turks are natural born shits, and that it has nothing to do with their mothers.

[EVENING]

Tonight's concert at the Music Academy was the vocalist Sri V. Ramachandran. A star he was, too. He would sing to the violinist, and the violinist would sing, via his strings, back to him. He would sing to Sri Dorai, who was playing the mridingam, and Sri Dorai would return the compliment. Then Sri Swami on the violin would sing to the mridingam. Sri Dorai would sing back to Sri Ramachandran, and the three of them would sing to each other, and to us, their loving audience. I don't think the music ever moved beyond the notes of E, E-flat, F, and F-sharp. And yet out of these few sparse notes, the musicians carried Theme and Variations for Two Hours. I was thinking that when these concerts began, sixty years ago — in 1926 — the English ruled India. And the concert goers of England were going gaga over Frederick Delius, William Walton, Percy Grainger, and Sir Edward Elgar. The BBC would play "English Art Songs" — strictly hot-house stuff — on short wave, and the colonialists would listen, and bethink themselves cultured. They'd eat bad English mutton and blood pudding, cooked indifferently by puzzled Indian cooks at the Racquet Club, complaining all the while about the servants, wondering why their lives were so doltish and dull. While all they had to do — if the spirit and adventure had moved them — was to walk down Poona land, eat some thali at the Shiva Restaurant, and repair two weeks of the year to the Madras Academy of Music for a good dose of Carnatic Music.

I suppose that is why it is so easy to loathe the English. They lived in India as Bumps-on-the-log for some four hundred years — and made only the most cursory attempt to love the musics and foods and language of this most rich and provocative of cultures. They, the raj, lived under their own oppression: the noose of the Anglican Church, the poverty of the Victorian moral system, the desert of English art, and the gross inability to open eyes and ears and hearts to the rich Carnatic culture that could dance circles about those fey, long-suffering, straight-backed English matriarchs. What do the English have to show for four hundred years in East India? A large export trade in Major Grey's chutney.

DECEMBER 22

Adela claims that there are two types of bananas in India.

"What are they," I ask.

"There's the big ones and the little ones. The big ones are great."

"Yes?"

"And the little ones taste like Tampax."

Me: "How do you know?"

Matrimonial Ads in *The Hindu*

Bridegrooms Alliance invited for convent educated graduate girl, home-loving, 23/152, medium built, good looking, wheatish complexioned, vegetarian, Star Pusam, wears spectacles sometimes, of affluent parents, Tirunelveli Saiva Vellala Community. Groom should be strictly from same community, smart, around 27/30, clean habits, post graduate in engineering, medical, C.A., IAS, PHD, well settled in India, but preferably USA/abroad. Reply with horoscope, bio-data, family details at first instance.

Brides Suitable proposals invited from respectable, well to do parents of tall, slim, fair and beautiful Nair girls, minimum graduate, preferably convent educated, age 20-22, by Nair parents well settled at Vijauawada in Industry and Business for their second son, 26 years, tall, 174 cms., well built and handsome, an absolute teetotaller, nonsmoker and having an exemplary character, M.Sc.Tech. First Class, Geo-Scientist, O.N.G.C. at Madras, gazetted Grade A, Rupees 2,600/-plus house rent and car allowance, possessing car. Preferably from Madras settled families. Details with horoscope.

Bride & Grooms Alliance for brother and sister, Tamil Gownder, boy 30, Goodlooking, income 2000 and sister 24, Goodlooking, domestically trained. No dowry. Simple marriage. Mutual preferred. Caste no bar. Reply with full details.

[NOON]

We have a personal ghost we call Fred. He is a sepulchral Indian, middle-aged (if one can tell age here), the usual polyester short-sleeved shirt hanging out over his white dhoti, thick glasses, imperfect hearing.

We call him Fred because the first time I met him at the Music Academy, he pulled out a worn and much looked-at calling card of the noted ethnomusicologist from U.C. Santa Cruz, Fred Leiberman. He had evidently known (or haunted) Leiberman at previous concerts or in previous incarnations.

I made the mistake of telling Fred — Indian Fred, not U.C. Fred — that we were staying at the Hotel Savera next door to the Music Academy. So yesterday, just after waking, as I am starting to get dressed, in my hotel room, in walks Fred. I can't believe this invasion. To get rid of him, I do everything, pushing him away with my hands, waving bye-bye, shouting "Go away" and "Come back later!" but the more I try to get rid of him, the closer he stands, half-bent over, trying to hear me, or understand me, for on top of his other problems — like animal obtuseness — he seems to be a tad bit deaf. So there I am, waving this Indian away from me, and he's standing there bent over, his big ugly hairy grey ear about an inch from my mouth, not being able to near, nor understand, why I am so agitated. Finally, by dint of vigorous shouts, and brusque waving, I get him out the door, which I then lock.

Later, when I tell Alex about this, he seems unperturbed, even when Adela reports that Fred is lurking about the hallway near their room. "Different culture," says Alex, by way of explanation. "They aren't taught any system of privacy," he says.

"Well, how in the hell can I keep the old galoot from coming in my room, without knocking, when I'm not prepared to receive him," I ask Mr. Smarty-Pants.

"I don't know," responds our answer to The Culture Gap. "He may be associated with someone else important. You don't want to insult these people," he says, showing how quickly *he's* been enculturated. I am not so easily taken — especially when it involves strangers in my bedroom at nine in the morning, when I am at my most vulnerable and mussy. "I just don't like it — even if he is a close friend of U.C. Fred. Why don't I send him down to you," I offer. "We'd rather you keep him," Adela says.

An hour later, as we are eating at the New Woodlands, I spy Fred, larking about behind the door to the kitchen. I can see him looking at us through the glass pane, but when I try to point him out to Adela, he's gone. Alex thinks that I am seeing things, but then confesses later that he spotted him over in another part of town. He'd gone over to Transformer Alley to see if he could find an adapter for my word processor. If you want a sari, you go to the part of town where they sell saris; there'll be twenty-five sari shops right next to each other. If you want a harvesting machine, you go to the street where they sell harvesters — there'll be a dozen stores in two blocks. All the transformers in Madras will be sold on Transformer Alley — all you have to do is find it.

Now, Alex walked over there — about four miles. I'd be the last to say that he is hard to follow, even in a city of 5,000,000 people. He's six-foot-four and walks like a tank; no, more like a penguin — his arms fixed at a permanent 160 degree cant on the right, 200 degrees to the left. He bobbles from side to side, as if they had done bone-fusion on the knees. It's all done with a singular, absent-minded determination — plowing over cows, cow shit, pedicabs, and people. It has the élan of the blind and the thought-engrossed.

I am not saying that Alex would be that hard to follow, but it does seem a bit strange that Fred Leiberman manqué should pop up next to him after he reaches Transformer Alley, handing him the wrinkled and grey calling card, bowing over with courtesy, or deafness. Adela and I later claim that Fred is a practitioner of teletransportation, which in this city of a million or so wheeled vehicles is probably the most sensible method of getting about. Fred doesn't look hardy enough to follow Alex over mountains of people and shit for a solid four miles. "He has to be doing a bit of mystical flying about," I tell them. The fact that Fred could find Alex four miles from here makes them ready to believe anything.

Even though I am 12,000 miles from my sweet bed-and-board, I am still given to my morning libation — come hell, high water, and Indian Fred — of hot tea with lots of hot milk. I drink it half-and-half, which scandalizes the cognoscenti but satisfies my palate. The only concession I make to India is that I take also a slice of fresh papaya, with fresh lime juice.

Now you'd think it a simple feat for room service: tea, hot milk, papaya, and lime. The cutting edge is the milk. I always ask for two milks. I always get a thimble-full of milk and a mountain of tea. The tea pots come with magnificent foot-tall red tea-cozies, crowned with the official insignia of the Hotel Savera. But no matter what I say or do, I am left with about two drops of milk. I complain to Alex, and he tells me that when they were here in 1973, they could never get coffee and ice cream served at the same time, which is his particular weakness. He'd order them together, but they'd come apart. If the coffee came first — he'd wait for the ice cream to appear; but by the time it arrived, the coffee would be in terminal chillblains. He'd order the ice cream first — but it would be a puddle by the time the coffee arrived. They'd try having Adela order the coffee, and Alex the ice cream — but it never fooled the kitchen help. One or the other would never come. I said that probably there was some taboo in the Hindu culture against the coffee-bean being consumed in proximity to the vanilla-bean.

❧ ❧ ❧

I listen to all the radio I can get on my Sony. There's not too much. In the morning, I'll listen to classical Indian music on one of the two Madras stations. However, by 8 a.m., one station had gone to wretched Indian movie music, complete with soap commercials, and the other into long readings from Tamil epic poetry which normally I adore, but not in the morning. So I adjourn to the 19 meter band for the BBC news and news background. "This is London," they say, and they give us the best, most unbiased, measured, intelligent news of the world. What a testament to Lord Reith! Elections in Singapore, miners trapped in Utah, bombings on the straits of Hormuz. At four or so in the afternoon, All India Radio comes back on, well rested after their half-day hiatus.

❧ ❧ ❧

Adela and I spend the morning writing post-cards. After coming 12,000 miles, we're damn well going to prove to all our friends that we are here. Some of the cards I write are the wish-you-were-here variety, but I send off to my lawyer the card I have been sending him, with slight variations, for the past twenty years. The rules are simple: the post-card has to have a vulgar picture on it. In Spain, it was quite easy — I'd get one of those 3-D Jesus-On-The-Cross-With-The-Blood-Leaking-Down cards. On the message side I would write in large clear letters (so the mailman, and all his partners, and all the secretaries at the office can read it):

Dear Hunkums:

I miss you so my darling. I think of you every night. How lonely it is without you I'll never forget that wonderful night in Granada and all the things that happened to us it was the prettiest night of my life. The baby is fine but Mother is beginning to ask questions please send the $$$ you promised at once [underlined three times in purple]. I miss you smack-smack-smack [painted red lips here]

Your flower
Snookums.

With great regularity, Lawyer has been getting variorum editions of this message since 1962. I am not about to let him down on this trip. On a card backed with a nice blue-faced representation of Krishna, I write in sober black ink:

My dear Mr. B:

I have been retained by one "Snookums" in what you call in your country a Paternity Suit. She claims that the three children, "Tootsie," "Hunkums," and "Mikey" are, in law and in fact, in loco parentis. You have been adjudged neither guilty nor non-guilty on three counts of perjury, paternity, and praecox, but you are hereby advised to send the $$$ you promised at once.

Sincerely,
Ravi C. Shankar
Barrister for the State of Madras

Mucous is "unclean" in India. Thus The Daily Puke. Indians spend the first few minutes exhuming it from their throats and lungs, getting it onto street and floor. Since spittle is also unclean, only the unclean can play reed musical instruments that involve spittle — like the nagaswaram.

And since spittle is unclean, one is not to lick stamps, at least not in public view, in the Post Office. Stamps are to be stuck on with water and sponge, or with glue. Adela tells me that there is a sign in the Calcutta P.O. absolutely forbidding the licking of stamps under penalty of law. In Madras, when she went to mail off our seventy-five post-cards to the seventy-five friends to let them know we are in India, she has to enlist post office help in sticking the hundred-and-fifty (two on each card) stamps and the other seventy-five "Via Air Mail" stickers. Then, after that, the cards have to be taken to the Cancel Man (on Cancel Alley?) so he can mark them up and make damn sure that they won't get ripped off and reused. This means that Adela spent about an hour inside the P.O. The first assistant tried to bring her dibs and dabs of glue on his fingertips, but then she persuaded him to take her and the cards over to the glue-pot. After they got that done, they had to go down the street to Sri Cancel, and that took another twenty minutes. When they were done, Adela offered him 2 rp., and he told her it was going to be 15 rp. for his assistance. That did it. Adela will put up with poverty and dirt and garishness — but being tampered with by Public Servants? Never. As we were departing, he whined a bit about "baksheesh," but she was adamant. I am surprised he tangled with her. I know Adela is a teddy bear — but when she gets her back up, she's more like a grizzly. "At the end," she said with ill-concealed satisfaction, "even the 2 rp. looked good to him."

DECEMBER 23

At the Theosophical Society a Dutchman we ran into looked like a Dutchman, acted like a Dutchman, even walked like a Dutchman. But when he opened his mouth, he spoke English with a perfect Indian accent — complete with sing-song voice. It was a shock: we associate that accent with the Indian physique; to have it emerging from one who looks so

Northern European jars our particular cliché reality. It put me in mind of a friend of mine who lived in the Rhone Valley shortly after WWII. There was a French woman who had lived with an American soldier for a year, and since he was Black, and from Alabama — when she opened her petite French mouth, her words came out heavy with the accents of the poor black American south. It's the juxtapositions that get one — the shock of the unexpected. Just like Adela says — we are always reacting to anticipated reaction.

When we were telling Alex about this, I said "I couldn't understand a word he was saying." Alex still claims that Indian English is a definite and consistent variation on English English — as regular and ordered as the English spoken in Ireland, or Bermuda, or America.

❧ ❧ ❧

Alex says you have to hear some bad Indian music to know the good. Today, I went to hear J.K. Jesudoss, obviously of the movie-idol school of singers. He had a rich black beard, flashing eyes, a white cotton shirt open half-way down to the navel, a luxuriant growth of black chest hair. It is the custom in Carnatic concerts for friends and devotees of the musicians to sit in the lotus position on the stage while their idol is doing his stuff. Evidently Jesudoss is just such an idol — because the stage was jammed. Every seat in the auditorium was taken. Later Adela said that she thought he was pretty bad. "He hasn't suffered enough," she said. The best part of the concert was the mridingam and ghatam, the latter being a large crockery pot which is played with fingers and heel of hand, just like what we used to call a "bongo" drum.

Adela said she was seated in the very top balcony, next to a very fat woman. Adela is herself built on the order of the Queen Mary. She said: "The two of us make quite a pair, sitting there next to each other, competing for the arm rest. She looks just like an angry mother-in-law, glowering at me, at the audience, at the singers, the ushers. When Alex gets up there with us, it should be quite a team." However, this may never happen. Alex is sick with a cold.

When Alex is sick, he has a style of his own. He either sits slumped over in some tiny chair — with his huge physique perched at such an angle that you know he's miserable, with his six-foot black woolen scarf wrapped about his neck.

This position alternates with the Sepulcher Layabout. Alex lies flat on his back in bed, fully dressed, some frail cover over him, lying like an Egyptian pharaoh, his huge feet sticking straight up out of the covers. He doesn't read, nor listen to the radio, nor watch TV. When you speak to him, he answers in listless monosyllables. He is fully intent (right concentration, in the Indian mode) on Being Sick. He is certainly not intent on overcoming his misfortune, and going out in the world. No. His job is illness, and there shall be no distractions; none at all, for example the many concerts he came so far to see.

Item from *The Hindu* for today:

DISPUTE HOLDS UP BURIAL OF A BODY

From Our Correspondent

Erode, Dec. 27.

A body could not be buried because of a major dispute between non-Harijans and Harijans of Bangalapudur village in Gobichetipalayam taluk on Wednesday.

Subbe Moopan, of Varapalayam, died on Wednesday morning. After religious rites, the body was on its way to the burial ground in the afternoon.

As the road to the burial ground was full of ruts and water was stagnating, it was not possible to carry the body along the road. Hence the mourners wanted to go along a nearby road passing through the Harijans' colony. But the Harijans would not agree. The body was placed on the road bordering the colony. The Harijans offered to carry the body along the usual route but the non-Harijans would not agree to it.

Efforts by Mr. T.K. Subramaniam, DMK candidate contesting the Sathyamangalam Assembly seat and Police and Revenue officials to effect a compromise failed. The body, which remanded on the road for 36 hours until 3 a.m. today, was taken to the Gobichettipalayam Government Hospital and deposited with the mortuary.

The Bangalapudur Police have registered a case against 56 Harijans for rioting and wrongful restraint under Section 147, 148, and 341 IPC.

DECEMBER 25 [MADRAS]

"Have no desire for what thou seest. Desire not, desire not. Desire; desire. Have no desire for desire. Desire and deliverance must be simultaneous. Voidness, voidness. Non-voidness; non-voidness. Non-obscuration; non-obscuration. Obscuration, obscuration. Emptiness of all things; emptiness of all things. Desire above, below, at the center, in all directions, without differentiation.

"When all this had been explained in detail, and the guru had assured Padma that he would realise the essentiality of all doctrines, Padma praised the guru."

— THE TIBETAN BOOK OF THE GREAT LIBERATION

When I come back from the concert of Carnatic music, the untouchable who sweeps the hotel driveway with a broom (made of about three pieces of straw) is commissioned to push my wheelchair and me up the driveway. He is as black a person as I've ever seen. His skin is so black that it's hard to see his eyes, except for the bare edge of the whites. The details of nose or ears or skin are completely blotted out. Unfortunately, his mouth is outlined in white — which may well be the beginnings of leprosy. Ay! His tall thin body in his loosely fitting green uniform tells me he is seventeen or so, but he has the typical Indian young-old face — so it's really impossible to say. I slip him five rupees for pushing me a hundred yards. Alex tells me that's probably a week's salary.

Alex is obviously feeling much better. His sickness seems to have abated, and instead of lying in bed staring at the blotches on the ceiling, he has started reading maps. Maps of India. He comes 12,000 miles to lie in his hotel room in India and look at maps of India.

Adela and I repair to the restaurant at the top of the building for supper. The hotel help are out on the roof next to our window, erecting a papier maché angel with electric lights placed about head and wings. The lights are powered by an evil-looking transformer that sparks and groans each time the lights blink. I say to Adela: "And lo! An angel appeared atop the Hotel Savera, and the many guests were sore afraid." I'm sore afraid for my personal safety as my room lies more or less directly under the buzzing and sparking light machine, and it's eleven floors to the ground, a long way to fly unless you are of the angelic persuasion.

The people here are wonderfully late with their Christmas decorations. It was only on Sunday that they got the tinsel and bells up in the lobby. The hotel management made the mistake of calling Alex and asking him if he would play Santa Claus in the Hotel's Christmas Disco. Little did they know that they were dealing with a dyed-in-the-wool Existentialist in terminal agonies of a rare and mysterious affliction known as Head Cold. He refused to say how he responded to their request.

Alex confided to us yesterday that he thought he had tonsillitis. "Dengue Fever [pronounced 'ding-ey'] too, I suppose," I said. Only those of us who have known Alex for a lifetime know that for him a cold takes the form of a disease that can only be cured by a week in hospice — a month if he's lucky. Extreme unction does not include his playing the role of Kris Kringle. In a few days, he will open the curtains, and will venture out on the streets of Madras once again, commenting often on the miracle of his recovery, the miracle that he did not pass away in the clutches of this rare and exotic disease.

The tea and milk man wished me "a Merry Holiday" this morning. Since our trip here was an attempt to escape the foolishness of a certain American holiday, I might have snarled at him if he did not essay to make my day brighter by bringing lots of hot milk with my tea.

I told Alex and Adela that the Pope gave audience, which was dutifully broadcast by the BBC this morning. In keeping with the good-will and joy of the season, he had announced that all war and poverty were caused by "atheism." I, for one, approved of his safely ignoring 2000 years of simony, Christian-sponsored wars, inquisitions, witch-hunts, torture of "heathens," and death to the children of Islam. "That man gets wiser and more humble as he gets older," I told them.

I thought for a while about salvation. It seems to me that the real salvation of Western Civilization is not in Christianity with its obviously dotty Pope and cursing, snarling Jerry Falwells. Nor is it the attempted superimposition of Eastern religion on the U.S. à la Bhagwan Rajneesh, who said, recently, and rather petulantly, I thought: "Perhaps it would have been better had I never come to the United States" (thus recognizing what we have known for centuries — that is, we have no real religious toleration in America, especially for prophets). Americans love the violent fundamentalists, and honor the biases of the mainstream churches, certainly mock the true revolutionary spirit of religions — but visionaries we detest. We label them as heathen, and through the press, we hound them unmercifully until they say or do something very unholy. Then we can say: "See. I told you they were up to no good. Did you hear that? He said that sex between married couples was all right, if both parties agree. Did you hear that?"

It seems to me that the real salvation of the Western world is not through following the fake godheads, but through psychology and psychoanalysis. What it preaches (tolerance, understanding, non-violence, peace within and without) makes it quite holy. And its prime prophets — Jung, Milton Erickson, Fritz Perls, Harry Stack Sullivan, Virginia Satir, Carl O. Rogers — all bespeak a system which, since it embodies understanding, must therefore encourage tolerance and acceptance. Giving credence to the existence of a devil must, by definition, spawn self-hate. A Big-As-Life Devil, soon enough internalized, must make for paroxysms of battle within, between what is, after all, an imagined good and bad. It is this split, this civil war within, that makes the Fundamentalists so vicious, so quick to pretend away Jesus's own call for peace, love, and toleration.

The psychological school, on the other hand, recognizes that pain is created because we had to survive growing up — no matter the psychic price. The "devil" (hate, anger, rage, self-destruction) is a necessary part of us — not to be assassinated or butchered out of the psyche, but laid to rest by understanding and tolerance of the self.

The thing that saves psychology from attack from the religionists is that it pretends not to be a religion. Thus it can be all the more powerful and subversive, a loving subversive movement.

DECEMBER 26

I listened to Radio Moscow some today, then to an American religious station. The Russians were jamming the religious station. Jesus! What the Kremlin doesn't know is that the American religious broadcasters jam themselves. Listen for three days and one could die of brain-fever. Why they take the trouble to jam International Family Radio is beyond me. The Russians just don't trust their own people, do they? I can't think of anything more noxious than a country that doesn't trust its own citizenry to separate the stupid from the good. By jamming the broadcasts, Moscow is making them more enticing. They are actually giving glamour to those dusty, fusty Bible people droning on about Matthew X, 14:12. They are making it far more important than it is — they are attaching grace to it, by trying to destroy it. I wonder how long it will take Russia to make it into the Twentieth Century.

No matter how we try to avoid it, the radio is filled with Christmas Music. All India Radio gives a stirring performance of "The Twelve Days of Christmas" with the Lawrence Welk Plasma Band. It may be The Day After here — but on the other side of the date line, happy, angelic children are jumping out of bed and racing to the tree and ripping open packages with exclamations of joy and rapture.

Indians don't nod their heads. They don't shake them. They waggle them. When they are wobbling their heads about on their necks, they can either be saying yes or no.

We feel guilty because I only get to one concert in four at the Music Academy which, after all, is ostensibly our reason for being here. But we do get a full dose of Carnatic music on All India Radio Madras — at least for an hour in the morning, and then again in the late afternoon. A majority of Carnatic music, I find, uses the same tonal intervals, theme-and-variation, as "Mammy's Little Baby Loves Shortnin' Bread."

Yesterday, Adela had an attack of what she calls "The Existential Angst." "I didn't even want to go to the Madras Aquarium," she says. Since Adela is a super-active buyer, shopper, walker, investigator, viewer, rider, walker, experiencer (the perfect active fascinated interested tourist, the Renaissance Woman of Tourism) it was very bizarre that she retreated into her hotel room for the day. But then again, I feel the same way today.

I just don't want to deal with India. What I want is out. I hate the hotel, the help that speak such a strange English. I don't like any part of this trip. I think "Why don't I just go out to the Madras Airport and buy a ticket to Singapore. Then I can be done with the crowds, cows, exhaust, men-in-dhotis-hauling-huge-wagons. Who cares about India, anyway?" As I am thinking this in the bathtub, the maid rings the room door-bell about fifteen times, just because he knows I am in the bathtub. "I'll just take off," I think, "send a telegram back to Alex and Adela to bring all my stuff. It's just too much." I get out of the tub, and look at my figure in the mirror, and think "God, look at that." I think about how many exquisite meals and thousands and thousands of bottles of beer it took to get me that physique. I go to the window, somehow get over the guard-rail, and throw myself off the porch, scattering myself all over the screaming tourists at the outdoor cafe below my room. They were just sitting down to a BLT on toast and... wait: no, I mean I look gloomily out at the smog, the street jam-packed with people riding, walking, running, slouching, shuffling — with their bicycles, and cows, and goats, and pedicabs. "If I see one more third eye painted on just one more wrinkled brow," I think, "I'm going to puke, just puke."

❧ ❧ ❧

Later I explain it all to Adela and Alex. "I'm not going through mid-life crises," I tell them. No, I'm going through mid-trip crises. We're at the half-way point of the journey, neither here nor there. And as with all crises, we get the five Kübler-Ross stages: anger, bargaining, depression, denial, and (finally) acceptance.

And I get it — acceptance, that it. I go over to the National Museum — to see endless statues of Krishna, Devi, Mali, Malipuram, et al. It is a museum designed by, of all people, Col. Balfour of Balfour Declaration fame. I see Krishna in a hundred postures, live, fluid, moving, dancing — sculpture with form and motion captured entire. I wonder — yet again — how the Indians were such artisans of form in bronze while the English were still burning peat in their homes and eating rat.

Why do we travel? We travel to stir up the juices. And mine certainly have been stirred on this trip. I couldn't have invented that O-Misery-Why-Aren't-I-Home? anywhere else (certainly not at home!) It comes from being away from one's system. No *Los Angeles Times* in the morning, no morning mail, no writing at the friendly crowded desk, no making supper, sending out letters, laughing with friends, or standing in the courtyard, watching my chickens bicker with each other over a neighboring worm. Nope — stuck in India with Alex's

Head Cold which he was kind enough to pass along to me when he had done with it.

I am making myself live — recharging the batteries that will run me for the next six months.

DECEMBER 27

Adela says the caste system works even in this hotel. She says the people in the kitchen are probably Brahmins — because you cannot eat something prepared by a lower caste. She tells me about our friend Charlie who looked in a hotel kitchen once — and they had to throw out all the food as a result. His shadow fell on (or in) a pot of beans that were cooking on the stove, and since he was unclean, they had to dump it all.

I now have The Deluxe Super Special Gold Star and Brilliantine Alex Head Cold. I am usually so healthy I get the sniffles about once a year, for a day or two, but India has bugs I've yet to meet — they have germs I can only dream about. I wake up at two (and three, and four, and five, and six a.m.) so thirsty that I might as well be a sponge. Nose running, eyes filled up to here. Fortunately, I stole a roll of toilet paper from that wonderful Peninsula Hotel in Hong Kong. If I had to blow my nose on Indian toilet paper, it would sharpen my poor old schnoz to a fine red point.

To comfort me, Adela tells me about the time she and Alex were travelling third class on an Indian train, and she blew her nose on a hanky and then, unthinking, stuffed it back into her purse. "The other passengers were revolted," she tells me, "because mucous is unclean. They were crawling the walls. You can guess what they thought of me." As she is telling me this, she is laughing. Adela has a sonorous set of laughs that play through her mouth, throat, and chest like Bach on the organ at Braunschweig. She starts up here, rolling her eyes, then the laugh descends a roller-coaster down around her diaphragm, pulls it up around her chest for an arpeggio, then reëmerges from her throat for a finale. People meeting her for the first time think of her in terms of the cliché plump and jolly woman, who laughs all the time. But to know her is to know the multifaceted dimensions of one who — like all the rest of us — laughs, but who also, like the rest of us, cries, is sad, wonders what it all means. She is a wonderful travelling companion — and I am lucky to be here with her, especially when I am feeling so bum.

❧ ❧ ❧

Adela says she went to see one of the Tibetan lamas who've settled in the Northwest after he got chased out of Tibet by the Chinese. She said the Chinese invasion — and the resultant diaspora of the lamas — is probably one of the most hopeful things to happen in our century. The resettlement of the holy men from that tiny mountaintop land called Tibet will give the whole world what it needs — a healthy dose of wisdom and spirituality at the time that Western Christianity is turning so cruel and barbaric.

She went to hear one of the speeches of the lama. It was devoted to meditation. "He said it had to do with breathing, and having right thoughts while breathing." Such a simple thing. Who would, for a moment, think that wisdom could come from concentrating on something as simple as breathing. Putting one's full attention on the breath going into the nostrils, and coming out of the nostrils — even while you are walking or doing the dishes or trying to get to sleep.

"He said one thing that stayed with me, about the flow of living. Blink — you're twenty. Blink — you're thirty. Blink — you're forty. Blink — you're fifty. Blink — you're sixty. And soon, you're gone. It happens so quickly."

And it's true. Here I am past the half-century mark — and I still think I am twenty-five. When they ask me what it is like to be fifty, I respond "Delusional." The signals are strange because of what we've experienced. I feel like I am ten sometimes, like when I am watching my chickens pick at the shit in the yard. But then I feel like I am sixty-five when I have something to do that I don't want to do. Most of all, I do not subscribe to the belief that one exists at one age until the birthday, and then one moves on to the next year. That's not how it works. Time runs across us like waves, back and forth, like waves, and we charge backwards and forwards across ages, depending on what we are thinking, on what memories we are collecting, on what our tasks are at the moment, on how we feel, on how we react to our environment. This morning I was old, now I am young, this evening I may be a child, or middle-aged.

And then: Blink — it will be gone.

❧ ❧ ❧

The guy who cleans my room may leave yesterday's *Hindu* on the floor just where I left it because he thinks I want it there; he thinks I left it there for a purpose. I see him as reacting to poverty. It is a huge advantage to work at a hotel where tall Americans hand out five rupee notes as tips — and he doesn't want to do anything wrong, so he does nothing, or very little, and whatever he does, he does wrong. My room looks like a garbage dump. He doesn't want to throw out my apple cores, or the half-filled beer bottles from three days ago which are starting to developing a vegetative life of their own. The only way to create order in this sty is to do it myself or to leave town — which I will do tomorrow.

Leaving tomorrow! Thank the Lord! I know all this will be funny and wonderful a month from now, but right now I want out. So I have fears. I have heard so many Indian bureaucracy terror stories that I figure getting my hostage ticket from customs will turn into a scene from Kafka's *The Castle*. I am sure they will create a scene in which I can't have the ticket because the word processor which I have checked through to Bangkok is no longer with me, and they will claim that I sold it to some Indian Shylock and I'll be left sobbing at the departure gate, waving goodbye to Alex and Adela because Mother Indian just doesn't want to give me up.

The main problem is that I don't speak Tamil, and I can't stand being in a place where I can't talk to the taxi drivers. Or — worse — where the beggars are talking about us and laughing. The Big "P" for tourists — language-barrier paranoia. For instance, when I am walking in the public market in Guadalajara, and some kid says to his friends: "Mira, el viejo con muletas" ("Look at the old man on crutches"), I can turn to him and say: "Tú! No sabes que hay que tener respecto por pobre los turistas?" ("You! Don't you know that you have got to have respect for poor tourists?"), and he cracks up and I smile and I've got a new friend. Here, even when they're supposed to speak English, I'm blessed if I can understand a word. "Ved Mehta said they spoke English at home," says Alex, but Mehta came from an upwardly mobile middle-class Brahmin family — not some poor street-sweeper family in Madras.

We had an exciting outing to Mahabalipuram yesterday. Most exciting. Mahabalipuram has some of the largest outcroppings of shore temples in all of India, created some 1500 years ago, and, according to my guide book (which tends to be somewhat sensational) "they are notable for the delightful freshness of folk-art origins in contrast to the more grandiose monuments left by larger empires... The shore temples in particular strike a very romantic theme with a full range of emotions and are some of the most photographed monuments in India..."

The taxi driver was kind enough to show us a full range of emotions during the forty miles between Mahabalipuram and Madras. He took vehicle and passengers at speeds as near to Mach 1 as possible, which he showed off at close hand to various cows, pedicabs, bikes, trucks, busses, and humans. He did this not only at maximum speed, but at maximum noise level — in other words, he drove with his horn, not his brakes. Each new adventure, each new possible head-on, each new juxtaposition of passengers and wall, tree or truck provoked colorful comments from Adela in the back seat, such as "Thrill-a-minute" and "Alex, would you ask him to stop so I could walk back to Madras," and "I just don't care to be maimed in an Indian hospital." At one point Alex, who seemed to be enjoying the scenery far more than white-knuckled me or blanc-mange-faced Adela, said "O, I think I see a dye factory," and she said "That's spelled D-I-E" and I: "How can you read signs when we've passed the speed of light?"

Adela and I marvelled at the fact that the driver had lived to such a hoary age of twenty-five or so, but then she claimed that he was really twelve and had just aged rapidly through his many experiences on the road. There was one point of delicious contretemps where a bus, a big green bus, a big green tall bus, filled, crammed rally, with some 160 Indian innocents, was coming at us from what appeared to be a speed of between 100 and 200 mph. It was one of those magic moments where time stands still. The bus was flanked by a bevy of pedicabs to port and a big dead tree lying half in the road to starboard. For our part, we had responsibility for a mass of young, virile, certainly not ready-to-die bicyclists on our right, and a monster ox cart — rather a water buffalo cart — to our left, complete with boy in dhoti urging water buffalo along with stick.

Now I did not want to be responsible for that boy being taken early to the grave, nor did I wish to be responsible for his water buffalo's passing (nor, indeed, my own), so when the driver took in the situation and *speeded up*, I did what any sensible and right-thinking responsible American would have done in a similar situation: I bowed my head and closed my eyes. "Mama mia!" said Adela from behind, if not under, my seat. Alex later showed me the smear of water buffalo snot on the taxi's left rear bumper. Adela commented that I looked "quite nice" with my hair sticking out in all directions; she wanted to know the name of my hair-dresser.

It certainly was worth it to visit Mahabalipuram. It is a wonderful little town if you like beggars without arms or legs, or sullen-faced Indian boys with postcards for whom the word "No" means "Could you waggle those cards in front of my eyes some more until I say *'No'* again, and then come closer and do it some more?" Sometimes, from between the hands, heads, cards and stumps, I did get a glance at a carved elephant or a cave, but beggars and sales folks were quick to rectify that wrong by filling the gap with big green coconuts which they offered to decapitate with a particularly evil-looking machete and then would sell to me for a mere arm or a leg (mine, I think, more than their own, the way they were twirling the machetes about.) At the holy site of the Five Rathas, we were further entertained by two dark and surly Tamils along with their various uncles and cousins, fighting over a bus seat, making the universal sign of mayhem and loathing. The screaming and name-calling went on for no more than an hour.

At the shore Temple, I almost got a gander at the stone carvings and a breath of fresh air until they wheeled out the beggar with no legs and arms, riding on the back of his sister. I figured that if I turned away, they might go away, but no: sister and back-pack hove into view again, and yet again, and yet again. It was blackmail (or backmale) pure and simple: "You're a tourist, now let me show you what human misery is really like. I'll do it graphically, close up, so the point won't be lost on you." I thought my being a quasi-basket case myself might entitle me to a few brownie points but it just meant I couldn't escape them so easily — they doted on me. I asked Alex how he dealt with the beggars, and he said "What beggars?"

After some time of trying to see the forest for the trees — we gave up and went off to the Village Inn, which had been recommended in my Moon Guide. It was like going from the Carnarsie Line Subway in the Bronx to the Four Seasons Restaurant — only nicer. Out the door of the dining room was a garden, and beyond that, a lagoon. It was warm, a lush early afternoon. The sky was clear and blue. The two Indian boys had shed their lungis and were swimming and laughing and playing in the calm waters. Like boys everywhere — they were ducking each other and splashing, racing against the horizon with its three straw-thatch huts. The coal black outlines of their bodies were limned by the sunlight, and the red-yellow sands of the beach seemed to float them right off the ground. "They've staged this just for us," I thought. There was the sweet smell of frangi-pani in the air, and the sharp aroma of seafood cooking over the nearby grill. "They're making up for all that hubble-bubble at the temple — they cast this scene just for us." The boys came out of the water, and put on their lungis, and discreetly used them as bath-tents by pulling off their red bathing suits from under and squeezing out the salt water. Alex and Adela and I ate prawns, obviously fished out of the self-same lagoon this morning, grilled to too much perfection over charcoal for our delectation, moments ago.

The whole scene reminded them of Sri Lanka. "One time we were walking down a dirt road there," she said, "past a lagoon just like this one. It was a tea-plantation. All the way — we passed just one placed, a shop, out by itself in the middle of the plantation (it was called "The Gregory Peck Tailor Mart") and the air was just like this, soft, and warm, and gentle. And we walked and walked, and when we came to the end of the road, out there in the midst of all those tea plants, there was this huge reclining buddha, of stone, this giant carving, lying down, in the middle of the plantation, with a smile on his lips.

"It's not all paradise, though," she said. "In one village in Sri Lanka we went into a grocery store, and there were three beans and one egg for sale. That's it. The village was starving. We didn't eat for two days. There were no restaurants, there wasn't any food anywhere. It's funny: we travelled for almost three years, through Bangladesh and Pakistan and Iran and Turkey and Afghanistan — and that was the only place we came to that had absolutely no food."

I wanted badly to travel to Sri Lanka, but the Tamil nationalists had just started a war there against the Buddhists. I gather these Tamils were not unlike the Indians who had been mugging each other and blackmailing us earlier today. If I were the Prime Minister of Sri Lanka, I would be quick to get me some ferry boats and some guns, and ship all the Tamils back to Mahabalipuram, out of the hair of gentle folk, back here where they can harass the tourists at their leisure, be as unpleasant as they want, make trouble for all those innocent visitors from Germany and England and America.

There were some porkers in the garden there at the restaurant, wild boars, with pig-eyes and smiles on their long hairy snouts. There were also chickens — but no cats and dogs. When we were driving back to Madras, at those times when Adela didn't have her eyes closed in silent prayer, she told me about the dogs in Bali. Evidently every household has its own wretched mongrel, and at night, they bark. "You can hear the one next door to you start up," she said, "then the one next door to him starts barking. Then the one next door to him, and the one next to him, until it circles around to the furtherest edge of the village — goes to the furtherest point of your aural horizon. Then you can hear it coming back, all the way round, circling the village, at first distant, very distant, then getting louder and louder, this wave of barking, until it comes back to the house next to you, and then to ours, and then back to the dog who started it all. And then he starts again, the circle begins again. It's very hypnotic. You can't sleep. It drives you crazy."

Then she started talking about Afghanistan. They were there before the invasion. They loved it. "The Afghanis are noble and crazy and never ever servile," Alex said. "If you treat them with respect, they'll treat you with respect." Adela said she liked the Afghani gas stations the best. "There's gas all over the tarmac, and the guy will be filling your tank, smoking this cigarette, crushing it out on the ground. That's how crazy they are."

When they came into the outskirts of Rudbar, just off the 120 degree Afghan desert, they went into a store and there was a cooler filled with big bottles of icy water, with beads of frost on them. "We asked the owner if the water had been boiled. We asked him three times. He assured us that it had, the bastard. So we drank it right down. We were laid out the next three days. While we were rolling about in our beds, we could see out the window where he was filling the bottles out of the stream right next to the cesspool. He capped them all himself." Evidently the only safe water to drink is out of pipes on the streets. They were put in by American engineers, drilling down to 1200 feet. The Russians gave them highways, and the Americans gave them water.

"Why didn't you drink the beer?" I said. "It's a Muslim country," she pointed out. "The only thing they had besides poisoned water was a soft drink that was made out of melted lollypops, you know the ones that no one would eat in the third grade, so you gave them to the stupid first graders. That's Afghani soda pop."

Alex described what it was like to have their Jeep break down on the Afghani desert, outside of Qandahar. "It was the timing gear, it had to be the timing gear — everything went wrong," he says. "Here we were on the desert, hotter than we have ever been, and everyone — I mean everyone — warned us not to be out on the road after nightfall, because of the brigands. We had been following a Land Rover, driven by an Englishman — and he was overheating. I told him the only way for him to tow us without blowing up his engine was to turn on the heat. So there we were, going along the Rigestan Desert, us and this Land Rover, them with the heat turned up full blast, their arms and legs hanging out, the doors pushed wide open so they wouldn't get parboiled."

Alex and Adela say the town of Qandahar is the second most evil city they ever went to. (The first was Londi Khotal, in Pakistan, where everyone carries machine guns on the street, as casually as briefcases in New York or a loaf of bread in France.) "Qandahar is a city of thieves — everyone calls it that. It's nightfall. There are no lights anywhere. You'd see some huddled figure, with glinting eyes. And everywhere, the smell of hashish."

"But we lucked out. We went to the one hotel in town, and the owner was a jewel. I thought it would take us three weeks to get another timing gear. Can you imagine being stuck for three weeks in Qandahar?" It's like that contest: first prize, you get a week in Qandahar. Second prize, three weeks in Qandahar.

"To get the timing gear, I would have had to hitchhike back to Bam, in Iran. That was the last place I saw a Jeep parts store. It's five hundred miles each way, across the desert. But the hotel owner said I shouldn't worry. He took us to the market the next day, and there was a brand new Jeep timing gear. It was a reject. It took me two days to install it. Everything in their market was reject from America. The gears, the machinery, the tires, the canned food. You'd open up a can of tuna with big red 'X's' marked across the top, and it would explode. Afghanistan lives on rejects from everyone else in the world."

❧ ❧ ❧

Just before we get to the hotel from our long trip, we stop at a traffic light on the road. The driver stops in just the place where Adela's face is on the level of the fuming exhaust pipe of a Very Big Green Bus. "It's just like smoking thirty packs of cigarettes," she says. "Only I don't even have to smoke them. I wonder how many years this is taking off my life. It'd be ironical, after this taxi ride, to die of asphyxiation two blocks from our hotel." Adela claims that most trucks in India don't have any mirrors on the door on the driver's side. "They've all been broken off, on the highway, passing, too close to the trucks coming from the other way."

Adela says that while we were in Mahabalipuram, some guy tried to inveigle her into watching a cobra-mongoose fight. Mongeese — in terms of attractiveness — are right up there with civets, vultures, and possums. "The thought that I should pay to see these two beasts fight each other!" she said. Pfaugh! It would be like watching a fight to the death between Bishop Maher and Jerry Falwell, or Jimmy Swaggart and Frank Sinatra, or Roy Cohn and the U.S. Army: what a friend of mine used to call "a nest of vipers."

[LATER]

My head cold has gone into overdrive, and my nose leaks like a baby's bottom. I lie in bed, dim-eyed, my head a balloon, and think on beautiful words. Today's favorites — the 'S' words: Sarcophagus. Sycophant. Scoliosis. Slipper-wort. Snavely. Sargassum. "Sar-gass-um" I say over to myself, savoring its flavors on the stopped-up nose. Sartorius (Faulkner loves that one — it's the longest muscle in a man's body). Sleeve. Sleazy.

And then the 'G's.' The first golf-ball: gutta-percha. Gnostic... a fine nasal word for the nose-bound. Gooey; gooney bird. O you gooney goofy gold golf-ball like a granitic gladiola. You're too, too gneiss. O gosh, there's that ghastly ghat-going gnat, ghoulishly known as a grebe. Gnostic — all those 'gn' words deserving a gnashing under the guzzling gorse-bush for their gnomic twist of the double consonantal gnu. "Gnothi seauton" — "Know thyself." Sage advice, goo-goo grace with your gummous gum rash. A gizmo gizzard with glad-rags and glandular grace. Gor!

And thus I entertain myself in the great cavern theatre of the mind when I come unglued and eyes and nose go out of commission!

DECEMBER 29, 3 A.M.

I woke up thinking about American tourists. Americans are the true International Travellers. We cross most borders freely, are welcomed freely. Half of it has to do with money: Americans drop $$$ like cockroaches drop eggs — randomly, everywhere.

The other half has to do with politics. Because the politics of America are so benign, Americans are mostly apolitical. There aren't Americans killing each other to vote as they do at the polls of India (fifty-six dead so far in this election). If we had shooting at the polls, it would be a scandal of major proportions.

We don't have the urge too often to murder in order to solve our political problems. We aren't like the bomb-throwers of the Balkans, or Indonesia, or Sri Lanka, or Belfast. Ours is a politics of benevolence, not of desperation.

Our government has been in business for over 200 years. We did most of our power-bashing/political spoils system during the first century of our existence. No foreign power has ever touched our soil. So many of the denizens of America are rich, confident, knowing that there are always ways to buy power with money; buying being far easier than bombing — because it preserves the apparent order. Money is so genteel, and the way we spread it about is not unlike spreading Chunky-Style Jif on Wonder Bread.

We go over our borders and into the world outside like babes. The travel columns of the *Los Angeles Times* are filled with questions — not about the politics of where we go — but, always, "How much should I tip the taxi-driver, the waiter, the bell-boy?" "What are the liquor laws; how many bottles of whiskey can I bring back?" We Americans wish only, nay, we're eager, to conform to any and all rules, customs, edicts, and requirements of the countries we visit.

We can and do travel into the rawest dictatorship in the world, but we will merely complain about the surly service at its local Sheraton. We go to places where would-be political reformers are castrated, shot up, have their hands cut off — and we fume about being overcharged by the bag-boys at the airport. We visit dictatorships where opposition newspapers are bombed into silence, and we complain about the taxi-driver who took us the long way 'round to our restaurant.

The world's issues don't concern Americans. American travellers are "clean," e.g., none of us will be asking the president of Brazil unseemly questions about torture in prisons — rather, we'll want to know when the Carnival begins. We wouldn't question the president of Indonesia about murdering his opposition; we just want to know why the power was off for three hours last night so we had to stay in our room, drinking gin rickies.

Sweet innocents! We want our swimming pools to be clean, our service to be prompt, the bathrooms to be sanitary; we want our maids to be polite, our visits to be neat. The policemen who abound in San Salvador, knocking on the doors of the dissidents, hauling them away at 3 a.m., will certainly not be knocking down the entrance to our hotel room. We travel as angels — loved for our largesse, mocked (but not too loudly) for our innocence, welcomed everywhere.

❧ ❧ ❧

One critic said that the head-cold is the hope for the future of America. All interns have been spared yellow fever, the pox, whooping cough, malaria, kidney stones, polio, diphtheria, tuberculosis. Their only experience of physical disease and suffering will be the annual sneeze — swelling adenoids, drippy noses, stuffy head, red-rimmed eyes. It becomes a humiliation device for these otherwise arrogant preppy would-be doctors. Through the cold, they learn, for the first time, how vulnerable the human body — if only for three days — and how strong our dependence on good health for good will and happiness; they learn, once and for all, just how miserable we can be. So let us sing a short hymn of praise for the Common Cold — which has so much to teach us, and the medicos.

I take a cold pill, which is evidently laced with some sort of exotic narcotic — beginning to love everything (even India!) I look at my journal, the book in which I entrust all my hopes, dreams, angers, bitternesses, passions, wonders, delights. I write: "I love this book. Its expensive hard blue cover; its well-constructed pages, with their simple one staff red line down the inner page, with the thirty or so light blue lines going across on the horizontal." The pages each have a simple stamped number ("199!") atop, and the edges of the pages are dyed a light green. Sing praise to Mr. Boorum and Mr. Pease, of Elizabeth, New Jersey, who for so long have provided the covers for my heart. They have constructed a book that not only deserves but gets my deepest thoughts, delights, fears and dreams.

[All while this is going on, the pill has, in addition, switched on my mental muzak — which is intoning the words and music to a song from 1946, named "Tico-Tico," viz.:

Oh tico-tico tic/Oh tico-tico tock
Oh tico-tico is the cuckoo in my clock/
And when it's time to woo/
My tico sez "coo-coo"/
And when it's not, my tico-tico
Sez it's not...

etc. etc. God! The tapes Tin-Pan Alley set going forty years ago, across America, still grinding on in our heads with a certainty of idiocy which can never be stamped out.]

It's time for me to get up and pack. Our plane leaves in five hours, and I damn well don't want to miss it. A head cold and eternity in India: no.

DECEMBER 29 [EN ROUTE TO KUALA LUMPUR]

I was convinced that Mother India wasn't going to let me go. Awake before dawn, packing (at three a.m.!). A cat-nap between four and six a.m., accompanied by endlessly chattering brain dreams. Up again at six with what my *Foreign Travellers Disease Book* describes as "the meatus" of my nasal passage so swollen that I could not breathe through nostrils without use of pickaxe and shovel.

At the airport in Madras — the customs man, the one who hijacked my ticket in exchange for my word-processor — is nowhere to be found. I cool my heels outside the customs shed for an hour, listening to the adjutants chuckling over the Tamil version of "Ozzie & Harriet" — they are watching on their three-inch Muntz television set. The official appears a few minutes before flight time, filled with apologies and forms for me to sign. I am so ready to be gone, to be done with India, that I would award him with the Word Processor if he would just let me go. [Sings] "O let me goooo, Mother India, let me goooo."

Over to the terminal, thinking "Well, India has me just where she wants me. Sick, tired, nervous. I'll get to the ramp of the airplane and then they'll call me back, tell me I can't leave until the whole problem with the word processor is solved, which will take six months." There are a thousand people or so swirling around the ticket counter — Indian ethic doesn't call for orderly lines — a milling mass, yelling, holding up tickets, trying to catch the attention of the two harried representatives of Air India. By this time I am sick of bloody India — all I can see and hear about me are the press of people, and the flies, and the beggars, and the ersatz English I can never understand. "Well," I say to myself — "if it doesn't take off, or take me with it — I guess I could go back to the Savera," but it's a damn lie. I'm 12,000 miles from home and I'm blessed if I want to spend the rest of my life (or the rest of the day) here. I look over at Alex and Adela in another line. They are even further back than I am — and yet seem idyllically peaceful, as if this proximate airplane will never take off without them or — if it does — that it makes no difference. "I would rather spend a day, a week for Christ's sakes, driving back and forth to Mahabalipuram in a taxi-cab rather than return to that hotel," I think. Just another eager tourist, ready to fly off, even if I have to rev up the damn plane myself.

When we finally get on the jet, it's held up another fifteen minutes, then twenty-five, then forty. "O no," I think, "a bomb threat." Or maybe they want my word processor back. Or perhaps there are mechanical problems. I envision 189 Indians and three Americans and 600 pieces of baggage weighing 30,000 pounds all being unpacked and set back down on the ground again — we passengers pushed back into the fly-speck terminal again, to wait for, say, the annual 1997 flight. "Why don't I stay home and grow pansies and chickens," I wonder to myself.

Well, we do take off, finally, and the answer to "Why travel?" is the same one each time: travel gets the glands up. It stirs the broth, pickles the pot, makes us active (and worried) and in our activity (and worry) it engenders the juices of creativity and thought.

I hate it and I love it. The streets of India, the Carnatic music, the crispy bread, the exquisite chutneys and exotic foods — coupled with the beautiful boys in their long dhotis: all these balance out the stumpy beggars, the snotty babies, the German cockroaches in the hotel (and the equally obnoxious German tourists at Mahabalipuram), the smog and car-horn-mad wheeled populace of the city. Now that I am away from it, I can see it as the perfect Hegelian synthesis — the thesis of travel, the antithesis of reality, the synthesis of the two into Experience, growing, keeping the pot boiling, not surrendering to old age, or the ease of day-in-day-out in a lotus-infested cottage in California. The confident me just has it too easy — we have to test the foundations on which we survive. The sacred balance point between potential (getting up and out) and kinetic (existing life). On the road, all forces come into union — the good and the bad, the wondrous and the horrible, the tedious and exciting, the unnerving and comatose. To travel is to be free, to try out all the devils and angels that run us.

On our first stop, the stewardess announces in a pleasant monotone: "In Kuala Lumpur, the penalty for illegal drugs is death..."

[EN ROUTE TO BANGKOK, 9 P.M.]

We have, I think, in my fevered state, possibly wronged the sun all these years with our arrogance: thinking of it as a thing, rather than a friend (or at least, as a friendly foreign correspondent). Perhaps it is but one of a huge family — its brothers and sisters the stars — who talk to each other endlessly (sometimes about us!), occupy a different time-dimension than we do and have some notion that we humans — beasts that we are — don't really exist. All the while we, in our puny way (through nuclear bombs, say), attempt to imitate the family of suns, all the while not acknowledging the existence of creatures which are, after all, right under our noses (or over our heads).

It goes beyond the Peruvian concept of the sun god, which is merely anthropomorphic. We must think of the sun as a huge, gaseous brain, floating about in the dark of space, filled with the essence of humanity: thoughts, loves, truths. Its involved thought processes convert to light, heat, electro-mechanical waves. We can tap into them if we dare. Thank god the sun does not presume to punish us for our hubris — the folly of equating ourselves to it, ignoring its parallel existence.

❧ ❧ ❧

Some attendants at the Singapore airport (they recognize me from three weeks ago, even though I am so very different now) ask me how I liked Christmas in Madras, and I respond "It was terrible." I didn't think of it as being so tedious when I was going through it — one can soften any blow — but in retrospect, it reminds me of Dallas, where I lived, in perceived equanimity, for two years and a half — and which I did not see as being so hideous until I finally got the hell out of there. Madras just isn't my city, as it is for Alex and Adela. I told them the last time I returned to Spain that I had found most of my now-joy in Barcelona and Madrid, places I shunned in 1960. I change, as do the cities: paradises of yore can turn stupid and boring the next time around.

The change-over in Singapore from Air India to Air Thai is like going from cattle car to private sleeper. I suppose I like

Air Thai because I am a plutocrat. Smoked salmon and impeccable service for the few. None of that messy democracy that Air India represents, where the fares are low enough that everyone can fly it. Air India is so democratic that I found a bug flying steerage — buried deep in my goopy rice jello. Unfortunately, he had been baked to death in his little roachy juices. I pushed the pesky treat underneath the plate. I wasn't about to embarrass the stewardess in sari serving us. I debated some whether to continue eating (the pudding, not the bug) because it was the only worthy part of the meal. Suffice it to say there were no archies, baked or no, on the Air Thai flight.

Alex leaves us in Singapore to fly back to the Northwest. Adela and I go on the Bangkok, to the hotel that is said by all to be "the best hotel in the world," the Oriental. We find out when we get there that, because it is so crowded, Adela and I are to share the same room.

Now Adela, as much as I love her, has apnea. That means she snores at night. No, she doesn't snore. She whistles, sighs, sings, moans, rasps, hoots, calls out, wails, rails and flails in her sleep. No sooner had we put out the light than she began her concert, obligattissimo. I am beside myself... actually, I am beside her since the hotel has only a queen size bed for us to share. Our nuptial night! As the symphony goes into the second movement (with tympani), I think "Maybe if I turn her over she'll shut up," but when I put on the light, I find that she is already face down.

I get up to put in my earplugs (I travel prepared). I would like, at this point, to say a word about head colds and earplugs: avoid them. The ear-plugs amplify any and all internal sounds, the usual smacks and swallows and gurglings and bargles that go on, unnoticed, inside of all of us. The noises are at such a low decibel level that normally we can, and do, safely ignore them.

Not with ear-plugs. If the main tenet of Yoga Buddhism is that by concentrating on our breathing we can achieve enlightenment, then I recommend the heady mix of head cold and ear-plugs. And I find myself, with all the inner and outer noises, faced with the too difficult choice between listening to Adela's "Aida" or my own.

The ear-plugs are of that rollo-plast variety that you heat in your fingers to make them soft and moldable; then they get inserted into the ears. After stuffing my tubes, I go to the sink and brush my teeth. What a racket: I can hear the sound of every bristle across every molar. I had always thought tooth-brushing to be a fairly quiet and sedentary activity, but in reality, it's avalanche time to bicuspids every time we put brush to gum. Do teeth have ears?

So then I get back in bed. Despite the elevated air pressure in my ears due to the plugs, with eustachian tubes at eight atmospheres (the residue of our recent flight), and the final duet from "La Traviata" being sung nearby, I figure I can get at least a bit of sleep before dawn. Foo. When they say we hear through our fingers and skin and bones, they're right. The lights go out, Adela pauses, then crashes into a Fourth of July John Phillip Sousa Special such that it penetrates these wax plugs, and with my own trombone section, I feel like I'm the hero in 2001 out near the wastes of Jupiter, listening to every internal, intergalactic and universal noise.

Most people at this point would laugh philosophically and turn on the light and read *The Seven Story Mountain* or some such. Not me. I lie there for a few years or so, cursing the travel agent, the Orient Hotel, myself, the King of Siam, and Adela's adenoids. It isn't until the sun drifts up (a few eternities later) that I forgive all and fall to sleep.

Sometime later, when we wake up, I offer to 1) order up some breakfast, and 2) pay for Adela's sinus operation. I call up room service and say "Send up one Apnea Curette, on the double." No, wait — I call them and say:

"Do you have any fruit?"

Room Service Lady: "Yes, we have flute cocktail."

Me: "Is it fresh?"

She: "O yes sir — it's flesh..."

DECEMBER 31 [BANGKOK]

"The grass may be greener on the other side of the fence, but it's just as hard to cut."

— LITTLE RICHARD

Since Adela and I are a pair of natural storytellers, already the tale of our night together is beginning to grow flowers and amazing shoots and roots. Chris — my old working partner from twenty-five years ago — lives here in Bangkok, and he is the first one we regale with the details of our honeymoon. I tell him that Adela is the first woman I had slept with since 1968 with apnea.

Adela (interrupting): "I have what?"

Me: "You have apnea."

Adela (voice rising): "I have a penis?"

"No. Apnea. Apnea!"

"What's that?"

"It's when you sleep and don't sleep."

"It's when you sleep and don't sleep," she repeats dumbly. Christopher tries to change the subject, but neither of us will let go; we've been traveling together through the wastes of Southern India too long for that.

"When you're asleep, you relax to such a degree that you literally start to suffocate," I explain. "You wake yourself up to catch a breath, then you drift off, and then you start to lose it — so you wake up again. You may think you've slept from eleven to seven — but you may only get four or five hours of sleep a night. You've got apnea," I say, definitively — but then again, I don't have my Merck Manual with me, and I may just have made up the word, as I am wont to do. Maybe the right word is "angina" or "intaglio" or "euripides" — something like that.

Adela and I tell Chris about our fascination with riddles. She said the earliest one from her childhood she could remember was:

Q. "Does a fish smell?"

A. "Not if you cut off its nose."

I pointed out that this was simple Northwest Juvenile Humor. I was born in the South. Florida jokes are more complex. "There was one my sisters used to ask me all the time," I say. "It was 'What's the difference between a duck?' It's zen if you think about it," I say, as they are puzzling it out. "What's the answer?" Silence. "The answer is: 'One leg is the same.'" There is another silence after that, a long one, and I know it's time for me to take my afternoon nap.

❧ ❧ ❧

Adela is feeling morose because Alex has gone back to the Northwest, and all she has is whiney me trying to get the two of us to an Ear, Nose and Throat specialist. We change hotels early the next day, get ourselves a suite with two separate rooms in a fancy-dan place called the Dusit Thani (which I immediately dub "The Lusitania"). After we move in, she goes to the novelty shop downstairs, and buys a pair of plastic glasses frames with a fake black moustache and eyebrows. It's the superimposition of Groucho Marx on her rather sweet Renoir face. She wears it nonstop. We order up some Thai Lemon Shrimp Soup from room service, and she answers the door in disguise. The waiter seems oblivious to bearded ladies but I find it more than distracting to share my lunch with one. I tell her about the very cosmopolitan New York chansonnier Spivey from my long-ago cosmopolitan youth. Spivey operated out of a twelve-table, pea-sized nightclub on the upper east side where she entertained the Smart Set and me and my drunken prep-school set.

She was a florid lady, with a grand past and a greater girth. She would come out, sit herself at the piano, and with a tumbler full of gin before her and the husky voice of a genuine functioning song-filled alcoholic, would launch into one of her rather daring (for the times) songs, such as

On the fourteenth floor of a walk-up flat
I used to keep an alley cat.
Each night I'd take him down the stairs
And waited while he got the air.
He grew up fast and developed a yen:
No sooner was he in than he was out again.
I hated to spoil his fun,
But I knew what must be done.
So I took him to the vet
And had his profile bobbed;
And when he sat down, he said:
"Hell, I've been robbed."

Or:

She was only a bearded lady
In love with a Surrealist,
They'd walk in the park
While she wore a rose in her beard
And he wore a lamb-chop in his boutonniére.

Actually, Adela is somewhat given to surréalisme herself, at least in her speech. As I am singing (or talking, or sleeping) she utters paradoxical, out-of-order statements such as "My dogs are barking" (she was afoot most of yesterday in the alleys of Bangkok) or "I feel like I'm on a boat," or my personal favorite, yielded up at totally random intervals, any time of the day or night: "I am a farmer outstanding in his field."

I tell her about how Chris and I met when he was trying to get a degree in Black Studies at Howard University in Washington, D.C., and I was trying to get that damn permit from the damn government for what I had hoped would be the first listener-supported community radio station in Washington, D.C.

Well, it was dark times for us all. It was 1959, and the country was being run by a good-natured ninny by the name of Eisenhower. Chris had just graduated from Oxford (he had grown up a product of a mixed English-Afrikaans family in South Africa). He had come to Washington to learn about black life and culture in the U.S. He lived with a poor black family which, in pre-Kennedy Washington, was considered to be quite radical, as was his attendance at the all-black Howard University. It was a frustrating time for both of us. He could scarcely come to grips with bizarre United States, and I could get no one in the government to pay any attention at all to me and my application: they sat on it for so long that I thought that they would hatch it or that I should go bananas. We had no air-conditioning in the $35/month office that we shared.

Washington, at that time, was a place where new ideas were not encouraged. In fact, the policy was to bury anything that might cause discomfort, strangeness, change. It was a 1920's Southern town with an 1870's political mentality — not unlike the city I had grown up in. Chris and I were both filled with the fires of change-society. We were both college graduates, twenty-five, angry at our different countries' political systems, impatient that government should be in the hands of the fogies and the fearful. We had no idea that, in a year, a man would be elected to the presidency who would strive to move this country along another course. We were so close to the oppressive nature of Washington at that time that we couldn't sense that we were part of a force for change that would revolutionize not only Washington but the world as well. When that change finally came about we were both gone: me to Spain to abandon America (for a while, anyway); he to work for the government of a small, newly-emerging African nation of a million people.

Ah, Chris. We were bathed in the same broth of frustration and despair — and out of that came our friendship. As well out of our frustration and despair grew the knowledge that made it possible for us to act later — much later. We learned the system well enough by our failing that we were able to go on later to succeed, beyond any of our wildest dreams. I learned how to use the rules of the FCC to get what I wanted; he became the head of an international banking organization for all of Southeastern Asia, floating huge loans for third world countries (on which he is considered one of the few free world experts).

I hadn't seen Chris since the shared misery of colonial Washington, and here he is in Bangkok; it's instant rapport — or re-rapport. I was so shy back in the 50's that I had few friends. He was one of the few — true-blue, loyal. We lounge around in his apartment overlooking the Bangkok Racetrack and our words flow so easily; the cheering of the race-track crowd accentuates our memories. How nice it is to reconnect with a friend who, unlike so many of the others, is not balmy, or alcoholic, or destructive.

I tell Chris that one thing I like about Thailand is that it has a currency called a "bhat" (as in "going bats"). Also, we find the "Teachings of Buddha" in the hotel room, right next to the Gideon Bible — although the "Teachings" have been sanitized and updated to make Buddha sound like a slightly paunchy Jesus — with nothing of the paradox of Buddha's real teachings. They don't mention, for example, his saying that he was just a Second Rate Master; saying that the fourteen real Buddhas had all lived before him, and they were so perfect that they lived out their lives in secret, without anyone stumbling over their sanctity.

Chris says that Thailand is amazing. "No one can figure it out," he says. "The army controls two of the four national television stations, there is a monarchy, the bureaucracy tries in every way to hamper the development of the country — and yet it is alone in the world with a seven per cent annual growth in gross national product — and it is a net exporter of food while still feeding its own population."

He tells me that Thailand was one of the few countries to join with Japan and Germany to declare war on the United States in 1941 — but at the end of the war, the U.S. was so frantic to keep Southeast Asia from going Communist that we poured aid into the country. "Japan came in here during the war," he tells us, "and the Thais said 'Here, take it.' They're so benign. So at the end of the war, Japan made huge repatriations — but this still doesn't explain Thailand's prosperity."

Chris is a goader. "The Third World needs your kind of radio. Why don't you move here and start showing people how to use the media. Can you imagine a Community Station in Bangkok?" It makes me weary even to hear him talk about it. "There is a kind of lunacy in believing that one can, single-handedly, change the world," I tell him. "That kind of hubris can drive you looney." Still, as he says "Why don't you come here?" and "The Third World countries need you," I can feel that tug, that I'm-gonna-change-the-world-even-if-we-have-to-cram-change-down-their-throats feeling that Chris and I had back in 1959. God, we were piss-and-vinegar back then. And I suppose our pissiness paid off: he's a star in the complex of Third World Finance, and I affected the media as much as possible or necessary. We both changed the world some, but how different it all is when we look back and see how we did it. When they cheer the horses at the Bangkok Del Mar Racetrack down below, they might as well be cheering the two of us, in our lonely fix-the-world stance.

On his fifteen story balcony, we overlook a city the size of Houston. Below us, in two water tanks, I can see some young Bangkok males in their skivvies, jumping in and out of the water. I wish my glasses were better. Chris wants us to stay over the weekend, but I demur. "Come on," he says: "I'll take you to a real fishing village. They have the best seafood restaurant in Thailand." I note that he hasn't lost his gift for hyperbole.

He tells me that all four television stations in Thailand go off the air from six p.m. to eight p.m. to save power, not only from the television transmitters — but the added bonus of 10,000,000 television sets turned off for two hours. It is a novel conservation method I never thought of before. It might be the answer for the United States. "You're in this Thai village, at seven in the evening, and everyone is talking and visiting, eating food at the stalls," he says. "Then — bang! At eight p.m. they've gone back to their tv sets, their bicycles all stacked up, not a soul on the streets."

"That's the answer for the American angst," I think. Turn off all the television stations in the early evening. "People will start being nice to each other again — they'll meet each other over the backyard fence, walk about the neighborhood, visit, relearn things about themselves, their families and their friends that they've long forgotten," I think. "We've been coming at it the wrong way — trying to wean the kids from television. What we have to do is to wean the tv sets from the TV signal."

Chris still thinks that TV can be a force for change, and for good. "All they do is show those terrible action/adventure soap operas from Hong Kong," he says. "What a waste!" he says, sounding like me in 1959 [How many times did I make that speech?]

"You're wrong," I tell him, me not sounding like me in 1959. "Read Marshall McLuhan," I say. "He says that it makes no difference what you show on TV. Content is totally unimportant. Rather — what is important is that television exists, and that people watch it. The programs they see — Bill Cosby, Barnaby Bear, the Five O'Clock News, Hong Kong soap opera — it makes no difference." I tell him about the famous HEW study that proved that violent hyperactivity of kids occurred after watching television — and it made no difference if it was Sesame Street, or The Flintstones, or Hawaii 5-O, or The Dick Clark Show.

"It's unimportant what they are watching," I explain: "They — all of us — are being revolutionized by the mere existence of television, and radio, and telephones, and copying machines. No one, I mean no one knows the true effect of the media."

I explain the Russian Fallacy: "The government of Russia thinks that the citizens will not go crazy, change, act differently if the content of programming is regulated. Thus, no Playboyski Channel — and lots of opera and ballet and stolid newscasts, tractor production information. Great!" I explain that the very existence of the television set is the revolution — and they don't know it yet. "They've been much smarter with regards to the copying machine: no Xeroxes outside of high government offices. That's smart censorship — for awhile."

"The South African government was much shrewder — at least until five years ago. They permitted no television whatsoever. Then they fell into the same trap: 'We'll let television in,' they said, 'Only — we'll regulate what is shown.'" They thought that would prevent change, uprising, revolution. "Keep the natives watching crop reports and official government news," they say. They are convinced that will prevent the masses from changing, growing, growing more sophisticated. They are ignoring the fact of the tv set: what it does to one's view of the world, to family structure. They can present the most benign programs, think the country will be safe. How wrong they are. McLuhan always said that the most revolutionary program on American television was "I Love Lucy" — because all those absurd situations were acted out against such luxury. It wasn't the comedy or the human interactions that got some villager in Africa or in Indonesia. No, it was all those backdrops: stoves and washers and dryers, that amazed, hungered the foreigners. It will take the governments time to realize what they have done, so irrevocably, so casually. Yet all they had to do was to read *Understanding Media.*"

Chris — evidently fascinated by my insights — yawns and interrupts to say that we have to leave if we are going out to eat. "I'm going to take you to the greatest Thai restaurant in Bangkok," he says.

I have to confess he is right, or — based on the fact that I have eaten in but two places in Bangkok — I should say I suppose he is right. My favorites are the vermicelli, fried dark and crunchy, served with raisins and sweet sauce. And turtle eggs in soup.

❧ ❧ ❧

Turtle eggs! What memories they bring back. And such a homely item too. Looking like nothing so much as a white ping-pong ball, with a dent in the side.

It all takes me back to 1944. John Z. Founder, the only man in Jacksonville with a 100-foot yacht, invites our family to go along on a trip to Jekyll Island. Founder is a choleric sort, with a large stomach, a tribute to many chicken-fried steaks, plates of grits, apple pies and eight or ten shots a day of bourbon and branch water. The moon of his tum is only slightly more prodigious than his nose, certainly equal to the nez of J.P. Morgan — finely laced as it is with a delicate vein system, as detailed as that of the colorful planet Mars.

The passengers on our journey consist of my father and mother, and six children — from older sister to eleven-year-old me — and Founder's family: children and mother (a new mother, the old one having been recently discarded, worn out like a shoe by his high living and "other" ladies) and innumerable servants, pilots, navigators, cooks, nannies, and maids.

Jekyll Island is a seven-mile long strip, facing the Atlantic Ocean, a few miles from Brunswick, Georgia, sixty miles from our home port. Up to 1930, it was the place for the industrialists of the northeast seaboard to winter (Miami Beach had scarcely been invented by this time). When we visit the island, the ancient castles are turning decayed, being revisited by the jungles of South Georgia. Amongst the trellisses and the silence, Spanish moss and vines, slash pine and palmetto — the mansions are falling to the prevailing forces of entropy: reverting with clay and mud and moss and creepers and vines to a natural, shadowed, and pristine state. Deer, rabbit, wild boar and possum have taken up habitation in places once reserved for the frock-coated millionaires, chantilly-lace wives, debutante daughters. Jekyll Island is reinvesting itself with its natural state.

The only time to hunt turtle eggs is during the first full moon in June. It is then that the high tides help the great sea-turtles come lumbering out of the sea. They move awkwardly with flippers meant solely for sea-travel — pushing their way across the narrow beach to the sand dunes where they can dig a hole and drop three hundred ping-pong balls which are the hope for sea-turtle future. The eggs are left there, buried a foot or so under sand; the hot sun does the work of gestation, and thirty or forty days later, dozens of smaller versions of their two-ton parents come cascading out of the nest, down the hot sands, to the waters of the south Georgia seas where they can swim to safety — if they escape from the thousand natural enemies of the shore: raccoons, and possum, and wild dogs, and sea-gulls. And man.

Today it is illegal to hunt the turtle egg. But in that far-off time of my youth, we still thought the wild resources of land and sea to be infinite — and if we dig up two dozen nests to eat what we could, and throw away the rest: what does it matter? Such an innocent time with that largesse of Nature. We had no idea in the world that man could in any way impinge on the bounty all about us. Thus the annual turtle-egg hunt, using the great floating limousine of John Founder of bulbous nose and belly.

At night as we come down the beach we see the dark shapes moving out of the ocean, making their way across an intervening strip of white, then pushing into, punching down the sea-wheat that rises above the high tide line. We can see great dark clocks spawned by the ocean come out of the waters to leave the burden of a new generation to feed on the future.

There is no mercy. They may have arrived before us, left before we put in appearance among them, but they have dropped a clue — an upheaval attesting to their presence: a trail up the beach, punctuated by points where flippers dug into the sand to get purchase, to carry them to a tell-tale depression in the dunes where the burden (the burden of the Lord!) is released and covered; and then yet another trail they take to return to the sea. Like mothers of every spawn, there is no way these creatures, with the weight of their days, can hide the path to their progeny.

We dig and we dig, and we take and we take. Easter egg time — filling great croker sacks with the round still warm white fleshy eggs. At one point, my brother clambers atop a turtle and for a brief stymied moment she tries to accomplish her nature's driven purpose with a hundred pound boy riding her. He is at that moment a figure out of mythology: with his dark face and his white garb, some statue from millenia past — a figure of the god's world atop the black and moving earth. But she surrenders to fear, turns back to the sea with her burden undelivered.

And later, as the engines turn in boat, and I am lying on the deck, trying to force my eyes to stay open in light of the great moon that rides above us like a wheel — Philip the cook comes to me, with three just-boiled turtle eggs. He rips a wedge from the top, fills them with a hot savory sauce, and shows me how to take the warm grainy concoction from shell to mouth. Delicious! I fall asleep to the seas of motion and the wheeling light of moons, and the black-timed bodies of great sea creatures that turn and turn below us, the delicious burning taste of their unborn children in my throat.

❧ ❧ ❧

Jung says that the major figures in our life (figures of love, hate, fear, anger, passion) have all come to us by the time we are ten. We internalize them at the same time that we are internalizing the language, the ethics, the morals of our world, the mannerisms that we grow up with.

We learn our love-hunger early on. We fall in love, starting at age zero (or thereabouts) with perceived knights, beasts, fairies, devils, mothers, and gods. By the time we have passed the first decade, we are already programmed for our times ahead. Much as a girl, before birth, contains all the ova of all her would-be children within; and much as a boy, while still in the womb, has had his first erection and orgasm (they say it comes at the moment of birth, when the meatus is dragged against the walls of the cervix), so have children established the loves and hates and obsessions that will accompany them, nay, drive them through life.

It is possible to reprogram some of these shadow plays that we carry about with us. Powerful psychedelic drugs are useful for this: LSD, Peyote, Psilocybin, "Magic Mushrooms." (That is, of course, why they are outlawed in what we are fond of calling the "civilized" world.) Psychoanalysis — in all its many manifestations (psychotherapy, group therapy, counselling) has the same effect and — although painful, and slow, and tedious — may be successful. Both represent a mode of exorcising the ghosts that we have internalized to survive the shark-infested waters so romantically called Youth and Childhood.

Another way to beard these spooks (the spooks we must please) is through death — either self-imposed, or by means of wars, crimes, terrorism — e.g., force whole civilizations to commit your suicide for you. Death solves so many problems — especially the one brought on by immense internal pain. There are no end of politicians, leaders, ministers, presidents, popes, caudillos, politburo chairman who are willing to commit us to death to recompense for their own miseries left over from thirty or forty or fifty years past: their virulent, grim, hag-ridden childhoods. Because they cannot vitiate their own spooks — they are kind enough to volunteer to kill the rest of us.

In addition, the "proud flesh" of youth can be expunged by religion. And here I am not speaking of religions which externalize the black forces from within by labelling them 'devil.' (In this bleak form of god-worship, 'Thou shalt not kill,' is given footnote status, as: 'The turning of the other cheek does not apply to communists, infidels, Cubans, liberal humanists, North Koreans, Viet-Cong and other heathen. Onward Christian Soldiers,' etc. etc.)

Here, rather, I am speaking of religions which strive to be honest, which do not brutalize their adherents nor their 'enemies.' Quakerism, for example. Seventh Day Adventists. Catholic mystics. Hindu holy men. Greek Orthodox Saints. And most of all — Buddhists. Those who can say, with honesty and grace: "It would kill me to kill another human." Those who know that the master lies within, and if we pretend he/she/it is above, below, out there — then we are condemning our selves to hideous pain and condemning our families, peers, nations to brutality. No wonder ignorance is the only sin in the Buddhist creed, for they have found that the answers do not lie in temples or in war or in plastic Jesus statues on the dashboard: but, rather, within the heart. That dark, never moving, ever changing never-to-see-the-light baby that lies within, never touched by light, only to illumined by our sacred, arcane, truth-seeking dreams.

JANUARY 1, 1985

We go to the Wat Fra Keo — the holy grounds of the King of Thailand. What is to be said that hasn't been said before? It is a dream shrine. It is bigger than I ever imagined. The juxtapositions of the spires, and the dragon's points, and the lions, and the smooth, breast-like cupolas. All overlaid with a gold-leaf that pulsates in the sky-blue. A complex of complex spires, and edifices, and gold (and silver) roofs, and bells, and saffron-dressed monks, and wall paintings, and golden buddhas.

I think about the residuum of Christianity: the holy artifacts and cathedrals of Europe. The effect of them is always to brutalize with sheer massiveness — a construction of dark and heavy blocks of granite. The Wat, by contrast, is a lively and joyful interplay of gold and silver and bright colors, the play of the senses with patterns in the sky, catching the lights in a thousand different ways. European cathedrals — with their dark and cold and harsh interiors, catch one by one's fear. The wat — with its riot of colors and smells and wind chimes —

catches one in the passion: it bespeaks a religion with a sense of joy and fun, a religion that can take itself seriously or not — whenever and however it chooses.

The primary symbol of Christianity is a gaunt man with huge spikes driven into his body. A man with a wasted face, with blood leaking from head and side and hands and feet. Coarse wood riven into his extremities, flesh and bones crushed: the tortured corpse of a man tortured and mounted on cross-purpose stanchions.

The vision of our god hung up like a piece of meat (which is why they have to call him "the Lamb") is at once garish and barbarous. That people should worship before the crossed timbers on which his body was brutalized is almost as bizarre as abasing yourself before a noose or an electric chair. What kind of a society can we run, what sort of peace can there be in a state religion which used such blood-stained objects as its highest artifacts? There is a particular vulgarity in martyrdom (in any form: a suffering mother, a dying god). That we idolize such martyrdom does incalculable harm to our capacity for love and sweetness.

The contrast with Buddhism is startling. There, the master figure is huge and pacific, often smiling. His eyes are veiled; he is sometimes even shown in the reclining position (can you envision Jesus on his side, resting, with a beatific smile playing across his lips?). The message is one of inner quiet — gleaned not from battling with the changers in the temple or the Romans, but from exploring the gentleness within. At one point in his life, Buddha gave himself hunger and pain and suffering, and learned that hunger and pain and suffering are not the answer: rather, he found, the answer is in the soul within, the soul which lies pacific, the golden heart that runs all of us — when we permit it, which is accessible by penetrating the ugliness without.

Adela and I notice that there are very few pigeons at the Wat. Our guide says it is because of the sticky powder that the monks use to prevent the birds from landing. I think he just doesn't know. Pigeons know where the real holies are at. They'll hang out at (and poop all over) St. Peter's and Westminster and St. Patrick's and San Sebastian and Notre Dame — but not the Wat Pho. "It's just like I told you," I tell her: "The Buddhists come back as hummingbirds and monarch butterflies and doves — while Christians are stuck with returning again and again as fleas and Norway rats and Black Widow spiders."

JANUARY 3
"Let a hundred flowers bloom."

Chris takes us to one of the legendary Bangkok sex shows. All sex shows all over the world take place in a terrible milieu: tiny tables, smoky rooms, minuscule stage, watered-down drinks, sleezo maitre'd.

Still — there is something special about this one. I have to confess that I never guessed that one could introduce such an alarming number of artifacts into the old squeeze-box — making what a contemporary rock song titles "the place where the sun don't shine" a veritable lost and found depot. Mercy me!

For instance, on arrival, there's a hefty lady on her back on stage, extracting what appears to be plastic daisies or doilies, a long string — a very long string indeed — of flowers of such quantity that it would have shamed the ladies at the North End Begonia Society.

Then shortly after — after our being served the usual tenth-of-an-ounce of whiskey — another lady arrived to indulge herself in an involved and intimate way with several large bottles of Coca-Cola, both empty and full, or (at times) halfway between the two. Then we got the Camel show, where cigarettes (not a dainty one or two, but whole pack) were placed *in medias res*, promptly lit, and puffed, in a great cloud of smoke, giving us a real fear for the safety of the patch-of-lawn of our supine friend. All the time, a choice selection of music belted forth from the speakers, including (but not limited to) "You Can't Always Get What You Want (But If You Try Sometime You Just Might Find You Get What You Need)."

The trick-of-the-week for those few of us still functioning was the Banana Shot — said artifact which was cast forth, not unlike an ABM missile from a silo, to great and amazing heights. All our Early Warning Systems had gone off by this time, making the next six tricks anticlimactical, including darts shot with remarkable inaccuracy at red and yellow balloons suspended overhead. It all reminded us of Samuel Johnson's tale of the walking dog: the concern was not that it was done well, but that it was done at all.

The finale was the Usual Act of Congress taking place with grunts and suchlike between a husky young fellow and a slim-waisted little thing who earned my respect by staying firmly connected all the while she was thrown about the room by her consort. When the Master of Ceremonies announced that the next act was the Ping-Pong Playoffs, followed by the Razor Act — we high-tailed it for the door. I mused for a while on humans' — at least Porn Parlor humans' — insensate need to show strange objects addressed to commodious privates, objects that would not normally be expected to be found in or near such places. Chris insisted, absolutely insisted that the final act of the evening came when the indefatigable young man placed his factotum on the counter and his lady friend addressed it vigorously with a sledgehammer "to blow the wax out of his ears." *Maxima cum laude.*

❧ ❧ ❧

One of those books I so favor lately states that all time is going on simultaneously. Thus — the creation of the earth, and its consequent destruction, are both happening right now. The fall of Carthage, the first presentation of Hamlet, the death of Hitler, and New Year's 2551 are all here with us at this moment. The first meteor attack, the last monster attack, the rise of the dinosaur, the decay of the Cretaceous era, the last man on the last beach taking his last breath: all are happening at this very juncture. There is no temporal difference between now and then, then and now. It's all the same.

❧ ❧ ❧

Adela says that I hum constantly. When we are puttering with the morning ablutions, I might be humming "Tea for Two." As I drink my last glass of brandy for the evening, I might be rendering (to the best of my ability) Bach's B-Minor Mass, or something out of Philip Glass. When we had our fight yesterday at the Wat (I told her she was always trying to dominate me; she said I was too bloody competitive) I might have been belting out the Götterdamerung. And when we went boating yesterday it was "Cruisin' Down the River."

That boat trip took us into the klongs to the west of Bangkok. The canals of Bangkok proper have been paved over for the cars — or are so heavily polluted that they are dangerous to be on or near. But to the west we were able to enter into the lives of people as they must have been fifty or a hundred years ago. Thousands of homes, shanty style, opened onto the canals. Men with elaborate tattoos bathing in the waters. Long boats — as long and narrow as any Venice gondola — being poled by slender Thai women. The dhoti as bathing tent: one changes clothes under it, slipping a bathing suit on or off.

Kids pissing in the water — just to see it splash. An old monk doing the same, only he turns his back to us in modesty. We pass, in our long boat, a dozen wats: at one, a dozen young monks in saffron robes are descending like ants from one of the towers. There's an old fashioned single-pole long boat, followed by a water taxi with thirty-five passengers. Two kids swim out of the water, jump onto the front of our boat. We give them each a bhat which they clench between their teeth as they jump back into the water. The inboard motors are set at high angle for the long propeller shaft — and the motors themselves are painted red and blue and gold, even one with a pair of eyes.

Clothes are hanging everywhere; we pass a casket-making factory; ducks are in duck heaven; there are cannas everywhere. Bangkok grew up on water transportation — it was known as the Venice of Southeast Asia — and only recently have they destroyed all the past for the ubiquitous automobile.

[LATER]

When we go to the Crown Bank to cash travellers' checks, the cashier counts them out and then says "Pee-pee-tao." That becomes our theme song: every time Adela sees something strange or funny, she pokes me and says "Pee-pee-tao."

We go to the Wat Pho — which we immediately dub "The What Fo'" — and I spy two "Thermostat" hair drying machines (beauty shop variety) outside the temple. We decide that they are some sort of new religious artifact to be worshipped. As we leave the Temple of the Reclining Buddha, we see the following scenario:

Man, wife and one-year-old son on bench, under bo tree. Child crying. Wife tries to quiet child. Child continues to cry. Father drops child's pants, applies his mouth to child's member. Child quiets down. Adela looks at me, wide-eyed. I look at Adela, wide-eyed. What in the United States could get someone a sentence in the Greybar Hotel for thirty years is done without shame, without fear, in a wat, in Thailand.

❧ ❧ ❧

When I part from Adela in front of the Hotel Lusitania, me on my way to Tokyo and LA, she staying behind for Kyoto and the volcanoes of Hawaii, I hug her and say to her "You're a farmer outstanding in my field," and she whispers "You're an outstanding dork to travel with but I love you."

Trips are like love. If nothing else, each one teaches you a bit about yourself. Trips are not all travel poster sights and agreeable natives. There's jet lag and communication breakdown and homesickness and befouled toilets. Each trip has a lesson for us. My 1984 summer trip to Spain, France, and Italy taught me not to drive myself so endlessly. It was a big change for me — because for thirty years I had prided myself on the fact that I could go anywhere and do anything. Now, at age fifty-one — it's no longer the way to travel. This time I paced myself: an hour or two in the morning, an hour or two in the afternoon out in the world; the rest of the time reading, or listening to the radio, or looking out the window.

JANUARY 5, [10 P.M., TOKYO]

At the Narita Hotel, the bellboy explains everything, everything: shower, refrigerator, tea maker, television set — and refuses to take a tip. He was so polite that I am sure he would accompany me back to the United States if I so asked.

And in the bar, every time the bartender shakes the cocktails, he gives it the precise fifteen shakes, tapping the shaker exactly, so, at the end, everyone is endlessly cheerful, pleasant, thoughtful, courteous, kind, etc. Everything is ordered; and compared to the confusion and anarchy of India, it is a pleasure — appealing to the Prussian in all of us. I regret that I have only given myself eighteen hours here.

And so, my last night abroad, I have time to muse on my trip, here in the Sashimi Room of the Nikko Hotel. I count the hours between me and home. (Will I be setting down thirty-one hours from now? No, it must be twenty-eight. Let's see, it's three a.m. in Los Angeles, but it is also yesterday — perhaps tomorrow is thirty-eight hours behind us. Who invented the execrable system of time zones? No doubt the bloody British in their miserable Greenwich.)

I wonder how some expatriates survive. If one loves one's home, it becomes hard to stay away past the break-even point which I put at the standard two weeks, as in "two-week vacation." How did Henry Miller, T.S. Eliot, William Burroughs, Henry James, Paul Gauguin, Christopher Isherwood do it? I remember my two years in Spain — and the longing for absurd American things. I would catch myself dreaming of chocolate malted milkshakes, hamburgers with lettuce and mayonnaise, and most of all, for some reason, BLT on toast.

I absently order some raw oysters, and in the American tradition (in my head, I'm already home!) polish them off in about two minutes. Oysters and hot sake! The Japanese gentleman next to be seems agitated by the way I down them so grossly, so quickly. He's been loitering over his half-shells for an hour, nibbling a cracker from time to time, meditating over his meal, as a good Oriental traditionalist must. What is it they call it? The Oriental Clam? (Or Oyster.)

I muse over my three-and-a-half weeks out of America: the good and the bad of it: the Carnatic singing in Madras, waking to the sounds of the Indian instruments being played in practice next door to our hotel room. The streets filled with bicycles. The thin, absurdly thin Indian women three-eyeing their way down Krishna Road, in gold and green sari — their one possession before them, a bony water buffalo, which they guide by means of a stick applied to thin hairless flanks. And the gold-skinned boys in their lungis in Mahabalipuram, bathing in the lagoon — bathing dreams of paradise. The wonderful Peninsula Hotel in Hong Kong where room service brings special knives for cutting the pears and bananas. (And who can forget the Banana Catapult Show in Bangkok?)

Then there's the bad of it: a monster head-cold in Madras, invented by Kali. Being threatened with maiming and death on the Tamil highways. Indian Fred following us all about the alleyways of Madras, teletransporting himself into our very hotel rooms. Fighting with Adela over what is, after all, her personality vs. my personality (travelling together for three weeks would be hard even with St. Jude). The up and the down, the eternal yin and yang.

❧ ❧ ❧

I am musing on The Journey — feeling at one with the great world travellers of the past (Kubla Khan, Boswell and Johnson, Robert Byron) and Richard sits down next to me at the bar. English, grown up in Singapore. Nineteen years of age, being deported from the United States, he tells me, at once, no shame, after being jailed for transportation of drugs into Seattle. He had been in King County jail for over a month — and was being returned to the arms of his unwilling parents and his all-too-willing (he claims) thirty-two-year-old Russian lover lady. The American Immigration Service and the British Consul have conspired together to make possible Richard's sudden trip south.

Ah, Richard: you do introduce me to the madness of the English-speaking culture again, don't you? A 1980's Dylan Thomas, Holden Caulfield, Jack Kerouac. Brash, noisy, loudly proclaiming his four-year dependence on morphine; that wild pride, which the young seem to favor — proclaiming the body's weakness, needs, tolerance, its survivability. "Have you got any painkillers?" he says — shouts, rather — in case anyone might have any doubts over his wicked Western ways. Crazy, Richard, jangling all over the place, the spawn of Western Victorianism, the kid who will do anything, say anything, announce his lunacy with pride: "I'm cold turkey for the first time since 1980," he tells me.

How many time have I met Richard before? In San Francisco, in London, Spain, Amsterdam, all over the world — on the run from Immigration, the police, families, the world. There was Tommy in St. Louis who, when we wasn't shooting meth, wrote some of the most exquisite poetry, played the most exquisite harmonica. Or Rick from Portland, who just couldn't stay away from airplane glue, for Christ's sakes: one of the most brilliant artists I've ever known, a mind turning to oatmeal under the constant onslaught of toluene. Rod, in Málaga — who described what it was like to be searched by the police on the streets of Berkeley when he was holding a "balloon" of heroin in his mouth, ready to swallow it. "If I did it —

I knew I had exactly twenty minutes before the rubber burst and killed me," he told me, with that mix of pride, excitement, delight at his own wickedness.

Richard is brother to them all: just as bent on "totalling" his body. He and his Christopher Robin face, his lean, still (miraculously) functioning body: it is for him, and Ricky, and Rod, that all the drug laws were written. It is because of them that they are so useless. They are clever as cats in evading them. Noisy, proud, arrogant, and charming: who can resist this madness?

Richard was delivered in handcuffs to Japan Airlines in Seattle. ("How do you respond to 'Smoking or non-smoking?' when your hands are behind your back, in cuffs?") Richard, the Charles Baudelaire of the nuclear age — willing to shoot or snort or inhale anything, anything that will take his brain on some merry chase — a merrier chase than the normal dull-brain muddle. "They caught me because of the tracks," he says. "Look," and he proudly pulls up his shirt-sleeves to show me his needle marks. I can see nothing. Maybe the light is too dim, maybe he doesn't have any. Who knows, who can answer? — for after all, we are dealing not with Richard the voluble who sits with me, swizzling sake like it was shortly to be rationed. No, we have here a dream-fantasy of a picaresque character: an anti-hero compiled by his own brain, speaking (with wit and verve and complete fantasy) to anyone who will listen. Richard, convincing all, if possible, of the truth of his fabricated persona. We both know he is spinning tales. Not necessarily about being a junky, or about being caught. Presumably, that has happened before, will happen again. No, what he has to do is to catch me in a spiel with his wit and beauty and brainset; to use his narcissism to convince me (and him) that he is a master confidence man; that he's the elusive and charming Don Juan/James Dean/Thomas DeQuincy. Being caught is just a glitch in the roller-coaster that he has ridden so wildly, for so long. He is a confidence man, his brain skewed by arrogance. Man-power turned on its head —

knowing that even if he is nabbed, he'll be able to talk his way out of it. This gives him a double system: if he doesn't get caught, he's mocking, masterfully mocking the system. If he does get caught — no difference! He'll worm out of it somehow. Both sets seed his imagined power. A no-lose situation; a perfect balance of potential and kinetic energy, fighting to a stalemate.

❧ ❧ ❧

So here I am, 6,000 miles from my home, with my beautiful, alive, funny, smart son... so beautiful and smart and alive that he is going to maim himself — die with all that monster destruct-desire intact. Richard, my handsome, tall, funny, articulate boy, the flower of western English-speaking culture. Given so much, he has to take even more, extract a price from his arm, suck the richness from his veins, take away from that which had been so generously given.

"You always get out, don't you?" I say.

"Out of what?"

"Out of trouble?" I say.

"No, no — you don't understand. The British Consul had to bail me out."

"And who got them to do it?" I ask.

"They did."

"Your father did?"

"No, no — they... no, yes, maybe you're right. Yeah, I guess that's what happened..."

Never thinking ahead — the perfect Zen Now: never examining consequence, responsibility, lines-of-power. "You always get out, don't you?" I say.

"I don't know. I don't know. What's wrong?" he says.

"O nothing, nothing," I say. I refuse to tell him that I am grieving over him — grieving over me, me and this beautiful tall flower cowboy-ruination-junky inside all of us. He sweeps through our lives like a cyclone: knocking out power lines, uprooting the flowers, tearing them to bits, or setting them, so artfully, intact, in the carcass of the house; the cars in the trees, the chickens denuded, squawking.

"Do you know I've put $25,000 in my veins in the past four years — and I haven't stolen a thing," he says, and I feel for my wallet. "I broke down," he says. "After I'd been in jail for three days... I broke down and cried. I hung onto the bars and cried. And there was this black guy, this huge black guy. He was OK. He held me, told me everything was going to be OK... Hey, listen, thanks for talking to me. I really appreciate it... and the drinks."

"I'm just another one of the countless people you've got wrapped around your finger," I tell him. "Do you want to go to your room, or mine?" I will go, first, down to the desk, give them my wallet, passport, travellers checks to put in their hotel safe.

"We can't go to my room. There's a guard there. No — I think I'll just stay here for awhile. Listen, thanks for everything..." And he takes my hand and looks in my eyes, laughing, the nuclear Holden Caulfield looking into me and smiling. It's the smiles that do it, right? Smiling that wide warm gentle loving fake smile — the all-encumbering smile of all the miscreants of all times, so taken with themselves, so taken with what they can put over on the world, so taken with taking the rest of us so completely, knowing we'll give them everything, even without their asking; giving them our Christly tears, for Christ's sakes.

❧ ❧ ❧

Twenty hours later, I am looking out the window of Flight 50 — Narita to LAX. Dawn — those spectacular 36,000-feet-up-in-the-air dawns that we now take for granted — lancing the arc of the earth with such blues and golds. Our flight has gone to the east, and on reaching the California coast, will turn to the south. Seven miles below me I can see the peninsula, the bay that so astonished the Spanish in their tiny barks, three centuries ago. They saw the land cascading wild to the waters' edge; trees, austere trees, rising up like monoliths, spiking the fog that lapped at the water-ragged edge. The relief of the peninsula so astonishing; the land so naked, so uninhabited. The thin grey thumb of it outlined atop the grey sea, the grey inlet, descried as in a thousand maps from the past; yet by no cartographer's art is it as spectacularly subtle as this.

"It's a damn good thing I didn't take up with that junky," I think sleepily. I huddle in my seat with a blue blanket up to my chin. "That's all I need — some twenty-year-old James Dean, getting me hooked on him." Going crazy with crazy Richard. My own personal hobgoblin, waiting there in my veins, ready, just for a poke (a pig in a poke) to come frothing out all over the place, capturing me (innocent me) for the next thirteen years. I — Richard's slave — howling through yellow dogsbody streets of Singapore, screeching into every hole in the wall for his next fix. Jesus! That was a close one.

We turn — and the grey-on-grey bas relief of the vision edges behind me. Crazy Richard! His flight was to leave at ten. The telephone in my hotel room rang once at eight, and then gave up. Thank god I didn't get to it in time. "Say, how'd you like to?..." he would have said. And I, boob that I am, would be heading back into the swarm of Asia with him, my blood in his blood, his curse my curse. It was a close one for both of us.

I have journeyed. I have gone into and out of the dawning again. It blasts the dark edges out of our existence as it has for so long. It flares into our lives (as it has for so long — for all of what we call time) with a welding of desire and fulfillment, a mass that turns all it touches to gold, all it touches to ash. "How was your trip to India?" they'll ask me when I get home. "Did you have a good time in India?" "India?" I'll say. "India! O no! I said I was going to Indiana. Kokomo. That's where I always go for Christmas. I wouldn't be caught dead in India. What lunacy that would've been!"

[1985]

THE REDWOOD FORESTS OF BAJA CALIFORNIA

AUGUST 22

Q: What is quicker than the wind?
A: Thought.
Q: What can cover the earth?
A: Darkness.
Q: Who are the more numerous, the living or the dead?
A: The living, because the dead are no longer.

— *THE MAHABHARATA*

Several years ago the missions of [Baja] California were accused at the Court of Madrid of trading with the English. Yet there is nothing in California except wacke [composite dirt and stone] and other worthless rocks, and it produces nothing but thorns. If the English would accept these and in return import, above all other things, wood and shade, rain and rivers; then to be sure, a trade of great advantage for California could be established with Great Britain. Otherwise, there is nothing to trade. Wood and water, stones and thorns, are four elements of which California has an unbelievable scarcity of the first two and a great surplus of the others. Nothing is so common in California as rocks and thorns, nothing so rare as moisture, wood, and cool shade. It is not necessary to be afraid of drowning in California, but it is easy to die of thirst.

— *OBSERVATIONS IN LOWER CALIFORNIA*
FATHER JOHANN JAKOB BÆGERT (1771)

I suspect that our place out in the Sonoran desert, the place the natives call "Nomirage," is really part of Baja California. The only difference I can figure between Nomirage and the tiny town of Colonia Progreso, a short hop to the south, is that ultimate delusion, the international border.

Colonia Progreso is considered, by all concerned, to be a town in Baja and part of Mexico. Because I have an ounce or two of Mexican blood lurking about in the sweet corners of my heart, I am convinced, and will be convinced until the day I die, that Nomirage is the last (and most northerly) outpost of Baja — and that we (the old Korean War vets, the rednecks, the desert rats, the alcoholics, and the unrepentant hippies who live here) answer to the governments of the United States and California not as a necessity, but rather as a courtesy. Take Smitty, for example.

Behind our place there in the desert, on the adjacent piece of property, is a trailer, sitting on its own sun-blasted acre of land. The trailer, a 1955 twenty-five-foot Sundance, is owned by a geezer named Smitty. He must be a WWII vet. Like many of the old ones in Nomirage, he's come out there to live cheaply, to be by himself, to be left alone, to die.

The desert around him, as deserts can and will, and loneliness, as loneliness can and will, turn Smitty balmy, and angry. He builds a huge fence around his sandpile, a fence with bands of coiled flesh-ripping metal ribbon on top of it. He mounts a sodium-vapor light on a pole, which at night casts raw shadows over the fence, his dogs, his trailer, his life. And if, during the day, you go to his gate and call out to him — he stumbles out, his front dirty with spaghetti sauce, his pants wet and foul. He snarls at you. "Get the goddamn hell off my property," he'll say. He'll glare at you, and snort, and spit. He stands there, swaying back and forth, smelling of piss and age and anger there in the desert heat.

Smitty erects a big sign that tells people to stay off his land. It says that the property is guarded by vicious Dobermans, only he spells it "viscous dobarmans." The sign is right:

they are viscous. There are seven of them, and they go about in a viscous pack — a yelping mass of creatures screaming at the moon all night and at each other all day, never shutting the hell up so you in your once-quiet cabin next door can have some peace.

These beasts must be the logical extension of Smitty and his tortured mind. They are the Hounds of Hell that I remember from a piece of juvenile fiction I read so long ago, a pride of dogs so ugly and noisy and gratuitously mean that surely no one wants to mess with them, nor their master.

❧ ❧ ❧

A couple of months ago, in the middle of the day, a typical summer day on the Sonoran desert, when the heat blasts the world flat, blistering the hills and the tamarind trees, singeing the catclaw, burning up the Mormon tea; on a typical day like that, Smitty has an attack. He staggers to the telephone and calls the Nomirage volunteer medicorps, and they come right over, sirens screeching, trucks filled with respiratory equipment and volunteers eager or, better to say, mildly willing (all of them have had experience with Smitty before) to save him.

They can't get past the dogs. Every time they try to open the gates, the seven black and white Dobermans snarl with their ninety-six paired teeth, keeping the volunteer corps away from the door. Those dogs mean business; there's no way to get past them. Fred Wise of the Nomirage volunteer medics radios in to El Centro — thirty miles to the east — so that the Animal Control people can send out someone to get rid of these howling creatures. While all this dialogue is going back and forth between the El Centro Police, Animal Control, and Fred Wise, they can see Smitty through the trailer window, yanking at his shirt, staggering about, trying to get the door open, trying to get out to save himself from his confounded dogs. But he can't get the trailer door open: it's too complicated for him, befuddled as he is *in extremis*, what with the three bolt locks, the cross-bar, the latches. He can't get them all undone right because he has set it up so they have to be sprung in a special way to keep out the thieves and bomb toters and ax murderers that swarm over the desert in Nomirage, outside there, lurking in the shadows of this blast-furnace desert, in the 110-degree heat, there in Nomirage, waiting to get at Smitty and his tomato-paste shirt-front, his droopy old pants.

Animal Control arrives at last, but Smitty has fallen away out of sight. The Control man races out of his truck, takes the mace and the steel-reinforced antibite mittens, reaches through the gate, grabs the snarling yowlers, one by one, wrestles them to the ground, drags them away across the sand, throwing them in the mesh holding tanks at the back of his truck. By the time they get to Smitty, his body is twisted down on the dank, shag carpet on the floor, his face red and apoplectic. They hook him up to the resuscitation equipment, but it's just too damn late. Those creatures, those *beasts* that were to watch over his dark days and brilliantly lit nights, to pit their lives against all comers, they did their job so very well.

❧ ❧ ❧

Consciousness converges with the child as a landing tern touches the outspread feet of its shadow on the sand: precisely, toe hits toe. The tern folds its wings to sit; its shadow dips and spreads over the sand to meet and cup its breast. Like any child, I slid into myself perfectly fitted, as a diver meets her reflection in a pool. Her fingertips enter the fingertips on the water, her wrists slide up her arms. The diver wraps herself in her reflection wholly, sealing it at the toes, and wears it as she climbs rising from the pool, and ever after …

— AN AMERICAN CHILDHOOD

The gods are very crazy, or perhaps very angry, here in Nomirage. The wind is coming down out of the Rumorosas, shaking the house, yanking at the windows, pulling at the crossbeams — the wind tearing through everything with its hot, midnight breath. And Smitty is fit to be tied, storming around the house, rattling the cage. "It figures," I say to myself. "Smitty's so dumb he doesn't even know that he's dead, so he comes over to bother me at three a.m." There's certainly nothing for him to do next door, since they dismantled the sodium-vapor light, took the seven hounds (and their teeth) away to the pound, got rid of all the locks, nailed the doors and the windows shut to keep out the the wind and the sand.

First Smitty rattles the bed, but that doesn't talk to me. The hot hurricane blasts down from the Rumorosas so often that I don't even notice the bed and floor and windows shaking. Since we're a mere thirty miles from the butt-end of the San Andreas fault, this shake rattle & roll is as common as the black widow spiders that operate out of our half-assed basement, along with the four-, five-, or six-inch scorpions that turn up under my pillow without my specific permission, or the earwigs who move into my shoes during the night

The wind and the shaking and the three a.m. noises are like the desert creatures, so common that we don't even notice them, so I don't notice Smitty even though the house seems more rattly and bangerous than usual. But I have to confess to you right here and now that I firmly believe in any and all spooks — possessed, dispossessed, friendly or no. Smitty must know I believe in the dead nonworld, so he rattles my bed and — getting no reaction — starts pulling on the back of my nightshirt, like some absurd child. That does it. They can talk to me or through me and rattle my cage, but when they start pulling on me, that's it. I turn on the light, knowing that the only way to get rid of the old sucker is to read a book and pretend he isn't there. It's obvious that he, in concert with my usual insomnia, will not let me sleep any more tonight, so I rouse myself, drink a glass of icy milk, check what's left of my face in the mirror, look in on Eve and JD (sound asleep:

they've got better sense than to be bothered by alcoholic spooks) and give myself over to a night of reading.

I woke in bits, like all children, piecemeal over the years. I discovered myself and the world, and forgot them, and discovered them again. I woke at intervals until, by that September when Father went down the river, the intervals of waking tipped the scales, and I was more often awake than not. I noticed this process of waking, and predicted with terrifying logic that one of these years not far away I would be awake continuously and never slip back, and never be free of myself again.

Annie Dillard comes from that same source as so many of us: the rich, overconfident post-World War II America, where everything could be accomplished, where we were given a life in families who cared for us, more or less, did their best for us, more or less, gave us a seamless childhood of friends, food, clothing, houses with enough rooms, brothers and sisters with enough interest, friends with enough diversity — and most of all, permission for us to grow into ourselves as best we were able.

Writing autobiography is hard, for one has to take all the confetti, the colored bits of memory, bring them together into a gestalt, as if they all had meaning. One can lard autobiography with uniform themes, like cruelty (Richard Wright's *Black Boy*) or rough humor (Betty MacDonald's *The Egg and I*) or melancholy (Singer's *In My Father's Court*) — but Dillard has chosen to tell us her childhood out of the stuff of poetry, tie the whole together in the style of James Joyce, Vladimir Nabokov, Jean-Paul Sartre:

Children ten years old wake up and find themselves here, discover themselves to have been here all along: is this sad? They wake like sleepwalkers, in full stride ... they feel themselves to have just stepped off the boat, just converged with their bodies, just flown down from a trance, to lodge in an eerily familiar life well under way.

AUGUST 24 [EN ROUTE MULEGÉ]

The three of us are perfect traveling companions, since we have known each other for so long that there can be no unpleasant surprises, hidden personality tics that could disastrously affect a trio on a ten-day journey together into the hot wastelands of Baja, the great thin, dry, fingernail paring that is Baja — a thousand miles long, peopled with ocotillo and creosote and brittlebush, filled with snakes and waterless wastes and high, dry, untouched mountains, with, still, and occasionally, the rare oasis. And at the edges, the Baja nature jokes: the blue-footed booby; the fabled boojum tree; a land so dry that although it is immediately adjacent to the richest state in the richest country in the world, remains its own desolate place. This, of course, has saved it from being turned into another potbelly like Palm Springs, Marina del Rey, La Jolla.

We drive across the border into Mexicali — then turn west towards Tecate. The climb from the Sonoran desert into the alto plano at 3,000 feet carries us through some of the most spectacular scenery in this hemisphere. It reminds me of the "Picos de Europa," the Cantabrian range in northern Spain. The rocks, the Piedras Grandes, great thighs and bellies and biceps and backs of granite: enormous rust-colored, rounded boulders, sensuous in their roundedness, with a rusty tinge, rocks dyed by a thousand thousand years of two-inch-a-year rainfall. Boulders crowding each other and the whole landscape so that the eye is dazzled by the enormity of them piled asymmetrically against each other, split, leaning crazily, perched at the edge of hills, rivulets, canyons — flowing out of Dylan Thomas' giant,

there this night I walk in the white giant's thigh
Where barren as boulders women lie longing still
To labor and love though they lay down long ago ...
Now curlew cry me down to kiss the mouths of their
dust.

We drive between the backs and the thighs on a thin line of black asphalt (no shoulders, mountain sides to the left, sheer drop-offs to the right) Mexican Federal Highway Two, twisting and angling among boulders so huge as to dwarf the few cars that push up towards the aching blue sky. This is the main route between the fifteen million people of Mexico City and the million-and-a-half people of Tijuana, so we have these busses zooming up to our back bumper, and then, when there is a milli-inch space ahead, streaking past us in a blast of diesel fumes. The kamikaze school of bus driving is in style here, and the steep two-lane black-asphalt narrow crowded highway is the perfect place for a driver, on the upgrade, to test his (and our) manhood: to race past us blindly, heading towards the curve that lies just ahead of us.

In Mexico highway deaths are not only courted grandly, they are rendered full tribute *in situ*. Every mile or so, a metal cross blooms, with its tiny bouquet of plastic flowers, to show those who tempted the gods — and lost. Specific warnings about intercity travel hubris from the past. Even more to the point, there is the Mexican method of dealing with wrecks: they leave them lie. Car bones appear at the edge of every curve, at the bottom of every slight "vado" — moldering in their final resting place (stripped of anything worth saving: tires, motor, universal joint, headlights, mirrors, seats). The bones of *el carro* and the bones of the earth linked, often decorated, Indian-blanket style, in white or black or red paint, with square-limbed Mexican characters, reporting that Miguel loves Teresa, or Louisa is desired by José, or, in one case, that the carbones have been visited and marked forever by the *The Ba Ha Ha Phantom*.

AUGUST 25 [ENSENADA]

When the good Señora Serpiente undertook to pinch our poke, she did not pack a forty-five (what is that old wheeze? "She said she felt like a young Colt, but she looked more like an old .45"). At least we couldn't see the gun in her hand, *per se*, but that did not deter her from 125,000 pesos worth of highway robbery.

"Sí, cien veintecinco mil. Sino, si no quiere," said the Señora, shrugging her shoulders and moving towards the door. "If you don't want it." And she has us. The last beds in Ensenada — the last beds within fifty miles of Ensenada, so said the lady at the tourist office. "She doesn't *look* like a mugger or a bugger," I whisper to JD and Eve as she is getting out the sheets. But I feel, somehow, that she has introduced something hard into a tender and very private part of our anatomies. A hard, cold object, a long, hurtful one, introduced into that private area where one sits, where rests what's left of the assets we had come to treasure over the years, before their final demise at her hands.

Still, the good Señora opens up her door to the weary American travelers, loans them her beds, for the night: beds out of antiquity, perhaps artifacts of the Aztec period, wardrobes created long ago, replete with a rich supply of old straw and curlicue springs; beds designed for Tom Thumb (and his lovely wife Tomessa), beds sitting lumpily there in a room dainty with pink walls, green ceilings, black flies, alongside the main roadway running between Ensenada and Tijuana, filled as it is all night with the roar of the thousand or so Peterbilts hurrying north and south at speeds approaching Mach One. But at least we weren't sleeping entangled in each other at the back of the van: we're in our own beds, with the happy cantadores below us, the Mexicans who love ranchero music so much that they are willing to share it with all the tourists, all the night.

And then there is the *pescadera* — the fish factory. In Ensenada they take fish fresh from the sea, nice, fresh, flapping, friendly fish, live and healthy and otherwise inoffensive, and they let them sit around for awhile in the sun, until they're good and dead, a little rank, maybe, and then they grind them to a paste — head, scales, guts, roe, and all into the grinder. Then they let this fish-paste sit out in the sun for a day or so more to get more redolent; then they burn it, cook it up — sending great gouts of greenish yellow clouds out to the heavens, and with the prevailing wind from the north and the west, the visitors to Maison Señora Serpiente get a whiff, in fact, get many, continuing, all-night whiffs, direct from fish factory to us. It's shipped over, via airmail, this vicious, nose-twisting, brain-baking, uterus-shrinking, teeth-clenching, scrotum-tightening, bowel-churning, malodorant, mephitic, nidorous, putrid Stench. The only other time in my living memory that I have been kept awake by the effluvia of the nights was when Rover cornered two skunks, not one but two, in the basement of the camp house, right there under my bed. Rover and I spent the night tossing and turning and whimpering at the sheer animal power of it. That's the power of the *pescadera* of Ensenada, visiting, as if some great god, our rooms, our nights, and our sleep, or what is left of it.

AUGUST 26 [GUERRERO NEGRO]

Q: Give me an example of space.

A: My two hands as one [bringing the two hands together in the prayer position].

Q: An example of grief.

A: Ignorance.

Q: Of poison.

A: Desire.

Q: An example of defeat.

A: Victory.

— *THE MAHABHARATA*

The Mexican government has caused a monument to be built at the joining of North Baja California and South Baja California. It is an abstract rendering of a great steel bird, at least we think it is a bird, with metal wings, stretching upwards forty meters, with an angular metal body, and metal feet pushed out in front of it, the whole hunched over itself so strangely that it may be something else entirely — like one of those monuments around the Kremlin, entitled "The Joy of Peace" or "The Second Five-Year Plan."

Coming into Guerrero Negro on Highway One, there among the yucca and piñon and agave and barrel cactus, it rises up, the spirit and hope of indefatigable Mexican uselessness. You can see it from twenty-five miles away, and as you get closer and closer, it gets bigger and uglier, until at last there you are, the road (and you) circling about this ludicrous metal figure, now — already at ten years of age — rusting and flaking, because it was set a couple of miles from the sea, at the coldest and wettest and windiest part of Baja, here at the center, the umbilicus of north and south.

This monument, constructed to immortalize the joining of the two halves of the State of Baja, the meeting of the new 1359 KM road, stands there abstractly, uneasily, resting on its base which in turn rests on the edge of a huge square colosseum, complete with a thousand cement seats, all carefully numbered. Then next door, there are two concrete bunkers, cement structures set part way in the ground, one marked "Museum," the other marked nothing, and each bunker — like the many seats — resting vacant, and wind-blown. The museum has a dozen or so just-above-ground windows, with the glass panes carefully pried off so the wind coming off the Sea of Japan howls through the holes, as it slices, too, through the thousand invisible spectators, sepulchral on their cold and pile-inducing seats. And above all, the bird towering, and all empty, all, except for, in the sky, a single gray gull, riding the cold wind (stirring about the papers and the Bohemia cans), a wind coursing down through these dilapidated structures which were constructed, no doubt, to commemorate the history of a blighted region just before its burst of prosperity, but which, either through *mañanaism*, thievery, or — most probably — sheer forgetfulness, stand here bleak and forgotten, symbol of the eternal hope of poor Mexico and its eternally hopeful government which caused to be built here a great monument five hundred miles in either direction away from the citizenry necessary to commemorate north and south coming together along this tiny black spider road that, like the bird itself, is no monument except as to the very vast enormity of barrenness that we know as Baja.

"Somehow the monument and the boojum tree — the two things that rise above Baja — are intertwined," I think. Both are the ugliest structures imaginable. The bird — which JD dubs *Gooney Bird Descending* — is brother to the boojum which rises out of this blasted land and which looks like nothing so much as the wrong end of a carrot as seen from underground. If they wanted to go to all this trouble, how much more appropriate it would have been for the government to have erected not a metal eagle but a six-hundred-foot steel boojum, the bulk of it tapering to an ugly yellow steel blossom at its very top, metal yellow flowerlets which could be used for an observation platform, with — for steps — the dark sticks poking out of the sides of the bare creature (as they do), so one could mount scarily all the way up to the verge. All monuments worth the name "Monument" must be available for human involvement, even if it is making it possible for us to crawl up in it, look out of the top of it, then crawl back down: the Statue of Liberty, the Eiffel Tower, the Washington Monument.

❧ ❧ ❧

As we pass down through Guerrero Negro, JD points to the garbage at the side of the highway. He opines that Baja California's Route One must be the longest running garbage dump in the world. In and near the towns of San Vincinte, San Quintín, and El Rosario, whole fields are covered with waste paper, tin cans, plastic bags, plastic containers, empty bottles, fluff, and general detritus. He says that these are a type of farm peculiar perhaps to Mexico — "Trash Farms" — places where they grow trash for export. He says it is an easy crop to produce, doesn't demand much watering, and is only matched in efficiency by "Dust Farms," also endemic to Mexico, where they cultivate great quantities of dust which can be gathered up and exported as easily, whenever there's a windstorm. He points to one dust farm which is being prepared for export at this very moment, possibly across the road in front of us.

As we wait for the dust to clear, I tell JD and Eve my favorite Baja story, which is from the last time I was here, several years ago, when Gerry and I were traveling north from Santa Rosalía. We had been stuck in Mázatlan for something like three days trying to get on the ferry that would take us across the Sea of Cortez to Rosalía. We went down to the terminal repeatedly to wait in line to get tickets, but Mexicans wait in line like the folks in Bombay do, that is, they don't. So we got trampled twice, and on the third day, the way we got the tickets to get out of town was to camp out in front of the ticket booth at six a.m. and, even so, got the last of the beds.

The ferry was everything that you would expect on a Mexican liner. It was August, so they piped a little extra heat into our squalid cabin. This didn't seem to affect our roommates, the two Mexican truck drivers who fell asleep at departure and did not awaken until arrival. We found out that they were musicians as well as teamsters, because they sang for us, through their noses, all the long night. Our headboards were set as close as possible to the adjoining engine room, with its 1912 Bucyrus-Erie thirteen-cylinder 40,000-horsepower engine — so their bugling should have made little difference; but what with the heat register turned up full blast, and the music, and the engine room, I think Gerry and I, between us, were able to stalk, trap, and wrestle to the ground something in the area of ten to fifteen minutes of sleep during that long and tedious night.

When we finally drove off the boat in Santa Rosalía, looking for a place to rest, it turned out that there was a convention of the Stupid and Noisy American Visitors Association in town who had taken up all the available rooms (noisily) so we were forced to head north. We ended up driving for ten hours, across the desert, because we could find no place for the night (nor the day). I was convinced that we were going to spend the rest of our lives wandering, driven from place to place, turned away at every door, finding no place to lay a weary head.

Finally, it was night, and you aren't to drive at night on Mexican roads, ever, because you'll be run over by cows and overbearing trucks. I was resigned to die, in the dark, my foot on the accelerator, my eyes crossed, somewhere near Santa Inez, when there, over the next rise, came this apparition out of the night: in the very middle of nowhere this huge hotel, illuminated by giant spotlights (electricity so hard to come by in the desert), a tender vision if there ever was one. The castle was complete with fountains, red-tile floors, deep beds, and lovely Mexicans dressed in white uniforms with gold tassels. "I thought we had died and gone to heaven," I tell JD and Eve. "But there was only one problem with heaven."

"What was that?"

"Fake air conditioners. They ground up the air and spewed it out — but didn't cool it. A special for the American tourists. Since we demand air conditioners in every room, the hotel gave us Placebo conditioners."

AUGUST 27 [SAN IGNACIO]

Indians do not make a clear distinction between facts and ideas, between ideas and words; they have never clearly recognized the principle of contradiction.

— LOUIS DE LA VALLÉE POUSSIN

JD claims that Baja is the land of mirages. He proves that with the car radio. He's a radionut, so to travel with him is to have your normal ordinary dumb Federated radio perform strange tricks. Driving along the western shore of Baja, some 500 miles south of Alta California — he is able to tune in KUSC's low-power repeater in Santa Barbara. FM repeaters are limited in range to a maximum radius of twenty-five miles, but because of "ducting," the signal is guided along the warmer air just above the ocean. At the same time, we see mirages along the edge of the horizon — trees and bluffs which are over the edge of the earth — but which are projected above it, looking wavery and inconstant. He tells me that they are related. All mirages — visible, audible, tactile, ductile, the primitive mysteries of Baja — are all related.

To be with JD is to be in radio magic. The last time we traveled together was several years ago in Italy. He wanted me to hear Radio Gabon on the fifteen meter band. He says it is the best shortwave broadcast station in the world, so he took my little Sony, and hung it under the bed, with the spiders and the slutswool, and there, and there alone — under the bed, that is — we were able to get Radio Gabon, which was, that day, in total cultural reversal, playing 1930s Blues, the Memphis Jug Band. So if you get down on the floor, there in the Hotel Londres, in Venice, just off the Main Canal, and put your ear near the radio next to the bedsprings, you can hear "My Baby Rocks Me (with a Steady Roll)" and "The Santa Fe Blues" seeping into a room from 4,500 miles away. What we are doing is experiencing the radio magic which is JD's specialty — because he is a radio fool — building and operating strange radio stations when he is not seeking them out along the cold tiles, under the springs, there in the Hotel Londres. All about us now, there are signals coming in everywhere, and all you have to do is to figure out how to pluck them from the timbrels of the æther, like we are doing, driving down the finger of Baja, listening to the beauteous Vivaldi *Beatus Vir* — coming to us from a station 650 miles away which is, technically, not expected to transmit more than a few miles (FM is defined as "line of sight"). It is these mysteries and contradictions that delight my friend JD, president of the Radio Nut Association.

Twenty-five years ago, when we first met in Seattle, I went over to his house. He had put the antenna of his Hallicrafters shortwave receiver in the freezer of the refrigerator, because he said he wanted to hear the local service of Radio Moscow, beaming out of Olëkminsk, in the Central Siberian Uplands, the frequency of which he had selected out of his short wave guide. He said that because Olëkminsk was located up there near the Arctic Circle, and its transmitting antenna was resting in the cold, cold ground — it would be best to duplicate the conditions of transmission, so he planted his receiving antenna in the freezer of the refrigerator, and I knew then that I had stumbled over a genuine Radio Fool, a man driven to lunacy by transmission alone — one who was completely, and happily, deranged by all the RF that has been beating in on his poor brain since (or perhaps before) his conception.

And as he was showing me his coiled-copper receiving-antenna residing in the freezer of the GE SuperTemp, trying to explain this stupid theory of supercold transmission to me, a theory that was contrary to every logical principal of physics ever taught me, all of a sudden the Hallicrafters shortwave bloomed into life, there behind the heavy dark burnt umber rotating dial, and a music came wavering in (as shortwave music will, wambling through the force of the cosmos): we heard the song of two women, presumably two Russian women, singing full-throated contraltos, a duet so haunting, so filled with sadness and might, that I knew that somehow JD had created his own law of physics, and thereby had tapped into the soul of that sad country, so that it could reach us through the dark airs with the music of a people locked in the furtherest reaches of Mother Russia, souls out of the great permafrost, words and voices roiling slowly out of the hearts of the powerful earth women, two peasant women conjoined with the soul and the universe, and the great night sky, and all of us transfixed there in a place so far distant from the night, these two great souls bearing in on us.

I have to tell you that no matter how hard we tried after that, with refrigerators, antennas, freezers — we were never able, ever again, to pull that sweet sound out of the æther, as if the local service of Radio Moscow had been struck dumb by our finding it, but, more likely, by the freak transmission condition (the zodiacal placement of the sun, the periodicity of the moon, the ellipsoidal conjunctions of Sirius, the phalangeal rotation of Kohoutek). We never could find that exact combination again, and for that reason the song of the two earthen Mother Russia souls would never be duplicated for our ears, at least, not in this lifetime.

❧ ❧ ❧

As we drive along, we are having one of our usual interminable debates about radio, the æther, frequencies, governmental policy. JD claims that the reason there isn't enough spectrum space in the United States is because the federal government owns and monopolizes over eighty percent of it. Our available AM, FM, and TV bands are miniscule when you compare them to what the feds have sequestered away for god knows what nefarious purposes (spying, wars, international ruination, and the usual public policy activities of your usual twentieth century governmental seek-and-destroy entities). For the hundreds of broadcast frequencies available to each region, there are three or four thousand more owned by the federal government under a variety of jurisdictions, and kept out of the hands of the ultimate consumer (us). Thus, our government (for some anachronistic reason, they persist in calling it "capitalistic," as in "the American Capitalistic System") is powerfully socialistic when it comes to eminent domain, the ownership of the hectares of raw land in the western United States, and the stewardship of the longwave, medium-wave, shortwave, high- and ultra-high-frequency bands.

JD: What I would like to do is get some of these frequencies away from the government — set up a series of special bands, one for each interest group. Free speech. Every possible political group would have their own reserved frequency.

ME: The anarchists?

JD: Yes.

ME: The socialist workers?

JD: Yes, those too.

ME: The John Birch Society?

JD: Of course.

ME: PAW? AIM? The ADA? The IUD?

JD: All of them. Everyone gets to broadcast, whenever and however they want. It will be designated as the Political Band — for all political interests.

ME: I'm for it. A Political Band. And since I've always liked march music, I want them to set up something for the John Philip Sousa fans, like a Brass Band.

JD: Right! That too. And for Caribbean music, a Steel Band. And for the latex industry ...

ME: A Rubber Band?

JD: And for the FBI ...

Eve: The FBI, the CIA and all spying services get a Watch Band.

Eve is an information junkie — and because she is a radio person too, it means she can't get through the day without a dose of National Public Radio. Here we are hundreds of miles from the U.S. border — and she wants to hear "All Things Considered." You need to visit with Nina Totenberg? The Radio Freak will take care of all your needs. JD goes to work, mutters and curses, and then there she is with some AM station from Tucson that does NPR. It fades in and out with all this talking about Bork — but there it is, at 1550 kHz. Driving past elephant trees, senita cactus, yucca, and the sweet organ-pipe cactus (that fed the Indians for so long in this dry and hungry land), those smooth-voiced Americans are telling us more than we want to hear about the Straits of Hormuz, keeping us world-nervous even though we are so far from home.

AUGUST 28 [MULEGÉ]

In Mission San Ignacio and in others farther to the north, there are persons who will attach a piece of meat to a string, swallow it, and then pull it out again, like pearl fishers pulled out of the water, repeating the performance a dozen or more times in succession for the sake of prolonging the taste and the enjoyment of the meat.

— *OBSERVATIONS IN LOWER CALIFORNIA*
JOHANN JAKOB BÆGERT, S.J. (1771)

Our first evening in Mulegé we go to the Candide Restaurant. We sit out of doors, on the patio, so we can eat while enjoying the wasps and gnats that fly into our eyes and up our noses. The waiter is a hectoring little hunchback named Toulouse-Lautrec (Pancho Toulouse-Lautrec, that is) who can make no sense at all of my impeccable Spanish, as I can make no sense of his Mulegé accent — except to understand that they are all out of fish, clams, seafood, meat, vegetables, bread, and tortillas. The three things they do have in abundance are warm Bohemia, crying babies, and, "Callo Empanizada."

After we order three plates of crying baby, I mean Callo, Eve wants to know what it is, and I explain, in the simplest way possible, that "pan" means "bread," so "empanizada" must mean that the Callo is "embreaded."

Eve: Embreaded? It's going to be "embreaded" What does that mean? And what's "Callo?"

Me: You know what "encrusted" is?

She: Yes.

Me: And you know what "endive" is?

She: Mmm.

Me: Need I say more? It means "fried."

They turn to watch the antics of the black dog Lobo. Lobo has taken an immediate fancy to me, or rather, to my groin. He rests his big, ugly, flea-bitten nose there, seeking scraps. "Shoo," I say, making weak motions with my hand, but he snarls at me (and into my groin). Evidently in Baja dog language "Shoo" means "Stay!"

"What does "Callo" mean?" persists Eve.

Me: *There's* the mystery. The closest word I can come up with, using the usual etymological keys, leads us to believe that it has something to do with "street," or "calle." They probably have the same root, or route.

Eve: As each other?

Me: As each other before they had begun. Did you get that? *Route!*

JD: We're going to be eating fried street?

Before I can answer that question, Toulouse-Lautrec brings in three plates of breaded and fried potholder.

As we chew on this for awhile, Eve points out that the Candide is "an unhappy restaurant." Indeed, the patrons are sourfaced, a man and wife over in the corner are going after each other with blancmange, the owner's children are having tantrums in the kitchen, two cats are fighting in the oak tree behind me, and there is a palmetto bug crawling up my leg. I tell them about my fungus.

"This subtropical air has a very strange effect on my feet," I explain. "My fungus has been an old friend for forty years, now. Each night, regularly, I sprinkle some Desenex on it, which it slurps right up, licking its little fungoid chops, sitting up, rolling over, and begging for more." It is one of those *quirks*, like my dewlaps, my twitches, and my rotund personality that I figure will be with me until I die.

But down here, something goes haywire. The symbiotic relationship that me and my fungus have had for so long gets topsy-turvy, and it begins to send tendrils far beyond its usual nesting place between the fourth and fifth digits. And the scabies which has contented itself with a place on the cranium, at the back, near the bald spot, starts south, down, all the way down to meet the fungus coming up from below. "Sometimes I think I am just a big Horn and Hardarts for all the various bacteria and funguses in the universe," I tell them. "A larder of delicate flesh. All the people in the world, and they choose me, and invite all their microbial friends down for dinner. 'We've been munching on Amantea for so long,' they tell their pals. 'He won't mind. C'mon over and join us. You'll bring the wine?' And they show up with their families, and their families'

families, and all my doctors and sorcerers shake their heads, and sympathize, and show me their *own* cases of fungus, and I know the meaning of lifelong attachment."

It sets me to thinking about this thing we call body, and how it is given to us, to most of us, in a relatively pristine condition, and then over the years we give it, or are given, these scars, kinks, and twists, some of which are temporary and some forever, or at least *our* forever: the exact place where you broke your wrist, the fungus under the nail, the scar where you cut yourself just above the kneecap, piles, varicose veins. They're not about to go away, but rather like tenants who refuse to depart, they become a part of you and your world. We age, and we (and they) are written on this huge scroll called Body. These unbidden ride-alongs take the journey as seriously as we do. They've signed up with this vessel for life, and stay with us until the end and will, I guess, reluctantly pass on to fungal heaven with us on that day when the train finally pulls out of the station.

AUGUST 29 [MULEGÉ]

Q: Which animal is the slyest?
A: The one that man does not yet know.
Q: Which came first, day or night?
A: Day, but it was only a day ahead.
Q: What is the cause of the world?
A: Love.

— *THE MAHABHARATA*

Last night Eve said that Freud's novels were as good as Dostoevski's, but instead of the four Brothers Karamazov — Ivan, Dmitry, Alyosha, and Smerdyakov — what you got were the Four *Bothers*: Id, Ego, Superego, and Libido. This observation threw her sullen audience into gales of silence, so we hastened to finish our hotpads, retrieved my groin from Lobo, thanked Toulouse-Lautrec for a terrible meal, and disappeared back toward the hotel.

The Placebo air conditioner in my room thrums, *sotto voce*, goes into a deeper thrum when the condenser kicks in, every twenty seconds or so, continues this deepthroated noise for a minute or so — and then kicks off. It can drive you crazy when you are trying to sleep (or trying to go crazy). I lie there for an eternity or so, anticipating the musics of the air conditioner and the leavings of my brain: thoughts, memories, ideas, plans, hopes. I fall to thinking about the last time I was in Baja.

After our fever-torture ride, when Gerry and I finally got to our room, there at the Miracle Inn in Santa Inez, we'd been conjoined to the car for so long that our bodies were sweaty, aching, tired. Once in our room, we strip and shower, and as the hot waters flow over us, he washes me and soaps me down from the top of my head to the bottom of my feet, and I do the same for him. I can't vouch for me, but I certainly remember Gerry: perfect, at least to one observer's eyes — no bald spots, no inner tube about the waist, no saphenous veins.

Then we fall into bed, not even bothering to eat, so tired that we don't even turn off the light, just pass out in the bed.

He wakes me several hours later in a fugitive dream, racing along the shore, feet kicking out at the sand, eyes moving about under closed lids. I wonder if I am part of his dream: running with him through this dream surf, kicking at the dream waves before him, alive with the dream pleasure of being alive. Chimera motions are filled with effort, and float at the same time. The waves arch perfectly, catching the turquoise light without flaw. The sun is heatless, the motion goes on forever. Bodies move, and move, then are quiescent. Gerry's feet stretch across the foot of the bed, then turn inwards, like a dream. "Wake up, Gerry," I say, and shake him. "Wake up." He turns, and the dream is gone. Gerry is powerful when awake, vulnerable when asleep, missed when gone.

"He's somewhere around here," I think, thinking of him, now that he is (unthinkably) gone. Maybe he is out for a walk on the night beach, as he is wont to do, so full of life, not willing to waste any part of it on sleep. I'll go outside, and there he'll be in the distance, the black shadow on the moon-white shade, caught by reflections that run across the waves, a shadow so far away that it becomes part of the night. "He's somewhere around here, I know," I say to myself. And when he returns, I'll be able to lean over, and, by listening carefully, hear the great sound of his heart, the great, warm, generous heart that moves so perfectly, perfectly in his chest.

They say that these afflictions we call love are shadows out of our childhood. A father or a mother, a brother or a sister, an uncle, a cousin maybe. Our child hearts become forged into a diamond point of love at age four or five or six. We love, with a child's mute love. It's one of those prints we make in kindergarten. We take the wild rose, and put it in the press on top of the blueprint paper — flatten it out under the glass cover. We put it out in the sun a few minutes, and then take it inside, into the darkroom. We turn the key, take the paper out and slip it in the water, and child-magic, the wild rose appears there, before our eyes, the background light blue, the shade dark and flat, a still image of the wild rose. We throw away the rose, but over the years the image stays: faint but always there, just enough of an image to bring back that particular day, the acrid smell of the darkroom, the thin aura of the fields, the frail scent of the wild rose.

Our childhood loves are imprinted on the soul, and that imprint stays with us all our days. It's an image that holds all subsequent loves. It's a time left over from forty years ago on this earth (an earth that no longer even exists): a shadow-love which taught us, for the first time, that we could be immersed in the very existence of other humans, and thus be capable of mountainous feelings, feelings of divinity, feelings of absolute, unbroken, unmitigated love. We learn, too, that as humans, inducted as we are into the fraternity, we are capable of the dying fall when we lose that love.

In honor of that flower, and that dark room, in 1940; in honor of that faded, flattering image: we'll spend the rest of our days attempting to reproduce it, days in which we try to replicate the flower of it and equally, and as virulently, replace its loss.

❧ ❧ ❧

I loved my boyfriend so tenderly, I thought I must transmogrify into vapor. It would take spectroscopic analysis to locate my molecules in thin air. No possible way of holding him was close enough. Nothing could cure this bad case of gentleness except, perhaps, violence: maybe if he swung me by the legs and split my skull on a tree? Would that ease this insane wish to kiss too much his eyelids' outer corners and his temples, as if I could love up his brain? ...

When rage or boredom reappeared, each seemed never to have left. Each so filled me with so many years' intolerable accumulation it jammed the space behind my eyes, so I couldn't see. There was no room left even on my surface to live. My rib cage was so taut I couldn't breathe. Every cubic centimenter of atmosphere above my shoulders and head was heaped with last straws. Black hatred clogged my very blood. I couldn't peep, I couldn't wiggle or blink; my blood was too mad to flow.

— AN AMERICAN CHILDHOOD

We try to write the memories of the flower into our journals. The journals, always at our bedsides. Dreams, memories, expectations, euphorias, dolors, rhapsodies, lamentations, promises to improve, promises to keep, so many promises to keep. For me, fifty-four volumes for some literary executrix to wade through, all arranged by date, hour, and city (if travelling): thoughts, observations, feelings (or imagined feelings), ideas for stories, angers (temporary, permanent), psychological assessments of childhood (or of yesterday's argument), telephone numbers, loves, lost loves, anticipated loves, anticipated loves lost, pretty words to remember ("peckerwood," "drosophilia," "maladive," "effluvia," "gutta-percha"), for possible pretty poems:

The drosophilia comes crawling,
Crawling onto the gutta-percha.
"Peckerwood,"
Says the maladive, bird-in-hand:
"Peckerwood effluvia" it sings.

And, as well, for comparison, bits of real poetry that strike the fancy:

Along the edges of the river
the night is turning moist
and on the breasts of my little Lola
the branches are dying of love ...
The night of anise and silver
sparkles along the tiles of the roof.
Silver of gutters and mirrors
The anise of white thighs ...
The branches are dying of love.

— F. GARCIA LORCA

Date of first journal entry, June 30, 1977. First sentence. "What is this misery?" A doldrum, a barely remembered plaint from so long ago. What other way to start out the first of fifty-four Domesday Books than with this interior Greek chorus in mortification. Wading through this mopish river we call life, in the middle of yet another attack of neurasthenia, transcribed dutifully in the diptych. If we have nothing else to show for our wormwood, there are, at the very least, words. All else may disappear (dreams, pretensions, hopes, desire, love, lust, wonderings, wanderings) but there'll always be the words, pouring off the page, onto the floor, clogging the drains, gushing willy-nilly into the kitchen, flooding the hallways, filling up the rooms, pouring over the transom, spilling into the streets, mucking up the neighborhood, so the mayor has to call a special meeting of the council, saying "We have to do something about these words, they're flooding the whole damn city!" They clog the freeways, bring interstate commerce grinding to a halt, immerse all buildings to their tops, making everything useless, this endless outpouring of words!

❧ ❧ ❧

The Journal — I must tell you — is no different than the slashed wrist or the swallowed bottle of pills. It becomes the symbol of Woe. Unless one is starving, or dying from some intractible, wasting disease, Woe cannot be seen. There is no accepted way to elevate the doldrums so that others can smell, taste, or feel them. Tears are not acceptable. Whining, not tolerated. Complaining: no — not in America, Land of the Brave. Therefore, we are forced to mutilate our bodies ... or write.

You don't see my *Weltschmerz*? Look: I have thousands of pages to document it. Eileen Simpson says that when she was working with ten- and twelve-year-old orphans in Nashville,

> *these malnourished, undersized boys with pale, wizened faces [which] seemed to be from Dicken's day ... Each carried, or rather clutched, a small wooden matchbox which he let go of reluctantly, and only on the promise that it would stay where he had put it on the testing table in front of him. What was in the box? "Things," they said. One of them, a recent arrival at the school and younger than the others, allowed me to look into his. It contained a canceled stamp, a bit of twine, a paper clip, a single jack, a marble: his possessions.*

We are all orphans, we all have to have a simple possession, something to fall back on. A matchbox. Leopold Bloom's bar of soap. Stephen Daedalus's ashstick. C. Amantea's fifty-four journals, with their 570,000 words.

On the other hand, my friend JD collects seconds — Leap Seconds. A couple of years ago when they were going to sew an additional second on Universal Mean Time (which they do every now and again), he tuned into WWV for the occasion. WWV is the official U.S. government time station that broadcasts on medium and shortwave. The broadcast consists of metronomic peeps, and then, on the hour, a voice saying "Universal Mean Time, Fifteen-Hundred Hours." And then there's a sound of weeping. It is appropriate that *someone* mourn the passing of time, n'est-çe-pas?

JD wanted to be there listening to WWV at the momentous occasion of the Leap Second so he could add it to his collection. He claims that the fact that they have to stick an extra second into the time bank now and then is because "the earth moves around rather unscientifically: it doesn't conform." As he is telling me about this very important occasion, I have a picture of all the Scientific Goonheads of the world gathered about their shortwave receivers for the Big Moment, when the Leap Second is added forever to the universal clock works.

It's not unlike another Leap Second, that of *The Mahabharata*. *The Mahabharata* is the epic of India, an epic fifteen times longer than the Bible. Peter Brook recently boiled it down to nine hours, and gave his version of it on stage. One could choose to go to the all-in-one session (taking up a whole Saturday), or go three evenings in a row. We went to the latter.

It was a grand experience, an epic play, with epic actions, gods, characters, and dilemmas. There was Vyasa, the writer of *The Mahabharata*. The writer writes himself into the play as a seedy old bum, and despite the fact that he created it (and himself), he never seems to know what's going to happen next.

There's Yudhishthira, who can never tell a lie and who, as much as anyone, is the hero. There's Krishna — the great, blue god of the Hindus. At the beginning of their epic battle, Arjuna — soldier, brother of Yudhishthira — appeals to Krishna, asks him to be his charioteer. Arjuna says that he is afraid, that he cannot go to war. "I can't bring death to my own family. How could I dare to be happy again? No, I prefer not to defend myself. I will wait here for death." Then the following dialogue takes place:

Krishna: *Victory and defeat, pleasure and pain are all the same. Act, but don't reflect on the fruits of the act. Forget desire; seek detachment.*

Arjuna: *Yet you urge me to battle, to massacre. Your words are ambiguous. I am confused.*

Krishna: *Renunciation is not enough. You must not withdraw into solitude. You must not stay without action, for we are here to serve the world.*

Arjuna: *Yes, I know.*

Krishna: *You must rise up free from hope and throw yourself into the battle.*

Arjuna: *How can I put into practice what you're demanding of me? The mind is capricious, unstable; it's evasive, feverish, turbulent, tenacious. It's harder to subdue than taming the wind.*

Then Krishna "murmured in his ear:"

Krishna led Arjuna through the tangled forest of illusion. He began to teach him the ancient yoga of wisdom and the mysterious path of action. He spoke for a long time, a very long time, between the two armies preparing to destroy themselves ... He showed him the deepest movements of his being and his true battlefield where you need neither warriors nor arrows, where each man must fight alone. It's the most secret knowledge. He showed him the whole of truth; he taught him how the world unfolds.

And that is the Leap Second of *The Mahabharata*. For what Krishna is whispering in Arjuna's ear, just a mere moment on stage, is the entire *Bhagavad-Gita*. Like the æons of the stars themselves, this lovely document has been compressed down to a whisper, an aside, on the stage, before the battle. The philosophy of the ages, crammed into that single moment.

Whether it is The Leap Second or the entire *Bhagavad Gita* as a moment or the comedy of fifty-four journals — it is enough to save us from ourselves, isn't it? The cure for the *taedium vitae* of our nights, all the brooding of our days.

SEPTEMBER 2

Just below Mulegé there are a series of beaches, all part of the Bahía de Concepción. We drive through a brown and stony wasteland, with only lava flows and cardón cactus for relief from the stoniness of it all — and then we come over the hill and there is the beach spread out before us, tucked into a cove, hills all about on three sides, turquoise waters to the east. The sand is brilliant white, and there are twenty or thirty deserted straw shacks set about to protect us from the worst of the sun.

We drive down to the beach, park near the water, spread the towels, get out the cooler, and put ourselves into the waters, the earthen, warm waters of La Bahía de la Concepción, the Bay of all our Conceptions. All day we float there on the water, take our rest on the sand, or in the shack — talking sometimes; not talking, others.

And when I am in the waters, with my mask, I think I am turning into a fish, floating over the bottom of the bay three or four or six feet below me. There are a hundred minnows that come to nibble at my fingers. There are a dozen large fish that rest in the floating shadow of my body; I become a great white whale rolling about in the warm waters.

I have assumed this mask, no different than the masks used in Greek dramas, because it is a mask to disguise the world (and me) from the fact that I am probably not a fish. A mask that allows me, still, to play at being a sea creature, hovering over my brothers along the bottom: the turbans racing awkwardly along the rocks, the clams lying about like Christmas presents, the goatfish and garden eels, the purple spirals. The multifarious creatures lie so easily below, as I float along, until, at one point, I come upon the doubler crab. John Barth once talked about the doublers, in love (as it were):

> *With a great sense of well-being I tossed the last hard half of my breakfast biscuits at a doubler crab mating lazily*

just beneath the surface. As was their *custom, the gentleman did the swimming while the soft lady beneath, locked to him with all her legs, allowed him his pleasure, which might last for fourteen hours. Crabbers refer to the male and the female thus coupled in their sport as one crab, a "doubler," just as Plato imagined the human prototype to be male and female joined into one being. My biscuit landed to starboard of the lovers, and the gentleman slid, unruffled, six inches to port, then submerged, girl friend and all, in search of the tasty missile that had near scuttled his affair.*

We're sea creatures, the crabs and I, back where we began; half in the waters and half in the air. I am part of the shore, part of the waters; I am the waves and the light — and these are the rhythms of my childhood. The waters of the sea, as much my home as the land.

We develop a beach style. Eve will often sit up to her waist in the water, reading her book, her great floppy hat making her look like one of the naiades. JD will be off in the deeper waters, standing, bent over, mask on face, leaning over the secrets which lie below him, at his feet. I float about, held a few feet above the seafloor by the salt waters, as I drop my hand down to weave through the fish, pick up a clam, then float it back, touch the limpets and chitons, dig up some sand so that the hundred minnows will fill it with their curiosity, thoughts in and about the hole.

Floating at one with the sun and the water and the sand. There are times during the days when we go back to Mulegé, so briefly, and while there, we find ourselves longing for the beach: the streets are scorching, the sweat comes so readily in the damp atmosphere. We stop by Panaderías Lolita to pick up some bread and cheese and ice and mineral water — and then we come back to our home in the water again.

Sometimes, when the sun is at its highest, our scheduled nonschedule brings us together in the straw shack, and we lie there, out of the sun, talking about this or that. At those moments, we are in no way connected to the world — that real world out there, the one we come from, the one we have to return to, someday. Someday.

Nearby, there are four or five fan palms, joined at the base, set in the sand a few feet from the waves, looking like nothing so much more than every cartoonist's vision of a desert isle. Birds flit in and out of the fronds. Eve says we should look them up in our bird atlas.

"Look at the red-breasted one up there," she says, pointing.

"Where?" I ask, hopefully, trying, squinting through my lenses, against the light of the sun, trying to see the tree, much less the bird.

"There," she says — "see, it has a green head, and fulvous wings."

"Fulvous wings?" I say. "What color is its tongue?"

"Orange," she says, "with tiny veins of green."

"The truth is not in you," I tell her. "You're suffering from Mythomania." But I dutifully get out our worn copy of *Captain Wimbey's Bird Atlas* to look up this red-breasted bird with yellow wings, and the green-veined tongue. "Here," I say, showing her a likely looking one, "It must be the Flammulated Fly-Catcher, with its 'low bubbling or rolling cry of Prrrrreep-prrrrreep.' Listen!"

We fall silent. "Cheep," go the birds in the tree. "Cheep-cheep," they say. Eve points out that the Flammulated Fly-Catcher does not have a golden beak, and certainly not an orange tongue. Furthermore, it nests only in Squaw Valley. "O.K.," I say, leafing through the pages, "How about ... here! The Slaty-Tailed Trogon. 'When mating, it goes 'cow, cow, cow.'''"

"Cow-cow?" she says, doubtfully. "Cheep-cheep," go the birds in the tree.

She pulls on her straw boater. "The truth is not in you," she says, pushing herself out to sea.

Later, as the sun yawns, and starts to stretch out to rest, I put on a tape of some Russian songs. I drink a bottle of Corona, eat some Gamesa crackers. The sounds are magnified in the late afternoon. Eve and JD are together, in the water, looking at something in the deep. The shadows grow towards them. I listen to these songs from the mountains of Georgia. It's the sound of people from far away, singing about *their* loves and *their* nights and *their* souls. The quiet, the growing shadows, and I think about the people 12,000 miles away, thinking that the music I am listening to is really no further away than our souls. "These voices, these people, no matter where they are from, they're human," I think. It is as if all humans are visiting together on this planet — and happen to come together this evening. This sweet and silent beach, the waves rubbing against the shore — and we are all together on the land, on the face of the earth, with these words. Whatever they may be, these are the sounds of humanity, and they tie us together in the universe.

❧ ❧ ❧

San Quintín ... [is] an ugly town with an even uglier reputation ... the Hotel La Pinta in San Ignacio is overpriced, and the Motel La Posada has a very good restaurant, but the service deteriorates if you order the cheaper items on the menu.

Loreto is a drab town with a poor beach which boasts a fine museum and a few cheap hotels.

The Hacienda is untidy and carelessly run, but has a good bar.

Santa Rosalía has a dirty beach and sparse accomodations.

— THE 1987 *SOUTH AMERICAN HANDBOOK*

"It's a good damn thing we got out of there when we did," I tell them as we drive north.

"The bugs?" JD asks. For indeed, as we loaded up the car, the gnats and mosquitoes and horseflies had discovered us, especially me and my sweet, savory blood, which they tried to steal for the care and feeding of their own obnoxious progeny. And while not nibbling away at my neck and arms, they would buzz my ears to let me know they had my number.

"No," I say. "It wasn't the bugs. It was that I began to believe that if we didn't get the hell out of there, we would have had to move into that straw shack, spend the rest of our lives there, pothering around, plucking clams and crab and fish from the sea to broil over the fire, picking up bread and beer and *limones* in Mulegé to tide us over. If we hadn't left when we did, we'd have been a disgrace to all parents and friends, since they had naïvely thought we were going to be coming home some day. Can you imagine the three of us living in a five-by-seven hut with a three-mile wide front lawn? For the rest of our lives." We all sigh.

We head on north, then east — back into the desert, out of the steamy heat. We are leaving our seaside freedom, going back to our routines. Our sublime time together makes us a bit silly. JD finds "All Things Considered" on the radio again, and I tell Eve and JD of a program I am planning, a radio program for the Little People of the world — midgets, dwarfs: the Short Folk. It will address their needs, and will be called *Small Things Considered*. JD starts in on his theory about Taco Bell. Here he is referring to the telephone company of Baja — whose lines, carried on spindly, bent, and twisted old-man canes at the side of the road, accompany us northwards. He says the engineers of CEPSA — the Mexican Highway Department — visited the United States and found that all the highways have wires, on poles, alongside them. They weren't sure why, but they felt it was essential for the road, so they came back and — zotz! — Taco Bell (and Tel) was born.

The desert here is spectacularly dry, and desolate, and brown. As the sun dies in the west, the cirio trees are lit up by the last of the rays, giving them an especially bristled otherworldly appearance. They certainly are the ugliest thing going, outside of Kansas City, with their large, pale trunks growing narrower and narrower, coming to a point, sometimes curving over themselves in strange loops, and with prickly branches sticking out all over. The romantic priest Fr. Junipero Serra, who explored Baja two hundred years ago, and could find good in even the worst of land and life, despised them as "a tree utterly useless, even for fuel."

A rainstorm comes up, as happens occasionally in this part of Baja, a torrent which showers us thoroughly and then is, as soon, gone. JD makes me stop the car so he can remove some boulders that it brought down into the road, because that's the kind of person he is. "What would happen if they had a race along this road — and someone ran into one of those boulders," he says. "All Things Considered" babbles on about American mine-sweepers, far away, troubles so far away from us now, but now coming closer.

JD has been reading *The Arabs* and thinks he has solved the problem of our conflict with the Iranians. He says that all their violence comes from their being Muslims. He claims that the Muslim mentality leads to all their frustrations, which they try to solve with war and other antagonisms. He thinks that instead of dropping torpedoes on them, we should torpedo them with love — Porky's style.

"We've spent a hundred billion dollars on 'the Iranian Problem,' and what do we have to show for it? What we have to do is make Iran a part of the solution, instead of part of the problem," he says. "We have to appeal to them in the only way we *can* appeal to them."

He calls it "The Jim Beam Solution to International Conflict." The U.S. military will contract for 50 billion mini-bottles of booze, along with balloons and an equal number of videotapes. The bottles will consist of Jim Beam, the balloons will be used to float them and the tapes softly to earth. The tapes will consist of special, educational programming put together by the National Science Foundation, the National

Institute of Mental Health, the National Security Council, and *Playboy*. They'll be specially-produced programs that will appeal to the brighter side of your average Iranian male. Instruction will be in the form of ladies and gentlemen, in the buff, rolling about in beds filled with couscous and lamb stew. There'll also be your regular, old-fashioned bondage (with *shadoofs* and *djellabas*) and a couple of camel — not donkey but camel — shows. The usual intellectual dialogue of "Sex-cetera" and "Electric Blue," along with the usual grunts and pants, will be translated into Farsi. The Air Force will balloon these gifts not only to Teheran, Qom, Abadan, Tabriz, but out to the heartland, into the deserts, up in the mountains, to the shore. At the same time, the Japanese will deliver, gratis, apparently by mistake, to each and every village, tens of thousands of disposable, battery-pak VCRs.

Love will do the rest. These videos should serve to dispatch 500 years of the call of the muezzins. Soon enough, your average Iranian will begin to figure out what he has been missing all these years under all those veils. The tapes will reveal to the fellahin a whole new world filled with ludicrous breasts, ribald posturings, long nights spent panting on the waterbed. Soon enough, western culture will come clear. The average Iranian's anger over what he's been missing all these years will be tempered by his greed not to miss any more. The National Security Council and the National Science Foundation, we speculate, have — between them — enough money stored away under "entertainment" so that no one in Congress will probe "Operation Bunnyhookah" until after it's over and done with, and a rousing success. In this way, the plan will not violate the usual foreign policy operations emanating from secret White House subbasements.

"You have saved the peace," Eve and I tell JD. We are swept aside by his prescience. We instantly award him a brittlebush staff with crown of boojums for a job well done in the service of humanity.

SEPTEMBER 3 [SAN IGNACIO]

... the Old Gentile (Indian) did not flee. It was soon evident from his actions that he neither cared nor feared any one or any thing. During his talk with us, in the very midst of all the people, he squatted down, and having no clothing to remove he proceeded to relieve the demands of nature even as he kept on talking! And when he finished, he was as happy as he was relieved!

— *THE JOURNAL OF PADRE SERRA*
MAY 20, 1769

In the midst of the bone-desert lava-flow lies this oasis, the clear and lovely lake at dusk, surrounded by tule and palm trees. The mission, dating from 1786, is exquisitely designed, decorated with several irregular points atop the structure — a half-dozen giant strawberries — and a dozen or so round windows, spotted here and there, surrounded by faded red rings and diamond-shaped workings. There is the usual huge, wooden door, with elaborate, black-metal hinges. It's dark and cool inside.

"It's funny," I say. "When the Spanish padres came through, their first thought was always about building a mission." The Indians were perfectly content to go around eating the piñoles and sweet cactus and mescal, dressed up in their birthday suits. But the Spaniards wanted to have some symbol of their religion: they wanted to clothe the land (and the Indians), so they caused to be built thirty missions thoughout Baja California. They, like the architects of Manhattan, had a definite (and intractable) edifice complex. And the missions were all the same: imposing, cool, tall ceilings — a relief from the blasting heat outside — but always with the feeling of prison, with twelve-foot heavy doors, the black metal bars and hinges.

The next day, as we drive west and north, I catch myself thinking about Father Serra. We're going along the same trail he took, although at a slightly different speed. The good father marched north from Loreto, a hundred miles below Mulegé — from March 28 to July 1, 1769. He and his followers went by foot across some of the most parched, dry, inhospitable, burning hills, arroyos, and mountains in the world.

To read his words, one would never think that he was trudging along through a wasteland, with his soldiers, a few burros and Indians, and the newly appointed Governor Portola. In fact, reading his entries, one would think we were on the road to Paradise. Which, romantic that he was, perhaps was true.

At San Andres he wrote:

> *What we saw was a vast extent of good land, all prairies and well watered. It is an excellent site for another good mission and ranchería.*

On May 16th, he paused at

> *a pleasant spot called San Juan de Dios. We found here plenty of water, pasture, alders, tules and a bright sky.*

And on June 13:

> *The explorers sent us word about 3:00 P.M. that we may take our choice of two good watering places. The first is three leagues from here; the second is five. Both have plenty of sweet water, with abundant pasture for the stock. God be praised!*

Even at those places where there was absolutely no water, he could find *something* of interest, such as on June 2, when he reported the discovery of "Rose Canyon:"

> *I have noted the beauty and abundance of flowers. To indicate the truth of this, when we arrived at our camp site today we found here the Queen of the All — the Rose of Castile. As I write I have before me, a stem on which there are three full blossoms, several buds, and more than six whose petals have fallen.*

Was he as deranged as Columbus — to whom he bears no little spiritual resemblance? Or was he just an optimistic talespinner? Maybe the father had a necessary supply of bunkum in his soul, something appropriate to other salesmen that were to appear in Alta California a hundred years later.

It may have had to do with the fact that if he were to report honestly on the barrenness of the countryside, it would be the end of any and all further exploration or interest from the Spanish Crown. By sending back glowing reports of verdant fields and potable water — even hinting at a good silver mine just waiting to be worked — Serra was making sure that his own stupendous efforts on this godforsaken peninsula would not be in vain.

Perhaps it is wrong to call him a liar. Perhaps it is best to think of him as a romantic, the Don Quixote of the desert, a man who was able to find flowers and trees and good, sweet water where no one before (or since) ever has been able to do so. There has to be something daft, indeed, about one who presumes to walk eight-hundred miles up the most barren peninsula in the world, claiming all the while that it is in the service of The Divine ("I have undertaken this journey to the Ports and San Diego and Monterey, for the greater glory of God and the conversion of heathen to our Holy Catholic Faith," he wrote).

Serra's tale is not only one of romantic tale telling. It has the feel, as well, of tragedy to come. Not for the Spaniards, certainly — they had the cross and the musket to protect them. It was ruinous, however, for the Indians, the happy "Gentiles" that the Spaniards met. For them, the crossing of paths was as much as if they had met Mr. Death himself. Instead of the crucifix, it would, perhaps, have been more appropriate for Serra to carry a Death's Head on his breast. For he, the soldiers, the priests, and the Spaniards who followed over the next decades were to leave behind them diseases — mostly syphilis — that killed off 50,000 Indians and laid waste to a whole innocent culture. In less than a century, the Indians who roamed Baja California would be reduced to 2,000 in number by a hideous corruption of flesh presented, gratis, by the followers of Serra. This is a priest's report from a mere fifteen years later:

The missions of San José, Santiago, Todos Santos, San Javier, Loreto, San José de Comondú, Purisima, Concepción, and Santa Rosalia de Mulegé are on the way to total extinction. The reason is so evident that it leaves no doubt. Syphilis has taken possession of both sexes to such a degree that mothers do not conceive, and if they do conceive, the fetus is born with little hope of living. There are three times as many adults who die as there are babies born.

A special gift of the soldiery, the camp followers, and the religionists of Spain.

For that reason, Serra's descriptions of the "Gentiles" is especially piquant — for it was one of the last times that they would be so free and alive, so free of the European sicknesses. Their innocence has the hue of tragedy because they were so eager to contact these strangers, showing them their naïve way with possessions.

So many came that I could not count them. But their amiability soon degenerated into familiarity. If, in token of friendship, one placed his hands on their heads or shoulders, they would immediately repeat the gesture upon us. If they saw us seated, they would sit right down beside us. They showed an acute desire for anything they saw or fancied — not stopping at petty things at all. They begged me for my habit. They asked the Governor for his leather jacket, his waistcoat, his pants, and in fact, all the clothes that he wore!

Excellent conceit: wanting "all the clothes that he wore." We'd be the last to think of Serra as obsessed, but he mentions a dozen times that the Indians were as naked as on the day of their birth:

I found myself face to face with a dozen of them, all grown men except two boys, about ten and fifteen. One fact impressed me, a fact which I could not believe when I

> *read or heard it: — they went about stark naked just like Adam in Paradise before the Sin. Thus they came among us. We mingled with them a while. But although they saw us completely dressed there was no evidence that there was the least blush of shame among them for their nakedness.*

Lo! the poor Indian. And denizens of the east came to them, and would clothe them, and tell them right from wrong. And there would be nothing to fear:

> *I made them understand that henceforth a Padre would be stationed here, pointing him out to them and calling him Father Miguel. They and their friends should come to visit him. They should tell their friends that there was nothing to fear, for the Father would be their best friend. The soldiers who remained with the Padre would not harm them, but would do good things for them. They must not take any cattle which roamed over the open country. They should come to the Father in case of necessity, and he would do whatever he could for them. These and other things we told them, and they listened attentively, seeming to understand. Thus it appears to me that they are ready to fall into the apostolic net ...*

Fall into the apostolic net. The naked Heathen. Now saved by the Holy Church. Animals now saved by the bald man with the piercing eyes and the heavy cloak. "The Father would be their best friend." "There was nothing to fear." Nothing to fear.

> *They do not need food — for they are big and fat! Because of their great stature, the Governor thinks they would become fine grenadiers ...*

They are fat and big now, big enough so that the Spaniards think of turning them into soldiers, the Army of the Cross. Lo, the poor Indian! So happy and fun loving, so curious about these interesting people from another land, men — no women — with their burros (how the Indians loved playing with them) and these funny shaped body-encasing, coarse materials they called "clothes." Lo, the poor Indian, who, in such a short period of time, would be devastated by the sicknesses that ran through the hearts of the holy Spaniards. It was only a century and a half later that Arthur North was to write:

> *The end of the Baja California Indians is near at hand. The Pericues and the Guaycuras are now practically extinct. Of the former thousands of Cochimis, perhaps a hundred still survive. Of the northern Indians there survive today remnants of the Cocopa, Catarina, Yuma, Kiliwa, Pais and Diegueno tribes, but only the first names can muster more than a hundred individuals.*

Those Indians who did not die, who became part of the missions — the few who were not murdered by the social diseases out of Civilization — would be treated so wretchedly with scourge and rod meted out by the Spaniards that one commentator opined that the Indians would most certainly be better off dead rather than saved.

> *A mother with a nursing infant took a notion to let me hold her baby in my arms for awhile. And thus as I held it I could scarcely resist the desire to baptise it before giving it back to its supper.*
>
> *I gave them all the Sign of the Cross, and I taught them to say "Jesus! Mary!" I do for them what I can, caress them as I may — And thus we journey onward.*

That sweet infant with such a short time to live.

❧ ❧ ❧

Q: What is your opposite?
A: Myself.
Q: What is madness?
A: A forgotten way.
Q: And revolt? Why do men revolt?
A: To find beauty, either in life or in death.
Q: What for each of us is inevitable?
A: Happiness.

— *THE MAHABHARATA*

"He might as well have put the Ultimate Curse on them," I tell JD and Eve. "There aren't any of them left — not a one. And they want to sanctify the old noodle-head, make a saint out of him."

We fall to silence in the proper rhythm of the road. We fall silent in our drive, and drive and drive. I feel as if we were on one of Kerouac's runs across America, barely stopping: a few moments here for gas, a few moments there for some water. A brief stop to eat.

We are now on our own goose chase. Like Chaucer's pilgrims, Fr. Serra, Jack Kerouac, we must have a touch of that romantic beatitude in the heart. We drive, and drive, and drive ourselves some more. The land no longer is a part of us — but a great, wheeling scenery forever falling behind.

We are going home, and our minds are already home, and the desert is no longer with us, but something to get through so we can be done with the trip, get back to our lives, return to whatever we were before, whatever we'll be after Baja. We drive and drive, the sun behind us, the sun to the side of us, the sun going down, the sun gone, the night sky blaring with a thousand stars. We pass back through Guerrero Negro, San Quintín, Cataviña, Rosario de Arriba (Get-Up-and-Go Rosary!), Santo Telmo, Ensenada. We are *On The Road*, in one of those endless journeys that leaves you dazed and befuddled, but you don't want to stop, can't stop, will not stop. The journey becomes its own creature, it moves us on its own, we cannot be rid of it.

By midnight, north of Ensenada, I see that they've planted great stands of redwoods on both sides of us, alongside the "cuota." Giant redwoods, crowding in on each other and on us — towering over the sides of the road, thousands of them. "How in the hell did they get these trees all the way down from Alta California? And how in the hell did they get them to grow in this desert?" I wonder. The great, dark trees all about us, climbing up the hillsides, hanging over each other, and the road. Huge trees, tall and wet, surrounding our lonely road with shadows of darkness.

We are in the footsteps of Serra, Portola, and Bægert, de Galvaz, Cabrillo, and the mad "filibusterer" William Walker — who sailed into La Paz a hundred years ago with forty-eight men and proclaimed himself ruler. All of us delusional. We all see this barren land and make of it exactly what we most desire — superimposing on it Paradise: filling it with sweet waters; hiding in its hills mythic silver mines; mythic rivers filled with creatures that make huge, black pearls; planting — as one might plant divinity — great stands of towering redwoods. It is no accident that the peninsula commences at a place called El Arco, the arch, a magic arch formed by the sea out of solid rock. In Spanish, the word also has the connotations of rainbow, the sign of good luck, and prosperous journeys.

It is no accident, as well, that the peninsula concludes in the wilds of Tijuana, with its arch to the country next door, the customs and immigration arch. It is a place, too, that collects our fantasies, a place of wild passions, fantasy nights of exotic and drug-filled lust, and the ultimate dream of all encaged, Anglo-Saxon men — a city without any restraint, without any regulations, without any laws to bind, whatsoever.

❧ ❧ ❧

Q: What for each of us is inevitable?
A: Happiness.
Q: And what is the greatest marvel?
A: Each day, death strikes and we live as though we were immortal. This is the greatest marvel.

— *THE MAHABHARATA*

I am not to tell my two companions about the stands of redwoods passing us on either side. I won't tell them until we get through the border, out of the Land of the Visionary Madmen, into the Land of the Pragmatic. I will not reveal the extent of the mirage until we make the last miles home, out of this bone-dry madhouse that stirs us into such a grand fecundity. We do not brake for hallucinations.

We — all of us seers who journey to the south, and there have been far too many of us — should not be frightening, those who lack the romantic lunacy of the *Don Quixotes* of Baja. We must protect them from the dreams that have come to us on our journeys: visions of salvation, visions of tall, kind, trusting Indians (stark, staring naked). Visions of unrestricted passion, visions of wide, white, open beaches, sweet, turquoise waters pouring out of a bone-dry and dusty earth, and, not the least, visions of huge, wet, dark, towering, ever-so-quiet, redwoods. Apparitions out of this land of Ultimate Projection.

Baja is the last refuge of such innocence — the last hope of the servants of God as well as the servants of lust. Even the original inhabitants were not spared such lunacy. With all their sensibility about clothing, the foods of nature, and the shelters of stone, the Indians also shared a touch of the Baja Head Balmies. As Fr. Bægert, certainly the most acute and stolid observer of the land, good burgher that he was reported:

> *some of my parishioners believed themselves to be descendants of a bird, others of a stone which was lying not far from my house, while others dreamed of something different along the same lines. Each dream in turn was more absurd and more foolish than the other.*

Each dream. More absurd, more foolish — than the other. The Truth of Baja. The tale of the visionaries and madmen; and, ultimately, the tale of all of us.

[1986]

REFERENCES

Observations in Lower California, by Johann Jakob Bægert, S. J. University of California Press; 1952.

The Floating Opera, by John Barth. Avon; 1956.

The Mahabharata, by Jean-Claude Carrière, translated by Peter Brook. Harper & Row; 1987.

An American Childhood, by Annie Dillard. Harper & Row; 1987.

Dario, The Journal of Padre Serra, translated by Ben. F. Dixon. Don Diego's Libreria, San Diego, California; 1964.

On Being Mindless, by Paul J. Griffiths. Open Court Publishing, Box 599, La Salle, Illinois; 1987.

The Forgotten Peninsula, by Joseph Wood Krutch. University of Arizona; 1986.

The Magnificent Peninsula, by Jack Williams. H. J. Williams, Box 203, Sausalito, California; 1987.

THROUGH COSTA RICA WITH DRUNK AND CAMERA

There are many types of cold drink, made either from fresh fruit, or milk drinks with fruit or cereal flour whisked with ice cubes. The fruits range from the familiar to the exotic; others include cebada (barley flour), pinolillo (roasted corn), horchata (rice flour with cinnamon), and, according to one Michael J. Brisco, "chan, *perhaps the most unusual, looking like mouldy frogspawn and tasting of penicillin...*"

— "COSTA RICA"
IN THE 1987 *SOUTH AMERICAN HANDBOOK*
JOHN BROOKS, EDITOR

In essence Matter is a veiled form of Life, Life a form of veiled consciousness.

— SRI AUROBINDO

Those ninnies at Eastern Airlines managed to lose our baggage for ten days. I suspected we would be in trouble when, on the day of our departure, they put San Jose tags on our luggage, and I said "How do you know the difference between San Jose, California and San José, Costa Rica?" "Oh, we know," the ticket lady said, reassuringly. I found out later that she had been working there a week as a trainee, and that, despite my helpful comments, she didn't know beans about the difference between the prune pits of Santa Clara County and the coffee beans of the Talamanca Mountains. For ten days we were required to borrow toothbrushes and straight-edge razors from the hotel help, cover our nakedness with banana skins and papaya leaves. The eight books that were going to entertain me on dull drives to dark volcanoes stayed safely there amongst the smog and freeways of the South Bay for almost two weeks, while I read the Costa Rica telephone book (twice) and the directions for evacuation of the hotel room in case of fire (twenty-seven times) in Spanish, English, German, French, Urdu and what I assume to be Japanese.

The one book that crept into my carrying case was Ralph Metzner's *Opening to Inner Light*. Since I had so little else to read, I savored Metzner's newest work with all the cupidity of a widow with her fabled mite. I gave myself the reward of but one of the available chapters per day. I started my study in the bathtub of a morning, and nibbled on the rest of it on and off for the rest of the day. It worked out just fine: a more interesting and delightful book hasn't been conceived of since Emanuel Swedenborg's *Oeconomia regni animalis*.

Metzner has conceived of the work as a description of "human evolutionary transformation" experienced by people all over the world: in their religious works, their myths, their language, their tales, their holy practices, their beliefs, their "primordial images," their dreams. As he says in his preface,

> *The essential human process of evolutionary growth is described in similar terms in all major cultures and sacred traditions all over the world.*

For example, in retelling the common myth of a "Journey to the Place of Vision and Power," Metzner refers to the Tao, Walt Whitman, the Old Testament, the New Testament, the "Red Road" of the Sioux Indians, Mohammed, Joseph Campbell, Mircea Eliade, R. D. Laing, the Sufi sage Ibn al'Arabi, Lewis Carroll, the legend of Odysseus, the Babylonian Ishtar, the Egyptian myth of Isis, the Huichol Indians of Mexico, the 12th century German Benedictine mystic and seeress Hildegard von Bingen. It is an exhausting compilation of the great writers, prophets, visionaries, and religious figures and documents of the world, and it is a testament to Metzner's persuasiveness, or else the paucity of alternative reading materials, that made it possible for me to get through this particular philosophical/theological work. One is quite overwhelmed with its richness, and I found it not unlike the tea they serve in North Africa, an aromatic tea so supersaturated with sugar that it makes one's teeth sing and jangle in the close harmonies of the Egyptian singer Om Kalthoom. Indeed, if one is to find fault with Metzner, it has less to do with his willingness to go everywhere on earth, to draw his examples from all peoples of all periods, as his need to compress it all into one 180 page tract. As it happened, I read it at exactly the proper pace—with few if any other distractions, which tells me that it is to be read slowly, savored, to be marked and re-read. I think, however, we might do well to get Metzner a grant from the Theosophical Society of America to expand the work into ten or twelve volumes for its second printing. We, and the world's metaphysics, deserve no less.

Tentative, as if fording a river in winter
Hesitant, as if in fear of his neighbors
Formal, like a guest
Falling apart, like thawing ice
Thick, like an uncarved block
Empty, like a valley
Obscure, like muddy water.
Who can be muddy and yet, settling, slowly become clear?
— THE TAO TE CHING

My travelling companion is an alcoholic. That's why, during the course of this tale, he will be known as Al.

Travelling with alcoholics is very simple. You always know where to find them. They are in the nearest bar. And if you want them not to go out and get lost in the evening, you give them unlimited line-of-credit with room service. And when it's time to drive somewhere, you get them up to go before eight in the morning, before they've had a chance to assimilate the leavings of one hangover with the beginnings of another.

My friend Al is, as is true with many alcoholics, funny, wise, kind, generous, thoughtful, brave, understanding, true, and true-blue. He just has this kink in his personality, his wonderful personality: when he goes into a bar he orders two beers with two double jiggers of tequila for "chasers." Those are boilermakers. That's his first order: more come soon after, in five or ten minutes. He just wants to be damned sure that he doesn't run out of booze before the bar does, or before he assuages his terrible terrible thirst. Since Al is one of my best friends, I wasn't going to let a little thing like him passing out on the cold floor of the bathroom, getting rolled in the taxi coming home, or smelling like a sewer most of the time keep me from travelling with him. I figured it would be educational for both of us.

The country of Costa Rica is rich, at least compared to its neighbors. They call it "the Switzerland of Central America." There are only a few klunkers, some things that don't appear in the official histories, or travel guides. One is that the country practiced active and militant apartheid until about twenty years ago. The blacks were confined to the Caribbean coast and were not permitted into the piedmont region until the mid 60s. The faces on the streets of San José—in the high Central Valley—are almost uniformly white, or very light.

Then there is this war, this *war* going on about 300 miles to the north, this war, brought to you by the CIA, and various multinational corporations, and several strange nation-states, not satisfied with poisoning their own wells, wanting to poison a few in this idyllic waterspout of land that arches down from the underbelly of Texas and California, down to a tiny waist called Panama, then on into that center of American needs and addictions—Colombia.

Many of the twenty countries South of the Border have been chosen (by us, not necessarily by themselves) to manifest the psychotic bifurcation of North America. We want these countries to have capitalism, we think, but only as long as it contains a dollop of state-sponsored socialism for the very wealthy.

Like colonial powers of all times and all persuasions, we savor exporting our desires, our dreams, our addictions, and our lusts. Too steamy for our own shores—we relegate our Sins to countries like Peru, the Dominican Republic, Colombia, Belize, Mexico, the Philippines—much as England a century ago would relegate its dope-heads and philanderers and pederasts to Nairobi, India, Egypt. That left England, as it does us, free to pretend the purity of the Christian Home State. Castro knew this. He didn't want to free Cuba from Fulgencio Batista as much as he wanted to free it from being the whorehouse and opium den for the United States. To this day, his memory is reviled in America because he wasn't content to expropriate our oil refineries and banana plantations; no, he insisted, as well, on closing down the pleasure palaces, the way stations for gringo lusts and passions.

No wonder we're *still* so miffed at him. Revolution-schmevolution. It's our pent-up libido, and his fake puritanism, that bug us so.

The Zen Ox-Herding Allegory *may be regarded as a metaphor for the process of unifying human and animal consciousness. The ox symbolizes the wild animality of the human and animal consciousness... the steps of the process are (1) searching for the ox, (2) seeing its tracks, (3) perceiving the ox, (4) capturing the ox, (5) taming the ox, and (6) riding the ox home. The sixth step represents the stage where the wild animal within has been transformed into a trusted ally. In the next phase, the seventh picture, the man sits contemplating in the moonlight outside his hut, and the animal is gone. The ox, the commentators tell us, is "symbolic only," or has been "transcended..." The eighth picture shows only a perfect circle. "Both ox and man transcended," the text says. "Everything merges into nothing, like a snowflake in a raging fire..."*

— OPENING TO INNER LIGHT

The streets of Costa Rica are filled with god-beautiful people. None of the noseless faces, leprosy-stained, leg stump and jawless nightmares out of the streets of Saõ Paulo, or Bogotá, or Mexico City. Every citizen of Costa Rica gets free medical care; all get electricity and water—no matter how far up the mountains they live. A modified socialism, as cooked up in 1942 by the head of the Catholic Church, the head of the government, and the head of the Communist Party.

The streets of Costa Rica also run thick with music. What we call "salsa," what they call "musica tropical," is everywhere, pouring out of the cars, running in the gutters, floating down from the very sky, snowflakes of mambo and bongo—snowing down from everywhere. The sun and the clouds mix with the music, great billowing gray-white clouds streaming across from north to south through the winter sky, the music leaking up from the very gutters. Moving sky, filled with song, a feeling of impermanence in a land which owns several active or near-active volcanoes.

On our way to visit Volcán Poás, we drive through Heredira, and start up a mountain road surrounded by lush fields, filled with grass and trees, cows and horses, all robust and healthy looking. "The Switzerland of Central America." Perhaps. If so, it carries three great advantages over its European counterpart. First, there is no snow—except rarely at the very highest peaks. Second, there are no cuckoo clocks to make a tootling idiot of something as important as time. Third (and perhaps the most fetching), we don't have to put up with any prissy, self-centered, arrogant dumpkoff Tyrolean hotel keepers. Our caretakers here are all sunny, polite and kindly.

The road to Poás is delightful, winding up and down the flanks of the volcano, with grand vistas of the intermontane around San José. Trumpet vines, great black-and-green butterflies, white snowflake moths, potty round fat trees, fat cows, fat chickens, fat babies. A land so lush that the fence-posts themselves sprout leaves and limbs and roots.

We stop at a cafe called "Paradero Chubascos," and if there were a Michelin guide to Costa Rica, there would be a little red man seated in a little red rocking chair, with a single red crossed fork-and-spoon, to tell us how peaceful it is. We order two cocos—a fruit-juice cream mix—and two "platos del día," along with a bottle of red wine, imported, as it turns out, from Chile. The view over the bucolic valley is exquisite, the clouds make funny faces as they pass by (clowns and goats and pigs and even cow faces to reflect back on the contented cows there below). The sun shines brightly, and Volcán Poás politely refrains from hawking, belching, and spitting up as we eat our sweet vegetarian soup and *carnitas*.

Somehow, the owner has called in the CIA, or the gods, and was thus able to determine that my most favorite music in the world is romantic guitar music from the Yucatan of Saul Martinez and Chalín Cámera—so when we are nibbling on our dessert, they sing about love, "un rayito del sol"—a little ray of sunshine, and our lives, our lives are, for the moment, for this moment, made perfect, what with the wine and clouds and horses and lush greenery and the temporarily quiescent volcano and the raylet of sunshine. I ask the owner of the Paradero if she is afraid of "terremotos" from the temperamental Mr. Poás, who has been known to eat whole cities for breakfast, and she says "What good would it do?" Besides, she points out, with more logic than my own, there are more earthquakes in Los Angeles than there are here. She says that the volcano spouts out ash and rock into the air from time to time—but the fertile flow has given the valley such a richness and lushness that it is one of the most beautiful and best growing areas in Costa Rica.

As we are talking, Al finishes eating, strides out and lies on a bench in the field, near a stream which laughs and giggles nearby, and I am so struck with the beauty and health of the countryside that if I had had one more bottle of that Chile tinto I might well have asked for the hand of the kind and good-cooking Señora Chubasco so that I could spend my salad years there under the volcano, praying to the gods of slumber, eating of her wonderful repasts. Before I can make a fool of myself, Al bestirs himself, and we find ourselves back on the road to the mountaintop.

Al is scarcely twenty, and he has never driven before, but since I need a driver, he has been elected. On our first day on the road, the day before our trip to Volcán Poás, we get into our renta-car in front of our hotel in San José. There is now, I trust, a C. Amantea Memorial Foot Marker on the floor of that Toyota Celica, on the far right side, where the passenger's pedal extremity should go. As sure as I am sitting here, I wore that area down smartly as Al was learning to navigate and as I was wondering whether to carry through on my proposed myocardial infarction. By nightfall of his first full day of driving, he had driven through a crowded pre-Christmas town crowd to the south of San José, squashing but one spotted dog, grazing two older grannies (who had not that much longer to live anyway), wiping the snot from the noses of a dozen or so sullen Brahman cows, and flattening one fresh-faced teen-aged girl in the prime of her life. He was, I believe, most grieved by this last, as he has this thing about teen-aged ladies, but if I am to have good memories of that day of learning to drive, I would prefer to ignore her rites of passage, and his own, and instead recall, warmly, our trek across a two-foot wide plank bridge that meanders over the Costa Rican version of the Grand Canyon. God knows how we found this most ancient of suspension bridges built, they later told us, sometime towards the end of Columbus' third trip to the New World.

Some may say that the bridge with its wet planks and invisible barricades wasn't meant for automobiles at all, but I am here, a living testament to the falsity of that claim. Our long, long drive, there at the 5,000 foot level, with Al navigating and me correcting his course ever so pleasantly as the tires ventured over the nebulous edge of the rotting planks, was a marvel of good sense and timing, and I understand that I have been nominated for the "Henry-the-Navigator Award" for service (and aplomb) during times of extreme duress.

After our journey was concluded, and we spent the next hour or so kissing and caressing the very earth, Al wanted to know how I had managed to locate on the map such a scenic drive, with such a funny bridge, and I had to confess it had something to do with down-home blind luck, if not the Blind Staggers. I do say I was hard pressed to justify it, much less, subsequently, even locate it on my map. Conversations with hotel management and the tourist liaison at the San José Chamber of Commerce confirms that our day's journey was none but the figment of our rich Anglo-Saxon imaginations, a drug-induced dream: such a frail bridge over such an elevated canyon—where the very cows and sheep visible below were but toys, and the roaring river but a rivulet—has not, cannot, and does not exist, they tell us. Except, as I say, in our very dreams.

Man has no permanent and unchangeable I. Every thought, every mood, every desire, every sensation, says "I..." There are hundreds and thousands of small I's, very often entirely unknown to one another, never coming into contact, or, on the contrary, hostile to one another, mutually exclusive and incompatible. Each moment, each minute, man is thinking or saying "I." And each time the "I" is different. Just now it was a thought, now it is a desire, now a sensation, now another thought, and so on, endlessly. Man is a plurality. Man's name is legion... There is nothing in man able to control this change of I's, chiefly because he does not notice, or know of it; he lives always in the last I... This explains why people so often make decisions, and so seldom carry them out.

— G. I. GURDJIEFF

Al and I decide to go north from San José, so, early on the morning of the 21st, we head north on the Inter-American Highway, going through Puntarenas, Cañas, and La Cruz. The highway takes us from the mountainous area of Costa Rica—almost 3,000 feet above sea level—down to sea level, so we go from a chilly, temperate climate to a hot and moist environment in less than four hours. The road is wide and well-paved. The truck and bus drivers are not of the kamikaze school so common in India or Mexico or Spain, where one crests a rise in the two-lane road to find a twenty-foot tall megabus filled to overflowing with 200 or 300 passengers, bearing directly down on one. The traffic here is moderate, the speeds reasonable, and the vistas, wildlife, and roadside greenery are breathtaking. Al and I find ourselves enamored of bushes, vegetation, and certain trees of the weeping willow family, the latter being so elegant that we want to carry them home with us.

At one of our stops, the barkeep shows us his tame howler monkey. Al, enamored of all wildlife, brings the monkey a beer, and stands there as the creature sips the brew, using him as a tree trunk. I can see them now, in the shade of a great wide oak, the monkey intertwined so completely with Al, that it is as if he were a great oak. Al is shirtless, and the gray-faced tan furred "mono" is entwined about his tall frame, one arm about his neck, the other hand in his hair, legs twined about Al's waist, the tail curled about his upper thigh, the two of them so totally intermeshed, a loving Laocoön, that I find myself envying that languorous creature, wishing I could use all my members as successfully as this furry little beast. I think of Al as some sort of a monkey himself, with his huge brown eyes, and open face, his eyes of such dimension to capture one entire, his great lanky legs and arms (he's 6' 5").

"He had such pretty lips," Al said, later, "I wanted to kiss him." The two of them were so entranced with each other that it is only with promise of more monkeys (and peanuts) down the road that I am able to convince him that it is time to move on.

As we get closer to the Nicaraguan border, the road gets more and more deserted, the vegetation dryer, more barren. We pass through several checkpoints, like all military checkpoints, except the civil guards are hopelessly drunk. We stop in a roadside bar near La Cruz, and the lady does not understand my request for "cerveza." I thought it was a universal word in all hispanic countries for beer, but the word here, I learn from her, is "spumo." And when I ask for a sandwich ("san'weesh, bocadillo, o tapa")—she brings us peanuts.

Al—a perfect product of American television—wants to drive on into Nicaragua. He's been conditioned to associate the country's name with glamorous sweaty dark faces in fatigues, toting bazookas through the jungle, fighting The Enemy. I point out to him that, what with the hostilities, it will take anywhere up to eight hours to get over the border. I figure we can look at the barren wastes of Northwest Costa Rica from here, rather than looking at the barren wastes of Southwest Nicaragua from there, since they are probably all the same. "Besides," I tell him, "the war is 300 miles from where we are now, and our renta-car doesn't provide bullet hole insurance."

"That's what would happen if we went up there—they'd shoot at us?"

"Probably."

"Bitchin'," says Al, full of youthful enthusiasm.

"You can understand their reluctance to make it easy for us to get in," I say. "After all, our government is essentially at war with their government."

"Why are we fighting them?" he says.

"Our government doesn't like their government?"

"Why?"

"Beats the hell out of me. But what we've done is to get the CIA to contract with a bunch of pissed-off dissidents so we can dump millions of dollars in tanks and bazookas and bombs and 'aid,' so they can kill off a few thousand peasants, make the world safe for democracy, or what's left of it."

"I don't understand," he says.

"I don't either," I say, "and I don't really think those lardheads in Washington do either. Anyway it's a mess, and

I'm not about to be standing in long lines to get over borders, to get shot at in some dumb war."

So we turn back, and drive to the coast, turning at Liberia, some 9,000 miles from the other Liberia, and pronounced lee-burr-REE-uh. It is from there that we drive to Coco Beach.

I got a dog a cat a mouse a rat
A fly (he don't die) and a little gnat
Dumb girl stupid as can be
All the guys call you fast
But I call you slow
You're always sniffin' or givin'
Somebody a blow.

—RUN DMC

Al's favorite rap group is called Run DMC. Since I have little interest in Run DMC, or rap music of any genre, we keep the music low when I am in the car. But whenever I leave—to go look at something, or go to the bathroom, whatever—the car blossoms into great gouts of drum and voice, filled with a fly and a little gnat so that the vehicle threatens to levitate with the sheer volume of noise. Al uses such music, like sleep, or alcohol, to wrap a cone of silence about himself, so that people like me won't be bugging him.

We drive over to the town of Coco. I am in a fretful mood, what with my sleeplessness and all. The natives who only yesterday looked so frolicsome and languorous today look stupid and dull. The kids are gnarled, the trees have turned bleak, the road dusty, the houses overcrowded, and all the tourists noisy and goofy looking. I am not about to look in the mirror.

"You said some things last night I don't even want to remember," says Al, over coffee and strong cream. The sea slaps against the beach nearby.

"It was awful," I say. "I didn't sleep a bit. Did you hear that old geezer next door go to the bathroom?" We are about to laugh, but then an American comes by, a man who's built on the same general lines of a garbage truck, sporting, too, the same general air of friendliness and warmth. Al met him yesterday. He talks at length, and with high volume, about AIDS.

"That's what they get for giving it to each other in the ass," says the man. "If fags want to do each other up the ass, they get AIDS and they deserve it." Garbage Truck stops to shake hands with us, and I hesitate a moment, worried as I am about catching something.

The sea looks polluted and murky, the headlands scrubby and awful, and the black sand on the beach is littered with paper cups, cans, wrappers. If we hadn't contracted to go out on a fishing boat at noon, I would suggest that we depart at once—but Al wants to have a chance to fish. We drive over to the hotel, and down to the beach. They put us in a rowboat, and Cap't Manuel and first mate José take us out to the boat. They start it up, and in a few moments we are trolling the green waters, leaving those dark and pestiferous clouds behind.

A hundred or so friendly pelicans skirt the waves about us, the breeze is gentle, the sun is gentle, the day is so gentle, and my god, isn't this what we live for, to drink beer and troll and crest the waves, the sun licking us like kittens, making us warm and comfortable in the brightness of this superb day, with the breezes tucking about us, moving us here and there. Later, when they ask us how we did on our fishing trip, I tell them that we caught about 80 - 150 fish about this long (both arms outstretched), and, when I get enough of that whopper, I tell them that, through some magic we are yet to comprehend, we caught two goldfish about *this* long (thumb and forefinger held about two inches apart).

It is not unlikely that there is a pivotal moment at some stage in the body's reaction to injury or disease, maybe in aging as well, when the organism concedes it is finished and the time for dying is at hand, and at this moment the events that lead to death are launched, as a coordinated mechanism. Functions are then shut off, in sequence, irreversibly, and while this is going on, a neural mechanism, held ready for this occasion, is switched on...

— *A MELORIST VIEW OF DISEASE AND DYING*
LEWIS THOMAS

Al is cheery and attracted to all animals and children. In the course of our journey, he befriends little girls and boys, even those with ugly faces and thick glasses and dumpy drawers. And his interest in wildlife is not restricted to humans: cats, chickens, deer, monkeys, and an amazing variety of puppies, shaggy monsters, ferae naturae, flea-bitten bitches with curled tails, spotted, mange-ridden dogs with purple salivarous tongues and a breath that would curl the bark of a tamarind tree at five hundred paces: all turn limp and loving in the huge hands of huge Al, with his huge eyes and even larger heart.

We drive down towards the ferry that goes to Puntarenas. The road to the boat is barely shown on our maps, and the natives whom we stop and ask about it say that it leaves at eleven, it leaves at two, it leaves every hour, it leaves once late in the afternoon, it leaves at six in the morning, it leaves early on one day and late on the next, it leaves once every three days, only on the odd days. The only answer we didn't get was a consistent one. Since our pursuit of it is down a dirt road heavy with skinks and lizards—a road that runs on gravel and twists for forty miles—it gives us some pause. "Once we arrive," I tell Al, "if it's gone, we will be spending the night in the bush with the night beesties, waiting for tomorrow's boat."

The beesties. The beesties of the jungle. That starts me to thinking of a trip I made several years ago, somewhat north of here, from Acayuacan to Tehuantepec. I was travelling with friend Sam'l—and we came to be lost in our renta-car much as Al and I are now. I think it all started with our powerful thirst, and the intervention of Our Lady of the Streets.

Acayuacan in April can be hot, and Sam'l and I have bought a dozen or so Corona beers—the elixir of Mexico. We are looking for some way to cool them down. We have ice and beer but nothing to put them in, together, safely married. The day is a Mexican feastday, so all the bucket shops are closed. Finally, in an "Ultramarino" we find and purchase, at arm-and-leg prices (Sam'l's arm, my leg) a Pedro Domecq cooler. The catch is we have to buy, in addition, three bottles of wine, one white, one red, and one rosé.

As Sam'l is wrestling the chest and beer and ice into the car, a wrinkled Nahuntl comes up to us and holds out her claw-like hand, asking a contribution for her own personal foundation. I try to figure out what we could spare—and since all Mexican rosé I'd had before was no better nor worse than an expectorant, I give it to her. It disappears quickly behind her bulky skirts. I thought I had done a good deed, but it must have been a profoundly bad wine. That was the only reason I could figure for the events of the next twelve hours.

We head south from Acayuacan. The first mistake is our picking the El Diablo Hotel in far off La Ventadora for our stay that night. The sun drops into the sea as suddenly as it does in all tropical environments, and after getting lost in Salina Cruz, we go down a winding road (not unlike the road to our ferry)—to find that the hotel is full. That's when I say: "It's only eight. We can make it to Puerto Ángel before eleven. It's a nice road along the shore..."

So we set off, violating the primary rule of travelling in Mexico (one does not drive after dark). We expect to pick up a bite to eat, maybe even a comfortable motel, as if we were just outside of Philadelphia, rather than in one of the most desolate parts of Mexico.

Our ratty little map does not show that the road goes up and down, up and down through, by, and around the twelve huge hills we encounter in the first thirty-five miles. Nor does the map point out that there is no traffic on this road, none at all. Not one car, not one smelly noisy blatting Pemex truck. Driving in an unknown place on a winding road up and down the hills with no lights, no towns, no traffic whatsoever—well, it comes, after a while, to be unnerving. Especially when the highway is surrounded on both sides by swamps. Swamps that are dark and dank and mossy and impenetrable. Swamps that seem, at times, to contain vague hulking, slow-moving shapes, dark shapes, dark and odd shapes that, from time to time, move, along with us, just next to the car. Dark creatures with funny eyes, and strange spider-like limbs.

"Sam'l," I say at one point. "Do you notice anything?"

"What?" he says.

"Do you notice anything funny?"

"I notice that we haven't eaten for almost eight hours. I'm hungry. I'm getting sick from hunger."

The tone of his voice makes me unwilling to share a few monster stories, so I relapse in sulky quiet. We drive on for a few more years, and Sam'l complains several more times about the lack of Howard Johnsons. I keep my eyes straight ahead, ignoring the fervid roadside activity to the left and right of us.

At one point, he insists on pulling off the road into what looks like a village. Since the interior car lights don't work, we take the map out before the unnaturally dim headlights to see if we can see where we are going or where we have been. I point out to him that there is a previously unannounced hole in the map where the road should be, so we don't really know if the road goes on the Puerto Ángel or whether, a few miles up, it feeds directly into the swamp where we would be eaten alive.

"You're getting pretty silly about this swamp stuff," he says.

As he is saying this, I notice the denizens of this dark village are congregating near us, preparatory to marching over to murder us. "They seem awfully quiet," I say quietly to Sam'l, nervously hoping he'll get the damn car going and out of here. From all over, they drift towards us. I move as quickly as possible towards the car. As we pull out, finally, Sam'l states that we are going on to Ángel, hole-in-the-road map or not.

"You can't," I say.

"Why not?" he says.

"I remember now, yes: there was a roadside café. Right—it was about ten miles back. That's right," I say, "and the sign out front said 'hamburgesas'—and it had a picture, big juicy rich thick hamburgers with lots of fresh tomatoes and lettuce and steaming French fries, and you could smell the meat cooking. Good chocolate milkshakes, too."

"Shut up," he says, but he does turn the car around to head back to Salina Cruz.

After a few minutes, he begins to question me specifically about the size, shape, location, and approaches to this mythic restaurant. Since I am busy counting dinosaur eyes to the right, I don't pay much attention to this Inquisition, except to comment at one point that he would make a fine upstanding Torquemada if he has interest in such a career. He then says that if we don't find the restaurant in another three miles, he's going to pull over and go to sleep on the side of the road. It's hours past his bedtime, and if he can't eat, he's damn well going to sleep.

"You can't do that," I say.

"Why not?" he rumbles.

"Because," I say, "Because, the restaurant is just around this bend. Or the next. Yes, I remember it clearly now, just around this bend or the one after it..."

Did I create that restaurant out of whole cloth? Such desire for peace and security, especially when under attack by monsters: does it create a restaurant out of nothing but swamp and darkness? We've heard of the creation of mass feeding systems out of two fishes and a single loaf of bread—but is it possible for a slightly dog-eared writer and his grumpy companion to resurrect a humble Mexican eatery out of a haunted jungle?

In any event, this fantasy which was (I swear to you!) not there on our previous passage appears there at the side of the road, just as I had said. Six tables, three fluorescent lights (dim, but by god, they were lights), all under a thatched roof. There is a quiet Indian family which, little aware that I had but recently fabricated them, successfully fends off my caresses, kisses and hugs, and brings us heavenly tacos, delicious black beans, and eggs cooked in a sweet hot sauce.

"See," I say to Sam'l. "You just don't trust me. Here I am, taking care of your welfare, watching out for your hunger pangs, and you just don't appreciate me."

"We've been driving for twelve hours," he says, after finishing off most of the contents of my plate as well as his own, "I'm still going to sleep in the car."

And despite my protestations, and tears, my noisy rolling about on the ground, pounding fists in the hardpacked earth, he moves luggage and cooler up to the front seat and makes himself room to curl up and pass out in back. I tell him that by letting me drive, he's giving his soul up to heaven. He will have none of it. "Don't blame me if we crash," he says, comfortingly, and he falls asleep within a minute.

"To hell with that," I say, so I wedge my left foot on the brake, my right on the accelerator, and take off (slowly) towards the south. I notice that with Sam'l *non compos*, the dragon count goes up drastically. This surely has to be the darkest, bleakest road in the world. There is no traffic whatsoever except for the dark road-runners that lean forward every now and again to glare at me with their crimson eyes, or to breathe on (and melt) the windshield wipers. It isn't helped at all by the appearance of the moon, or what appears to be a moon. I am to this day unsure of where the Nahuntl Indians got that one—a bile-colored frogwort hanging there in the southern sky, darting behind the grey, fungoidal clouds, and reappearing every now and again to shed a little wan, useless, dusky light on us.

The return trip only takes somewhere between three and five years, and I make it fit as a fiddle. My friends say my new white hairdo is quite becoming, and I've been thinking of teasing it to look more distinguished. The doctor says my shakes will probably go away with time, and after he sedated me as heavily as he dared, he said that I should "lighten up." He suggested that I take a vacation. "Have you ever thought of Mexico?" he said brightly. "I think you'd like it there."

❧ ❧ ❧

Al and I make it to the ferry stop at noon, and they tell us that the boat leaves at two. We repair to a nearby eatery for lunch, and an American there asks if he can travel back to San José with us. Jack is almost seventy-five years old, and is truly, distinctly, and honestly one of the ugliest people I have ever laid my born eyes on. He looks like an old catfish—an old, wise, heavily scarred catfish. Jack grew up in Flushing, measures everything in "bucks" ("they charged me forty bucks a night at the hotel"), and lives with a seventy-five year old woman in Ft. Lauderdale. His wife died fifteen years ago, painfully, slowly, from lung cancer.

Jack was the Dentyne chewing-gum representative for Bergen County, New Jersey, for eighteen years. He ran a Howard Johnson's for a while, and lost his fortune on "an amusement park." ("I shudda studied it more," he says.) He's just another of the lonely and lost of the world, I think, moving around here and there, travelling, watching, sitting, going back to Ft. Lauderdale from time to time, to the tiny cottage, with the woman who lives there, whom he doesn't love.

"Why live with her, then?" I ask.

"I like coming home from a trip and finding things moved around some. Have you ever come back to a house you live in, and everything's exactly where you put it, nothing moved? I can't stand that."

I ask him what he does, and he says he travels.

"Do you have any projects, or a hobby?"

"No."

"Nothing?"

"I was thinking of taking up bridge."

"Bridge?"

"Bridge."

I said "Good Lord, Jack—why don't you write, or paint, or sculpt. *Bridge*? I think people go senile when they don't use their brains. Look at Grandma Moses. She wasn't really that good a painter, but she gave herself a new career at seventy-five. You could do the same."

Jack looks out the window, sucking on his Marlboro with his strange fish lips, with his rheumy bulging eyes. He says nothing. At least he wasn't—like so many older people I know—going on and on about his health or his duty time at the hospital. He isn't a whiner; he just keeps on keeping on, ugly as sin and travelling hither and yon. A feather, an old and very scraggly feather.

We sit outside, on the ferry deck, with the wind in our faces, the sea beneath us. Most of the other passengers seem content to stay inside, where it is insufferably hot—so there is plenty of room up front for Jack and Al and me. I watch the pelicans wheeling, turning, folding up their wings, plunging, bobbing up, and slowly lifting themselves off the water; or gliding, no more than a few inches over the swells.

Jack is interested in facts of exotica. "Take pineapples, now," he says. "Didja know that it takes three years to grow a pineapple, to maturity. Three years!" He stops and shakes his head.

"Can you beat that?" he says. "Three years." He shakes his head again. I agree that it is a long time.

When we arrive in the city, Jack will be gone. We were strangers yesterday, we will be strangers tomorrow, so I have no problem talking to him, asking him questions.

Once we get off the boat, and go through Puntarenas, we stop at a roadside cafe, me and Al and the old goat. We order some snacks: meat wrapped in fried tortillas, fried cheese. Delicious, delicious with our beer.

I ask him about his relationship with his roommate.

"No sex," he says.

"Why not?" I ask.

"Why bother?" he says.

Jack tells us his only child, a son, is thirty-five, and all his hunting buddies are dead.

"Are you afraid of dying?" I ask.

"No," he says, "I'm more afraid of living."

"What do you mean?"

"I don't want them keeping me alive."

I think of Metzner's description of the two phases of our lives:

In the first phase, which normally lasts from childhood to middle adulthood, we are becoming individuals in the sense of learning the ways of the world and involving ourselves in the demands of family, work, and society. In the second phase, which begins, according to Jung, with the midlife crisis, when we may find ourselves, like Dante, "lost in the middle of a dark forest," we begin the process of individuation, which involves turning inward. Now we have to integrate the shadow, balance the anima and animus, and reconnect with the Self, which has been all along and remains at the center of our being.

Al is just in the middle of the first phase, Jack well in the second, and I am between the two.

When we come out, Al starts kicking the soccer ball with two kids on a little plot of land in front of the restaurant. One is nine, the other twelve. They have smoky eyes and smoky skin and lovely coordination. Al is good, too—he kicks the ball up on the top of his shoe, and then across to them. You can see they are digging this huge American playing soccer with them. I love it, there in the sun, my good friend Al, who loves all, being the kind American with these kids, playing (nicely!) on their turf.

I bit it and spit it out
I did it all
I loved and laughed and cried
Did my share of boozing
I find it all so amusing
To think I did all that
And may I say, not in a shy way
(Oh no, not me)
I did it my way
The record shows I took the blame
And did it my way
Yes it was my way.

—FRANK SINATRA

That evening, back in San José, at the casino, Al and I meet up with Eutheria and her two merry consorts. She's forty, and her voice is a nicely enriched basso, made so by twenty-five years of cigarettes, gin, and love. Al and I can hear her whinny across several cubic yards of crowded casino. I had complained to him about this Siren's voice, but he was curious, and so we ended up at table with her, playing blackjack.

"Thirteen," she says to the dealer. "You dealt me a thirteen. O God, what am I gonna do?" One of her consorts, Rafael Fariña, looks at the dealer, and looks at her.

"Muy serio," he says of the dealer—very serious.

"O shit, go ahead and hit me." Jack of Spades.

"Damn," and she yields up her *colones* chip (about $1.50) and then digs out another, out of Rafael's side pocket, and starts the whole process all over again. Definitely poor-man's Twenty-One.

Love and sin and rum and smokes are evidently very invigorating. Eutheria doesn't look a day over thirty. She swears, giggles, downs huge margaritas, even outdoing Al, matching Rafael and the young Cantinflas drink for drink.

"I came to Costa Rica seventeen years ago," she tells me, "stayed for ten years, and lost $1,000,000 in the lobster trade." How can we doubt one so sincere and so lovely and so raucous?

"We were doing fine until the Russians moved in. The lobsters come down the coast, and the Russians park their boat factory just off the coast of Nicaragua, and put this hose, this *vacuum cleaner* down, and suck up all the lobsters in the western Caribbean. I hate Communists. They just suck 'em all up, pack them right there—on the ship—and ship 'em out to Moscow. So I lose a million dollars." She pauses to lose another $1.50 there at the black-jack table.

Eutheria claims to be living up in the hills "like a goddamn absolute Indian."

"I broke my goddamn leg falling off the Jungle Train last year," she says. "And the outhouse is a mile away from where I live. And I have to go out there with my crutches with those snakes hanging around, everywhere." I, her dedicated listener, go everywhere on my crutches, so I'm used to all these crutch-and-fracture stories laid on me; everyone has at least one—but this particular tale does seem to have a few new twists.

"Are they poisonous?" I ask.

"Who?"

"The snakes."

"O god. Are they poisonous? Every goddamn one of them. I hate snakes. And I don't have any goddamn water, either."

We talk for a while as she alternatively leans on Cantinflas for another cigarette, or leans on Rafael for some more affection or *colones*, the national currency of Costa Rica (the *colones*, not necessarily the affection). She tells us the story of her life. And we trade travel stories.

Eutheria has the infuriating habit of having been everywhere I've been, obviously having had much more fun—or having had more revolutionary turmoil, or meeting more exotic people—than I ever did.

"Yes, I was in England," she tells me. "I hated it, and Ireland, loved it, knew J. P. Donleavy, he was an absolute ass, and you were in Málaga? I was in Torremolinos, built a house right next to Ava Gardner, she used to come over with her horrid boyfriend, who was always trying to feel me up while she was out getting the wine, and you say you are going to Limón on the Jungle Train. Listen: be sure to take a bottle of booze, not beer, you don't want to piss with the train going like this..." And she lurches from side to side on her tall stool, and I try to steady her, fearing for the balance of her and Rafael and Cantinflas and the Twenty-One table and the dealer, and me, the whole room, from this swaying train and lobster lady of disaster. She spends her last *colones* hitting a quite good soft seventeen against the dealer's twelve, so we move over to the bar.

Eutheria has the vocabulary of a sailor, and she mixes Spanish phrases pronounced badly with a South Florida accent. She claims to have grown up in Madrid, Florida, and although I doubt its very existence, she assures me that she grew up there, and happily, too. She also seems to know every man in the casino. She waves her cigarette at the bartender.

"Manolo," she says, loudly. "I used to know him when he was thin as a rail, hair down to here," she tells me. "Manolo," she shouts, "¡Qué panzanita!" [What a fat little belly!] Manolo comes over and wipes the counter and trades a few old-time Costa Rica memories with her.

A few drinks later Rafael falls off his stool and announces to me and Al that we are invited over to their place "for a little toke."

"I bought some weed, just a little, just a poquito, eenie-weenie—for my fortieth birthday," Eutheria tells us. "I'll be forty in..." she pulls on Cantinflas' wristwatch, with his wrist in it, pulls him this way and that, and announces: "...in just fifteen minutes, I'll be forty. Can you imagine!"

I assure her that forty is a fine age, and that I can imagine, having passed that way too long ago to remember with candor, much less accuracy. "I had my nervous breakdown when I turned forty," I tell her.

"I suppose you are right," she says. She puts her arm around Cantinflas' neck, kisses him. "Listen, you both come on over, have a little smoke with us. *Fuma un poquita de ganja,*" she says, loudly. I tell her that as tempted as I am, since I am pushing a decade or so past forty, I'll beg off and go back to the room to read some Metzner and sleep the sleep of the just. The last I see of them is as a drunken eight-legged caterpillar, arm-in-arm, making their way down the stairs of the casino, down to the elevator.

"'Dios," they call to me. "Bye."

"'Dios."

"'Dios, 'dios," they call, now out of sight.

In his works Denial of Death *and* Escape from Evil, *Ernest Becker extended the work of Rank, Wilhelm Reich, and Norman O. Brown to argue that the repressed fear of death is at the root of much of man's evil behavior: we destroy one another in order to symbolically stave off our own fear of destruction. On the collective scale, the exploitation of this fear of death underlies the most dreadful phenomena of tyranny, oppression of the masses, war, totalitarianism and genocide.*

— *OPENING TO INNER LIGHT*

As usual, we are late getting to the station to catch the train to Limón. Five minutes before departure time, we arrive among the armies of people with their dozen dozen children and mountainous bags. We cross over the tracks, and a friendly porter pushes me up the stairs while the engine shuttles cars back and forth, threatening to squash us.

In six hours, the trip will take us from the heights of Costa Rica down to the sea-level jungles at Limón. As we go through towns, the boys wave and the girls shriek and run alongside us. We are doing ten miles an hour, they five or so.

The famous San José-Limón train is praised in many guidebooks as the ultimate journey, travelling the valleys of

Orosi and Turrialba, lumbering over great valleys filled with animals and people and the ever-present coffee plants. It is light and airy out there in those lush valleys, but our train to paradise—as scenic as it is—is noisy and dirty and bumpy and dust-ridden. The tracks were built before the Panama Canal (indeed, this was one of the first routes across Central America) and I daresay that they've done no maintenance work whatsoever on them since 1902. The coaches have the arched roofs and the lack of suspension so dear to railway buffs and people who lived a century ago. For the rest of us, somehow spoiled by buses and trains that work and don't jiggle about like a bowl of blancmange, we know that extended journeys like this could easily lead to rupture and fallen testes.

The towns we pass are noisome and dusty and dirty, the shacks unpainted, the villagers are as soporific as any I have seen anywhere. Indeed, only the animals seem healthy and alive. Great huge dun-colored horses, tawny stallions, white geldings, lithe mares. Huge, healthy Brahma bulls, trim cows, calves. Even the chickens are glorious—a country that cares for chickens has to be an honorable country: giant golden cocks feathering their Pertoletes, Rhode Island Reds, Barred Rocks, even the rare and exotic Bearded Favorelles, Naked Neck Turkens, and fuzzy white bearded silkies.

We asked our friend Francisco to drive down from San José to meet us in Limón, at the railway station, but when we arrive, he is nowhere to be seen. We've been jolted about in this scenic eggbeater with smoke and dust and eighty to ninety degree heat for six hours, and we are left at this siding with two worn benches in what appears to be a very seedy area of Limón. Al has a magic ability to stir up booze at any juncture, and he finds us six very cold Bavaria beers. We sit, nursing our bruises (and brews), gazing at the cinders, until, Lo, Francisco appears magically out of the dark and takes us to our hotel at the edge of the sea.

Francisco, like many people in San José, is very very light, and very slight, and sports a mere soupçon of a moustache. With his dark hair and nice eyes, he is a parody of a kind and civilized Latino. We go out with him to eat at a fish and stew restaurant in downtown Limón. We talk, we talk—and as is so usual with those trying to practice their language on someone else, he speaks to us in English, and we talk to him—on and off, in Spanish. He has lived in the United States for several years, and his English is quite good. He is also outspoken: he loathes the *contras*—says they spend all their money on arms, and that there is not enough money in Nicaragua left over for rice. "Perhaps they have no choice," I say, wanting to argue with him, but not too much. Political arguments are the province of long nights in the college dorm over Four Roses and too many cigarettes and pizzas. Now the wine is nice, as is the restaurant, and I ask myself if I really want to involve myself in a discussion of America's retarded foreign policy.

Francisco has lived in Missouri, Mississippi, and Miami. He says, "Some of my best friends are niggers."

"Pardon. I mean, *pardón*."

"I've really known some nice niggers, both here and in America."

"Francisco. That's not the right word."

"Oh?"

"No. Negro maybe. Black, yes. Or Afro-American. But not 'nigger.' If you talk like that in California, you're done for. The word is 'black.'"

Then we get on the subject of Germany.

"The Jews take all the money out of the country. They have no loyalty," he says, "just like they do here."

"Francisco," I say. "Have you ever heard of Hitler, and what he did to the Jews?"

"Hitler gave Germans national pride," he says. "He used his speeches to give people a good feeling about their own country."

It's funny, this thing we call prejudice. It's jarring when it turns up in the wrong people. If I were to talk politics to the garbageman from Coca Beach, I want to believe I could expect all this talk about 'niggers' and 'national pride.' But here's Francisco, of the nice eyes and perfect manners, going to school at night to study economics, working as a hotel clerk during the day. I am reminded of *The Stranger* and Camus' description of his father, a lawyer. One day he goes to visit court, to see his father at work. "It was the snakes, falling from his mouth," he says. It was the snakes got him, as his father argued to put to death a man sitting there in the courtroom. And it is the snakes that get me as I'm talking to Francisco, Francisco of the nice smile and nice moustache and good taste in wines.

Sometimes I have to take my own pulse just to be sure that I am still alive...

— ENTRY IN SPANISH JOURNAL, 1960

Al and I drive down to Costa Rica's Chuita Beach, on the warm and sweet waters of the Caribbean. Just outside of Limón, a crazy woman dances out on the street in front of us, her arms in the air, her face mad, as if she were acting out a scene from *Black Orpheus*. A few miles further on, Al drives the car smack dab into a vulture. He swerves to miss it, and then — flapping to take off — the beast comes down on the car's hood, rolls its eyes once, and flips over onto the roadside. Since Al loves all animals, even the death of such a leathery beast bothers him.

We head towards Bribri on the Panamanian border, and go over a slight pass, cut through the hillside. When we return, ten minutes later, there is a large mass of rocks spread over the roadway, and a cloud of dust rising up from it. If we had been three minutes earlier, it would have come down on us and bopped us on the cupola through the open roof of the car. "We might be in the wrong place," I think to myself.

Near the beach, we pass an abandoned white 1976 Chevrolet. Inscribed on the open trunk, in dust, are these words:

Poor Herb
Poor Poor Herb.

Well, you know me. I am not one to get worked up over curses, hexes, badlands and such — but I say to Al, "I am not especially keen on staying around here for the night." Al is busy trying to drive while scratching one or two of the estimated 1,000 mosquito bites he garnered in the Capri beach hotel last night. I didn't get bitten once, My blood is so pickled with bile that when they smell all that fresh young meat — Al — they decide to go high rent. "If you don't want to get eaten again for supper tonight," I tell him, "I think we can do better than to stay on this godforsaken coast." I suspect the goddess of the local natives comes to earth disguised as a giant bird-of-prey, and since Al just squashed her, we are probably better off in the mountains.

We drive back into Limón for lunch, with the thought that we will go west out of the city shortly afterwards.

A city's marketplace is its heart, and what you see there is what the city is. If that is so, we are well off to be out of here: I've never gone through a darker, more evil-smelling public market than that of Limón. The meats look to be left over from the Conquest. There's nothing that can cure hunger more quickly than pale tripe eviscerated from a diseased cow, fish with eyes that are sunken and dull, pigmeat left over from Biblical times, and all used as a feasting field by several thousand flies. We decide to push on with our hunger intact.

Little did I know how thoroughly we were to get lost that evening. I wasn't paying attention to our direction, because Al and I had fallen into another mindless argument about his being a boozer. Remember that book, *Games Alcoholics Play*? It says that every alcoholic needs a long-suffering wife (to suffer), a barkeep (to listen to the babble), fellow drinkers to feed the habit, and finally, a nag. Well, I elect myself to be Al's Nag. Me, of all people, needing, as I do, at least a quarter-bottle of Port to put me to sleep of an evening. "At least, at *least*..."as I say to Al during this particular quodliber,"...at least I don't have to have my bottle for breakfast, and another for lunch, and another for mid-afternoon snack. And another before supper, and another..."

"You didn't look too sober last night when we got back to the hotel, after all that wine," he says.

It is, as I say, a mindless argument, and it keeps us from paying attention to the road. As we start up into the hill country from the littoral of the Caribbean the road gets wider but emptier. It begins to rain. My road map, printed on the back of a matchcover, doesn't show any rainstorms — just a squiggly road to San Jose. The road *does* wind and turn, but there are no villages at all, like there are on my map. Just rain-soaked fields and roaring creeks. We come around a bend, and there is a landslide across most of the road.

"How long did it take Francisco to drive our car down yesterday?" asks Al.

"Two and a half hours," I say, eating my fingernails, the matchbook cover, and the matches.

"Did he mention any landslides?"

"Not a word," I say, making sure that my voice sounds even and natural. No sense in upsetting the natives. "He said the driving was perfect." There is no one in sight. We come around another bend — the rain getting heavier and heavier — and come to a cross-bar across the road with supports sunk in the asphalt. A huge black man, in yellow slicker, is tending several kerosene lamps.

"Why don't you ask him where we are," says Al.

"Oh, I don't want to bother him," I say.

"ASK him," Al suggests.

I roll down the window. "¿Qué pasa con la carretera?" I ask, in perfect textbook Spanish. "¿Dónde estamos?"

"Fo la tidica rodie asa freedlo," says the keeper of the road. He comes over and stands by the window. "Pooley quila? Seis sem'nes. Seis gorga low-dah."

"¿Éste es la carretera a San José?" I ask.

"Teedle puddle-hum. Foo tee laksae," he says.

"What did he say?" asks Al.

"Teedle poodle-hum. Foo tee laksae."

"What does that mean?"

"Beats the shit out of me. I think he's a Persian, talking to us in Farsi. Or maybe it's Urdu. It's not going to help us much just hanging out here, jawing with The Hulk. Let's go back."

"Why?" says Al. "Don't you want to find out what happened to the road."

"I don't even want to know," I say. "What little I could understand — he says that the road's been out for six weeks. Or else, it's going to take six weeks to fix it. Or maybe there are six Gorgons up ahead of us. We'll never get back to San José. We'll have to spend the rest of our miserable lives in Limón." Al backs the car around.

"Gracias, señor," I say, waving to the man.

"Boodley wimp," he says, smiling at us, "¡Fardle!" And he waves us goodbye.

"What was that?" says Al.

"Boodley wimp," I say. "¡Fardle! I know it's Spanish, because of the upside down exclamation point. But what kind of Spanish, we'll never know, and he ain't telling us. It might have been an ancient Nahuntl curse. You shouldn't have squashed that buzzard. I hope you don't mind sleeping in the car. I think we've caught the Traveller's Disease."

"What? The what?"

"It's called The Traveller's Disease. It's when you wake up on the road and you're lost. It's nightfall, and it's raining. There's no place to sleep, no one in sight, you're in a strange country. No one speaks the language, at least no language heard or studied on the face of the earth for the last five thousand years."

Travelling, travelling, travelling. It really does do something to you, doesn't it? It puts you up and it puts you down. It gives you something and it takes it away. As we plow back down the hill, the rain spattering our windshield, the black trees moving and writhing around us, the landscape absolutely barren of life and humanity — not even a cow or a goat — I think on travel, that cure for the soporific called life. Filled with ennui? Just take a trip through the heartland of Liberia, the mountaintops of the hairy Ainu Islands of Japan, the village of Rat, the jungles of Costa Rica. Need some excitement in your days? Try getting lost in a strange land at dusk with no lights, no people, no habitations, no creatures of the earth — only cascading rainstorms, dark waving laburnum and ominous grey-black orchids peeping out of the trees. And, for added pith...

"We're getting low on gas," says Al. "How come you didn't buy a map?"

"You didn't tell me to."

"You always tell me you're the navigator."

"Listen, I have taken whole convoys through the Chilean desert. I've lead caravans of camels into (and out of) the upper reaches of the Nile. I have brought professional climbers up to, onto, and down from the very tops of the Himalayas, the tiptop of the earth. And every damn one of these places had a sign or two or three — even the bloody Kalahari in Botswana had a sign, every 100 miles or so — to tell you where you were, or were not. And here we are in the Switzerland of Central America, and not one goddamned sign — except for that one over there. Pull over."

"Did you really go to all those places? What does the sign say?" Al asks when I get back in the car. I wring out my shirt, dump the water out of my shoes, and emerge from my wetsuit.

"Would I lie to you?" I ask. "It says *Rio Colorado*"

"What does that mean?"

"Colored river."

"Oh, there's a river there?"

"Yes, a very colorful one. And a very big one. And a very angry one. I suspect this bridge will be taking a long journey to the coast within the next hour or so. What did you say about the gas gauge?"

"It's just on the other side of the red."

"Which side of the red?"

"The dark side."

"The *dark* side?

"The dark side," says Al. He does have a way with words.

There are a few, a very few advantages to travelling with a boozer. One is, he isn't necessarily given to worry. I may be comatose with fear at spending the next twenty-four hours in a newly discovered rain forest in a leaky car soon to be eaten by night creatures or sucked into a rampaging river, and all the while Al will be singing tunelessly a verse from Run DMC,

I got a dog a cat a mouse a rat
A fly (he don't die) and a little gnat...

Another advantage of travelling with an alcoholic is that he will always have something stashed somewhere to ease one's jangled nerves. After a bit of high level denial, Al admits to having some tequila stored under the back seat "in case of emergency, or if we ran out." I point out that this might qualify as an emergency since we are lost at 3,000 feet somewhere in the heartland of Central America, with tree beasties all about. After he finds the bottle, I nip it several times to be sure that it isn't poisoned.

Travelling, travelling, travelling. Here I am, stout Cortez, staring upon rain forests (and empty gas tanks) with wild surmise. "It's like a merry-go-round to be in such strange straits," I think. "Sometimes it takes you up, sometimes it takes you down." It's like love: the very first love, the one you never get over. That love always with you, until you die. The good and the bad of it — the appalling innocence of dealing with one's own true feelings, perhaps for the first time ever. "You never get over your first love," a friend of mine once said.

"Or," I might add, "the first trip." The first real journey alone, away from one's heritage, family, anger, needs, previous lives. The first adventure of them all.

❧ ❧ ❧

Rikkō and Master Nansen were conversing. Rikkō said, "The philosopher Jō once said 'Heaven and earth are of the same root as me. The universe and I are one.' It is really strange." Nansen pointed at a flower in the garden and said to Rikkō, "When people look at this flower, it is similar to a dream."

— *THE SOUND OF THE ONE HAND CLAPPING*
YOEL HOFFMAN

In 1960 I travelled to Spain because I was convinced that America was on a doom course, that if I stayed around any longer, I would be pulverised in the fight against The Red Devil of the East. I knew that when and if I ever came back, there would be a pit where New York City used to be. I had to get out. I had to go somewhere so I could stop dreaming about the flash of light baking child shadows on the schoolroom walls. It was a time when a pleasant old golfer ran the country and let foreign policy decisions be made for him by a Presbyterian Banker who was very righteous and who had dewlaps fit to kill.

I drifted through Europe. In England I was stopped by a Bobby for pissing in a dark alley. He threatened to arrest me. Later I read of Robert Graves' response when he was caught in the same act of relief, in London, possibly by the same Bobby: "Sir, I hope you realize that you are addressing a member of the Middle Class." It is said that the Bobby apologized.

I went on to Copenhagen, and haunted the streets at night with a Scots guitarist. We'd go into the dark bars, singing and passing the hat. We would sing Bo Diddley and Bobby Darin and Muddy Waters songs. While my friend was collecting money, I would sing "Home on the Range" and "You Are My Sunshine." We made enough for him to take the train to Paris.

It got colder in Copenhagen as the fall progressed. The friendly streets ceased to be thronged by friendly natives. I stayed indoors at the Youth Hostel and ate lots of Danish bread and Danish butter. Someone at the Youth Hostel told me about the sunshine and beaches and the cheap rent in Torremolinos.

In the jet going between Copenhagen and Madrid, I filled out an absentee ballot for the American presidential election. I chose Kennedy over Nixon. We believed then, really believed, that the country could be enhanced by a young neo-intellectual from Harvard. We had never heard of The Bay of Pigs or Nuclear Confrontation on the High Seas or French Indo-China.

I stayed at another Youth Hostel on the outskirts of Madrid. It was my first brush with the smell of poverty — the dust and the stink of it. All cash receipts were kept in an old unplugged GE refrigerator wrapped about with a chain. Our big activity of the day was sitting on the steps outside the office, drinking five-cents-a-shot Fundador Brandy and watching the liver-splotched dogs licking, sniffing, and humping each other in the courtyard. The Falange Juventude held meetings in an adjacent room, singing jingoistic songs, off-key, marching about the building with fake rifles.

I took one of the trolleys to the airport and got a flight down to Málaga. My ink pen leaked all over my shirt which bothered me because I was travelling light: two shirts, two pairs of pants, socks, chain-knit olive-drab sweater, 1955 J. Press hound's tooth jacket, portable Remington typewriter. We landed in Málaga after sunset, on a Sunday evening.

Paul Theroux claims that when we come into our own destined part of the world, we know it at once. Málaga, in Spain, in November of 1960, gave me just such a feeling. The air was nectarine. The Hotel Niza (I always think of it as *my* hotel), had been built in 1894. My room faced out over the Plaza Mayor. I went to sleep with the balcony doors open, and was wakened at ten-thirty at night by the sounds of voices, thousands of voices. I thought there was a riot. It was the people of Málaga, babbling to each other, and to me. Strolling, endlessly strolling. The voices drifted up the five stories to my room, along with endless clouds of fragrant black *Faros* cigarettes. Café con leche, coñac, lottery tickets ("¡Me queda el gordo!" — "I have the big one!") The bourgeoise, the beggars, the cripples, the fat and the thin, the old, the young — an entire society turned out for my arrival on that Sunday night. It had been a long trip, and although I put in an appearance on the balcony, they never stopped to notice me.

It took me a week to find a house. This was, you must remember, before the deluge. In 1960 only a few thousand tourists had found Spain. The Iberian peninsula had been cut off from the world for two decades. It had also been cut off from time. Spain in 1960 was America in 1900. Street-cars, black taxis (pre-war Mercedes the most favored), street vendors; they turned off the stop-lights at one in the afternoon.

I took the narrow-gauge train to Torremolinos. Too many tourists. The next day I took the train east, to the town of Vélez. Halfway out, we passed through Rincón de la Victoria. There were a dozen or so cottages, a piece of white paper tied to the bars over the windows. That meant the houses were for rent. I had a place to stay. Me, and my typewriter, in Spain, 1960, by the sea.

❧ ❧ ❧

Each morning I would get up, put on in the same grey shapeless pants, the same dusty cordovans, the same olive-drab sweater. I would write some, then take the train from the village into Málaga. It ran directly in front of the house, and from there to the rocky coastline near El Palo, with the two tunnels, and then on into the city. The engine was built in Brussels in 1905. There was an engineer, a coal-shoveler, and a ticket-taker. There was a single coach, marked "Second Class." Often I would stand on the platform, with the ocean on one side, the villages passing by on the other.

Málaga had blue-white inlay mosaic patterns decorating the sidewalks of the main plaza. Beyond were a thousand dark shops. Almost everyone was dressed in black. The children were muted, diminutive adults. I would shop, walk the streets, drink coffee, take the train home alone.

Supper was at 8:30. That was a concession to me. Most Spaniards ate at ten or eleven. Four kids from Rincón de la Victoria would come to eat with me, at my house, at my request. They kept me from being lonely. José, Marcellina, Enrique, Pacque. They told me the gossip of the village, laughed with me and at my Spanish as they demolished mountains of food. They had never eaten so well. They went from suppers of bread and olive oil to heaping mounds of gazpacho and paella, with vegetables, salads, fish and wine. The good food had an alarming effect on their skins, their face color, their activity. When I first met them, they were dust color, same color as the dust of the main street of Rincón de la Victoria. After several months, their faces turned bright, roses appeared on their thin child's cheeks.

José and Marcellina would go with me into Málaga to shop. We left in the late morning, when the sky was so blue it seemed to lift the mountains off their green-brown pedestals, elevate them into the air, into that pure, clean, breath-taking sky-blue sky. We would make a circuit of the meat markets and the public market with its mountains of beans and vegetables. We would look in all the shop windows. Marcellina would beg me to buy her a pair of shiny black shoes that she saw in the window of the zapateria. We would go to the newsstand — I couldn't break myself of the habit of the *International Herald-Tribune* — then we would go to lunch. We'd eat garlic soup, omlettes, drink beer.

❧ ❧ ❧

Our lives are defined like tangerines. My time in Spain was a colorful period of my existence. When I try to peel it, to see what's inside, I find a dozen perfect segments, with little white strings of memories.

I remember one night lying alone. It is past midnight. It was early in the spring. Fishermen are off the shore trying, with their bright lights, to pull a few more fish from the depleted Mediterranean. Their lights come bright through the bars, limned on the far wall of my bedroom. I am afraid. I am not sure of what — but I remember being afraid. And then I hear someone walking down the railroad track, singing a Flamenco song, one that Manolo Caracol made famous. In those days everyone, it seemed, sang Flamenco, and it wasn't just for the tourists. I drift off to sleep.

The days are stark, and blue. They drift by like scenes out of Gaugin that narcotize the soul. I open my doors and windows to the sea, and to the life around me. As much as possible for one from another land, I come to have a peasant rhythm to my life. A storm comes, and the run-off soil turns the waves to blood.

There are no real seasons in this part of Spain, but there is a general warming in March. I start to travel some, staying away from my cottage by the sea for a week or so. I travel with Jean-Louis.

He's my age, from France, with a face like a Modigliani drawing. His skin is dead white, his eyes the color of dark marble. He wears heavy denims and a thin grey sweater. We travel through northern Morocco, by train and by bus. I know a Quaker, working with the Algerian refugees in Oujda. We go to a camp, meet some refugees. I ask them questions, which Jean-Louis translates, and then they answer, Jean-Louis translates that. "The Algerian people are looking for a place in the sun," one of them says. "We will finish this war, and be free, and have our place in the sun," he says. I watch Jean-Louis as he translates these words for me. I think of how bright the sun in North Africa. I think how dark and mysterious Jean-Louis' sloe eyes. They are merry when he talks, and he uses his hands like an actor in a French movie. I am well taken with him.

We go back to Spain, to La Linea de la Concepcion, then Seville. Jean-Louis decides to go north. We make arrangements to meet in Madrid. I take the evening train back to Rincón de la Victoria. It is late when I arrive. I get off the train, and José is waiting for me at the station. He has been meeting every train for the last two weeks. In the dim light of the station, I can see that his skin is starting to turn dusky again. His eyes have lost some of their brilliance. He is standing on the platform, looking out to sea, out to the Atlas Mountains to the south. I am standing next to the tracks, perhaps three feet below him. He looks out at the everfolding, neverchanging sea. I try to think of something to say. He doesn't look at me: his hands are in his pockets. I touch his ankle. It is such a thin and frail ankle. He says nothing, I say nothing. I have broken the rhythm of his life. Before he knew me, he worked in the olive fields for fifteen cents a day. He is back working in the same fields again. It is time for me to go.

The day before I leave, Marcellina comes to show me the box of momentos she has of me. There is a lock of my hair, and a photograph — already going yellow — that we had made, the three of us, in the Alcalá in Málaga. There are a few other odds and ends: a poem by William Carlos Williams[1] I had torn out of the *Herald-Tribune*, a green plastic spray bottle of Mennen deodorant that I favored in that bathless environment.

I fly from Málaga to Madrid. Jean-Louis and I are to meet in the Plaza del Sol. When I arranged the meeting, I didn't know that the Plaza del Sol extended for three blocks, and contained, at the minimum, in the evening, some five thousand people on paseo, going round and round. I am out there every

1. I.

women your age have decided
wars and the beat
of poems your grandfather

is a poet and loves you
pay attention
to your lessons an inkling

of what beauty means to
a girl your age
may dawn soon upon you

II.

life is a flower when it
opens you will
look trembling into it unsure

of what the traditional
mirror may reveal
between hope and despair while

a timorous old man
doubtfully half
turns away his foolish head

III.

a bunch of violets clutched
in your idle
hand gives him a place

beside you which he cherishes
his back turned
from your casually appearing

not to look he yearns after
you protectively
hopelessly wanting nothing.

night, and I think I see him, but when I race to catch him, he's gone, or it's just a shadow, or it's a person who has a big nose or funny eyes, doesn't look like Jean-Louis at all, Jean-Louis with his long, thin, slightly askew face, his way of loping about with his hands in his pockets, his sardonic down-turned lips. I see him twice if I see him at all, but I can never catch up to him, and after three nights I give up and book passage on a flight for New York. Just before I am to leave, I go to the movies. They are showing *Black Orpheus*. The dubbing into Spanish is terrible, the singing is off-key, but I cry through the whole thing. I sneeze a lot so the people around me will think I have a cold.

❧ ❧ ❧

I entered the Buddhist life when I was a small boy. I have grown old now. Confronted with people, I now find myself powerless to save them. I used to discipline myself in order to help people some day when I became enlightened. Contrary to my expectation, however, I have become a fool...

— MASTER JOSHU AS QUOTED IN
NINE-HEADED DRAGON RIVER
BY PETER MATTHIESSEN

It turns out there's a bar around the next bend on that Costa Rican road, and when we stop and go in, and they show us on the map where we had made the wrong turn at Siquirres. It's sixty or so kilometers back. By the time we retrace our path, it's quite dark. The road to San José is twisted, and as we get further up the hill, it becomes foggy as well. One of the most gloriously sited roads in Central America, and we can barely see to the edge of the road, much less the mountain scenery around us. And the foggier it gets, the harder it is to know exactly where the road is: there is no center stripe, no sign of the terminus — and I suspect, as we get into the highlands, that there are many deep and dangerous drop-offs on both sides of us. After three hours of driving, at ten miles an hour, Al says he is falling asleep. I suggest we stop off at the next roadside cantina.

It is warm and cozy inside, and there are several drunk Costa Ricans, standing at the bar, sitting at one of the two tables. They invite us to join them at dominoes. Since I had, in my shady past, lost more than once in that innocent game, I defer and let them inveigle Al into it. The barkeep serves us several beers, and a *boca* which, according to my guide book, is "a small cooked delicacy, often delicious." Our guide writer had probably never been to the Cantina Descanso in Villa Quesada. The *boca* consists of baked spider attached to fried cane, all of it interlarded with, well, lard. I know that in some countries not to eat a gift of food is considered next in the line of sins to stealing another man's wife or sleeping with his ox, and can result in immediate execution. However, to eat this particular *boca* would, I knew, result in a lingering death, so I manage to hide the unconsumed portions behind me, down behind the ledge of my stool, near the fat snoring dog. La Fida the dog has a good sense of survival. I shove her with my toe, to try to tempt her to eat, but even with all those nice doggie sounds the bitch won't touch it. Al confesses later that the reason he made so many visits to the WC in the middle of the domino game was to disgorge that part of the *boca* he had hidden in the back of his mouth.

While they are busily poisoning us, the natives are also beating the pants off Al at dominoes. After one disastrous deal, they hand out the next set. The man with yellow fangs and evil eye sitting across from Al plays the double sixes, and the troll of the big, bepimpled nose lays down a six and a one. Al plays the double one. "El culo," says one of the men, a scrofulous old geezer with one eye. All the men at the table laugh.

"What did he say?" Al asks me.

"He just called you an asshole," I translated.

"Why?" says Al. His eyes narrow a bit.

Old Red-Eye picks up the domino, and points to the one-spot. "That's known as *El Culo*," he says, smiling and winking at me. I am fascinated. I have never seen a one-eye man wink before. Every time he does it, it looks like he's telling me to go to sleep. I explain the symbolism of the dot to Al.

"Don't let it disturb you," I tell him. "It's just a joke. They know you are going to beat the pants off them." The bar keeper tries to pass off another Spider Supreme on me, but I convince him that we've just come from a huge meal down the road, so he sets the two of them in front of Al who tries hard to pretend they aren't there.

An hour later, relieved of 500 or so colones, we get back on the roller coaster ride to San Jose.

"I don't know how they do it," says Al, in frustration. "I always thought I was pretty good at dominoes."

He drives on, but he finds, after awhile, that he is getting sleepy again. He pulls a casette out of the glove compartment. It is a tape containing the music or whatever they call it of a riot squad called "Iron Maiden." He turns it on at full force.

"Do you have to play that so loud," I say. I point out to him that my ears are about the only undamaged parts I have left on my tired old body, and I have a grudging affection for them and what's left of their abilities to distinguish one sound from another. I would hate to have them burnt out so soon, I tell him, leaving nothing behind but mudflaps, good for nothing but parking spectacles.

He drives on for two or three miles, then he turns down the screams and gnashing. Down, say, one-tenth of a decibel. He then tells me, very patiently, in one of those flat monotones given to late teen-agers of America, and presumably the entire world, when they know they are speaking to a dolt: "I am very tired. It is late. I can barely see where I am driving. I've never been on this road before. It is a long way to San José. If I don't have something to distract me, I could drive off the road and we are all dead. Understand, *culo*?" Al is not given to speeches, so I consider I've had quite a talking-to.

"Show me the way to San José," I sing tunelessly to myself. Evidently the music works. We get to the city at midnight. It is possible that the screaming furies saved our lives — but if you tell anyone that I have even begun to like "Iron Maiden," I will deny it all the way to the grave.

Food and long drives evidently have a salutory effect on one's stamina, because no sooner do we get to the hotel and eat than Al goes out "to party," his need for sleep completely forgotten. I go on up to the casino to see if I can help the state of Costa Rica with its balance-of-payments problem. There are a couple of old American geezers sitting there at the one functioning blackjack table, both quite drunk. One of them looks not unlike William Casey, the other like Enver Hoxha. Casey is trying to count the cards, in time-honored black-jack fashion. He's so drunk he can't remember what comes after five. The only thing he's doing, in contrast to me in all my sobriety, is winning.

Every two minutes, as he starts to count the cards, Casey says, as regularly as clockwork: "I'm getting so old that I can only count to twenty." Pause, and then: "But if I take off my pants, I can get up to twenty-one." Hoxha gurgles in laughter, then coughs fit to die. Casey repeats his two lines something like fifty times in the hour, and Hoxha loves it — each time. I finally retire since my debt-to-assets has fallen so drastically. As I pass out of the casino, I can still hear Casey muttering, "I'm getting so old that I..." And Hoxha laughing, wildly, then lapsing into a phleghm-riched wheeze. "We're all getting so old..." I think.

Given the weird events of 1986 - 1987, maybe it *was* Casey and Hoxha.

❧ ❧ ❧

There is a reality even prior to heaven and earth;
Indeed, it had no form, much less a name;
Eyes fail to see it; it has not voice for ears to detect.
— "ON ZEN," BY MASTER DAIO,
QUOTED IN *NINE-HEADED DRAGON RIVER*

One of the big attractions of Costa Rica is volcanoes, so the next day Al and I elect to take our hangovers up to Volcan Irazú. The Costa Rican Highway Authority, as always, shows its fondness for putting signs about for every two-bit piss-ant creek in the land, but for nothing as important as a 10,000 foot volcano. Therefore, at the beginning of our excursion we spend some of our happiest hours meandering the suburbs of southeast San José, asking the natives for directions to the nearest volcano, having, in the process, an opportunity to get to know many if not all of the dead-end streets in the area. However my navigating skill, honed by the simple expedient of craning my neck out the window and peeking through the clouds at the highest nearby mountain, makes it so that we arrive at the road to the crest well before early afternoon when the clouds, according to the guide book, will close down the volcano for the rest of the day. The navigating I do puts me not too far down the scale from Vasco de Gama. The dialogue between captain and navigator in the engine room goes something like this:

Al: (at junction in road) Should I go right or left?

Me: Unh — go right (pointing).

Al: You say "Go right," but you're pointing to the left.

Me: Unh, oh, OK — go left then.

Al: Don't you know the difference between your right and your left?

Me: You know, I could never figure it out. After all these years, after all my education — I still can't tell the difference between my right and my left. Each time, I have to think about it. Actually, I'm sort of proud of it. All of us need something to be classically dumb about. For me, it's right and left.

Al: I was like that once. Then I figured out how to remember.

Me: Does it work?

Al: Yes.

Me: How do you do it?

Al: I just think about my nuts.

Me: Oh. You just think about your nuts.

[Silence]

Me: How does thinking about your nuts help you to tell the difference between right and left.

Al: My right nut is bigger than my left one. I just think about that when I am making a turn.

On the winding road we soon leave the clouds below us. On both sides are lush farms, fields heavy with corn, barley, or most often, clover. There are cows and horses so healthy that we might well be in Colorado or Oregon. The road is deserted, the air fresh and heady, and as we drive, I fall into a brown study, as I so often do, on the meaning of life. The Meaning of Life!

When I was in college, it seemed that that was all we ever thought about. The question of the meaning of life in that far-off time seemed to have all of us quite bedazzled. I must have studied at one of those Meaning-of-Life colleges. Some of the teachers had come to us out of WWII France, England, Belgium, and Scandanavia; a few of them had been in the Underground. Their experiences with casual human cruelty, torture, and murder gave their philosophical questions a bit of pith. One does not ask silly questions on the nature of existence after spending five years evading the SS at risk of torture and death.

Few of these teachers were traditional Christians. This had the advantage of eliminating all those easy answers about God and Man so favored by American Baptists, Charismatics, Evangelicals, and other frauds. These survivors refused to accept the unexplainable by burying it in sentimental bible-worship. Some of our teachers might have been agnostics — but I believe the majority were Existentialists, Buddhists or

Quakers. Because of their backgrounds, it was given to them to wonder more seriously and more paradoxically about The Meaning of It All. And an Existentialist doesn't necessarily deny the existence of God — he just wants to know what the hell the divine means by all the ugliness laid down as an inescapable part of man's lot.[2]

Total and brutal warfare gives a piquancy to the question of man's destiny, and his relationship with the divine. It is no accident that our thinking was shaped by the writings of Sartre, Unomuno, Malraux, and Camus. *Man's Fate*, *The Stranger*, *Darkness at Noon*, and *The Plague* were our bibles. Especially the latter. Sometimes I remember regretting that I had not had a more traditional education, filled with traditional philosophers — Whitehead, North, Nietzsche, Kant, Descartes. The Existentialists set forth the question of man and his gods in a particularly troublesome fashion: "Why did they choose to put us here in this place, in this time, with this particular *set?*" (Religion, like philosphy, always prospers with paranoic references to an unseen, undefined "them," "they," and "their." Which is, perhaps, why religion, philosophy and paranoia have so much in common.)

Now of course I think it has to do with that grand paradox from *The Name of the Rose:* "I know. And I know I know. But how do I know I know I know." But then, thirty-five years ago, I had no such paradoxes to save me. The Buddhists are right. There is, can be, and will be, forever, no answer — outside of absurdity. It is like the koan related in Yoel Hoffman's *The Sound of the One Hand*,:

At the end of the summer session, Master Suigan says to the people, "I have been talking to you brothers for a summer; see if my eyebrows are still here."

"The thief is afraid," says Hofuku.

---

2. It put me in mind of that charming dialogue reported in one of the works of John Cage:
Question: If God is all wise, all seeing, all kind, and all loving, why is there then so much pain, misery, hunger, desperation, and sickness on earth?
Answer: To thicken the broth.

"It grows!" Chōkei says.

"The gate! The gate!" says Ummon.

Whenever we start wondering "What does it all mean?" or "What is the meaning of life," all we have to do is remember "The thief is afraid" or "The gate! The gate!" Maybe that's the only answer there is. And then the circle begins again. "They — whoever they are — why did they choose to put us here, in this world, at this time." The final paradox.

"Got it!" says Al.

"You've got it?" I say. "The answer..."

"Of course. There it is..."

And, off to our right, or left, up on the dark crest, touched by clouds, the Volcan Irazú.

I had some doubts if we would be able to visit the irascable Volcan. The cone is some five hundred yards from where we are stopped by the surrounding fence. I know I can't make it on my crutches because of the deep ash — and my Quickie wheelchair is more suited for the streets of San Francisco than for the ash-heaps of Irazú. Fortunately Al, when he isn't dead drunk in some alley, spends his time lifting weights, so he wrestles me and the wheelchair up an ash-strewn, eight percent grade in less time than it takes to say "Existentialism." Soon enough we are at the mouth of the volcano, looking a thousand feet or so down into the depths.

The streets of San José were warm when we left, so we assumed that Irazú would be as warm, or at least heated by great sulfurous clouds of gas. But the wind is blowing fiercely, and the crater seems lifeless. The surrounding area is powder grey, dusted everwhere with the leavings of the last great eruption in 1968. The only colors about us are the dozen or so tourists strung out above us, on a higher parapet, in their orange, blue, and brown sweaters. To the south, there are three or four red-and-white broadcast towers. At the bottom of the crater of Irazú, way below, there is a noxious-looking, lake-sized, yellow-green stand of water. As we remain there on the lip, shivering and contemplating the impenetrable depths of that hole, I think that I have not beheld such a moving sight since I went on a high-school tour of the main factory and surrounding slag-heaps of Bethlehem Steel, in Allentown, Pennsylvania. Rainstorms had left several such colorful yellow-green, ominous-looking puddles in their wake in the grey tailings all about the factory.

"The problem with a volcano," I tell Al, "is that it is all potential, no kinetic." Like a fifty-year-old whore, it shows all the ravages of time and past profligacies, but very little in the way of contemporary *Sturm und Drang*. Such quiescence is boring. I start to yawn, but at that moment, the ground shakes — at first a little, and then more heavily. The green-and yellow waters slosh about in the crater. I can see tiny waves lapping the edges as a huge jet of steam streams out of the ground on the far side, half-way down the crater. Out of the corner of my eye I see the tourists scattering, running for their cars. I think it's some joke, something put on by the Volcan Irazú Chamber of Commerce, perhaps, but then great clouds of debris start to fall downwards, into the cone, mixing with uprushing jets of steam. There is a strange flashing at the bottom of the crater. "Let's get the hell out of here," I yell at Al, but my chair has been jolted, and I find that it's beginning to slip down towards the pit. I try to reverse the motion, but the wheels slip from my hands. As the earth rolls and tumbles, I try to reach Al.

"Hold on," he yells, "grab on to something!" The air is filled with a loud shrieks of escaping steam. Boulders roll down towards the center of the inferno. I can feel Al's hands grabbing at the back of the chair, but it is too late. I am lurching forward, slipping down, slipping, irrevocable. Heat and fire surge up; I can smell the thick sulphur, feel it burning my face as I begin downwards...

❧ ❧ ❧

"This greater depth of realization," he wrote, "came later while I was in America, when suddenly the Zen phrase hiji soto ni magarazu, *'the elbow does not bend outwards' became clear to me. 'The elbow does not bend outward' might seem to express a kind of necessity, but suddenly I saw that this restriction was really freedom, the true freedom, and I felt that the whole question of free will had been solved for me..."*
— *WHEN THE SWANS CAME TO THE LAKE*

"The trouble with volcanoes is that they are only history," I tell Al later. "I can't think of a sillier way to spend an afternoon than looking at a dead hole filled with dirty water, surrounded by grit. Whose idea was it to come up here, anyway?"

"You're the tour guide," he says. "I just go where you tell me."

"Why are you looking so nervous?" I ask him, as we start back down the mountain road.

"You didn't notice that when we got in the car I put it into reverse by mistake and almost backed us off the hill at the edge of the parking lot."

"You're right — I didn't notice," I say. "I'd be nervous too. Jesus. The next time you want to go up on some mountain top, I think I'll stay home and read the *Areopagitica*. What'd you think of my eruption?"

Al yawns, and asks me when can have lunch, and a beer or two or three. All we have to show for our time perched up there is ash everywhere. You roll through it or walk over it, and it gets on your hands, on your clothes, in your shoes, in your hair, ears, eyes, up the nose, in between the toeses.

We stop off at a beer garden half way down the mountain. The bar-restaurant has a view of the San José intermontane that would bring tears to the eyes of even the most vapid traveller. We are able to test this, because nearby sits your typical vapid traveller, a pilgrim from Woonsocket, Rhode Island. As Al lights up his first beer of the day, I fall into conversation with her. I tell her that I have never met someone from Woonsocket before, and she says that during the time she's been in Costa Rica, her camera has been stolen, her bunions have been erupting, her hotel is right next to the bus depot, and she had the worst Christmas meal of her life at the San José Holiday Inn ("It was the giblet gravy. I knew giblet gravy would talk back to me. I don't know why I et it.") As part of a package tour of Central American, she has been on the go for ten days, fifteen hours a day. She can no longer remember whether yesterday they toured one of the coffee plantations on the eastern plateau or a jute factory near Bagaces. She has trouble telling the Panama Canal from the Golfo Dulce. She sure as hell can't remember what week it is.

As I listen to her, it occurs to me that the Ugly American on an U. S. Development Corporation project has been replaced by the Whining American on prepackaged tour. Nothing goes right: the beds are too hard or too soft, someone steals the cameras, travellers checks, luggage, toothbrushes, and passports. The water makes you sick, the food is too hot or too cold, and the nightclub tour is boring — it goes on too long, with strange people singing weird songs off-key in an impenetrable language. The museums whizz by in a blur ("I think it was in the natural history museum — no, it was in the Central Museum, where we saw those lovely fabrics, but the tour guide got us out of there so fast I didn't have time to find out where I could buy some...") The guide speaks English with such an accent that it is impossible to know if you are in the Cathedral San Cristobal, the Bar San Sebastian or the Escuela Paso Dobles.

She's brave, and hardy, our friend from Woonsocket. She won't give up, even though she feels like death. She paid her $1200 for this trip, her friends are expecting a slide show sometime in the next month, she's *committed* — damn if she is going to slack off after she's gone through all this torture. She'll stick with it to the last museum, fort, plantation, fiesta, nightclub, river, lake, or mountain until finally she's stuffed back into the jet for the trip back to Woonsocket. She'll return with too many woven straw bags, baubles, trinkets, bottles of rum, and colorful shirts which she will file away in the lowest drawer of the dresser in her late husband's bedroom. Once at home, she will complain in righteous indignation to her friends at church or bridge club or golf club about the tour leader, the beds, the busses, the watered-down drinks, the noisy hotels. She'll show them five hundred slides she took (she would have a thousand if they hadn't stolen her camera) including several of Raúl, the tour guide leader, who, as the year progresses, and memories get softer, will come to look more and more handsome, less and less dark and unctuous. His strange accent that bothered her so will become one of some nice movie actor she remembers warmly. In a few months, the whole excursion will be rounded smoothly, like a pebble, into a pleasant memory of a beautiful country with exquisite mountains and cheerful natives. By the time next Christmas rolls around, all her complaints will be gone, and our brave lady of Woonsocket will embark on yet another tour, this time a whirlwind visit to six countries of South America, or two weeks in nine countries of Europe, or perhaps the special Far East Tour (Thailand, Japan, Hong Kong, China, Macao, and Singapore), where again she will feel rushed, put upon, inconvenienced, misunderstood — and yet will be doing her duty as The American Abroad, the Foot-Sore, Angst-Ridden, Travelled America, learning of other cultures, other lands, other worlds, studying them all with appropriate industry, purpose and pain.

For our last night in Costa Rica, we go to the Bastille Restaurant. French food in Central America! Onion soup, shrimp in cream sauce, endive salad, cheese of the gods. Al tells me about the year he spent in the juvenile detention center. It was just before his sixteenth birthday. He had been arrested for being drunk in public, trespassing, stealing. After a dozen or so warnings, they sent him off to "juvie" in Los Angeles. I remember it well. When I heard about it, I asked some friends to go up to bail him out, so he wouldn't get brutalized by the system, but his mother would not permit his release. She felt that he needed to be taught a lesson, that prison was the best place for him. She was and is a woman of the Fundamentalist persuasion.

"I used to dream of my friends Larry and Tom coming in," Al says, "coming right through the wall, in their car, coming into the cell to bust me out. I would lie in my bunk, and I could see the car smashing through the wall. And I would get in the car, and we would just drive off, go off somewhere to get a beer, be with my friends. And I would never have to go back again...

"After a few months, the judge told my mother she could get me out by signing a paper agreeing to take charge of me," he said. "She wouldn't do it. She told the judge that God had told her not to." She's one of those who claim to have a direct line to the divine. Like Jimmy Swaggert and Pat Robertson expecting us to believe that the same diety that creates the Clouds of Magellan, a hundred billion supernovas, and the black holes of space spends his (or her) off-hours jawing with them about the length of jail terms for delinquents, good investments on the stock market, another bubblehheaded fundraising scheme in Tulsa, OK.

"Did they do anything to you?" I ask Al.

"Did who do what?" says Al.

"Did anyone, while you were in prison...you know..."

I butter a stick of the hard, delicious homebaked bread. Al is so tall, and wiry, dangerously handsome. His eyes are out of the oceans. The two weeks in Costa Rica have added to his lustre.

"You know what I mean..."

He looks at his plate. The waiter comes over and asks if we need anything. "No, no," I say, laughing. "I think we need more wine."

"And I would like another beer...no, *two* beers," says Al.

"One litre of wine and two beers?" says the waiter.

"Two beers," says Al.

"You and your double beers. I'm surprised you didn't ask for a triple shot of tequila..."

"Waiter!..." he says weakly, and laughs at me. His eyes turn merry.

"Did you notice that girl behind us," he says. "God, she's beautiful." He keeps turning to look at her.

"There are some things about you that worry me, you know?"

"I've got to get to know that girl. Look at her face. Do you think she's looking at me."

"She has no choice, they way your are waggling the semaphores, ogling her. Have you no couth?" Al is deep in the stage of thinking of all females as the original Madame Ovary.

"He has to get it out of his system," I think. "He has to burn all that anger out of his system." He appears to be so at ease — what is the word they use, so "cashh" (as in "casual") yet he has to drink so much beer, tequila, whiskey, bourbon, scotch, vodka, gin to rout the awful thirst of rage, to assuage the burning instilled by the people that wanted to shape him in the way *they* wanted rather than the way *he* wanted.

And the only way he is going to be done with it is by doing it. Lectures, insights, The Nag will not change him. Al has been "social worked to death." You can't be a juvenile delinquent in this society without falling into the claws of the innumerable MA's from some fleabag school of Social Work. He's heard all the lectures about "rebellion" and "family systems" and "resistance" a hundred times before, and he's built in the appropriate resistance to being told about resistance. We are better off with his making goo-goo eyes at the girl behind us rather than me getting on his two beers, his self-image — all that twaddle about the psyche so rich in words and so lean in power to change.

We go out onto the street. The whole place is bedlam. The way they celebrate New Year's in Costa Rica is block off the streets so that the young can go out and throw things at each other. The boys and the girls will hold in their hands a stick with a paper coil on it. If they see someone they like, they flip out the coil and it touches that person, stranger or no. And, too, everyone has a bag of confetti, and they throw it everywhere, filling the streets with tiny bits of colored paper. There are ten thousand people abroad in the streets of San José, most of them between twelve and twenty-five. This is a holiday and courtship ritual all at once.

I think of their peers in America: watching television, getting stoned, snarling at their parents, then whining to use the family car. No one stays home to watch TV on New Year's in Costa Rica. They are laughing, throwing their confetti, touching each other with the snake-of-wound coils; flirting, looking, gossiping, yowling in merriment. It reminds me so much of the streets of Spain that it gives me a great lump in my throat. I get Al to park me at the curb, so I can watch the flood of people, the waves rolling past. "It's a good thing I didn't give him that dumb lecture at the Bastille," I think. "I'd be just as dumb as Polonius ('Neither a borrower nor a lender be...')." I wonder why everyone wants to lecture him. It must be those eyes, those Al-eyes, those Owl-eyes, so wide, and impenetrable.

I turn to say something, but he's gone. We're close enough to the hotel, so that I can get home easily enough. Still, I know I won't see him for awhile.

❧ ❧ ❧

Our airplane is to leave the next day. We have tickets to buy, luggage to pack, passports to find, cars to dispense with. In my head, I am already home...

I sleep a few an hours. I keep waking, waiting for him to come back. Ten, noon, 2 P.M. — and still no Al. I go to lunch, come back, write in my journal, read some more from Field's book *When the Swans Came to the Lake*, about Rinpoche and his students at the Nyingma Institute in Berkeley. Tarthang Tulku would sit cross-legged before the class, and ask:

"What is thought? What is the difference between calmness and stillness? What is sound..." Rinpoche presented a barrage of exercises drawn from the vajrayana. He asked them to "sit in a chair for three hours and ask, 'What is the self-image.' You will get an answer," he said, "and then ask again, 'What is the self-image?'" He had people look into a mirror at the reflection of their own eyes for three hours at a time; he instructed them not to say 'yes' for a week; to keep silent for a weekend; he told them to count every thought they had for an hour...

and one student came up with "more than a thousand."

I go into the bathroom to look at my own reflection for awhile. What's the word in Spanish? *Cara.* Same root as "sorrow." I see one before me that's been through many a storm, laid on many a pillow, been kissed a few times, picked at — by me, and others — most every day for the last fifty-three years. Worn-down teeth, from brux. For those in the same room with me at night, it is said to be quite mad-making. Just call me Old Stumpy. Hair getting thin, but who wants fat hair? Nose developed quite a jut now and, at the tip, a rather attractive purple button. What is it they say? — the ears and the nose are the last body parts to stop growing.

Good dewlaps, though — make me look owlish. And the eyes. Aye — the eyes have it, or have had it: albeit, turning a little piggy, what with the weight of time and all, the skin pulled inevitably downwards. Once the eyebrows had arches not unlike those of Clark Gable's. But lately it's more like one of the Seven Gables — as in the House of.

If Rinpoche thinks I am going to spend three hours standing before the mirror, looking at this battlefield, he has another think coming, I think. Too many wars have been fought over the trenches before me. And all these years I've give it my best: hacked away at its growths, blown its nostrils, wiped its tears, fed its orifice, cleaned its protuberances, brushed at the once-curly dark locks, now looking quite pale and spare.

It was a good face, as good faces go, and as good faces go it went. I've been a loyal soldier, as good as it deserves, anyway. And it's done its job for almost five-and-a-half decades: keeping the bones under cover so as to not alarm the gentry, hiding various alarming thoughts over the years (thoughts that might well have landed me in the pokey for the rest of my days), smiling (or lifting the lips, at any rate) at people who were trying to be nice to me, or who might want to give me something besides a smack in the kisser; putting on the necessary snarls for those who might wish me ill or who are there to collect a bill.

All in all, neither of us can complain. We've been faithful friends for a half-a-century, asking little, giving much, the two of us, stuck with each other, through thick (cheeks) and thin (hair). Face, Mr. Mien (I mean) only looks put-upon when I abuse him with too much sun, strong drink, smoke, or shaving lotion. He only breaks out in bumps when we — or rather *I* — worry, drink too much Quik, or put him in the way of someone's wayward fist. Once, when I was but a lad, Mr. Mien developed some pits not unlike the Mare Imbrium, but that was just because he felt, as I did, that we were being picked on. Since then, it's been a friendly give-and-take between the two of us, for his countenance often belies the me that lies quivering underneath, even though from time to time, he will give me away: turn purple as a plum (with rage), white as ash (with fear), red as a cherry (in amusement), or green as a greengage plum (during certain nautical trips).

One time — I lost it. It was in the mad 60s. It took a vacation for most of a night. I had been experimenting with some uranium power out of a special plant, a highly concentrated fuel called peyote. In those days, it was all quite legal, so I ordered up fifty or so plants from Lawson's Cactus Gardens of San Antonio, Texas. The peyote came, along with a refund of $4.11 and a crabbed letter from Mr. Lawson explaining in detail how I had paid too much. The whole was franked with a Texas Department of Agriculture seal of approval.

Julie showed us how to take the buttons, cut off the grey fur, and cook them up to dry them out. We'd stuff them in Double-O gelatin capsules and swallow them down with lemon juice to counteract the alkalinity. I remember Julie, Warren and I sat around for a few hours, waiting for something to happen. I said that is was pretty dumb, since all it did was to make me feel like being sick. I looked over at my friend Warren for agreement, but he had turned into Prince Hamlet, which was pretty silly, since there was no play called for in the script. As I turned back to Julie to complain about this play-acting, she had turned into the great pink warm Gaia mother-of-us-all.

"Round and round it goes, and round;
Where it stops, there it will round
In the roundness of knowledge, back into itself"

she recited. "Where did she get that one," I said. "She's a goddess, and I never knew it before." Not only was she a goddess — she was profound. "O" I said, overwhelmed by what Al would call something quite "awesome."

Well, you've heard all those dope stories before, and none of mine are any more interesting or boring than any of the others. Like pain, or religious conversion, or love — drug visions are peculiar to the individual. The knot-holes in the walls of the house began to speak to me, *in my own voice*. An army of marching Chinese came through the living room, shuffling through, on their way out the door, into eternity (for all I know, they are still there, shuffling through). My hand became the hand of the colossus — such in interesting part of the body! Strange that I had never noticed it before.

I made a journey to the bathroom. It was a long journey, and a difficult journey, little different from The Odyssey, with dangerous beasts about. The floor of the shower, rough concrete, had turned into a mass of miniature volcanoes, puffing up little smoke-rings. The commode was filled with a dozen or so red string snakes, coiled up together, but then it turned into a friendly old man, friendly Mr. Commode, mouth wide, ready to accept anything I chose to give him.

I looked in the mirror, and that's when I knew something was going on. I wasn't there. In my place there was this stranger glowering at me. I was afraid to communicate with him. The more I looked at him, the more ominous he became. At one point his face began to melt like an icecream cone, and I looked down in the sink, and there it was, tutti-frutti. I knew it was time to retreat before all of me melted away. When I turned away — this is the strangest part of all — he disappeared, completely, into the void.

When, after a century or so, I managed to find my way back to the other room — not without many alarums and excursions — I stood there for a long time, watching Hamlet and Gaia motionless on the floor. I opened my mouth, but before I could say anything, this stranger chimed in: "You know, I know, at least I think I know, or *know* I think I know [pause for a week — they didn't notice] I *know* I've taken this pee before." That stranger (the one I thought I had left behind in the bathroom) was talking just like me, probably thought he was me, was standing behind me (probably) or even (the gall!) inside me, pretending to be me. I was fit to be tied. I hoped that Hamlet or The Gaia wouldn't notice the change, but I needn't have worried. He was no longer Prince Hamlet, nor was she Judy. The two of them had turned into the Himalayas.

Everyone has stories like this, and although the nightmares of subsequent journeys made me give it up forever — the god of the peyotl plant taught me one thing. He (or she)(or it) taught me that what we call Reality is an agreement, and nothing else. We have made a contract with ourselves, and others, that walls will be walls and people will be people and universes will be universes. Whenever we choose, however — and one can choose through the vehicle of drugs, or madness, or self-analysis, or meditation — whenever we choose, we can break these agreements about Reality: we can turn the Truth into anything we wish.

I know now why peyote, LSD, and all similar drugs have been banned, are the subject of so much propaganda on television and radio, in the press. If people were to learn, as I did, that Reality is a very fragile agreement made between one's self and the rest of world — if people realized that we have a fake contract with the world, a contract which we can break so easily — then I suspect too many of our operating systems (institutionalized fear, human isolation, economic competition, social hostility) would disappear. Thank god so few people know about it.

❧ ❧ ❧

"I am writing the memoirs of a man who has lost his memory"
— EUGENE IONESCO

"What a mess it would be if Al disappears," I think. I'd have to leave his ticket at the front desk, take off by myself. "Maybe he's decided to stay in Costa Rica," I say to mayself. These kids!

But why not? He could cash in the ticket, find a job, marry that nice Costa Rican girl with the nice face, the one we saw in the restaurant. They'll move to the coast, take a thatched shack beside the sea. She'll wear an orchid in her hair, they'll settle down and have four kids, *niños* with great wide eyes, and gentle ways. He will give up drinking, spend his days fishing, teaching his children to swim and to laugh. I'll fly down to visit every year, be the Godfather. Why should he even want to go back home? A lousy job tending gardens, a Jesus-bitten mother to nag him to death about his depraved ways. It will be good for him to stay — a whole new way of life, a new culture, a chance to learn a new language, to get away from things, get away from some bad memories.

I hear coughing in the hall. You can always hear Al coming, not by his footstep (he walks like a panther), but by his wracking cough. On top of his other travails, he's a two-pack-a-day man.

I hear his key in the door lock. Or rather, I hear the key rattling around, hither-and-yon, trying to find the hole. I open the door, he staggers past me, and falls into bed. He lays there moveless. I sit down next to him.

"You made it back," I say.

"Uhmn," he says. I help him take off his shirt. He turns on his side, hugs the pillow, looks at me for a minute with maraschino eyes, then shuts down the transmitters and receivers.

That smell. It comes out of the pores, doesn't it? The cells get so overloaded, they start pushing it out to the skin, to the world. Unlike a junkie — there is no way to hide this habit, unless you are born without a nose.

To love an alcoholic. ¡Ay, qué pena! Al's shirt is stained, his hair a mess, one shoe on, one shoe off. I pull off the other one. The socks are soaked, so I pull them off as well. I get a towel, dry off his feet. Fine, firm arches.

"Al."

" "

"We have to get packed sometime today. We leave at six tomorrow. In the morning."

" "

"We have so much to do. And," I add, "so little time to do it in."

" "

"Al, are you listening to me? If you are dead, you have to tell me, now."

" "

"I'm sorry I've been such a nag...about the way you live and everything. It's your own damn business, really."

His breathing is regular, his mouth slightly ajar. The fair hair, the gentleness of it all. I stretch out, lay there, for awhile, hold on to him. He'll never know, so filled is he with alcohol, and sleep; as I'm filled with...with whatever it is that takes you over, that won't leave you alone. Me and my alky friend Al: together here, close, close. His torso, the dark, bare torso narrowing down to those impossibly small hips, the start of the mysterious band of white. Two weeks in Costa Rica have made him appear quite dark and mysterious. So dark and so quiet: the mystery.

He turns on his back, lies so still, arms thrown above his head. The quiet after the storm. Open — so open, and so vulnerable. Lying there, the two of us. No one to know. No one at all.

❧ ❧ ❧

Keep your head cool but your feet warm. Do not let sentiments sweep your feet. Well trained Zen students should breathe with their feet, not with their lungs. This means that you should forget your lungs and only be conscious with your feet while breathing. The head is the sacred part of your body. Let it do its own work but do not make any "monkey business" with it...

Remember me as a monk, nothing else. I do not belong to any sect or cathedral. Not of them should send me a promoted priest's rank or anything of the sort. I like to be free from such trash and die happily...

— DEATH SPEECH OF ZEN MASTER NYOGEN SENZAKI

If they ever offer you a ride on LACSA — the national airline of Costa Rica — tell them you have other fish to fry. Please. It's strictly cattle-boat country in there. Especially at holiday time. Remember the old days, when *no one* flew on jets, when you almost had the whole cabin to your self? Then think about cattle boats. It doesn't help that in my head I am already home.

"I can't sit here," I say to the stewardess.

"I'm sorry, that's your assigned seat," she says.

"But I'm six foot four and this seat is designed for a midget. A *teenie-weenie* midget." They've placed me up against the firewall.

"I'm sorry sir. That's your assigned seat."

"I just can't stay here," I say. "I am not an accordion. Or a folding ladder, for that matter. It's too damn small." My voice takes on a certain pitch — I'm sure — like when one is trying to argue with the supervisor at the phone company.

"It's too late, sir. The airplane is about to take off." All the sunny people in Costa Rica, and where does LACSA find these snarling bawds?

"Do you always torture your passengers like this?"

"I'm sorry, sir, I can't hear you."

"I said 'Thank you.' "

"And put on your shirt — you're on an airplane now, not on some *beach*." This last is aimed at Al and his habit of taking off his shirt at the slightest provocation. He puts it back on, covering a torso I have come to know and to admire over the last few days.

I am rereading parts of *When the Swans Came to the Lake*. Like Buddhism itself, it is at once gripping, funny, paradoxical, mysterious. I read the chapter on Korean Buddhism. The author tells of the Seung Sahn who, after the partition of Korea, "disillusioned with politics, went up to the mountains to read Socrates, Spencer, and Rousseau." When he returned, one of his friends gave him a copy of the *Diamond Sutra*. "Ah! Buddhism's number one," he says, and he returns to the mountains armed with a special mantra of original mind energy. He stays in the mountains, where

> *...he ate powdered pine needles, bathed in the icy mountain streams and chanted for twenty hours a day. Demons, ghosts, tigers and snakes came to attack him, and visions of buddhas and bodhisattvas beguiled him. On the last day of his hundred-day retreat his body disappeared and he understood that everything he saw — trees, rocks, clouds, sky and crows — was his true self.*

It was said that Seung Sahn once encountered the Korean Zen master Ko Bong:

> *Master Ko Bong would only teach when he was given something to drink, and then only laymen and nuns, because, he said, monks were too lazy. People weren't sure whether Master Ko Bong was crazy or enlightened..."*

Seung Sahn asked Ko Bong to teach him how to practice Zen. Ko Bong gave him the classic koan "Why did Bodhidharma come to China?"

Then he gave him the response: "The pine tree in the front garden." "What does this mean?" he asked.

"I don't know," said Seung Sahn.

"Keep this don't-know mind," said Ko Bong. "This is Zen practice..."

❧ ❧ ❧

"What was your favorite part of the trip?" I ask Al.

"The train ride," he says.

"Yeah — you liked it because you could stay in the caboose. For me, it was The Hernia Special."

"What was your favorite part?"

"Well, I like it when we were in that shop in Coco, and I had to get a bathing suit, and I asked for a pair of shorts so I could 'nacer.' That was pretty funny — what I meant to say was 'nadar,' to swim. I said 'Quiero pantalones corto porque quiero nacer' which meant 'I want some shorts so I can be born.' I thought that was pretty funny.

"Most of all I think I liked Paradise Beach," I say. "You know, when I rolled myself off that boat, I wasn't sure if I could make it to shore. I haven't been swimming for a long time. It was a long way off, it was a little chancy. But I figured you could get me there. And besides, if I had to drown, better at Paradise Beach rather than the East River."

The airplane rises sharply over San José, and then heads north.

"I liked your driving," I say. "I think you were born with a steering wheel in your hands. You were great. Especially when we were going across that two-foot wide bridge, with the creaky boards, and the canyon down there, ten thousand feet below, with all the little teeny cows and horses. You were very brave."

He smiles. Perfect white teeth, a face touched by two week's worth of sun, and such a natural sunny personality. It's sad that I won't be seeing him after this trip. I shan't tell him, though; not now.

"It's a good thing you didn't tell me how far down it was," he says.

"You didn't know?"

"I didn't know to be scared. Do you know I cried last night when they kicked me out of the casino?"

"Bosh, that's the silliest thing I ever heard. I've heard of people crying when they lose money, but you're the first person I've heard of crying when you were winning."

"That's not why I was crying. I was crying because I was leaving my friends. They took care of me, got me back to the hotel. If it hadn't been for them, I'd be in one of the gutters of San José, and you'd be flying back by yourself."

He dozes off. While he's sleeping, I convince the stewardess that I'll die if she makes me stay in this seat any longer. She finds a place for me in the back.

"Two weeks is probably the best time to be gone," I think, after I've moved. If you are gone any less, you aren't gone at all. If you go for longer — it becomes an exile. "The secret of Costa Rica," I'll tell all my friends, "is that it's *Black Orpheus* all over again." The music everywhere, the dancing, the sounds of bongos drifting down from the windows, from out the doors, down from the skies, up from the ground. The sound of pulsing, tropical drums, rhythms forming a backdrop to our lives, the lives we choose to leave behind, the sounds of the spheres around us. The flowers and the music from back there.

When I get home, it will be raining. I'll go to bed, and lie there, a place so familiar. And when I waken, I will think the hills in the distance are the hills of Costa Rica. I'll be home; maybe. But then again, maybe not. Are we ever home? We go some place, and love it, and come back to what we call "home," but we are also still where we've been. Spain, North Africa, Mexico, Copenhagen, Costa Rica. I suppose you could even miss Transylvania, or Parsippany, New Jersey.

"I think I will become a Buddhist monk," I say to myself, pushing the seat back, letting the drone of the engines penetrate my bones. "That's the number one ticket. That'll solve all my problems. This love nonsense, wanting, always wanting. Always wanting things I can't have. I'm sick of it."

I'll shave my hair, put on the robes, become a begger on the streets of Calcutta. No — better — go into retreat in the mountains of Costa Rica, up there near the site of the Black Guard who spoke in tongues. I'll go off in the forest, eat ground pine needles, chant *Om Mani Padme Hum* twenty hours a day, watch the animals turn into gods, and the gods turn into animals. Bathe in dark streams, have visitations, laugh at the fact that I am to grow old and die near the crest of the last hill, with the flowers about me and the whole world at my feet. How was it the poet described it? "Somewher in a launde/Upon an hil of flours..."

No more of this world, and its needs, those needs always yapping at your heels, like a terrier. I'll become a Zen student and them, someday — ah so! — a master. I'll eat brown rice and sleep and they'll ring the bell to wake me at four a.m. so I can chant all morning, and wonder on the great Mu.

"What is Mu?" they'll ask me.

"I dunno," I'll say. "If you pronounce it with a long U, as in 'Mū,' then it becomes *Mew* and must have something to do with cats. If it's short, as in 'Mŭ,' then it's *Moo* which means it's probably all about Holsteins or Brahmans. Or Brahmins." That's when the masters will swat me with their kyosaku.

After seventeen years of this, they'll finally recognize me as a proper Zen master. Monks will come to seek me out on my mountain top, but I'll only teach nuns and laymen, and only if they bring me strong drink. I'll make up my own koans.

"Why must we meditate?" the students will ask.

"The red car in the garage, the television set in the study," I'll respond.

That's the ticket. A lifetime of devotion to being holy, holy like the lama of Crystal monastery, the one who they say is a very happy man...

...and yet I wonder how he feels about his isolation in the silences of Tsakang, which he has not left in eight years now, and because he is crippled, may never leave again. Since Jang-bu seems uncomfortable with the lama or with himself or perhaps with us, I tell him not to inquire on this point if it seems to him impertinent, but after a moment Jang-bu does so. And this holy man of great directness and simplicity, big white teeth shining, laughs out loud in an infectious way at Jang-bu's question. Indicating his twisted legs without a trace of self-pity or bitterness — they belong to all of us — he casts his arms wide to the sky and the snow mountains, the high sun and dancing sheep, and cries, "Of course I am happy here! It's wonderful! Especially *when I have no choice!..."*

I thank him, bow, go softly down the mountain. Butter tea and wind pictures, the Crystal Mountain, and blue sheep dancing in the snow — it's quite enough!

Have you seen the snow leopard?

No! Isn't that wonderful?...[3]

[1987]

3. from *The Nine-Headed Dragon River* by Peter Matthiessen.

PUERTO JESÚS AND THE KISSY-KISSY BIRD

NOVEMBER 26 [ACID ACRES RANCH]

We must invent the heart of things if we wish one day to discover it. Audiberti informs us about milk in speaking of its secret blackness. *But for Jules Renard, milk is hopelessly white, since* it is only what it seems to be.

— JEAN-PAUL SARTRE

Remember why you came here.

— *OUR LIFE WITH MR. GURDJIEFF*
BY T. & O. DE HARTMANN

D.T. claims that after ten in the evening, the truth is not in me. I tell him that he is lying; that the truth deserts me long before — usually around eight or so. I blame it on the various minderbinders they force on me in the disguise of "something you're really gonna like." In truth, the goods are an *olla podrida* designed to fry the brain and spoil what's left of one's reason and honesty. It is at these moments of weakness, for instance, that we start making up dishes for the world's starving and poor. It's not enough that we are eating our savory lamb stew, with onions and garlic and white wine, at the same time that 800,000,000 people on earth are lying about gaunt and hungry; not only do we indulge in such thoughtless behavior — we then have to talk about curing them, and their plight. I crunch down on a carrot, cooked in the blood of the lamb (with caraway seeds and white wine), and say "What we have to do is to take the most common disagreeable creatures, like rats, pigeons, roaches, seagulls, dogfish, and lampreys, and transform them into delicacies that can be enjoyed by the poor and benighted of the world."

After some discussion, and good-natured back-and-forth, and the termination of our meal, we come up with a list of dishes that will utilize these disgusting sources of protein, putting them into a more palatable form:

Seagull Bisque
Minced Mice Pie
Rat aux Fines Herbs
Gecko Kabobs
Beetle Tapas
Potage du Poisson du Chien
Sweet Potato Pigeon Pie Sparrow Flambé
Locust Compote
Lamprey Soup with Matzo Balls
Roast Buzzard with Green Molé Sauce
Roach Toasties

Our conversation drifts on, as these conversations will, there in Acid Acres, to the question of the Boojum tree. D. T. and Sybil have an especial affinity for this gross tree, the cirio, the pride of Baja California. They have one in their garden, which they kiss and fondle. They have promised each other that when they die and go to their separate rewards, in their new lives, when they finally meet, no matter their new form (man, woman, child, Gecko Kabob) the key word they will utter to recognize each other will be "Boojum." I point out to them that since the end of World War II, there has been a dramatic increase in the number of cirio trees sprouting in and around Baja, and D. T. refers to this as "The Post-War Baby Boojum," said remarks which may make one understand how truly tedious these late night extravaganzas can be, out there in the land of visions. My own memories of the evening are hopelessly clouded, due to some free-wheeling poison that had been placed, unbeknownst to me, in the firewater — presumably by my enemies — but D.T. and Sybil told me the next day, during that free-floating time when I had departed my senses, I came up with a plan to deliver Tibet from its terrible past and its equally miserable future.

A sojourner to that land, Ilya Tolstoi (grandson of the author) reported that the Buddhists of Tibet will not eat fish nor fowl because the creatures' bodies are just too small. To murder to eat is a violation of animal's rights to exist in this world. Tibetans do eat meat — but only the meat of large creatures, such as the yak. The logic is that they would have to eat twenty-five chickens, or two hundred fish (or a thousand snails, as in "let a thousand snails bloom...") to get the same quantity of foodstuffs that they get from one large beast. Since all life is sacred, if they are going to murder one creature (and consequently dim the opportunity to escape from the Endless Wheel), they much prefer taking their chances with yak. Thus Yak Butter Tea.

"The Japanese have made a breakthrough in the Tibetan Meat Front," I tell my friends. "Since Tibet is landlocked, fish is a special delicacy. You may remember that several years ago they discovered a peculiar breed of walking catfish in and about the waters of southern Florida." The Japanese, with the assistance of inbreeding, outbreeding, crossbreeding, bad-breeding, and just plain Oriental know-how, have managed to cross the Walking Catfish with the Blue Whale, and have come up with a baleen that can commute to Lḥasa, by foot — or, to speak more correctly, by fin. By the mere twisting of a gene here and a DNA molecule there, the Japanese have solved the problem of Oriental religious scruples, shortage of essential protein, and massive transportation of foods and goods into one of the most impassible regions of the world. "An army of walking whales are," I report, "as I am speaking to you this very moment, being herded up from Calcutta, up through Kooch Behar, stopping at the various Howard Fish Johnsons' along the way (which have been plentifully supplied by the USDA with krill by the ton for the occasion,) making their way to the kingdom in the sky. Whistling their way up through Lomdurup, and across Kampa Dzong, comes now a mountain of blubber for the poor and hungry of the Kingdom of the Sky."

NOVEMBER 27

Now that the April of your youth adorns
The garden of your face...

— LORD HERBERT OF CHERBURY

A giant boil has erupted just below my right cheek, to the starboard side of my mouth. A veritable Mount St. Helens, coming up from under my usually friendly and docile facial flesh. Like a visiting preacher who decides to come for a long visit, this *comedo* turns up unannounced, and stays long after it is clearly not wanted. For days I labor under the delusion that it will pass away unnoticed, but it begins to take over the whole right cheek and jaw. There's simply not room for the two of us in this parcel of choice and prestigious real estate.

Comedo decides to form a head just as I am preparing for a series of meetings with potential travel mates, so that when I go to smile, I fear that Krakatoa will erupt, flooding the plains, drowning the peasants, effacing whole rivers, caves, and crevasses that I've taken decades to develop. A rather interesting crease that runs from nostril to chin has been distorted and twisted; and the earthquakes that accompany the volcanoes have drawn and quartered a once-noble symbol of wisdom and suffering, my face.

I am as willing as anyone to put up with the slings and narrows of outraged pustules, but when they threaten to engulf my whole visage, I know it is time to take matters in hand. I suspect facial cancer, AIDS, or worse. Later I tell one of my friends: "I was in the emergency room, with bloody and dying accident cases, embolisms, heart attacks, and ectopic pregnancies. There I am taking up valuable emergency room time with what the doctor most sympathetically describes as 'an ingrown pimple.'" He advises me to go home and apply hot poultices, and when its term is up, they will operate. So I go home and stand over hot sinks and apply burning poultices to my already burning cheeks, until finally, one morning, I am standing there, sympathizing with myself over my too too morbid flesh, I burst into a grin, out of friendship and sympathy for getting myself in a pickle like this — and zoom, Etna shivers once, and cascades lava out to the furthest reaches of the terrain.

Later I try to explain it to my friend TG, who has had a few pimples of his own, but never a Whopperburger like this. "It comes and comes," I tell him, "It took twenty minutes for the well to run dry." The once shiny mountain turns dark and wasted. I can go out in the world again, smiling, proud to be an American, but all the while thinking, "It's hell to go through puberty twice." I am, temporarily at least, free to go to the passport office so I can get my certificate from the United States Government. I have truly been born, and am alive, and should be free to travel, like a bird.

When they take the picture of me for my passport I turn my face up and a little to the left, trying to hide the miserable intruder, but if you look closely, you can see the slight trace of an engulfment that once threatened to turn me into a two-headed beast. "You never would have known the head to address," I tell my friends later. "The one with two eyes, or the cyclops."

And thus, on my passport, because of that damned comedo, I am marked, for the next ten years, as a late-blooming teen-age pimple case.

NOVEMBER 28 [GUAYMAS]

The universal symbols of Mexico are dust, tortillas, babies, and rusted metal rods sticking out of the tops of concrete walls, or the sides of buildings. Grandiose plans never put into practice, the universal tomorrow that never came. Mexico is an ashheap of appointments made and never honored, ideas conceived and never brought to fruition, buildings partially erected — ones that were to soar — but that, for lack of plans, lack of money, lack of materials, never come to a conclusion. Concrete blocks half laid, window-holes in place but never filled with wood and glass, doorways firmed up but never closed, steel rods stabbing the sky like Don Quixote's lance.

— JOURNAL ENTRY

The hotel we are in has four leaks coming down into the bedroom. I call the clerk at the front desk, tell him about the four leaks. "Too bad," he says. We converse on like this for awhile, and then I say "Let me speak to your boss." He, breathing, and silence; finally, ominously: "There is none." When I wake up, it turns out that my driving-partner, Mark, breathing in stentorian fashion in his sleep is making the noise that preoccupies my dreams.

Mark is an eighteen-year-old juvenile delinquent loaned to me by his mother — an old friend — to help me get to the southern end of Mexico. He is tall, slight, and, at first, very silent. He affects one of those strange hairdos so favored by the young nowadays: skull shaved almost bare on both sides, hair long on top but pulled over to one side or the other. Since Mark's hair is as straight as an Arizona freeway, it falls down over the left side of his head, covering his several earrings, giving his whole cranium a peculiar lopsided effect, not unlike a weeping willow in a slight wind, the leaves and branches pulled inextricably over and down. It also gives him the option of constantly tinkering with his hair, brushing it out of his eyes, throwing it back, combing it vigorously. When he's bored, or when all other activities are out of the question, he does something to his hair.

Mark rarely speaks, but when he does, it's always to ask polite questions like "Can I go into town?" or "Can I smoke a cigarette?" or "Can I put on a cassette?" The first twenty-five times he asks me, I respond by saying "You are free to do anything you want. Anything." It is with great circumspection, I must report, that I resist my own mother's responses to the question "Can I do (this or that)?" "I don't know, are you *able*?" she would say, so tediously, and endlessly; but I now realize she was, in effect, telling me the same thing that I am telling Mark.

He doesn't speak any Spanish. I did several years ago, but a foreign language is like a well: if you don't use it every day, it dries up. The very first day in Cabron, we're eating tacos, and I want a Casera, one of Mexico's great contributions to Western Civilization, a Dr. Pepper-style drink, commonly known as a Sangría (not to be confused with the alcoholic drink of the same name from Spain). I call the lady over and ask her if I can have a "vasito de Sangre." My first Spanish statement in five years, and I blew it. "What I asked her," I tell Mark later, "was if she had 'a little cup of blood' for me."

Since we're in Mexico, all our mechanical accoutrements start to fall apart. Our first day out of Mexicali, the tape recorder on the car dies, and the clock on the dashboard goes into existential overdrive — the hours flipping by like seconds, and the minutes like, well, minutes. There's no way to shut the damn thing off. In early afternoon, the clock will report that it is 8:23 P.M.; at midnight — it's 11 in the morning.

We are driving across the Sonoran desert from San Luis Río Colorado to Sonoita, truly one of the most barren areas in the world. The November sun stretches shadows blue away from the stones and pebbles and occasional cactus. The car body shadow races before us. There is no one, no one for miles, and I am thinking about this journey, this, another in a series of journeys that I impose on myself to learn, as I must learn again, as we must all learn, that the ease and comfort of our lives are transitory; that nothing can be gained without change, a shift, without something new. Before the van on its black road, the mountains turn purple and grey-green, sharp edges cutting deep into the mauve of the dying sky, each in a mauve shadow. The few humans we see are frozen as we whirl past them along our narrow black trail. At sunset the road becomes a line cut into the sands but not a part of it, a darkened road floating through the desert, never to be in it but on it — rejected as illusion, out of an illusion of the desert; all of us rejected as illusion, all of us: me, Mark, the car, our few possessions, the road. We are made otherworld creatures, hurtling across sands that do not, and cannot, and will not possess us.

My mind is full of Gurdjieff. For the last few days I have been reading Thomas and Olga de Hartmann's book of their ten years with him. "If he were here," I think, "he would make us stop the car and start walking, taking all our possessions on our backs. If we were to ask why, he would say, 'Do it because I said so.'" And that would be the only explanation he would give us.

> *One of the principles of Mr. Gurdjieff's teaching [is] to make the pupils do something that is terribly difficult and demands all their attention and diligence, and then destroy it, because only the effort is necessary and not the thing itself ...*

"Ah, if he were only around now," I think: "I'd go seek him out — and he would dream up some stupid task for me." He gave the editor of *New Age* the job of digging a trench, just outside the kitchen at Prieuré. Since the man had never done manual work in his life, being the editorial type, he bruised his hands terribly on the rough shovel. Once a day Gurdjieff would go out and look at the trench, and criticize it some, make him get the edges more exact, bringing out some string to use as a measure of exactitude, complaining about it all the while. After a few days, the whole project was abandoned, "as we knew it would be," says de Hartmann.

I think on this strange Russian, with his narrowed eyes, and his cleaning brush moustache. I think of him lifting these upper class folks out of Petrograd, leading them to Essentuki, in the Caucasians, then down to Tiflis in Georgia, during the worst of the Russian Revolution — The Whites battling The Reds, both sides killing indiscriminately anyone who turned up between the lines — and like magic, Gurdjieff leads his band of a dozen or so Russian aristocrats between the trenches, through the Caucasus Mountains, across trails of boulders, past infested swamps, managing to avoid getting killed by the trigger-happy troops; and all the while, setting up these arduous terrible projects in the midst of this arduous terrible journey, making his followers take all the packs off the mules, carry the food and clothing and possessions themselves, leaving the animals free and burdenless, to caper along before them. And somehow getting them through, to safety, to Constantinople, and finally in July of 1922, to Paris, some of them half-dead with the journey. At one point, in the midst of this hideous journey, de Hartmann gathers up his courage, and goes up to Gurdjieff, and asks the question, the big question, ultimately, the Gurdjieffian Question, namely,

> *Have I now to place complete confidence in you, and fulfill unquestioningly all that you advise me to do?*

And Gurdjieff,

> *Certainly, on the whole it is so. But if I begin to teach you masturbation, will you listen to me?"*[1]

"If there were only a Gurdjieff around for us to follow," I think: "To command us, insult us, set impossible tasks for us, feed us awful food (at one time he made all his followers drink red wine, and eat bacon; a bunch of snooty Petrograd aristocrats, in Paris, dining on fatback and thin red wine, and nothing else).

"If we could only have him around, to have all the answers for us, even if the answers were, are as they often were, complete silence, or a simple 'Do what I tell you.' Ah," I think, "to have a leader like that!"

1. Significantly, later in the book, de Hartmann misremembers this question as "If I told you to masturbate, would you listen to me?"

NOVEMBER 30 [CULIACÁN]

When we die, whatever we think is going to happen will *happen. Thus, all those awful Baptists will go to a place where they play harps and fly about in white robes. Their god will have a white beard, blue eyes, and will thunder at them. They will live there for two or three or a dozen centuries, and after awhile they'll be bored out of their skulls, living lives as meaningless as their lives were always meaningless. After a few thousand years they'll finally figure out that they've blown it — that they've come to a hideous dead-end morass, a tedious hell of their own making.*

— JOURNAL ENTRY

In the restaurant of the Motel del Rio, they offer "Cheese and Ham Crips," "Cock Tail Fruit," "Briled Eggs," and "Baked Custar." And in the hotel, a sign says "Your Room Expires at 2 P.M."

1200 miles. Five days. The Rhythm of the Road has asserted itself. Mark and I are in the car six to ten hours a day. I get lost at least once, and explain to him (as in Las Mochis, yesterday, on a dirt road, with great mudholes) that we are not really lost at all, but that we are going North so I can find the road that goes south, to Culiacán. Then, when it turns out we're on the westbound road to Topolobampo, I explain that by going west, we can avoid the worst of the Sunday crowd in town, which might slow us down to the East. And we do avoid them, visiting the tiny farm of one José Martinez, who explains to us that Culiacán is not behind his farm, his chickens, and his pigs, and his ten children, wide-eyeing us, unbearably, inexorably, attracted to Mark's hairdo. No, rather, says Farmer Martinez, Culiacán is back the other way, from whence we have just come. He and his two eldest sons are kind enough to get us up and out of the mudholes, where we had sunk our trusty VW up to the axles. We thank him profusely, by means of 25,000 pesos, and I later explain to Mark that I wanted him to see how the typical Sinaloense farmer lived and worked —

making his living by raising jute, pigs, children, and the cars of stupid foreigners who venture out into his fields.

DECEMBER 3 [BARRA DE NAVIDAD]

When the Zen Master Bukko came to Japan, since he was one of the first Chinese to visit that country, he could not be understood. They wrote down his sounds literally for later translation. Thus many of his wise sayings were preserved — but they also preserved for translation (it was finally rendered in 1924) such phrases as "Come in! Come in! I have something to say to you."

— *ZEN AND THE WAYS*

I have invented a new meditation. I shall patent it, become a master too. It is perfect for what we think of as the New World. It is called Auto Meditation. While I am driving, I do Auto Meditation — or Automed, as it will be called. It works like this:

Instead of me driving the road, I let the road drive me. The car becomes a passive intermediary. As I lose myself in it, I don't move over the road — the road moves below me, or, at times, through me.

During Auto Meditation, it ceases to hurry by; it moves more and more slowly. The speedometer says 55 mph, but the road passes under us like a dream.

In Auto Meditation, one does not scan the scenery. The eyelids are half shut, the eyes are fixed on the pavement, immediately before the car, a certain distance in front. One clears the mind, meditates on the road as it is, not as it should be. The joltings and motion come more slowly; not only does the road slow down — the hours come to seem like minutes; the passing objects (cars, trucks, trees) turn into shadows.

I know that with Auto Meditation, the perfection of Self will come sometime in the future, when the speed of our passing the road and the road passing us reaches so close to zero that all will be as if we are moveless. Auto Meditation will permit us to reach a previously unrealized state of calm, even as the others around us are racing in a frenzy. With Auto Meditation we will be able to achieve a peace heretofore unheard of on the highways of the world.

DECEMBER 4 [BARRA DE NAVIDAD]

Nobumitsu cited the famous Zen phrase, "A finger direct to the human heart/See the Nature to be Buddha ... " He asked [Ekichu] for a picture of the heart. The teacher picked up the brush and flicked a spot of ink onto Nobumitsu's face. The warrior was surprised and annoyed, and the teacher rapidly sketched the angry face.

Then Nobumitsu asked for a picture of the "Nature" as in the phrase "see the Nature." The teacher broke the brush and said, "That's the picture."

Nobumitsu did not understand and the teacher remarked, "If you haven't got that seeing eye, you can't see it."

Nobumitsu said, "Take another brush and paint the picture of the Nature."

The teacher replied, "Show me your Nature and I will paint it." Nobumitsu had no words.

— *ZEN AND THE WAYS*

The waves come in from the East China Sea direct to Barra de Navidad. Even on a calm day, they hit the shore here with a peculiar force, sometimes shaking the whole building, built as it is right on the beach. Wham: they bang against the steep shore, and the floor shakes, then there is silence again.

Today is the day for nothing. The beach is too steep for me to get down. The water is filthy, and the waves are dangerous. So I read and write, and lie here in my bed and think, wonder where I was before the earth had any life on it whatsoever (a much more satisfying *sesshu* than "What was the face of your parents before they were born?" or "What was your face before your parents were born?").

Mark lived on a commune for years, and delights in telling me how much trouble he was for everyone. Here he was, in this ideal community, and he would steal money from the various rooms, rip off the whole-grain bread, spill jars of honey they were producing (at $300 a jar). He never got caught, or if he did, he would talk his way out of it.

ME: See, those commune people always treat kids like adults — so they teach you how to speak like an adult, and thus you're always talking your way out of situations. It's a scandal.

HE: You're right. Here I am with my hair shaved off half of my head, looking like some freak, yet I get away with everything — I never get caught.

ME: I have to admire you being so much trouble to all those people in the commune. You really tested their mettle, gave them something meaningful to bring up in their long, boring daily meetings. Congratulations.

DECEMBER 5 [PLAYA AZUL]

The important statues of Mexico are not to be found in front of important government buildings or alongside the roadways; no, they're the rusting metal rods, sticking out of the sides and tops of every house, building, and wall. I think my love of Mexico comes from the fact that it is a place constantly under construction, always unfinished, spare, without pretension. It is unbuilt, informal, free. Cats and dogs and chickens wander through the eating establishments. There are men gathered about talking, talking, endlessly talking, women carrying water, talking, talking, the goats and pigs and chickens, everywhere, the mass of children, many of them naked, most of them calm. There are archeologists who claim that the Chinese sent a fleet of ships to the east in the fifth century, and they landed near Colima. (People from that area are still described as "chinos" — in fact, anyone in Mexico in any way different is referred to as a "chino").

The entire populace of Mexico shows such calm in the face of earthquakes, fiscal breakdown, governmental disgrace, and the everyday collapse of cars, pumping systems, power, water, gas — what we think of as the essentials of life; the calm, that calm, that makes a child of six or eight able to sit, without fidgeting, for hours, with the family, or on a bus. It must have something to do with the complete unit of the family, responsibility universally shared, the Oriental calm.

Here, the children are an essential part of the workforce. Mexico is a Boyocracy. The boys, beautiful, dark-skinned, darkeyed boys, run the stores, run the taco stands, the grocery stores, the day-to-day businesses. Just outside of Barra de Navidad, the government monopoly gas station, Pemex, is operated by a boy who is nine years old. He takes care of the gas pumps. Another boy, presumably his brother, operates the diesel pumps. He looks to be about six.

In the United States, all this would come under the heavy hands of the social workers and the Child Labor Laws. The fantasy of America is that one does not exploit children by making them work. We have other ways: for example, we keep them in jails labelled "SCHOOL," complete with ID cards, cross-bars, locked doors, alarm bells, and security guards. It's a cynical way of keeping them off the labor market. The result, and Mark is a prime example, is boredom, ill-concealed anger, sniffing and smoking and swallowing all sorts of illegal things, unwanted pregnancies, and a rich blend of other anti-social acts. Boys hate being treated like boys, and want to be treated like men. So we do everything we can to isolate and humiliate them. They react by manifesting a deviant behavior which is their distorted fantasy of something we call Being Grown Up.

No wonder we are raising a whole generation of delinquents. Our system of enforced servitude to an outmoded school system has created a catastrophic double bind for our young, and the result is civil war. Our system holds children hostage to the 19th century Cartesian ideal of learning and abasement. By putting them in concentration camps, we destroy their morale, and turn them into violent sensationalists and hedonists. We have a war on our hands, and we call it

Juvenile Delinquency. It's no accident that the favorite song of ten years ago was "We don't want no education ..."

We only have to look to Mexico to find the solution. Those who want to go to school are encouraged to do so. Those who don't go right into the job market — with real responsibility, which isn't serving up pre-formed plastic hamburgers for Wendy's; rather, it is doing real tasks with real toil. The young men respond with responsibility and dexterity. One could say that the life for boys in Mexico is tough — but one sees so little of the mind-rotting, society-ruinating activities that we cultivate north of the Rio Grande. The tales of delinquent activities that come out of Mark's mouth — tales of stealing, snorting, smoking, and sheer destructiveness — are astounding, but as a good systems analyst would say, he is merely reflecting a breakdown in the operating modes. They send him to a shrink. "He's a nice man who doesn't understand," he says. The safest thing to do with an adult snitch — and that's what our shrinks have become — is to lie. That's what Mark does to survive: and he does it adroitly and well.

A bright sensitive intelligent American child has to go to such *trouble* to point out to his family, society, and the world how skewed our systems and values have become. He works overtime, for years, to demonstrate to everyone that our schools, systems of order, discipline and learning, are for the birds.

DECEMBER 6 [PUERTO ESCONDIDO]

When I dropped by Diego Rivera's house and found Lupe hanging from the top of the door while Diego was whamming her backside with a big thick board, I couldn't keep out of it. I rushed right in to stop this cruel treatment of his wife. And you may not believe what happened. They both turned on me, especially Lupe, and I was lucky to get out of the house unharmed. Neither of them has spoken to me since, and both were my good friends.

— *BURROS AND PAINTBRUSHES*
EVERETT GEE JACKSON

Mark and I do a road count on Highway 200 between Puerto Vallarta and Puerto Escondido. This is what we see:

- Eight dead dogs, with flies and vultures attached;
- One mama pig, with nine little piggies, with nine little piggie tails;
- One donkey, upside-down, feet in air, R.I.P.;
- One truck with the phrase written on the back bumper *Un mundo de ilusiones* ("A world of illusions");
- 17 civil guards with guns, who ask, each time they stop us, where we're going, and who help themselves to the pens, bank bags, and whatever else they find in the glove compartment;
- One lovely electric blue lizard, reported at twelve feet (me) and six inches (Mark);
- 6,573,510 school children, various ages;
- 503 taco vendors;
- Fifteen flat, flatter, or flattest birds;
- 912 Tres Estrella buses going between sixty and ninety-five miles an hour;
- Two amazingly velveteen, roseate sunsets;
- One sunrise: gentle green-blue-orange, sweet;
- Twenty-seven men with bent frames (Lord Buckley's phrase);
- Thirty-five women ditto;
- One Old Crone of beady eyes and moustache, vigorously attempting to wave down gringo VW bus, thinking it a public bus;
- Eight-hundred-eleven trucks belching great black gaseous diesel fumes, racheting through hill and dale;
- Seventy-three Brahmin cows, moving at between two and three miles per hour, firmly in the middle of highway 200, between Jamiltepec and Pinotepa National, despite all buses, trucks, and gringo VWs.

❧ ❧ ❧

Our night in El Carrizal spoke to my whole life's nightmares of where not to sleep. They're called "bungalows" — a circle of white plaster walls, a thatched roof, one leaky faucet in the bathroom. No windows, and although the cottage is on the beach, it is close and hot and dark: one can barely hear the sound of the sea. The door is kept shut to keep out the mosquitos, no air permitted, although there is a noisy fan that goes "thrwee-thump, thrwee-thrump" all the long night. For those of us who tear out whole walls in our houses for the privilege of doors and windows, El Carrizal is the worst of bad dreams — without windows, with a thatched roof so tightly woven one never knows if it is dawn, dusk, night, or full blasting daylight. The only break in the rhythm is the strange call of a strange bird, which comes by at strange hours, singing "O - whee, O - WHEE!" Mark sleeps like a top, snoring softly to himself. Later he tells me he doesn't understand my problem, he slept perfectly.

"I have this thing about rooms with no windows, and blank white walls, and slick cement floors, and doors that are shut to keep the mosquitos at bay, and things that go 'O - whee' in the night," I tell him.

Mark is protesting the fact that I roused him at five A.M. to continue our journey. He's at that age where he sleeps through everything, is perfectly comfortable sleeping a whole weekend, can sleep anywhere, so that when I get cranky or obstreperous, he just goes back to the back of the van and falls asleep, no matter how jouncy the road, no matter the number of trucks passing us by at high volume.

We arrive in Puerto Escondido, and after searching for an appropriate place to stay, we find El Motel Pescado Retirado, or the Shy Fish Motel. It's as fishy as they come. There are five out-of-commission state police cars parked out back. Of the twenty-six rooms, we occupy Number Nine, the rest are in total disarray: windows out, air conditioners dismantled, mattresses left in doorways, and Room Two, with eerie lights that come and go in the night. The swimming pool, brand new, clean, is never used (except by us). The American Express Card Squash Machine hadn't been operated in three years — it took the clerk practically that long to change the date. The bar is clean, the bottles untouched. All the help is noncommunicative, dwarfish, a mass of glinty eyes and furtive faces. Mark, who comes from a section of Los Angeles where drugs are manufactured extensively (the new cottage industry of the suburbs) is convinced it's a front for the DEA.

It's very tranquil since we are the only tenants. We figure they rent out one room, Nine, to tourists, to keep up the front. They refuse everyone else, claiming to be full. Indeed, as we are lounging about the pool, we watch four cars of tourists being sent on their way.

If El Pescado Retirado is a front, financed by the DEA, we'd like to thank them for the use of their excellent pool and services. The food was great, and since we were the only ones in the restaurant, service was top-notch — although some of the help seemed a little touchy and suspicious. They also forgot to bill us for half of our drinks, but we figured that making money was the least of their worries.

We would, however, like to complain about the bar-keep, who was named Alan (we figured after Alan Dulles, the founder of the CIA). Despite his surly ways, the drinks were excellent and powerful and Mark for one, who had never had a taste for sweet liqueur before, went away from one particular session beside himself with praise, head over heels in love with a drink called La Verga Chocolate del Mono.

We would like to register one other complaint. We understand the annual budget of the DEA is $500,000,000,000,000,000,000,000,000.00, give or take $100,000,000,000,000.00. If they could take, say, $600 of that and do something about the plumbing at El Pescado, we would be most grateful. The two taps in the shower disgorged, no matter how long we left them running, respectively, to the left, tepid water, and to the right, tepid water.

On the other hand, we would like to congratulate the operatives on their air conditioners. Real American know-how here. As opposed to most Mexican air conditioners, which make rich and powerful operating noises and deliver a handful or so of moderately warm air, this one, possibly newly sent over from Langley, delivered huge draughts of Arctic blasts directly onto my bed (and me). Since the windows couldn't be opened, and since no matter how long we played with the controls, the air conditioner was either *Off* or *Full-Blast*, it served not only to keep us toasty cold at night, but, especially since it fed right onto my back, served to exacerbate the problem I had been having with my neck after ten straight days of driving. Thus, for our stay in Puerto Escondido, whenever I was speaking with anyone, instead of smoothly turning my head, smiling, and talking as I had in days of yore — I was forced to twist my whole corpus, accompanied by a thrill of grinding bone and twisting muscle, giving out triassic grunts and little shrieks of pain. Having my head canted at such an angle not only made me look like Frankenstein's butler, but gave me the chance to observe things which had escaped my attention in the past — people's toes, dog shit, ground trash. It *did* make it difficult for me to drive, except by sitting in the driver's seat at a sideways rotational angle, steering with my elbow and my hip.

❧ ❧ ❧

"How does a three-legged dog take a pee?" Mark asks me from time to time. Mark and I have developed a certain rapport born of having been joined at the hips for two weeks, learning thereby that we share some of the same interests in the world: good food, good drink, and outright silliness — despite the thirty-five year gulf in our ages. For instance, Happy Hour is Joke Time at the Lost Fish Motel, and between us, we are able to dust off jokes so ravaged by age, so hoary and so wrinkled that one can hear the catacomb doors shriek as we haul them out for the delectation of the other. He insisted, for instance, in reviving — from the hieroglyphs at Nestor — that most wretched of kneeslappers, the Elephant-and-Bird Joke, which he plunged into despite the fact that I told him repeatedly, at great price to my lungs, that I had first heard when I was five years of age, and was not particularly interested in hearing it for the umpteenth time.

HE: There was this Elephant and a Tick Bird.

ME: A what?

HE: A Tick Bird. And the Bird asked the Elephant ...

ME: What's a Tick Bird?

HE: They really exist. A Tick Bird eats ticks.

ME: Off elephants?

HE: Off elephants. Anyway, the Bird asked if he could make love to the Elephant if he picked off all his ticks. So ...

ME: That's strange. I've never heard of a Tick Bird. I wonder if it's in Petersen's. Could you reach me my copy of *Guide to the Birds of North South-West Africa*?

HE: So he went to work, and picked off ticks, and it felt so good that the Elephant said OK, so the Bird finished picking off the ticks, and then started making love to the Elephant ...

ME: Are they large, these Tick Birds?

HE: No, they're really quite small, and over in a nearby tree, this monkey was watching, saw the Bird, this really tiny bird ...

ME: A Tick Bird.

HE: Right, a Tick bird ...

ME: As opposed to a Flea Bird. Or, say, a Mite Bird ...

HE: ... going at the Elephant, and the monkey thought it was so funny he dropped his coconut, which hit the Elephant on the head, and the Elephant groaned, and the Bird said "O did I hurt you?"

[Silence]

ME: Is that it?

HE: That's it.

ME: You booby. It's supposed to be "O darling. I'm so sorry. I didn't know I was hurting you."

❧ ❧ ❧

To penalize him for this Gravesend Wheeze out of the 18th Century, I resuscitate the one about the man talking on the telephone to the little girl:

ME: (Low Rough Voice) Little girl, is your mother at home?

ME: (High Squeeky Voice) No sir, my mommie's not here.

ME: (Low Voice) OK, little girl, is your sister there?

ME: (High Voice) No sir, my sister's not here either.

ME: (Low Voice) OK, little girl, listen carefully. Doo-doo, pee-pee, ca-ca.

Since Mark has obviously lived a sheltered life and has never experienced a lewd telephone call, it takes some explaining so he can get the point. He then tells me about being accosted by a man in a shopping center in Newhall. It was the dead of night, the place was completely deserted, the gentleman drove up to ask directions, and was completely nude. "I looked everywhere," Mark reports, "and I couldn't see a stitch of clothing. I think he was on speed, he talked so fast, and his thing was so *tiny*. That's what speed does to it, you know." I pointed out that the guy might have been going on so nonstop because of a certain fear of the police, or perhaps it was possible that he was a charter member of the Eenie-Weenie Club.

Mark starts in, again, on a litany of drugs, booze and sex. Like most of his generation he's immensely sophisticated in these matters, and all those lascivious and illegal adult activities that my generation, when his age, only dreamed about. I feel somewhat cheated. Back in those innocent days of post-World War II, at John Gorrie Junior High, the only drugs we were permitted were Camels, coffee, Jax Beer, and Four Roses. My tales of driving miles, blind drunk, on the back highways of Florida obviously pale by comparison to his frenetic world of peer group overdoses, busts, scores, girls going down for joints, drug-related thefts, visits to the emergency rooms, crack, police stool pigeons, and exotic drug rip-offs. Even if I believe only half of what he tells me, that half is dangerous and scary. He tells me of one trip on some derivative of amphetamine where "my heart stopped beating — I had to blow myself up to get it to start again ... " Or the time when he thought he was a balloon. ("I said to the doctor, 'look at my arm. Isn't it huge?' He didn't see it.") Obviously my tale of Tyler Potterfield drinking a fifth of moonshine all by himself and throwing up in the back of my mother's 1946 Plymouth coupé pales in comparison with his buddy on a bad trip, with black spiders crawling out of every pore of his body.

Mark's culture is frenzied, varied, and exotic. With so much going on, with so many choices, with he and his friends going to school drunk or stoned or zonked out on speed, acid, mushrooms, or whatever, I wonder that they have time to read Livy's *History* or solve a problem in trigonometry at all. Our culture more or less lived side by side with our studies — seemed to be equally important. His culture seems to dominate his world, with room for little else.

There is some good-natured jockeying between Mark and me for time on the car cassette machine (which miraculously comes back to life after he tinkers with it). My tapes of Vivaldi's *Gloria* or Atahualpa Yupanqui or the Dvořák Quartets take second place on occasion to The Dead Milkmen, a tuneless drunk by the name of Stephen Smith, or my personal favorite — The Bauhaus doing "Bela Lugosi is Dead." This part of the trip turns into less of a cultural study of the cathedral at Tepic or the mandatory visit to the ruins at Monte Alban — but rather, an opportunity for me to get to know the culture of my own country, one that has been growing up like a weed, unknown by me and my peers. The generations never speak, never will — and Mark's has less reason than ever to communicate with the elders — especially when the elders are represented by one N. Reagan whose innocence about drugs (*vide*, "Just Say No To Drugs") is so spectacular as to be charming. The media will kill a judge's nomination for doing what, after all, several generations have been doing for three decades — but neither Nancy Reagan nor the media mavens will listen to what the juveniles are trying so noisily to tell us: namely, that the arena for knowledge and understanding has shifted from the high school chemistry lab to the neighborhood chemistry lab. The wild pictures and visionary experiences that go on every weekend in the *corpus callosum* of Mark and his contemporaries is as fascinating a sign of change as we have had in 400 years of American history. It is being labelled Evil by those who should know better — and in their ignorance, they're becoming somewhat of An Evil themselves.

One can't help but have faith in Mark and his peers, but it comes from another direction than the coxcombs who run the War on Drugs. It comes from the fact that he and his generation have decided on their own what, after all, Marshall McLuhan proclaimed in 1962 — that television has rendered traditional schooling as vital as yesterday's mashed potatoes. The learning centers have shifted from these dark, isolated monoliths called "school" to the common protein we all share — the brain. Our sense of hope should come from the fact that Mark and his peers are willing to continue in their School Prison day after day (which they do with enough good will) while their real education gets to them on the side. The true learning process (via home computers, television, VCRs, and chemical experiments applied daily or weekly to the synapses in their heads) continue while they labor under this impossible system of education which would try the patience of a Job with the sheer schizophrenia of it all. That they can do it and remain cheerful and alive and funny and wise is the real hope we must have for them and for the future of this country.

DECEMBER 8 [PUERTO ESCONDIDO]
Sex is only a waste of time while you're not doing it.
— M. DUNSEATH

At Puerto Angelito beach you can damn near drive to the water — or within twenty feet of it. And because it is a protected cove, it doesn't have the suicide waves and run-back so common in this area, one that drags so many gringos out to sea each year to their eternal, damp reward.

I drive as far down towards the water as possible. Then I walk slowly down through the straws, boxes, baggies, bottles and Bimbo bags that make up the usual litter of your usual Mexican beach, slide down to the sand and haul ass to the water. Once in, it's paradise: I am free the bonds of gravity, and with my scuba mask I contemplate the great purple fish, the electric yellow eels, the polka-dotted blow fish, and the innumerable empty beer cans and orange peels moving about the bottom.

Two hours later, I return, wobble there in the sand, get through all the trash to the car, where I change back into my clothes again. It is a maestro performance, and I give a brief encore to the Mexicans who are watching every single move: I start the car, back up the hill, and slam right into an ebony tree growing there at the edge of the beach.

MARK: You drive up this hill faster than I ever would.

ME: Well I'm embarrassed about running into that tree and I want to get the hell out of here.

HE: Did it really embarrass you, all those Mexicans watching you?

ME: Actually, no. I did it on purpose because I was conducting a speed/velocity test for Consumer's Union on VW Vans to see how fast one had to back into a tree in reverse in order to leave the tree undisturbed but put $1000 worth of damage on the back bumper. Now I know it is 4 mph.

Later, I point out that the tree was not there at all. As we are reviewing the events of the day over a case of Corona beer,

I tell Mark that Mexicans are not as slow as all those stories would have you believe. "I put the car in reverse, turned around to make sure the way was clear," I say, "then I turned away briefly, and accelerated. In that split-second, an army of Mexican horticulturists appeared, dug a ten foot hole, planted a twenty-foot ebony tree, then disappeared, all just before I smashed into it ... " Mark agrees that all the mañana stories he's been hearing about Mexicans are indeed proved to be wrong.

DECEMBER 9 [PUERTO JESÚS]

After Mark and I have our fight (about him losing the room key) I adjourn to Loly's cafe to sulk over a pineapple fruit salad and an orange juice gin fizz. I pick at my meal, drink another gin fizz, and wonder what's wrong with me. Right next to my table is a cage, with a beautiful grey squirrel with lovely russet belly. At this moment, he's eating his supper, which is being fed him by the son of the owner of Loly's. Squirrel food consists of a large wriggly grasshopper. This must mean something. I take a bite of crunchy pineapple, and look over, and Squirrel is chowing down on the head of a crunchy 'hopper, and I look away, at the huge Ugly American sitting next to me telling me about his life in Mexico. Both of them are down-home Ugly. You can guess at the grasshopper, how ugly *he* is, especially without his head. The American ain't doing much better, even *with* his head. There's this swath of scar tissue across the lower jaw, and those funny round thick reflecting glasses you can never see through, and the dome where the hair should be is all red, sweaty and freckled. He has a torn teeshirt (labelled "Giants") with a prodigious belly poking out below it.

U. P. tells me he worked for United Press in Bangladesh ("It was just a job"), then he and his wife "sold Mexican" — bought furniture and clothes down here, trucked them up to their shop in San Antonio, sold them, then came back down to buy some more. They did this for twenty-five years.

U. P. had invited me to sit down at the table with him and Eve and Moise. I must have been disconsolate: never in a hundred years would I sit down with Eve, Moise, and United Press, unless I were Tennessee Williams, trying to weave a tale out of all this. I am too angst-ridden to do anything but mutter and drink orange gin fizzes, and listen to all their improbable tales. For example, Moise, Mexican artist, has been living with Eve, the dark and throaty American who jingles and jangles next to me, who used to swim naked in the bay of Puerto Jesús before it was discovered, back when it was a simple fishing village, where lonely American women could come and strip themselves down to the buff, and swim in the crystal waters of the Pacific. But things have changed, in the thirteen years she's been living here, and now she's living with Moise, and they are about to have a fight, because Moise, and perhaps some of the others around the table, with their woes and all, are getting drunk.

Carlos and Moise and Eve and U. P. are sitting together in Loly's cafe, brooding, them about dead wives, or *pinche gringos*, or rasty lovers — and me about grasshoppers, and troublesome American teenagers, and such. I hope they won't fight about feeding grasshoppers to squirrels, or about the language, or about getting drunk, especially the latter, because I am one of your passive drunks, where I drink and think of all the bad things I've done, am doing, will do in the future, so when I'm in that state, I am no trouble to anyone at all, except myself, being so tediously morose, and all. Having me around is like partying out with an old tired spongecake — no trouble at all.

U. P. is doing all the talking, anyway, doing something that drives me crazy, that is talking in English in front of a Mexican, as if he were some child, talking *about* Mexicans, his schtick being "the Mexican Mind" ("they can't fix anything, everything breaks down, they're useless around machinery; I can't understand the Mexican Mind."). Here we are sitting around, with a Mexican, like Moise, who can't speak English, except, I gather, an occasional "fuck, mon," and *he's* getting more and more sullen, and Eve, who has started saying that she's got a hard night ahead of her, that *he* is getting drunker and drunker, and since she is talking about Moise, she dare not look at him, nor mention his name, just refer to him in the third person singular.

Now, I may be drunk and sullen, but I figure that Moise knows that Eve is talking about him, and I pull myself briefly out of the great Pacific Chasm, the ultimate Dark Slough, and suggest that we all talk in Spanish, so that *he* won't think that we are talking about *him*, and his culture, like we are, and U. P. points out to me that he's never had the time to learn Spanish, lord knows, what with his business and all, buying Mexican; his working vocabulary, it turns out, after twenty-five years, is limited to "sí" and "no." "What am I doing here?" I think, ordering another gin fizz.

I turn off the movie around me, and start thinking about Mark. That bastard has honed down the Teenage Sulk to a fare-thee-well, so that since our battle over the room key, he has managed to be around me, but in such a way that he is able to be in my presence without actually communicating with me. He'll wake up in the morning, and while I am scratching myself, and yawning, he's taken a shower and slipped out the door, or maybe even out the window. He puts in a brief appearance around lunch time, to let me know he isn't dead, at least, not in the normal sense of the word, that is, and then he's gone again. Before supper time, I take the opportunity of addressing him directly, and as I do, he looks vaguely around the room, as if there were some presence around him, somewhere, but he's not exactly sure where.

"Look, don't you think this is getting ridiculous?" I'll say, and there is this mutter of a noise, somewhere in his larynx somewhere, and when I get up to get another beer, and come back, he has turned to angel dust again, is nowhere to be found. When I finally corner him in the patio later on, I say "Look, I am sorry I blew up at you. People can't travel together for two weeks without some problems." Silence. I then give him a fairly long and quite expert (and funny) disquisition on the Silent Treatment, which in the course of my life I had, too, brought to a high level of perfection. "It's very harsh, you know," I say. "Silence is a form of violence," I say. Silence.

It reminds me of something very similar I ran on my own father. Once, long ago, he did something to me I didn't like (he grabbed me and shook me, in a rage at me, a long-ago anger) so, in defense, I came up with the one weapon I had in my armory: namely, I turned into a spook. I would never talk to him, except in monosyllables. When I heard his car in the driveway, I was down the back steps and out of the house in a flash. My appearance at supper was brief, and silent. When we were forced together — on family occasions — I read (that was an accepted reason for silence in our world). Between the time when I was eleven and the time when I was sixteen I probably exchanged no more than a handful of words with him.

This was the man who was considered to be one of the brightest lights in the legal profession in this part of the country. He was a man who could woo juries, cause district attorneys to gnash their teeth, have judges marvelling at his astute knowledge of federal and state law; this was a man who before age forty was president of the bar association, a credit to his profession, a force in the state and regional legal establishment; yet I, his child, had managed to keep him at bay for five years with the one tool I could command — that is, by pretending that he didn't exist. Until the day in 1950 when he became a literal ghost, I was a figurative one.

When they brought me into the headmaster's study, that dark room, filled with books, and the smell of pipes and leather and solemnity, and said, "Your father is dead," I put my head down on my hands, perhaps for five minutes, closed my eyes — and had that feeling sweep over me, that great feeling of *relief*. That now I was free, that I would no longer have to be a ghost, that I was now free to live, and act and react, and never hide from him ever again.

❧ ❧ ❧

I think I probably saved the scene at Loly's Cafe last night. I became the ultimate *deus ex machina*. At one point I figured we had about five minutes before the floor show would begin. U. P. is telling me about the death of his wife: "They opened her up. Her lungs were shot. She was dead in a month. And I'm the smoker." He pauses. "I haven't been able to do anything since then. I sold the business. I travel around, here and there. I travel a lot. I've thought of going back into the business, but I've never been able to do it. I've got enough money, to keep on travelling. I guess that's what I'll do ... " And I look at him, trying to peer in through his huge round reflecting glasses. I see someone in pain, all of us in pain, that mute, inexpressive, awful pain. I see one who has lived out most of his life, and knows it, and doesn't have much left, and knows that too — someone who's travelled too far to go back, has practically run out of whatever it is that keeps humans going. I see before me a scared, fat, lonely man, too proud to ask for help, to come right out and say "Won't you help me?" Too proud to say it, but not too proud to hint at it — to let us reject the plea if we so choose.

I choose not to acknowledge it, fearing what would come next, and I think "If I were only Tennessee Williams ... " If I had the time, and the interest, if I were not in the Great Black Pacific Slough of my own, with all the trash and detritus and beer cans and lemon rinds and mango peelings ... if I could rouse myself, write up his story, in appropriate journalese, flesh out the tragedy of a lonely, isolated man, a man who's bereft: he and I would have a tale to tell, I suppose. If I wanted.

"Míra," I say, turning to Moise. "Que dices es la verdad. Hay un character en Mexico — un character lleno de amor, y alma — un corazón lleno de espíritu ..." and I'm off. It's enough to shock Moise out of his bitter brood. I've been sitting there for two hours, not talking, certainly not talking Spanish. He thinks I am another illiterate gringo. Well, I am — but when pressed by enough gin fizzes, I can come up with some of the damndest and most original groupings of words, the most outré collection of phrases — all born of a few years of high school and college Spanish, a year or so in Mexico. When I speak, as I am doing now, of the Mexican soul, the heart "filled with love, the spirit of that heart" — I may be speaking the most garish sort of gringo Spanish, never heard before on the southern coast of Mexico, with an accent out of the worst mix of Hollywood, Miami, and New Jersey — but no matter what the accent, Moise knows I am talking artist to artist, using the words he knows the best: "soul, heart, spirit." Artist talk, and damn the language barrier. Suddenly, the black moods that have been lurking about our table are swept away, two students of the soul of Mexico have found each other. U.P.'s monotone tales of the living dead are ignored; Eve's throaty projections of the miserable night ahead are for naught. Moise the Moody and Carlos the Broody have been brought together to transform all in a discussion of the world of souls and hearts, a discussion which will go on frenetically, with much fractured English and broken Spanish, for the next hours, as the two of them explicate to and for each other at great length with immense amorphous foggy clustering of words and gestures and logic exactly what constitutes Mexican Soul, Art, Love.

The remainder of the evening is a fuzzy babble. Eve and U. P. fade away. I recall at one point our gap-toothed fifteen-year-old waiter being hauled before the court of the table as an example of the best of Mexico, a young man with a proud heritage, one who should look to the future with a clear eye and an open heart because the best blood in the world runs in his veins. I seem to recall an extended discussion, somewhat later in the evening, at the door of the car, between Moise and me, but possibly others were involved, perhaps even the squirrel, and the grasshopper, whether I, in my present artistic condition, could make the long and arduous drive up to the hotel on the hill. As I embraced my new and lifelong friend Moise, I also embraced my car, and assured Moise that the car would make the drive all by itself, that we, the VW and I, had been together so long that it didn't even need me to drive it: all I had to do was to turn it on, step on the gas — and we were off. And even though Moise was my newest lifelong friend, he must have trusted me explicitly, or at least he trusted my car, because I awoke the next morning, safely in bed, knowing that not only did my kind van get me up the hill — it got me into the room, tucked me in bed, kissed me goodnight, and locked the door before tiptoeing away to the hotel lot for the night.

DECEMBER 10

The van wasn't the only one tiptoeing around. Mark appeared around three or so, got in bed, got out of bed, retched, got back in bed, got out of bed, retched, got back in bed, then tried to make it out the door this morning before I was fully awake.

ME: Mark.

HE: (Stopping at the door).

ME: Can we talk?

HE:

ME: This is silly.

HE:

ME: I refuse to live with a deaf-mute.

HE: (Looks out the window)

ME: Look, I was wrong, I'm sorry, I'm gonna go off and kill myself, I'm gonna stay in bed for the rest of my life. I blew it.

HE: (Looks at his feet)

ME: You should make up your mind. We can either stay here for a few days, go on — or you can go back home. It's your choice.

HE: (Mutter)

ME: I'm sorry, I can't hear you. On top of everything else, I have this ear problem. When people don't talk to me, I can't hear them.

HE: I'd like to go home.

ME: I'll be ready in a half-hour to drive to the airport. You'd better pack.

HE: I'm already packed.

ME: That's the first sensible thing I've heard from you for three days.

I have to go to the bank in Pochutla to get some money for the ticket. Mark insists on riding lying down in the back seat of the car. I keep wondering how I ever got tied up with this teenaged nitwit — how I could for a moment think this child was a smart, funny, proud product of late 20th-century American culture. I park the car in the sunniest part of the street outside the bank, roll up all the windows, lock all the doors. When I come back in an hour, there's no sound from the back seat. "My god, I've suffocated him," I think: "There's a dead baby in the car," I say to myself.

ME: Mark.

HE:

ME: Mark!

HE: (Grunts)

ME: We have about an hour left together. It would be novel, not to say civil, if you would sit up in the front seat here. We do, after all, have a few details to clear up before you fly off home.

"How can they be so pissy?" I wonder to myself. By not saying or doing anything, they can so enrage one. I wait a while, driving along, then say: "You know, one time when I was in college, I met this girl. She fell in love with me. I thought I loved her, too. Once, I went over to meet her family. This was back in 1956, and in our conversation before dinner, her father asked me if I had voted in the Presidential election.

" 'I voted for Adlai Stevenson,' I said.

" 'You voted for Stevenson?' he said.

" 'Yes.' I didn't think anything strange about that. Lots of people had voted for Stevenson that year, even though he lost to Eisenhower. 'You voted for Stevenson?' he said again, his voice rising.

" 'Yes,' I said.

" 'That scoundrel?' he thundered. 'You voted for *him*. How could you! How dare you!' And he got up, and paced the room, back and forth, red-faced, denouncing Adlai Stevenson, and me, as traitors, and ne'er-do-wells.

"I didn't say anything. I just sat there, and took it all in. But when I got up to wash my hands, I went on out the back door, and got in my car, drove back to school. When I got to my room, he called, almost the moment I got back, and I listened to his apologies. He asked me to come back — if not this very evening, sometime in the near future. I told him I would. I never did.

"I never forgave him for getting angry at me," I told Mark. "And I never forgave his daughter. She tried to talk to me over the next few weeks, but I had nothing to say to her. It was delicious. I never forgave the father for being such a boor; and I never forgave his child for having such a boor for a father."

There are two whopper hangovers riding alongside each other in the car this particular morning, so I'd be the last to say that I drove any faster than I usually do between Pochutla and Puerto Escondido, or that I made any special effort to hit the various potholes on highway 200, to follow closely any obnoxiously smelly diesel fume busses or trucks, but Mark *did* roll down his window and stick his face in the fresh air for most of the trip. In the airport terminal, I bought his ticket, looked at him for a moment, and turning, said "Well ... you're on your own, now." It was the only thing I could think of, except for the note I sent back to his mother:

Dear Rose:
Mark returned herewith. He's a good, possibly a great, person, but the trip didn't work out. He tried to teach me something about anger, and I tried to teach him something about forgiveness. We both failed.

Sorry,
CA

DECEMBER 11 [PUERTO JESÚS]
While he was at Lichfield, in the College vacation of the year 1729, he felt himself overwhelmed with a horrible hypochondria, with perpetual irritation, fretfulness, and impatience; and with a dejection, gloom, and despair, which made existence misery. From this dismal malady he never afterward was perfectly relieved; and all his labours, and all his enjoyments, were but temporary interruptions of its baleful influence ... Dr. Adams told me that as an old friend he was admitted to visit him, and that he found him in a deplorable state, sighing, groaning, talking to himself, and restlessly walking from room to room. He then used this emphatical expression of the misery which he felt: "I would consent to have a limb amputated to recover my spirits ..."

— *LIFE OF JOHNSON*
JAMES BOSWELL

You put me in mind of Dr. Barrowby, the physician, who was very fond of swine's flesh. One day, when he was eating it, he said "I wish I was a Jew." — "Why so? (said somebody); the Jews are not allowed to eat your favourite meat." — "Because (said he), I should then have the gust of eating it, with the pleasure of sinning."

— IBID.

Travel is madness. People babble at you in strange tongues, and expect you to understand. You are cut off from every comfort of the familiar and the easy. There is no connection to one's support group. If you are travelling with someone else, you are thrown together day and night in trying circumstances that would ruin even the most equitable relationship. If you are travelling alone, you are forced to walk alone, eat alone, sleep alone, recycling the oldest of thoughts, feelings, memories, hurts, angers, and dreams.

The money is weird, strange faces peering out of funny colored bills with peculiar words, signatures and watermarks. You don't even know what it's worth: 100,000 lire, 10,000 yen, 50,000 pesos. What's that in real money? you want to know.

People laugh at you, raise their voices at you, turn away from you, for inexplicable reasons. You do your best to imitate the mother tongue, but when you utter the sounds to someone, he either shakes his head and walks away, or answers you in a babble of words that are impossible to understand. No matter your education, intelligence, or social standing, you are reduced to the comprehension of a five-year old, the vocabulary of a three-year-old.

You haven't the foggiest idea of the operating rules, and the things you think you should be able to trust could make you deathly ill. "Should I even be bathing in this," you think, trying to keep the shower water out of your eyes and mouth. The food looks good enough to eat, but it could lay you out for a week. A mosquito bite could give you a lifelong disease. Danger and destruction lurk in the most innocuous looking places: light sockets fall off walls, live wires tumble about, door handles come off in your hands, shower heads bonk you on the cupola, and when you flush the toilet, it begins to boil up angrily, threatening to flood you and the floor and your room and the front desk with your own leavings.

Companionship is flaky, and today's best friend may be 6,000 miles away tomorrow. Fear of thievery turns one into a travelling paranoid schizophrenic: "Let's see, where can I hide the car keys while I'm swimming?" Certainly not in the car, or under the beach towel. "I suppose I should get a piece of string," you think, "and tie it around my neck, but suppose I were to lose it, how would I ever be able to drive home?" To make matters even more difficult, the country of your choice gets involved in a soaring inflation, so that you are never quite sure if you are getting a bargain or not, and when they cash your traveller's checks at the bank, they only have 5,000 peso notes, so they give you a hundred of them, and there is no way you can carry a hundred 5,000 peso bills around in your pocket without looking like an advertisement for instant hold-up and murder.

To journey is to test one's sanity. The last time I was in a foreign country, and my travel partner disappeared, I was in Southern Spain, on the coast, near the unfortunate and ugly town of Almería. I had rented a house on the Mediterranean, and now that I was alone, I had determined to continue to live in it. It was cold and bitter — Southern Spain is on the same latitude as Philadelphia — and that part of the country is noted for winter mistrals that come up from the south, blowing bitter winds, making one's days icy, one's nights a futile attempt to find a warm spot in an empty bed. The bedroom had a door that opened onto steps that went down to the sea, and one night I woke up to hear a dark furry creature shooshing up against the door, trying to get in, trying to get to me for god knows what reason. The wind had blown down the power lines, and for five days I was trapped in that house, with no water (the pump to the well was broken), with a cold and sullen maid who wouldn't talk, only looked at me out of withered eye-sockets. Neighbors all looked singularly hostile. I couldn't concentrate on any of the books I had brought with me, and I would wake up in the morning with a strange vision: before my eyes a tiny line, no bigger than a hair, on which were strung six or eight skulls, tiny skulls, some green, some blue, some red. No features, just wide vacant skull eyes and fleshless skull mouths. It did no good to shut my eyes (that's where they lived) and when I opened them, I was alone in my cold, bare room, the wind whistling in around the windows. A distant door would bang, the wind would whistle and cry — the wind that wouldn't go away.

When, finally, a friend flew in from the United States to rescue me, I had a hard time speaking; and for the next few months, I wasn't capable of acting on my own. They called it a 'breakdown,' but when they apply universal terms to one's own particular problem, it doesn't mean anything. For a long while there, I could never make up my mind, even about whether I was having a breakdown or not. I also couldn't make up my mind in the grocery store whether to buy chicken or ham, and I would stay there, rooted to the meat department for what seemed like hours, trying to decide. It was a time of peculiar mindless pain, and often the best decision seemed to be no decision at all.

This powerful memory gives a certain pith to the fact that, for the first time in fifteen years, I am now alone, in a strange place. "Perhaps I will go mad again," I write cheerfully in my journal. The ease of writing it belies my fear. Boswell says of the man for whom he has chosen to make himself the amanuensis:

> *To Johnson, whose supreme enjoyment was the exercise of his reason, the disturbance or obscuration of that faculty was the evil most to be dreaded. Insanity, therefore, was the object of his most dismal apprehension; and he fancied himself seized by it, or approaching to it, at the very time when he was giving proofs of a more than ordinary soundness and vigor of judgment.*

What we fear the most may well overtake us, and the very fear of being trapped in madness traps us. It's like one of those mythic creatures which you are better off not fighting: the more you fight it, the closer it draws you into it. One doesn't battle lunacy, because the battle alone can drive you looney. "I'm afraid of going mad," I once wrote, "and the fear of madness is driving me mad." "What ever I fight I shall become," wrote Tacitus. He was speaking of the battles from without — but it is equally true of those from within.

It is thus no accident that the night of Mark's departure is a night of bad dreams, with evil, Charles Dickens' nurses, abusing a rich old man. Evil students accuse him of being a Jew. They take away his cigar, and replace it with one with a firecracker hidden in it. Watching over this is a stark, wooden face mask drilled with three holes, two for the eyes, one for the mouth.

DECEMBER 11

The Mexican Great-Tailed Grackle, *Cassidix mexicanus*, Roger Tory Peterson tells us, is "a very large iridescent blackbird with a long, wide *keel-shaped* tail. Eye yellow." Then this:

> *Voice: Various excited, shrill, discordant notes, including a high, rapid* kee-kee-kee-kee-kee, *etc., or* kik-kik-kik-kik-kik, *etc.; a lower blackbird* check, check. *Also an upward slurring* ma-ree.

Kik-kik. Kee-kee. Check, check. That's not the half of it. What Peterson doesn't tell you is that the Great-tailed Grackle is at it from sunrise to sunset, with its variety of sounds, and that rather than transcribe them as "check, check" or sweet "ma-ree," — I would rather you imagine a Walt Disney cartoon of an office filled with busy machines, making all these busy electronic office machine noises, at full volume, at random times. Typewriters going, carriages banging back and forth. Electronic wheeps-and-bleeps of the telephone, amplified a hundred times. Dings and bings and rings. Beep-beep-beep: the busy signal (that's a favorite). Gleek-gleek: the adding machine adding. Shring, shring: the computer computing. Weep-weep: the telephone telephoning. Zuck-suck-suck: the computer printer printing. IBM Central Mexico has gone nuts in the trees of Puerto Jesús, with all the sounds of the central complex core raised in volume, speeded up, going on and on, from daybreak to nightfall. It's a madhouse out there. That's the musical accompaniment I want you to imagine as I continue my tale, especially this next part here. For there are times when the "wheeeepwheeeep" of the grackle is a voice laughing at me, all the days, and much of the night.

❧ ❧ ❧

As I look for a house, I live in the Hotel Sayonara, which overlooks Puerto Jesús. Each room is cooled by a Humphrey Bogart ceiling fan, and I spend many hours lying on my bed, staring up at the slowly rotating white blades, going round and round and round.

At the center of Puerto Jesús is a huge concrete wharf, built in 1925 for the coffee trade. Surrounding it is the arc of a clean, white, mile-long beach. This is surrounded by the many hills, with houses, palapa shacks, and dusty roads. The activities begin before sunrise, when the forty or fifty fishermen of town put out to sea, and return with their catch to sell on the wharf.

The hotel overlooks the wharf, and when the sun comes up, the unhurried glory of it, tied in with the turquoise blue of the water, all surrounded by peaks and rocky islands, the surf muttering at the shore, the children coming down for their early morning swim — it all seems so perfect, so perfectly beautiful. I sit for hours, motionless, watching it.

"I wonder if it is a question of madness at all," I write, sitting as I am on the porch far above the sea and the fisherfolk and the children. "Perhaps this is the usual overdramatization. It might be simpler than that. Maybe it is a question of whether I am a good enough companion for myself?" When I'm not looking at schedules of airlines that will return me to the United States, I keep nibbling at my fears, wondering where they might lead me. It's not unlike the tongue worrying the hole left behind when they yanked out the wisdom tooth.

"If I decide to stay," I tell myself, "my language should not be too much of a problem." At least not for me. I can understand myself fine. It's just all those people around me. For instance Manuel, the breakfast waiter idiot-boy of the Hotel Sayonara. I'm sitting at my table overlooking the bay, and I am reading the menu, which sports such items as "Clud Sandwich" "Fred Filled of Fish," and, to drink, "Bear." I am trying to imagine some guy named Fred, sitting here with his friendly bear, both chock-full of fish when Manuel the waiter comes up to ask me what I want for breakfast:

ÉL: ¿Café?	HE: Coffee?
YO: Si. Y huevos.	ME: Yes, and eggs.
ÉL: ¿Con queso?	HE: With cheese?
YO: No, solo. Como omelete.	ME: No, plain. Like an omelette.
ÉL: ¿Jamon?	HE: Ham?
YO: No.	ME: No.
ÉL: ¿Revueltos?	HE: Scrambled?
YO: No — como omelete.	ME: No — like an omelette.
ÉL: ¿Fritos?	HE: Fried?
YO: NO. Como omelete. Sabes omelette? (Points at "omelete" in menu.)	ME: NO. Like an omelette. D'ya dig the word "omelette," Jack? (Points at menu).
ÉL: (Sonríe, y trae huevos revueltos.)	HE: (Giggles, and brings scrambled eggs.)

DECEMBER 12

For this purpose, then, Tom applied to Mr. Western's daughter, a young lady of about seventeen years of age, whom her father, next after those necessary implements of sport just before mentioned, loved and esteemed above all the world. Now, as she had some influence on the squire, so Tom had some little influence on her. But this being the intended heroine of this work, a lady with whom we ourselves are greatly in love, and with whom many of our readers will probably be in love too before we part, it is by no means proper she should make her appearance at the end of a book.

— *TOM JONES*
HENRY FIELDING

The house across the way from the hotel is empty, and I find out that the owner is Emma, who runs the Escuela Palma Real. I go out to see her. I don't drink my usual three morning Coronas because I don't want to risk a beer, or bear, breath with a potential future landlady.

The school is located in Zipolite Beach. Zipolite is famous from hippy days as the Big Sur of Mexico. For years people came here from around the world to drop acid and moon at the sunset. It's on the very elbow of Mexico: the beach faces due south, and the ridge of hills that come down to the sea at the southernmost point here is named "Cometa" — Comet. As I am driving out to the school I pick up a German couple, and she sees my book of Tibetan Buddhism on the seat and says, "Ah, you read Buddhism."

ME: I try to.

SHE: Perhaps it is better to do it over there, to the east.

ME: What difference does it make? They all say the same thing. "Shut up the mind, make it stop babbling."

SHE: It's very hard to do.

ME: Tell me about it.

❧ ❧ ❧

The school, Palma Real, is set on five acres on the ocean, with extensive planting of coconut trees, thus the name of the school. It's two in the afternoon. Emma has not yet come back from shopping in Pochutla, so I sit in the dining ramada — a round structure with a woven palm roof, the sides open to the breezes and a complete view of the campus. Fifteen or so children are eating there, or being fed the spaghetti and watermelon 'liquado,' the lunch of the day. Some of the children are cerebral palsied, which affects everything: coordination, muscle tone, movement. Much of the food and drink they're being fed ends up spilled down their chests and onto their bellies. The ladies doing the feeding are hugging and tickling them, speaking to them in Spanish.

I learn later that Emma has a very good system of dealing with the hordes of volunteers who have heard of the school, and who come to Zipolete wanting to help. She puts them to work feeding José. José, who has cerebral palsy, in the U. S. would be defined as a basket case. Since much of the food that is chewed up is then regurgitated onto José's little front, one has to have a very strong dedication to continue to feed him, and after two or three meals, an even stronger sense of dedication to stay with the school.

When I write "campus" above, I probably give the wrong impression. When I think of campus, I think of cool green lawns, great oaks, stately buildings, ivy. The campus of Palma Real is three ramada huts set in a palm tree grove, all on a dry brown sand, packed dirt. Everything is in disarray (the power had been out for three weeks, and was to stay out for another three weeks). Into the dining area wander a multitude of children, ducks, chickens, geese, dogs, cats, turkeys, and pigs.

Emma doesn't come until four, long after lunchtime is over. I expect the founder and operator of Palma Real to be one of those tough talking, no nonsense, Jane Addams types from America. Perish the thought. Emma is stately, lovely, a blonde from Sweden, who arrives on campus in a jeep bulging with children hanging out of every window and door. So brilliant is she, dressed so coolly in white in this steaming environment, that I am quite overwhelmed.

I tell her that watching her and the volunteers with the kids can bring tears to the eyes. "You are very good with them, all of you," I tell her. Sweet Emma, with her cerebral palsied, poliod, clubfooted children, the retardees, the rejected from the poor Mexican families. She's one of those people who drifts through her days effortlessly, touching everyone, finding money and volunteers, talking calmly, radiating care and warmth. She in her white billowy dress, looking so regal, speaking in Swedish to her volunteers, in English to me, in Spanish to the kids.

The house that I rent from her is a bare bones building with two doors, no water, pigeon shit on the floor (and three live pigeons in the rafters), a dead yard filled with bottles, cans, stones, and candy-wrappers, and a bathroom with a dry shower head and no toilet seat. "I can see you've lived in places like this before," Emma says to me. "Why do you do all those things, for the kids," I ask her. "Sometimes I don't know whether I was sent to help them, as much as they were sent to help me," she says, so effortlessly, too wisely.

DECEMBER 20

i once heard the survivors
of a colony of ants
that had been partially
obliterated by a cow s foot
seriously debating
the intention of the gods
towards their civilization ...
insects have
their own point
of view about
civilization a man
thinks he amounts
to a great deal
but to a
flea or a
mosquito a
human being is
merely something
good to eat

— *ARCHY & MEHITABEL*
DON MARQUIS

In celebration of my last week at the Hotel Sayonara, before I move into my new home, I go to their restaurant and order the best in the house. Garlic Soup — spicy, a bit of tomato flavor, delicious, especially on a hot day. Then, *huachinango* — filet of red snapper. And for dessert, fresh fruit salad: watermelon, bitter orange, melon, pineapple, all topped with generous squirts of *limones*.

As I am chewing my way through the snapper, snapping at the snapper as it were, filling my journal with thoughts of the idiot day — speculations, peculations, and the like — I turn over a bit of fish and there, smiling up at me, is archy. You remember archy, of mehitabel fame, the cockroach who used to write letters to Don Marquis by diving headfirst off the top of the typewriter onto the keys. And here he is, on his death-bed, face up, smiling at me (if cockroaches can ever be said to smile), fried. I thought of all those jokes: "Waiter there's a fly in my soup," &ct. (although I always preferred: "How did you find your steak, sir?" "Oh, I moved over a pea, and there it was.")

So I move him over into open air, a respectable gravesite, at the side of the plate, muse on the rest of the snapper, think about going on with my meal — it was very tasty basted as it was with *sauce cucaracha* — think better of it, and leave him spread-legged there on the plate, in open sight. When Manuel comes to pick up the leavings, I have arranged archy so only an Idiot Waiter could miss him — but to make sure, I say: "Qué no come mucho" ("He didn't eat much") and Manuel wants to know what I am talking about, and I point at the little black corpse, and he starts visibly. When he brings the bill, in the place where I usually write the tip as "Propina 2,000 pesos" I write "Cucaracha 2,000 pesos."

Back in my room, there are swarms of mosquitos holding a convention in the bathroom. Usually they aren't a bother: I just turn on the Humphrey Bogart fan, which screws up their guidance systems — they can't navigate in a windstorm — but tonight something's wrong with the fan, so I have to sleep mummified in a sheet. It's one thing to come upon an squadron of mosquitos in the wilds of New Jersey or on the coast of Georgia or in the outback of Alaska. It's another to come upon them in the lower reaches of Mexico: just last week a visitor to this area was stricken with malaria, and my health department at home had given me a travel advisory against "Malaria and Dengue Fever." The latter I had never taken seriously, since I don't believe it exists (it's pronounced "Ding-ey Fever"), but I had read too many Joseph Conrad, Graham Greene, and Somerset Maugham stories to feel comfortable in the neighborhood of malaria. A mosquito singing in your ear here may be *the* one to bear the virus. Its sound, therefore, is a declaration of the possibility of the remainder of a lifetime subject to debilitating chills and fevers. Every time you look down and see the familiar red spot on the backs of your hands or on the ankles, you wonder if in a few weeks you will begin to turn feverish. A mosquito under these conditions becomes a real enemy, a danger to one's lifetime of health. And when you wake in the morning with a hundred or so bites, one gets chills and fever in mere anticipation of the chills and fevers that might come to pass.

DECEMBER 21
When a lady at the hotel says that I don't look *as if I am fifty-four years old, I blurt out "Es porque no tengo cara." I meant to say "I don't have any cares." What I did say was, "It's because I don't have a face."*

— JOURNAL ENTRY

My Christmas present to me: I move into my new home, despite the fact it has no electricity, water, gas, cooling, bed, stove, refrigerator. It does, however, have Nano. He comes with the house. Nano is short for Fernando. He walks like a cat, has black agate eyes, long Mayan nose, pointed chin — and that exquisite chocolate, semi-sweet (not bitter) skin of the Zapotecs of this area. I tell him later, much later, after he consents to drop his shyness, and is willing to speak to me, that I've started going out in the sun so much because I want my skin to become just as dark as his own. "Quiero estar moreno, tanto bello como tú." "Tú hablas Español muy bien," dice el. ("I want to be dark, as beautiful as you." "You speak Spanish very well," he says.)

Nano comes at eight in the morning and leaves at eight in the evening. For a five foot midget (he's only thirteen) he totes impossible loads (huge bottles of water, great sacks of groceries, barrels of garbage), keeps the house reasonably clean, drives with me out to the school every day, and into Pochutla to shop. For the first few weeks, I try to drag him into conversation, but his terminal shyness is such that it is futile. This, on the way to Zipolete Beach, on the dust and rock road with hairpin turns, for our daily trip to the school:

ME: What do you call those (pointing at goats)?

HE: Chivos.

ME: No, cabros (the traditional word).

HE: We say chivos.

ME: And those (pointing at a cow). Are those "chivos" too?

HE: No — vacas.

ME: And those (pointing at a black pig) — "chivos negros?"

HE: No, son puercos.

ME: There's a "chivo rojo" (pointing at a red rooster).

HE: No, es una mariposa (It's a butterfly).

Nano takes some getting used to. Since he doesn't judge my lousy Spanish, he is the perfect Spanish teacher. For $2.50 a day, I get a water bearer, house cleaner, factotum, travelling companion, jokester (I find out later), dishwasher, market shopper, commentator on life in the village (who's sleeping with whom; who are the town alcoholics; which mothers or fathers are beating their children mercilessly), cynic, and a walking dictionary — not only on Spanish in general, but on the peculiarities of the Spanish of this area.

❧ ❧ ❧

No running water, no stove, no running water, no refrigerator, no running water, no bed, no running water. That's my new home. If I seem to place some value on running water, it is because it becomes so important in its absence. I have lived in waterless environments before, and I move into this house knowing that there is a problem. But there's a storage tank, so I assume the city will fill it. I find out later that they fill it every ten days or so, and no more. I also find out that one flush of the toilet uses about a third of its capacity, one wash of the dishes a quarter, as does one small shower. In a letter I write to a friend, I report:

Our lives are ruled by water. If you live in the United States, water is that clear stuff that comes into the kitchen or the bathroom or to the spigot in the garden without question, need, effort, or argument. You drink it, bathe in it, spray the peonies with it, cook the beans in it.

Here, we have to wrestle it into our homes. They say the Mixtec Indian priests for this area who are responsible for the annual homage to the Water Gods haven't done their jobs for three years. The Mexican power coöperative delivered electricity into their homes for the first time in 1984 — and instead of dancing and singing or whatever they do to get the thunderheads rolling, they sit in their huts and watch *Rosa Salvage* or whatever other television serial is being offered in the evening. So there's been no rain in this southern part of Oaxaca for the last three years. The wells are running dry, the trees are dying, and Puerto Jesús is coming to look more and more like Central Baja rather than the lush savannah it once was. Dust is everywhere, pervasive, penetrating the cracks and eaves, mixing with the chorizo, getting into the frijoles. You brush your teeth with it in the morning, you go to bed with it at night. The once rather lush lawn of the house I have rented is now dusty and bare, and the tank that automatically piped in water once a day, fresh water from Zipolete Beach, now has to be filled by hand, by means of huge *galones* that we take to the river and fill on our daily outing.

It's not unpleasant — having this excuse to visit the Tonameca River, lounge about in it. I buy some inner tubes for the Nano and his friends, and a water mattress for me, so we splash around and laugh and throw dirty creek-weed on each other. But our visits would not be so frequent if we weren't coming back each day to fill the water tank. It's never enough.

It's a funny thing about the water here: it's poisonous. The liquid we depend on, bathe in, clean and scrub with, can be as dangerous to our health as, say, a poison, like fumic acid, or a pesticide. We're fooled because bad water doesn't smell bad, it doesn't look cloudy or funny in any way. It's just the same clear stuff that you put in a glass — it looks OK and it tastes OK, so you drink it down; and then six hours later, you are writhing about, holding your stomach, wanting to die.

The great clear waters that lave our lives and bodies are dangerous for the health, and can sicken one intolerably. The river water we seek out every day is just as bad as the well water, perhaps worse. There are too many cows, sheep, goats, burros, horses, and humans doing too many things in, on, and by it for it to be safe for consumption. We buy our drinking and cooking water from the water truck, in five gallon *garafones* which, I believe, if I may turn poetic, is one of the most sumptuous words in the Spanish language: gahr-uh-FON-ais. (Much nicer, for instance, than the *calumpe*, kuh-LOOM-pay, that which holds the *garafone*.)

Water, as you know, is heavy and awkward. One of the principal occupations of the region is transporting water. Since it is not brought to us by pipe (there is little for the local water coöperative to transport) it has to be brought in by hand, or by foot. This ennervating occupation — the passage of water from, say, the nearest well to home or store — is often accomplished by means of two buckets, strung at either end of a joist of wood. The man mounts the wooden piece across his shoulders, and the buckets swing freely on the rope at either end. I've often wondered why, in those pictures of Chinese water carriers, you see them exercising such an exotic dance, tiny steps as they carry the excruciating load. I know now: it is to keep the rhythm of the buckets down, so they won't swing about and slosh out the water. I watch dozens of water carriers mincing up and down the steep street in front of my house every day. It's a lovely sight, lovely if it weren't so heartbreaking.

DECEMBER 22

Fear of looking stupid chokes up many people. It is very unsettling for adults to be unable to communicate on what they feel is an intelligent and dignified level. No wonder the college graduate feels defensive when forced to say, "Want eat!" in order to find a restaurant. Swallow your pride and start talking: it's the only way you'll overcome the problem. I have never felt that remaining silent was preferable to a fumbling but honest attempt to communicate.

— PEOPLE'S GUIDE TO MEXICO

All major shopping for the residents of Puerto Jesús — outside of basics — has to be done in Pochutla (Oax)., population 25,000. I'd like to say that no wastebasket is complete without a photograph of the Pochutla main square, which consists of four cross streets, two elderberry trees (with no leaves), an old granny with rickets, and six woebegone dogs who spend most of each day licking each other's privates and tripping up the old granny with rickets. Pochutla is certainly the drabbest, dustiest, dreariest, dullest dingbattiest town the Mexican Chamber of Commerce has been able to cohere. It may well be the Mexican version of Odessa, Texas, Allentown, Pennsylvania, or Bend, Oregon.

Yet, after I have said all that, there is something ... something that you would never get in Allentown, Odessa, et al. In spite of the plaster-fall-off buildings, the bleak dark stores, a Bancomer that would put the offices of the Dallas branch of the American Civil Liberties Union to shame — despite all that — there is something, something besides the dust and heat and disarray and disorganization of it. It's not the Pochutla Town

Graveyard, with its electric pink, mauve, sunset green, and rank blue tombstones (complete with photographs of the deceased); nor is it the dusty, potholed, and rock engorged paths, called streets, which, likely as not, will dead-end into the town dump with its assortment of offal and unmentionables.

I would rather think it has to do with the street life. The streets are alive with vendors, gawkers, passersby — women carrying anything and everything on their heads (my favorites being the tiny girl with a bunch of huge white onions draped about her head like a living veil; the old fusty woman with a huge pie plate with two tiny pieces of pistachio-filled pie; and the lady with a huge bowl, with a huge, trussed-up, live rooster in it). The streets are alive, filled with people with two things in common — they are willing to talk to each other, and they will go anywhere to be out of the direct blaze of the sun: to the side of the bus, under a spindly mulberry tree, next to a building or the side of the cathedral: anywhere to be free of the blast of the sun.

The street life in Pochutla is what sets it aside from Bend or Odessa or Allentown, where the automobile and a variety of "health" and "business" ordinances murdered our street life and left us with pavement and parking areas and little else. In Pochutla there are an amazing variety of people selling an amazing variety of things out of buckets, baskets, handtrucks, bicycles, or trucks. And the selling, as is usual, is not the key: it is the leisure to talk and visit and gossip and watch the others and stare, on occasion, at the six-foot-four crinkled-hair and wire-rim glasses American on tall silver crutches, followed about by his five foot helpmeet, the one with the basket filled with celery, parsley, beans, potatoes, wine, and other items from the public market.

DECEMBER 23
Nabokov said the most frightening photograph he had ever seen was one taken of his family's house in 1899. On the front porch there was an empty perambulator, bought for his arrival. The photograph had been taken a few days before his birth.

My neighbors in Ocean Beach, the "born again" Christian folks, had a video camera. The husband recorded the births of each of his three children. "It's their favorite video program," the mother told me. "We play it for them over and over again..."

— JOURNAL ENTRY

Emma invites me to the Christmas party at the school.

ME: Can I bring some wine?

SHE: I don't like alcohol.

ME: Shit, Emma — I'm an alcoholic. What do you expect me to do?

SHE: You're an alcoholic?

ME: Yep. Four bottles of beer, a half a bottle of wine, and some sweet liqueur, every day, whether I need it or not.

SHE: You're not kidding.

ME: Nope.

SHE: Well, stop it.

ME: God Emma, I've been a boozer for forty years, and you want me to give it up for you?

SHE: Yes.

ME: Well, I'm not gonna do it. I like cough medicine too. If you want, I can bring that and pretend I have a cold.

SHE: I'll let you bring six bottles of beer. But you don't drink them all. Let some of the others have them too, OK?

It is only because I love Emma and her wretched school so that I even consent to this, much less going to a Christmas party, which I loathe. Emma is not only capable of talking me into almost anything — except giving up drinking — I suspect she may well be a saint. She's sweet, wonderful, resourceful, pretty, clear-eyed, caring, loving &ct. &ct. &ct., blah blah blah. Yesterday I took some gifts out to the school, and she gave me a hug, she and I both sweaty and loving it, and I told her that now that she is my landlady, she has to help me worry about such things as electricity. (The power hasn't been hooked up yet. I have visited the electrical coöperative in Pochutla many times. They are sympathetic, but — no juice.) She says she will talk to them. I bet she will. And they'll do something, someday. But it also means that she has to fit this visit to the electrical company with her shopping trips to Pochutla for 500 oranges, ten kilos of rice, twenty kilos of corn (for tortillas), twenty-five kilos of onions, and all the other stuff that keeps the school going.

Emma could be running SAS or SAAB if she wanted. But instead her love is for troubled, troubling, irascible, drooling, poor, malnourished, unloved (and some might think unlovable) Mexican children, and for them she schemes, plans, operates, fund-raises, all the while being charming, efficient, wise, kind, understanding, patient, &ct. She reminds me of some other saintly women I've known. They're definitely not of the Mother Teresa school — that is, so pure as to be somewhat suspect. They tend to be more of the Florence Nightingale or Jane Addams style. Whatever they need they get — and damn the torpedoes. On occasion, Emma has the vocabulary of a sailor, her deep throated resounding *NO* or *¡Cállate!* (Shut up!) is famous in the neighborhood where it can be heard for several kilometers. She can and does get angry, cry, grow impatient, yell, scream — but at all times it is her children who get her love and devotion.

Something as zany as Palma Real has been attracting attention since its beginning — it was started by a "curare" from California named Frank Douglas (a "curare" cures with the hands). Frank was accused by the locals of everything illegal, including witchcraft and practicing medicine without a license (the latter got him kicked out of Mexico for a while). When he died four years ago, the school fell into Emma's hands, and there were times when they thought the whole operation would have to shut down but she, by all reports, turned from a lovely hippy beach lady with the typical addled brain into someone who can and does run the operation with a fine instinct for what will work, and what won't.

As I am writing this, far away from her, I think on this lady, that I love, like so many do. We will do much for her. I see her now, in the plain thatch-roof, low-walled enclosure that is the center of the school. She is there in her white dress, with any number of volunteers around. She's three months *embarazada* — that strange Mexican word for being with child (when I was talking to one of her friends about her, he said she was a "Pregnant Mother Teresa"). She is surrounded by the School's Four Worst Cases — CP's with little or any motor control. She is showing two volunteers from Germany how to care for Paco: she has him down on the floor, on the mat, and is kneading him like a big wad of dough, which he somewhat resembles, explaining that for his muscles to stay in tone, and loose, such exercise is required every day.

The other children, the mobile ones, and the volunteers, friends, visitors, are sitting about on the low wall that surrounds the area, and as she kneads her loaf of Paco, she hands out instructions on the newsletter, the broken down Jeepster, the power failure, my power failure, the day's shopping — and meanwhile, the flies are buzzing us, the chickens and ducks and geese and turkeys and dogs are coming in through or by (at least half of the animals seem to have their own physical or emotional problems) and Emma, who scarcely seems to falter in the 95 degree, 95 percent humidity, she in her cool loose white cotton dress, has this power to bring us all together, to make us want to *do* something about these sweet sad malfunctioning children, the left-overs of a country with 84,000,000 people and too many sweet sad malfunctioning children.

If Palma Real existed in the United States, the state inspectors would close it down in an instant, because of the flies and chickens and geese and dogs and children being cared for not only by unlicensed volunteers, but by the other children. The building inspectors would come down on her for the wiring, the Health Department for the miserable sweaty stinky working conditions, the state licensing board would get her for unauthorized, untested, unacceptable employees (three of them are under eighteen). And someone, probably the State Clean & Cold & Efficient Department, would have them padlocked for all the cuddling and tenderness and — worst of all — the sin of sins, the fact that when one of the volunteers from Sweden was changing Maria's diapers, Maria being the ten-month-old retardee, that same volunteer was seen to be kissing Maria's bottom. Of all the Dark Sins in America — that clear and virulent act of tush love is the most abominable. Not only would the school be shut down in a trice for such abusive behavior (the newspapers and television stations would have a field day with it), both Emma and the volunteer would have to spend the rest of the decade in court defending themselves against the heinous act of Kissing Idiot Maria's Sweet & Tiny Bum! We'd never hear the end of it.

DECEMBER 25

Christmas Eve at the school is all that it should have been. One eccentric American did all the drinking, gave a sterling performance as the noisy Gringo, and proposed a toast "To those of us lucky enough not to have to spend Christmas with our families." (Someone replies "We're your family.") Emma is in her white pattern dress, floating over everything, her throaty voice alternating between Spanish, English, and Swedish. The two sullen German volunteers work with the children as if there were no celebration. Carlos, the thirteen-year-old club-foot, two spindly legs, going through the pangs of puberty while being faced with his own differentness at an age when all differentness is anathema, turns alternatively sweet and sullen. The drunken American who enjoys the same euonym reaches over to tickle him, and Carlos turns away, his child's face hard and bitter.

Stu and Nina, from Sweden, bring strange Swedish Christmas delicacies: porridge with milk and cinnamon, hot blueberry puree, shredded vinegar beets, red cabbage vinegar, and a light frosty strüdel. Swedish Christmas in Southern Mexico. Mark, one of the volunteers, like so many attracted to this place a little dotty, his face scabbed from a recent fight, hangs onto the edges of the party, watching over his children, the ones he thinks of as *his own children.* At the table are the kids, of various ages and complexions and problems: Fidel, of the huge eyes; Juana whose head won't stay up, so you catch her smiling at you toothily, her face at 90 degrees, her neck twisted at an impossible angle; Isabella, of the pop-eyes and the gimpy leg; José in his little basket on wheels; Marlena of the funny eyes; Dora with the bow legs; and from next door the cheeping of fifty chicks which, as if she didn't have enough to do, Emma has decided to raise as real chickens, instead of the half-breeds that swarm all over the campus.

It is very merry, and I am merry, to be with them all, at ten degree latitude, down here at the Southern corner of Mexico, the sweet hot fecund loving climate in this sweet hot loving fecund school that brings us all together for this brief moment in our scattered lives, knowing that we are not irrecoverably alone, knowing that there is hope, hope and kindness, even for the most forgotten of the forgotten, the poor and the unwanted of a desperately poor country where there are already too many poor and unwanted and forgotten.

DECEMBER 26

Such was the heat and irritability of his blood, that not only did he pare his nails to the quick; but scraped the joints of his fingers with a penknife, till they seemed quite red and raw.

— *LIFE OF JOHNSON*
JAMES BOSWELL

This is the The Season of The Fat Book, the time to read all those huge tomes that discourage one by their very size.

Thus I have brought with me *Tom Jones*, *Vanity Fair*, *The Way of All Flesh*, *Moby-Dick*, three novels of Faulkner, and *The Life of Samuel Johnson* by James Boswell. It is the latter that entertains most consistently and well. The contrast between the precisely detailed life in 18th century urban (and urbane) England and scattered life of 20th century rural Mexico certainly adds a pith to them both. Boswell and Johnson were endlessly needling each other, with their exotic English, their profound knowledge of the classics. *The Life of Samuel Johnson* is not exactly the history of a lone genius; rather, it is a drama, an extended play, a word-play between two eccentrics who cannot leave off going at each other: Boswell, the Scotsman, at odds with his father, too much away from his wife, the pursuer of the great, the man who must have spent as much time writing as being with the master of *Rasselas*, *The Rambler*, and the *Dictionary of the English Language*. Johnson a huge, cranky, immensely erudite maven of the language, constantly twitting and being twitted by his friend of twenty-one years.

Boswell may have loved the man for whom he was amanuensis — but he could never resist describing, with a surgeon's fine detail:

> *it is requisite to mention that while talking or even musing as he sat in his chair, he commonly held his head to one side towards his right shoulder, and shook it in a tremulous manner, moving his body backwards and forwards, and rubbing his left knee in the same direction, with the palm of his hand. In the intervals of articulating he made various sounds with his mouth, sometimes as if ruminating, or what is called chewing the cud, sometimes giving half a whistle, sometimes making his tongue play backwards from the roof of his mouth, as if clucking like a hen, and sometimes protruding it against his upper gums in front, as if pronouncing quickly under his breath,* too, too, too; *all this accompanied sometimes with a thoughtful look, but more frequently with a smile.*

Generally when he had concluded a period, in the course of a dispute, by which time he was a good deal exhausted by violence and vociferation, he used to blow out his breath like a whale.

This is the man that Boswell admits to loving too tenderly — but their snits were legion, and in their time together, sometimes they would go for a year or two without seeing each other. Like lovers, they would profess their affection, but always, one would have uneasy feelings about the other, some of which grew from their virulently opposed views on women and virtue, Americans, the Scots, Whigs:

Johnson: *Mason's a Whig.*

Mrs. Knowles: *(not hearing him distinctly) What! a Prig, Sir?*

Johnson: *Worse, Madam; a Whig! But he is both.*

Often the tension between Johnson and Boswell arose from their insatiable desire to hector each other — this being their dialogue shortly after Johnson completed his monumental *Dictionary of the English Language*, which he assembled single-handedly, with its 40,000 definitions and 114,000 quotes, drawn from every field of learning and literature. The project cost him nine years of labor:

Boswell: *It may be of use, Sir, to have a Dictionary to ascertain the pronunciation.*

Johnson: *Why, Sir, my Dictionary shows you the accent of words, if you can but remember them.*

Boswell: *But, Sir, we want marks to ascertain the pronunciation of the vowels. Sheridan, I believe, has finished such a work.*

Intermixed with these sharp and ironic exchanges would be sudden descriptions of Johnson's appealing human characteristics:

I never shall forget the indulgence with which he treated Hodge, his cat; for whom he himself used to go out and buy oysters, lest the servants having that trouble, should take a dislike to the poor creature.

Johnson was a melancholic (he said "Life is a progress from want to want, not from enjoyment to enjoyment.") He may have seen his peers, his history, and his language with the profundity of unquestioned genius, but he was, at the same time, a lonely semi-alcoholic and melancholic, one who was deeply fearful of madness, sickness, and death. He was the supreme savant of the language, the master of its history, its roots, and its beauty. His intellectual reasoning was superb; his emotional distancing was made possible by the language he spoke and wrote and thought. A show of human feelings was a weakness to be scorned and mocked. This was the same Johnson, however, who at the end of his life could write:

> *Oh! my friend, the approach of death is very dreadful. I am afraid to think on that which I know I cannot avoid. It is vain to look round and round for that help which cannot be had. Yet we hope and hope, and fancy that he who has lived to-day may live tomorrow.*

DECEMBER 27

Since reading Fat Tomes like Boswell's *Life of Johnson* is quite difficult by candlelight, I resolve to go to Pochutla, and not to leave the offices of the coöperative until I am satisfied and electrified. This particular day, it is hard not to leave the offices because I never get in: they are closed until three. So Nano and I go off to the Pochutla town dump to leave off some leavings of the new house. Someone had tossed a dead pig with its 10,000 attendant flies on the road leading to the dump, and many of the flies find much to interest them in our van — much more than the dead flesh of a dead porker — so when we leave, we take away many hitchhikers, little beasties who swarm about in the car, flying in our eyes, ears, mouths, &ct.

Back to the electric company: the offices are open, but no one is about who can help us, so we go to the local version of Safeway, the ConaSuper, which consists of six aisles: one given over to cookies and sweets, one to soap, one to alcohol, one to plastic doilies and oil, and one to votive candles. In a single corner lie the necessities of life: onions, beans, garlic, bread. There is a dark and streaked cooler given over to either butter or dead rats — but because it's so dark I don't investigate further.

Back to the electric company. With my visits of the past few days, I am becoming a familiar face. There is a long rambling discussion among the factotums about who I am, who Emma is, what her relationship is to me — and to the house (I am not yet ready to reveal the depths of my love for her). There is, in addition, some discussion about what a nice car I have, how much it must've cost, how long I've had it, and an even more detailed discussion of who's winning the local soccer game. Francisco Franco, who runs the Puerto Jesús division of the electric company, says that none of the employees ever works between Christmas and New Years, but if I could spring for some money so they could buy some pliers, they're fresh out ...

He need say no more: with 10,000 pesos, and an offer of at least part of a cooler of beer, and a ride, I get them into the van and truck them down to Puerto Jesús. The operatives from the electric company, led by General Franco, open up the meter and have the power flowing in two minutes flat. Unfortunately, a fuse keeps blowing, so the members of the Oaxaca Companía Electricidad, between them, take five minutes to fashion what we vulgarly call a shunt, with which they wire up my fuse box so I will never have to worry about burned out fuses ever again. Burned out fuse boxes; even burned out houses — but fuses; no.

It takes us an hour to empty the cooler, another half an hour to determine who is winning the local soccer game — and then they are off.

❧ ❧ ❧

That night there is a goodbye party at the school for one of the volunteers. I drive out the dirt road to Zipolete. Half way out, in a long and narrow part of the road, there's a stalled electric company truck. I half expect that if I pull out another 10,000 pesos, they'll become unstalled enough to move. Actually, a little push would get it out of the way. I lean out the window and make just that suggestion. Larry, the bulbous American with a bulbous nose and the canted eye, lurches over to the car, and burns my face a bit with his breath, and says "Hell, you know — yer not in L. A. now!" He says it six or eight times so I'll get the drift. Larry is an interesting case. He has been coming down here for twenty years. He's lived with the Sánchez family, helping them to fix up their house, helping to turn three of the five sons into active and garrulous alcoholics. He spends several months each winter with them. To this day, the Spanish words he knows are "Sí" and "No." This after twenty years.

"You know yer not in L. A. now," he says.

"Shit, Larry, I know I'm not in L. A. I just want them to push the damnfool truck out of the way so I can get to my party at the school."

Larry one-eyes me again, his other eye on the moon rising somewhat to the left of me, then he says, brightly, "You know yer not in L. A. now." I keep thinking we should be striking a medal for The Family of Sánchez who have put up with him, his boozing, his intolerable ways and his wall-eye all these years, putting up with this klutz for twenty years without a word of complaint.

DECEMBER 31

There is a bird that makes a strange 'tsk-tsk' sound at random times during the night. I call it the Kissy-Kissy Bird because that's what it sounds like. The noise seems to come from the wall, right next to my head. "Smack-smack-smack" it goes, very rapidly, at strange hours of the night.

— JOURNAL ENTRY

The smells of Mexico, in order of appearance, are: dust, exhaust, sweat, smegma, and Offal. Of the five, the one I still can't get used to is that awful Offal. I am not quite sure where it comes from, or where it is going, but I sure as hell know when it's about. It always accompanies a slow-moving, thick, greasy green-black line of waste product leaking between buildings, across dirt roads, down to the lower levels. It's hard to identify the ingredients, because one does not want to get too close without a mask, but I think, by smell alone, that it must contain at least a smidgeon of the following:

rotting food liquid
urine and/or stool
mop bucket leavings, after many a mopping
juices from the insides of old fish
animal droppings (a variety)
old, very old, very bad, cheese
pig scat
hen bane
asafœtida
eye of newt
dead baby

I actually had to give up eating at my favorite restaurant, Chez Pepy's, because there was a sizable Offal Creek running between my table and the ocean. Since the prevailing Westerlies were in my direction, all appetite disappeared in a flash. I attribute it to mere nasal weakness within my sturdy Anglo-Saxon frame, and, as well, the inability to eat tortillas and frijoles while breathing through the mouth. Nearby, whole happy Mexican families are downing great quantities of ceviche and fried fish and frijoles, drinking beer and soda — which is impossible to do while breathing through the mouth unless you are willing to drown. (It puts me in mind of a particularly noxious bathroom in the Texaco station in Pittsburgh; someone had scrawled on the wall "It's all right to breathe through your nose.")

Here in Puerto Jesús the Mexican military has an installation, and what I've seen of their drilling techniques, hardware, and armaments leaves something to be desired. I think that all they have to do is to corner the Offal Market, which doesn't seem to be such a hard call since it sprouts willy-nilly, in abundance, all over Mexico. At the slightest hint of invasion, a River of Offal would be laid across the battlefield, and I (for one) would guarantee that no self-respecting army in its right mind would cross such a barrier. Those foolish enough to do so would need instant mouth-to-mouth resuscitation and a year's R & R in Acapulco.

JANUARY 5

I suspect part of the problem comes from the dictionaries. My Collins Fontana English Spanish dictionary will have viejo verde *("gay old dog") but not a mention of the most well-used (and used up) word in the Spanish speaking world,* verga. Pinche *appears, but defined as "minion" — which is not what I think Diego means when Nano drops one of the waterjugs on his toe. And nowhere can I find* caca *— although they go to all the trouble of including* calera *("limekiln") and* caluyo *("Indian clog dance.") I suspect neither Mr. Collins nor Mr. Fontana of having gone further south than the donkey bars of Tijuana — if that far.*

— LETTER TO A FRIEND

Somedays I will sit on the porch, not reading, not doing anything, just letting my thoughts spin. The hates and loves and passions and fears and bitternesses of America are so far away, no longer stirring up the bitter brew, the collection of travails that clogged my mind 3000 miles to the north. I sip on a Corona Clara, ice cold, buried deep in the cooler.

Nano comes from school around two P.M. I tell him to make the bed and clean the kitchen. I have him load the water jugs in my car, and we drive to the river. We have Victoria's "Macumba" on the car tape deck, and I feed it full blast. I always pick up hitch-hikers — sometimes kids going to Pochutla to market; sometimes a whole family on their way to Puerto Escondido or Salina Cruz; sometimes an Indian woman carrying a bonita back to her family. We turn off on the road to Rio Tonameca. Two kilometers along and the river is before us. The floor of it is made up of stones and pebbles, so I can drive right on it. We go upstream, away from the Indian women doing their wash (many of them bare-breasted. "How like the 1960s," I think; and then I think, "They've probably been doing their laundry this way since 2,000 B.C.")

I pull my van onto the riverbed, the water half-way up the hubcaps. Nano takes off his shirt and shoes, wades out to the deep part of the river to fill the *galones*. I slide down into the water, let the waters bathe my hot body. I watch him as he concentrates on capturing water in the jugs. I see his form so filled with this-will-be, rather than this-has-been-it-too long. I ball up my fist, sluice water at him. He tries to do the same, can't — splashes me, laughing, his eyes so happy, making me happy that my shy Nano can be so joyful. Downstream, two Mixtecs bring their horses to the water, use them for spring boards to leap in the water. A couple of pigs go by, ferreting through the mud with their shovel-snouts. Further downstream, six or eight children, barebottom, are splashing, calling to each other. A pair of Orioles, yellow wings, black bodies, swoop down to bill water from the river, then ascend to the trees again. Upstream, a naked sixty-year-old Zapotec is soaping and rinsing himself. We are part of the river.

There are some goats way over in the field, and some roans. An eleven-year-old boy with a red bucket comes and pulls out some water and goes on up the path. There are green-yellow-orange clouds over near the mountains, and if you look upriver, where the water is moving swiftly, you can get a broken reflection of those clouds, pure undistilled Cezanne. Over the crest some swifts are turning and wheeling, making you wonder how they can stay together in such flight without bashing into each other.

In the bushes behind us there is a bird crying regularly and simply, "weet-weet." The children are laughing, their mothers are calling out to each other. The shirts and socks and shorts have been laid out to dry on the branches of the nearby bushes, sprouting there like huge improbable leaves of red, orange, green, blue and white. The air is fresh. There is a slight breeze. Every now and again, a yellow leaf will drift by to remind us of the seasons dying to the north of us. There is a peace and tranquility here which I had believed to be unattainable in this life and in this world.

I have put a tape on the cassette — some music from 300 years ago, by a squirrelly old genius named Bach. The chords of the *B-minor Mass* twist and turn, pulling against the sky, pulling, pulling something from the depths. Nano asks me if I am sad. "No, no," I say. "Sometimes we cry when we are happy," I tell him. "It's just as it should be," I say.

Soon enough he loads the jugs into the car, I hang my bathing suit on the outside mirror, and we drive back to Puerto Jesús. "¡Qué bueno que trabajas conmigo!" I tell him. "¿Te gustas?" "How nice that you work for me. Do you like it?" He is silent — not aloof, but silent — as we drive the road back to the great Pacific.

What is love, and what is life? I dream of dark corners, the bed wrapped in coolness, someone waiting in the next room so I won't have to be alone. Roberto, the young fisherman, comes by every day, after the catch. Sometimes he and his friends laugh at my accent which is coming slowly to recover five years of disuse. "Your Spanish is the worst — lo más peor — that I have ever heard," he says, laughing, imitating my accent. "Why does everybody in Oaxaca talk like they have rocks in their mouths?" I ask him. He brings kind Enrique, coal-black Negrito, wise Raul, brings them by to talk with me. I offer them a beer, marvel at the ease with which they move, laugh, enjoy my company, talk so easily to me and each other.

Later I sit alone at the wooden table, on the patio of my cottage, my new home, the one with all the heat and flies and ants. A couple of burros are making rutting noises out back. The radio across the street is playing loudly:

Macumba, macumba, tú no le casera,
Memorias mas fuerte que tú talisman,
El hombre que amo,
Memorias que suerte que lo amo,
Lo amo tanto.

I am drinking cheap tinto, the local specialty, being strong and thin and wiry, like the people here. I'm eating the crunchy pan *bolillos* topped with a round of the bitter vinegar cheese that Nano buys for me at the public market. I think I must be one of the luckiest people around, here at the edge of the Pacific, the Pacific which, at night, if you listen carefully, thrums so mightily against the rocky cliffs, near the mouth of the bay — thrumming as it has for a million years or so: rising up out of the darkness of the great Oaxacan Trench that lies just outside the harbor. The waves pound with a force borne out of that darkness, a darkness of the crevasses below and the mountains above — the dark of it all; the waves, "las ondas;" "el ondo" — the depths.

Down there in that rift, down there in one of the great cuts in the earth's seafloor, strange eye-lantern creatures and phosphorescent fish move about under a pressure equal to 200 atmospheres. These beasts move slowly, ferreting across a sparse and barren sea bottom. I am a mile and a half from them in the soundless dark, me in the warm air, with my wine, and cheese, the bread — Puerto Jesús and I — touched by this delicate veil, a sweet night breeze from the west. It is at this moment that I decide to return, briefly, to the north, to the world of clouds and cold and rain, the place where people who meet you on time, where telephones work, where there's clear water that one dares to drink. To the north, the land of fear and too much money and too little time. I'll spend a week there — ten days at the most — draw my life together, briefly, before I return to my beloved Puerto Jesús, my new home.

One of the most popular stories I told was my special abridged version of Cinderella, *with Cinderella working hard for her big, ugly, unmarried sisters — washing clothes in the river, cutting up tapioca for the pigs, and chopping firewood in the jungle. Along came the headman's son, who met her at an all-night rice-wine party and dance. Unfortunately Cinderella had to return to her village before midnight; otherwise, her exquisitely carved and painted longboat would turn back into a banana (I didn't know the Malay word for pumpkin). The headman's son married Cinderella and took her away to the mouth of the river, where there were lots of fish and fat pigs.*

— *STRANGER IN THE FOREST: ON FOOT ACROSS BORNEO*
ERIC HANSEN

The universe is a cobweb — and our minds are the spiders.

— VIVEKANANDA

JANUARY 17, 1988 [ACID ACRES RANCH]

It's dinnertime at Acid Acres. We are eating what one author has described as the "nut-flavored inner organs of animals." With our meal, Sybil, D.T., and I are discussing new concepts in science.

I tell them about the microphone, the smallest receptor *cum* transmitter ever created. "Recently developed by Japanese scientists," I tell them, "it is now, even as I speak to you, being placed around the tiny necks of tiny creatures of all descriptions — bees and ants, earthworms, even bedbugs." The most controversial and difficult placement of these mini-microphones, I explain, has to do with wiring them up to the ejaculatus.

"The technology is such that these transmitters automatically attach themselves to flagellates — and are thus not so much different than the radios placed on the migrating caribou. Scientists are thus able to listen in to the noises of a select sample of spermatozoa as they move upwards towards the lovely and mythic Garden of Zygote.

"To their astonishment, they've discovered that the little creatures sing and talk to each other," I explain. "Not in English nor Spanish nor Chinese — certainly not. Rather, they speak their own little patois, an Ur-sperm lingo so complex that it has taken researchers literally years to discover how to translate these snippets into our own languages.

"The Japanese have found that these flagellates are actually carrying on discourses — discourses that would be a credit to Socrates," I tell them. "They are discussing Hegel, or Heidegger, even their all-time favorite, Whitehead. They make good use of their cumulative wisdom as they prepare to shoot the Fallopial Rapids, before they dash their little brains out in that place where the sun don't shine. They even, it is said, have an understanding of time, and the ultimate futility of life. Thus, not only are their conversations animated — they are profound — as befits any sentient, thinking creature who knows that its stay on this planet it limited, both in time and in purpose."

This description of science in action is greeted by a wave of ennui that envelops all the dinner guests. However, not a moment passes before D.T., the head gummer, bests this tale of the Interuterine Algonquin. This is what he tells us:

"Modern doctors are very close to being able to take a person's head and transplant it," he explains. "The cranium (brain, eyes, nose, mouth, hair), they have found, can easily be transposed to another body. Thus, when the bag o' bones begins to go out on you, you can visit your local Body Shop, look through the selection they have in the wall freezer — and when you find one you like — pop you on it (or it on you, depending on whose perspective is being considered.) There you are with a whole new set of arms, legs, stomachs, thighs, cheeks, and toes."

D.T. explains all this in rich detail as we are chowing down on our scrambled eggs with brain, riñones aux fines herbs, mountain oysters flambé — and, for dessert, head cheese. I for one find the idea very appealing, for my body is one of those out-of-date models from the early thirties. The manifold is almost gone, the distributor shot, and I'm not even going to talk about the drive-shaft. The direction finders have seen better days, the headlights are dim, the horn is wambling, and the tail pipe needs replacing. The thought of trading this lemon in at the local Body Shop is more than appealing. Just this week — back from the first half of my stay in Mexico — a fever erupted, my ears started singing (off-key), and my eyes poured unexpected lacrymæ. My cells, I suspect, had become so acclimatized to the bugs of southern Mexico that all the parts of me went into active rebellion at American food and water.

"What's wrong with you?" my friends asked me.

"It's the local diet," I explain. "If I felt any better, they would have to lay me in the grave."

It is time to return to Oaxaca — so I can eat Mexican meals, drink their water — feel good again.

JANUARY 20 [PUERTO JESÚS]

What is the gain? The pig body is hard to give up; we are sorry to lose the enjoyment of our one little pig body! When I can enjoy through the whole universe, the whole universe is my body.

— VIVEKANANDA

I carry some presents back to Mexico with me. A box of felt-tip pens and a Walkman for Nano. Some Adidas for Roberto, the fisherman. I bring a bag full of presents — games, drawing materials, toys — for the children at La Escuela Palma Real. I buy a chess-set for Carlos, the club-foot. I buy a doll for María of the slow wit and sweet face. I buy a selection of toys for the sixteen other children. Finally, I buy a tiny soccer-ball key set for Diego, my good friend who works there, cleaning the grounds, climbing the coconut palms.

When I arrive, Emma, the head of the school, is, despite the wilting heat, so fresh in her white dress that I could hug her

— and I do. Her blonde hair, her eyes wide and green, her great soft lovely throaty voice. Her only concession to the heat is her moustache. For yes, and alas, dear reader, my lovely Emma — tall and regal — wears a moustache. Not for disguise (who would this angel have to hide from)? No — merely as acknowledgement of the day. Starting at ten each morning, until seven or so in the evening, Emma grows a clear liquid moustache, tiny droplets across the upper lip. Nothing else in the devastating scorching wilting burning of the southern Oaxaca day seems to faze or possess her.

Her airplane leaves at eleven the next morning. She wants to return to Sweden to raise money for the school. In the morning, two hours before take-off, the school jeep chooses to fail. "Since I am the school taxi-driver," I tell her, "I will taxi you to Pochutla and Puerto Escondido and the airport." We go to Pochutla, but the passport photographs aren't ready, she has no clothes for the cold, her papers aren't ready. Five years in Mexico, however, have given her what we now call "the ahorita method of dealing with the world." ("Ahorita" technically means "a little now." When you ask someone to do something, they say "ahorita." This means it will be done in five minutes or five years. It's far more prevalent than "mañana.")

Emma loves all her charges at the school without question — even the most homely and drooly of them. She, too, loves the prospect of journey. She loves me for taking her to the airport. She loves life. She loves the world. She even loves her passport photographs. Emma is addicted to a love of all things great and small — and all us creatures (great and small) thus react to her with love.

As we drive to Puerto Escondido, I ask her why she calls her rehabilitation center for the poor and despoiled and crippled of Mexico "a school." "You might call it a hospital," I say, "although that might be a bit grim. Or perhaps, 'Centro de Rehabilitación.' Maybe even an 'Instituto.' But a school!" We ride past the desiccated fields of southern Oaxaca, where a drought has turned the trees sear and brown, the grass dry, the streets to dust. Even through it is still morning, the hot wind lashes at us.

When I take my leave of our new, improved and up-to-date Mother Teresa — I hold her for a long time, there in the Puerto Escondido airport, the two of us in a sweat-filled embrace, and I whisper in her ear. "Remember, Emma, above everything else," I say to her, before she boards the plane for her 10,000 mile journey to the east: "Remember, no matter what you do — don't let them make an institution out of you. Listen to what I say: you are not now nor are you to ever be an Institution for Good," I whisper. And I turn, let her go — knowing she will remember my words.

I think later, much too late: "What an unkind thing to say to her!"

JANUARY 27

Weng told me the story of a diving ant that launches itself from the rim of a Lowes pitcher plant and plunges into the insect-eating reservoir of digestive fluid contained within the body of the plant. The diving ant rescues some of the insects by "swimming" them to the edge of the reservoir like a miniature lifesaver. Then the ant eats the insect...

— *STRANGER IN THE FOREST*

Puerto Jesús thus became a haven for the miscreants of America, dozens of elegant and not-so-elegant eccentrics. One of my favorites is a fifty-year-old by the name of Ernest. He's been living in this area for twenty years, calls himself a "healer," has had the usual checkered career of a late-blooming hippy, and specializes in curing young women of whatever might ail them. Mostly, I gather, their virginity.

Ernest is also a stonehead. He loves rocks, feels they are therapeutic. The way you do it, he explains to me, is to heat them up, lay them about on your body. He says I must try it. I don't have any stones, but he says I can substitute "tiny stones," e.g., sand. He says I should go to the beach with Nano and Diego, have them bury me under the hot sand. "Put a towel on your face — and be sure to have them bury your hands," he tells me. "Form your hands into a rod, hold onto it, holding onto the earth." He says the hot granite — that is what sand is — will be "good for your synapses." He then tells me that, in that position, I should practice yoga. He is intent on writing a book for quadriplegics which will outline the technique for this, what he calls "eye yoga."

Dear FAA:

I have been taking aerial trips over the past few years without notifying you. I do not like breaking the law, so I am writing you to get a permit. Please send me the appropriate forms for doing Astral Projection.

Yours in Truth,
Carlos A.

I suspect I am as Cartesian as one need be in this life. They had me read Aristotle and St. Augustine in college; math was always my best study; I always thought myself to be a master of straight-line thinking. I was raised in a family where the craziest thing we did was to get drunk on weekends at the Timuquana Country Club, tell slightly (only slightly) off-color jokes on a Saturday evening, and get carried home by a best friend.

We were shaped in as linear a fashion as the American educational system could create. We were expected to marry by age twenty-five in and among our own social level. We were also permitted to have one or two affairs during the life-long course of that marriage, but no more.

They would let us write poetry, but only for English class. We were also allowed to study Graeco-Roman statuary, Expressionist painting, Baroque music, and medieval illuminated manuscripts, but not too much, and in that order. Communicating with the dead was not encouraged, nor understood. Reading tarot cards was tolerated late in the evening, at certain parties, after certain quantities of drink. Attending American Indian peyote ceremonies was not encouraged.

We did not study the works of Madame Blavatsky or the *Tibetan Book of the Dead.* Palm readers lived in funny old houses on the edge of the industrial area; faith healers worked the other side of the tracks; and swamis wore funny towels and resided in India or in Pasadena. Tea leaves were merely to be cleaned out of the cup by the maid, certainly not read, and the *L'ao T'se* was literature, not a survey of life survival mechanisms.

If your dead father appeared in the upstairs hallway after midnight, you were not expected to speak to him — although you might tell an older understanding aunt about the visitation. The Ouija board gathered dust in the attic, along with whatever or whoever it was up there dragging the chains about on stormy nights.

Thus it is with some chagrin that I confess to you that over the last ten years or so I have become a card-carrying member of ABAPS, the American Body Astral Project Society. Furthermore, as often as I can possibly arrange it — and these things are not easy to arrange, even with spacial booking-agents and all — I am not only ready but eager to take any and all available future flights into hyperspace. And if you really want to know the truth, I confess to you here and now that if I had my druthers I would get the hell out of bed and go on out there into space and stay there from the moment of retirement until the morning alarm goes off at 6:30 if they gave me any choice on the matter. Why? Because it's a *kick*.

All astral travel, at least in my circle, begins in what we aficionados call "the hypnogogic state." In my youth, this half-way state between waking and sleep was a nightmare. It always occurred when you were just going to sleep or just waking up. You'd be almost asleep, but not quite; almost awake, but not quite. There'd be a loud buzzing in the ears; the body would be tingling, but not functioning; hands, arms, legs — nothing moved, no matter how hard you strained to do so. It was impossible to open the eyes. Your brain knew that you were there, but no one was home.

Sheer terror at paralysis: that's the first reaction. For many people, it is the *only* reaction. I remember straining — supreme will — to get the eyes open, to move a finger. Only when the "spell" broke could I come awake. Stuck there, I would want to shout, "Let me out!" I would strain violently to break the spell. One of my friends said that whenever he woke in that state the only way he could escape from it was by barking like a dog. (I once asked my college shrink about it. I described it to him in detail. He told me it was one of the first signs of schizophrenia.)

That was all I knew about it until I read Robert Monroe's book in 1977. At the time I was reading any and all mystic and Eastern writers available in America — including Alan Watts, Krishnamurti, Rajneesh, Vivekanada, and Sri Aurobindo.

It was Monroe's book that made the most sense. After all, here he was, an executive for the telephone company, telling the story of *bailing out of his body*. His simple style was so far beyond the other writers I was reading that it seemed to belie the bizarre nature of his tale. A businessman, describing the how and the why and the fact of astral projection, and his many journeys into space. At the time, it spelled freedom for me. We flew. And it didn't hurt us a bit.

Because of Monroe, the next time the hypnogogic state took me over, instead of straining against the chain of movelessness, I went the other way: I spun my body around — and took off. As I told my friends later, it was like being "bathed in diamonds." What had happened to me that night was something that would change, forever, the way I looked at myself, my body, the world, dying.

With practice, I evolved the following procedure:

1. Wake up in the hypnogogic state (moveless body; loud buzzing in the ears);

2. Transform the buzzing into a moving force to sweep the body from head to foot and back up again (Monroe's specific suggestion);

3. Using the spinal column as a locus, rotate the body. ("Think of yourself as a pig on a spit," I tell my friends, "with the rod going into the top of your head, and coming out from between your heels. Rotate the whole body along this axis");

4. This sufficiently frees the Other Body from the "Real" Body so that one is able to take off — zoooooom!

Unfortunately, in the hundred or so times since then that this has happened to me, I always suffer premature ejaculation. I become so agog at what I am doing that no sooner do I start spinning about the spit than I feel the power of it beginning to leak away — and then (oh, no!) I wake up. I pump away, trying to get this celestial body a-movin', heading out the window (or through the wall, it makes no difference) — but in my excitement, I blow it: no matter how I try to hold onto it, I end up back in my old chewed-up, dog-bone body again, in same old room, back there with my frayed and flattened pillows and covers.

It's taught me much, though. One is that the best way out of the deepest fear is to go directly into it. Being in the hypnogogic state can be raw terror. Not only is the body frozen, one's mind is very suggestible. Once — in my pre-flight days — I found myself not able to move, and I started imagining that the house was on fire, that I was stuck there in this moveless body, and I could *see* the flames licking the walls about me, see them vividly in my mind's eye. When I awoke, I was sweating, shaking, terrorized.

Nowadays, it's different. I just plow on into the hypnogogic state; and, just as quickly — and regretfully — find myself falling out of it.

FEBRUARY 1 [PUERTO JESÚS]
Life is but a dream of death.

— VIVEKANANDA

The moods are different when we don't have the games and toys of our day-to-day lives. No mail, no telephone, no bills, no *New York Times*. I waken and there is nothing to do except get up *there is nothing to do except get up* and I think "What am I doing here, why am I here, what does it all mean?" I am reminded of Eric Hansen's observations of his long trek through central Kaliman, waking one day to feel alone, although he has two guides with him:

> *I had chosen to come, wanted to come, but that did not dissipate the sense that I was isolated in a place that wasn't my own. I was completely restricted to a pace dictated by circumstances beyond my control: the weather, the moods of Bo 'Hok and Weng, and the availability of the wild game. I felt I had become fluent enough in Indonesian, but the cultural gap between my Western middle-class background and that of these two nomadic hunters had come to feel like a sociological Grand Canyon. The three of us had experienced so many intimate, humorous, touching moments, but I knew I didn't really matter to them. We were physically together, but separated by our histories, thoughts, perceptions, and expectations. To them I was a slightly amusing stranger who had some shotgun shells that they needed. One day soon we would say goodbye, and they would return to the forest without me. The likelihood that I would be forgotten troubled me because I knew that the memory of these months in the rain forest would stay with me forever. I needed someone to reflect the intensity of my experience in order to validate it. Bo 'Hok and Weng didn't think in such terms. They had a much more immediate sense of the world, based primarily on survival. I spent much of*

my time thinking; they spent theirs looking for food and a place to sleep.

Today, one of the school volunteers, Pedro Lorre, comes to visit. He works as an independent producer in Mexico City for a television company. He is another of those people whom I have met in Puerto Jesús, a person I would not ever have gotten to know under any circumstances any place but here.

I have had to become an expert on Mexican television. I watch it at Lola's Cafe; in fact — sometimes I sit there for five hours, drinking lime squashes and watching the train wrecks on Channel Two. Based on my extensive experience at Lola's, I tell Pedro that the main trouble with Mexican television has to do with mouths.

ME: Las Bocas (The Mouths).

HE: ¿Las Bocas?

ME: Sí — hay demasiado. (Yeah — there are too many of them.)

Pedro not only looks like Peter Lorre, he acts like him: when I say this stuff about the mouths, his forehead gets corrugated like a washboard, and he rubs the back of his crew-cut with the palm of his hand, looking away — muttering "Las Bocas."

"What it is," I tell him, "is that the whole of Mexican society has an Oral Fixation (una Fija Oral). When I watch the commercials, people are constantly putting things in their mouths. They are biting down on candy bars, sucking up on Pepsis, chewing their Bimbo Bread, nibbling at Fresa mints, puffing at Faro cigarettes, slurping glasses of Fundadore brandy. They do those things on American television, but nowhere in our commercial histography is there such a *fix* on lips." The Mexican camera positively dotes on the macro-cheilia. Endless zoom close-ups of things getting stuffed into endless holes — consumer products being consumed so, well, all-consumingly. "The zoom lens was invented so that the Mexican face can be highlighted *in labias res*," I tell him. "In one hour-long program I counted forty-seven pairs of lips smacking, smirking, slurping, biting, blobbing, chunking, chawing, chomping, champing and just plain eating." As well, the lips are having all sorts of screwy things being done *to* them; being licked, preened, painted, kissed, rubbed, wiped, fondled, pressed, stretched, smushed and smiled. "You know why you Mexicans do all these things with your lips? It's because you have problems with your oral nature. You remember what Freud said?"

Pedro wrinkles up his brow, shakes his head. An excellent question: "You remember what Freud said?" People are always frowning and furrowing over that one. Everybody remembers that Freud said something — but the question is what.

"The satisfaction and pleasure we bring from childhood comes from the union of breast (mother) and lips." I say. "The closest thing to a mother's heart is her breasts, filled with rich warm milk. The closest thing to a child's soul is this brand new sense apparatus poking out there at the top of that little wobbly neck: nose, eyes, mouth. It's a rounding, the warmth, the all-encompassing passion of mother for child, child for mother. It is not rare," I explain, "for little boys to have tiny erections while they are suckling, and for little girls to breathe rapidly." We pause to return Pedro's eyes to their huge sockets.

Then I explain to him that Mexican children are able to sit for hours, doing nothing, patient, moveless. I've seen them on buses, trains, waiting on benches — in physical attitudes that would drive American kids crazy in two minutes. And they stay there, patient, waiting, waiting, waiting. It's all tied together, I tell him. The Mexican society is a contented oral society, endlessly putting chocolate coated nuts, Coca-Cola, breath sweeteners, Bimbos, beer, cigars, Doritos, and cigarettes in this ever-needy hole: the center of the being, the always-taking-in, the greedy, always ready lip-pursed gape opening like some great warm inviting beast — the upwelled, outpooched, eternally wet, moving round orifice, always absorbing these tempting things that get pushed into its smacky matriarchal depths.

I point out to Pedro that the Mexican comedy program "La Loca" has a host who emerges from two ponderous living-room couch-sized rubberiod lips. "It's positively disgusting to see Rafael Caracol coming from a giant wet red plastic orifice," I tell him. I lean back, pleased with my ability to render words like "orifice," "smacky," and "matriarchal" into Spanish. Pedro nods and smiles and says that my theory is "very interesting."

FEBRUARY 5

How many goodly creatures are there here!
How beauteous mankind is! O brave new world
That has such people in't!

— *THE TEMPEST*

Pedro is to fly back to Mexico City today, and I offer to take him to the airport in Salina Cruz. Salina Cruz is where the Mexican government has chosen to put many of its smokiest oil refineries, but it is also where the original Amazonias come from — the home of the aggressive, snappish women who demand much and take no guff from anyone. I tell Pedro that Salina Cruz is the city of my heart's desire. He looks at me with his slightly buggy eyes for a half-a-minute or so. Not only does he look like he just got off the set of *The Maltese Falcon*, he has that slow way of looking around, disbelieving, Peter Lorre in the midst of the slow uptake.

As we drive to the airport, I tell him about the Morenos — literally "the browns" — on Mexican television. There aren't any. "Your prejudice is very revealing," I say. "There just aren't any blacks or browns." All the figures in the commercials, and the programs, look like members of the Spanish mainland upper class — or gringos who happen to speak perfect Spanish.

Pedro tells me there is a black he knows on Mexican television. "There aren't any talented blacks anywhere in the country," he says. And so we are, again, in the United States, in 1955 — the good and the bad of it: prejudice, bias, blindness; innocence, openness, naiveté.

On our way to Salina Cruz, we drive by the airport in Hualtuco and find a flight that will be leaving at two p.m. This frees us from the need to drive to the Jersey City of Mexico — gives us three hours to play, gives me a chance to experience what, I guess, I came so far to find. There at the hands of Prospero.

Someone told me that the beach at Coyula — just outside Huatulco — is a paradise, so we drive down a road of holes and gnarls for a half an hour. We stop at the gum-soda-and-tobacco stand (set up in the middle of the town square) and ask if there is a restaurant where we can eat. The man there says no, but then says he could serve us a lunch at his house. His place is a typical Oaxacan palapa — straw roof, large open windows, beaten-earth patio, shade trees. And there we sit, at the edge of the river, with the horses going by, and the breeze going by, our lives going by.

Our host is named Prospero. He is tall and regal. He smiles quickly, measures his words slowly. Like most Mexicans — in what must be a rite of passage not unlike the European circuit made by many Americans — Prospero has traveled north across the border, found it not to his liking, and returned. He now lives with his wife and two children in this wide open longhouse, where he lollygags about in his hammock, and prepares occasional meals for visitors. For us, today, the menu is:

Raw Oysters — served with chopped tomato, onion, cilantro, hot sauce, and *limon*.

Conch — cooked in its shell (same sauce).

Turtle eggs — fresh with sand, plucked illegally, yesterday, from the nearby shore. (We eat half of them cooked, eat the other half raw with the hot sauce.)

Cold Corona beer.

Nano and Diego, those little gourmands, eat as many turtle eggs and oysters as the rest of us. Pedro, always the director — this is one of his finest movies — is up and about in the kitchen, supervising Ms. Prospero on how best to cook the conch, how to boil the turtle eggs, how to make the sauce. It is a pity that we are not writing the Michelin Guide for Mexico, for surely we would give *Prospero's Café* three stars and a single crossed fork and spoon for simplicity and understatement. There is no sign, no menu — nothing but exquisite food, and quiet, and contentment.

Prospero doesn't seem that much like the Duke of Milan except for the magic of making a whole meal out of nothing. He stands on the beaten earth floor of his home, leaning against the pole that holds up his palm-leaf roof, speaking to us so easily and so familiarly, telling the tale of his life, interrogated as he is by the director and his side-kick, the noisy and nosy gringo. Prospero tells us about trips to the Sonoran Desert, Texas, Southern California. He rambles on easily about his times in Mexicali and Calexico and Los Angeles — an elegantly accented account of a saga that started out so primitively forty years ago (the family of fisher folk on the beach; life amidst the fruits of the sea) — then his travels to the land of gold. And now back, to live simply, serving simple meals to simple folk, like me and Pedro and Diego and Nano.

At times like this I think on what it is like to experience this Mexican world. I now am experiencing a life in which there is little necessity for me to do anything to get through the day. One must, I suspect, equate such days with one's own death. It is the Hindu concept that we will experience, at our time of passing, exactly what we think we will experience.

If I think, as the Tibetans do, that death lasts for exactly seven weeks, and, on the forty-ninth day, we see a spot of red and a spot of white (blood and sperm), and the sight of it so enrages us that we fly down to battle it, and thus get caught again in the mesh of life: if I believe that — then that is what will transpire.

If I think, as the Moslems do, that I will go to a fructiferous garden, filled with what is certainly, for the desert dweller, paradise (cooling fruit trees, great fountains of water) — then indeed that will be the reward.

If I have this vision of a white-bearded, green-eyed god, presided over by naked fluttering babes — then that will be my experience. If, as part of this, I see my enemies being roasted in a dark and sulphurous place, their flesh bathed in eternal fires, then, that too, will transpire: I will have a chance to experience what it is like to have my enemies in pain, will learn, slowly, horribly, the reality of their suffering.

And if I believe, as I most certainly do, that the end of the road for us is to be catapulted up into hyperspace, surrounded by great, turning, oracular, visionary experiences (experiences beside which the rings of Saturn are but tinsel) — if I believe that we will arrive there with all the sounds and visions and feelings we now have (and many, many more); if I believe this, then as surely as ashes from the fires fly upwards, it will be thus given to me. We will be orbited from our familiar world, deprived of the opportunity to read, or sleep, or go to the movies (or drink martinis, or eat hamburgers). We will be, instead, stuck with our own being and soul and mind for whatever term that we and they have chosen for us.

And in that perfect round we will find ourselves party to a total mobility, a total vision; total recall. We will find — again, as we have no doubt found so many times before — that we have but two exits: the first being to stay there in that waking mind state for years and decades and centuries and eternities, the chattering mind into eternity, *No Exit*. That is the one choice.

There is another, final, temporary choice — a terrible choice that will always be ours to make, if we want: the Choice of Choices. That is: anytime we choose, we can select to be returned to the earth, as baby, with all our eternity memories washed away, the great wonders of space teased out of us — temporarily. Back to earth again, to go through the pain of being ripped from the womb, of being child, of bearing children, of going to war, of getting love, of losing love, of fighting for survival, of being hungry, sleepless, and lonely; of losing body, of losing mind — of going through the life process yet one more time, for the 90th or 900th or 9,000,000th time — the choice we make not because we want life, to be back to this doubtful travail they call living; but because, without it, we would have to continue to live out of the present mind out there in space, with no diversion, no diversions at all — no sleep, no freedom from the us that is us — out there filled with nothing except the nothing that we choose not to choose.

And so, in nanospace, we'll find ourselves thinking: "I can't take this freedom any more ..." Being out there in the space of freedom with only our own mind-self for company can take us close to being devastatingly mad, with the ultimate fear and the ultimate trembling. It is then we choose, yet one more time (get me away from these thoughts!) to return to the Forgetful Non-Eternity of being human.

And so we resign ourselves to the saddest curse of them all: the loss of the glory of free universes. With appropriate reluctance, and fear, and the most divine celestial grief, we agree, for one last time (we think), to make the sad pact with that which lies all about (within and without). To return, yet one more time, to the nightmare pain of being alive, and human.

FEBRUARY 7

The usual daily round in Puerto Jesús is for us to go out to the school in the morning to pick up their list for the store, to buy them whatever they need. Then we (Diego, Nano, me, any other escapists) commute the half-hour to Pochutla. Today, the town square is filled with little tents set up for the public holiday, the feast of St. Pochutla. As I am making my way across it, trying not to get strangled on the tent cords all set at Mexican top-of-head height (directly at my jugular) the man at the children's plastic clothes tent watching me wending my slow way comes up to me and holds out 1,000 pesos — forty cents.

ME: What's this?
HE: For you, take it.
ME: Why?
HE: I want you to have it. It comes from my heart.
ME: Ay — que bueno. Gracias.

For me to explain that I had in my wallet enough money to buy his stock a dozen times over would have been a gratuitous insult. When I tell Nano and Diego about my new-found fortune, they are delighted. They want to set me up in the wheelchair, fix me up with a cup, have me dribble around Pochutla all day to pay for my vacation.

We go from there to the river, driving out onto the river bottom, water halfway up the hubcaps. The two of them get out to fill the *galones* and swim. The divine river — our own personal Ganges.

Several people are playing nearby. One of them — a man of twenty-five or so — drives his horse into the river, then uses its back as a springboard. He dives off into the water, but at one point, the horse shies, and to discipline it, the man pulls on its snaffle, with great force, pulling the beast's nose down into the water, forcing it to breathe water. It wheezes and shakes its great head, while those around the young man howl with laughter. Later, the man's dog — a spotted, mangy cur — pulls away from him as he tries to balance it on the back of the horse, so he throws it to the ground, takes out his pen-knife, pulls the dog's ears out straight, and slashes at them with the knife. The blood runs out — runs down the dog's neck, down its front legs, turns the water near the bluff red. When the dog shakes its head, the blood flies everywhere. Diego and Nano giggle at this drunken Mexican, what he is doing to his two creatures.

I have several choices. One is to report him to the nearest Humane Society. I think, though, that it's some three thousand miles to the north. A second choice is to try to impose my culture on him — direct the man to stop his cruelty at once: to stop being so brutish to his animals. The third, the most obvious, the one I choose — is for me to turn my back on him, to drink another beer, to wonder at the contradictions, the contradictions of my journey, the contradictions of Mexican life, contradictions of life and of culture. An hour ago, a poor stranger in this poor and strange land had offered to me, a gringo, a gift of what well might have been a half-a-day's salary — telling me that it came from his heart. Now, here at the river, an hour later, I am witness to the gratuitous violence of one of his countrymen on his two loyal beasts. While this is going on, my two good and kind young friends — Diego and Nano — are giggling at the drunken bestiality as if it were a comic scene on television.

As I am contemplating these universal contradictions, Robert Kennedy comes over to the car to visit. "My frien'," he calls to me. "My frien', 'ow are you?" In this incarnation, Robert Kennedy has come as a pal of the Animal-Slasher, so I try to ignore him, pretending to be deaf, dumb, and blind. Robert Kennedy is not to be denied. "My frien'," he says, wading over. He is a plump, dark Mixtec, with a startling series of moles growing out of his face and back. He yanks up some riverweed — he calls it "riz de agua" — and offers it to me for whatever it is that ails me. He tells me that if I rub it on my legs, I will be cured. "Here I am on my vacation, in the river of the gods," I think, "and two drunken Mixtecs have chosen to ruin my day." One of them trying to drown, then slash, his poor dumb helpmeets; the other who demands to talk to me in his awful English, running the Lourdes number on me.

Robert Kennedy sits himself down in the waters next to me, leans back, breathes out a hair-curling mix of mescal and molar occlusion, and:

HE: Where you fron, frien'?

ME: Germany.

HE: Wha' part German'?

ME: I'm sorry, I don't speak English.

HE: Wha' part German'?

ME: Baden-Baden.

I concentrate on my beer, the sky, the half-naked Indian ladies, up river, doing their laundry. A lovely day, the Mexican jays off in the trees, a great stand of ebony shading the deepest part of the river, the trunks dark and smooth.

HE: Wha's your name?

ME: Dietrich Bonhöffer.

HE: Wha'?

ME: Dietrich Bonhöffer Zarzuela.

HE: You know wha' my name is, Señor Zarzuela?

ME:

HE: Rober' Kennedy.

Well, that does it. He is such a merry drunk. Offering me some mescal, inviting himself at the same time to one of my ice-cold Coronas, which he opens and dumps in the river so he can fill the bottle with his poison. He then tells me his life's story, in miserable English, even though I tell him that since I had just flown in from the Black Forest, I understand only Spanish.

At one point, on the third drink, he draws up his pants legs to show me his scars, to advise me that he religiously uses the dark green venomous-looking river-weed to cure his misery, and advises me to do the same. "It will make you good again," he tells me, winking and smiling.

HE: Welcome ... How do you say "You're welcome?"

ME: Willkommen.

HE: You're Willkommen to our river. How do you say "río?"

ME: Wasser.

HE: Sí, Willkommen to our Wasser río.

ME: Danke schön. Ich kann in der Bahnhof nicht schlafen.

When I was in college, they put me in a course in which one was to learn German not from study, but from imitation. All our teachers were German; none spoke English. Ultimately, by dint of great study, I pulled a D, which I think they gave me just for staying with the course that was so obviously over my head for a full semester. I was, however, able to salvage two sentences, both of which come in handy at times like this. One of them is "Ich kann in die Nacht nicht schlafen" (I can't sleep at night) and the other is "Ich müss auf der Bahnhof gehen" (I have to go to the train station). Under stress, I often mix up the two of them ("I can't sleep in the train station" a/w "I must go to the night.")

HE: You got another bier?

ME: No, but you can have this ...

and I reach behind me, to the back seat of the car, and pull out a bottle of the awful anis that I had bought the day before, not the wonderful Spanish Anis del Mono that I thought I was getting, but a drear Mexican imitation — Anis del Mico, with the same cross-cut bottle: instead of tasting of paradise and cool winters at the edge of the cool Mediterranean, it's more like bad licorice and shoe-polish. "Here," I tell Robert Kennedy, "take it." And he does — standing up suddenly and plunging off down the river, striding mightily in the shallow waters, fearing, I suspect, that I might change my mind about gifting him with this unexpected treasure, a treasure he might lose if he waits around babbling too much longer.

In the light of cold winter nights in train stations, subsequent to this particular adventure, I have often wondered — and who is to say? — whether the Kennedy clan does indeed have a representative there on the Tonameca; a slightly dumpy man with warts and bad teeth and bad legs who tolerates his dog-abusing relatives, hands out river weed as a cure to any and all strangers, and joins with friendly (and unfriendly) German tourists to his unwanted company and his wretched English. Who am I to claim that he may not be the southernmost contingent of that omnipresent clan?

FEBRUARY 15
We are all who we are not afraid to be.

— M. DUNSEATH

The word in Spanish is "lágrima." A lovely, sad word. It is from the Latin, lacrima *— related to our own "lacrimal." It also has to do with a sadder word of the Spanish language:* lástima. Lástima *incorporates the ultimate, the last, what Faulkner called "the final main."* ¡Qué lastima! *they say. How sad! It has to do with grief and memories and tears. The tearing sadness, the lasting sadness not only of the young, but of all of us.*

— JOURNAL ENTRY

Nina asks me to go into Pochutla and buy the school a bag of mice. "A bag of mice?" I say. "A bag of mice," she says. I wonder about locating La Casa de Los Ratoncitos. "Where do you think I can pick up a bag of mice?" I ask Ginny — Nina's helpmate. "She was trying to say 'a bag of maize,'" Ginny explains. "It's the Swedish accent, you know."

We have all come to love Nina — Emma's temporary replacement at La Escuela Palma Real — because of her straight-from-the-heart, unobstructed, unhidden way. She's a younger, less complex version of Emma. Further, she's a person who has no compunction about unveiling her lovely self to the jape eyes of the men in and around the school or on the river — lovely Nina baring her soul and her all to the hearts around her. Her time in the river is another part of her sweet nakedness.

Lest I paint a picture of a young lady who is a bit too nice, or mice — let me tell you that at one point she reacted even as I would have to María, the two year old half-wit. María, usually quiet as can be, starts to cry, and then, with the perfect idiocy which is the hallmark of the two year olds of the world, cries, and cries some more, and then decides to cry some more, and then, as each of us tries to stop her, cries some more, and then, as we are throwing up our hands in disgust, she surprises us by crying some more. Finally Nina picks her up, and says, in perfect English, spoken, very loudly, approximately one half inch from Maria's red face: "Goddamn it, María, I don't even know what the hell you want!" And María, perhaps hearing the message she had been seeking for the first time, shuts the hell up, and plays sweetly and winningly at the edge of the river for the rest of the afternoon. We thought later the onset of the tears came from her distress at being set down by Nina when she, the naïad of Tonameca, went off to play in the waters. Perhaps that was it, for who would not bawl, and bawl endlessly, in being placed a distance apart from the lovely goddess of the deep.

FEBRUARY 20

I dreamed I was in the land of the white people. Their skin is white, their hearts are white, and they are simple and sincere. It is a very beautiful country. I think I shall go there.

— RAMAKRISHNA

Later, the soft night, and the Southern Cross weighing heavily in the air — and The Big Itch. I have been on the road too long. I lie awake too much of the night, thinking of my sweet home. I long for a hot shower (a hot shower!) and the morning mail call. I long to speak on the telephone again. I long to buy a leg of lamb, and roast it in the oven, a huge hank of lamb filled to overflowing with garlic, the corpse lavished with rosemary and lemon juice.

I long to wake up shivering in a room filled with an early morning mist. I long for a neighborhood with no drunken taxi-drivers blathering outside all night, no busses banging loudly down the street. I long for a yard free of porkers snorkling about my eaves. I crave a neighborhood free of donkeys who sneak up to my bedroom window, pushing me out of my early morning bed with their raucous braying.

I long to be able to sleep until seven or so without the neighbor rooster rattling my nerves. I long to go to the post office and find a letter that was postmarked earlier in the week, rather than earlier in the year. I long to go to the Safeway and see the meat waiting wrapped for me, not to have to fight off huge clouds of flies in the process. I long to buy fresh yellow crook-necked squash: to boil it and then mush it up with minced onions and butter, serve it with freshly ground pepper and chopped fresh basil.

I long to turn on the tap and get something out of it besides gurgles, spiders and diarrhea. I long to have the toilet work. I want to rinse face and hands and body in the morning with something more than three-and-a-half teaspoons of lukewarm water. I long to brush my teeth in something besides yesterday's stale beer. I long to get in my car without having to read the word "*puto*" writ large, in dust, on the back bumper.

I long to wake up and not be sweating. I long to sit in a café and not have to compete with the offal of last year's dead fish. I long to drink a glass of cold milk again. I long to come home and know the power will be on. I long to see a wasteful (and beautiful) grass lawn. I long to go out in the sun and not be slapped down to earth by the sheer force of the heat.

I long to spend one night without waking up to find the beaks of 1,000 mosquitoes penetrating ankles and wrists with their itchy peck. I long to leave some food in the kitchen and not wake up and hear a dozen feral cats fighting with each other over it. I long to see a dog that is not dying of scurvy or dysmenorrhea or fleabitus. I long to go home again.

As I lie in my bed, I can hear a pig going mad down the street — shrieking and howling in its dismal state of piggery. I listen to its cry of death. Through the bars of the window, I can see the Southern Cross — suspended in the sky, waiting, waiting, the Southern Cross waiting. I lie there thinking such thoughts that we collect in the corpus callosum on nights like this, nights when the mysterious Kissy-Kissy bird calls. "Smack-smack-smack" it goes, somewhere outside the window, in the ceiling, inside the walls, in rank parody of Hollywood Lips. "What can it mean?" I wonder. A secret night creature that stays about and — at odd intervals — perhaps when thoughts are drifting too far, makes the kissy-kissy noise to remind me of myself, my home, and love; to remind me of the love that I do not have, to remind me of the love that I want but that I do not have. To remind me of the love I want and cannot, perhaps will never, ever have; that perfect kissy-kissy love out of the scenes of our childhood. The wet Saturday afternoons of our Hollywood childhood, in the Fairfax Theatre, heavy with popcorn and jujubes; as always, the gun-toting hero, and the black-lace lady, fallen into each other's arms — and they turn kissy-kissy while we juveniles, restless, watch them involved in worlds so strange, so out of our ken; them and their twenty-foot heads, with great raptor beaks, feeding at each other with lip-smacking pleasure. Two giants, with giant crossed eyes, in lip osculation, jaws moving, feeding on each other — and we, the product of all this smoochy passion, wanting to get back to the shooting, horses barrelling across the desert, adventure of another sort.

For us on these Saturday afternoons in the hot black interior of the Fairfax: we seek to go beyond the unwanted mystery of the wayward buss. The mysterious birds, alighting in the trees around us — the mysterious dank dark-blooming Kissy-Kissy bird that appears so suddenly out of nowhere, cries out so, and then — just as suddenly — disappears. That is why I must leave my beloved Puerto Jesús. For awhile — for awhile.

FEBRUARY 28

God alone can worship god.

— VIVEKANANDA

I tell Nano that I will be going home shortly and that if he is wise, he should put as much distance between himself and any and all gringos. If one ever approaches him to work — I tell him — he should, slowly and carefully, say, "*no spika da inglish*" and run as far away as quickly as he can.

"Don't have anything to do with us," I say. "Why do you want to work for me anyway?"

"Because you have all the money," he says.

"That is such a lousy excuse. No vale la pena (it's not worth the pain)," I say.[2]

The Pox of Plutocracy. We invade this land of tranquil people and we leave behind a trail of frustration and angst. We are the invading army, as much as the Spaniards of five hundred years past. There should be barriers to keep us out.

The U.S. erects metal fences, hires 10,000 Customs and Immigration people just to keep the Mexicans south of the border — and it's all ass-backwards. These fences should be turned round the other way. Any Americans seeking to enter Mexico should be given deep (and painful) examinations, with seven-day visas, no extensions, forced to ante up a $25,000 bond swearing that we will not inflict our plague of needs, hungers, angers, hurts and wants on these gentle and good people. We should be required to pledge understanding that our psychic and emotional violence will not be tolerated south of the Rio Grande, that any American coming here and foisting off his brutalism on the innocents of this land will make him

---

2. Six months after this conversation, I receive this letter. The envelope is filled with pictures of watches, all cut from ads in the *New Yorker* that I left behind.

Hello, C. A. Amantea [he says]. How are you in your home? Things here are a little good and a little bad because I am sick and all the money is all used up and things are very expensive. We are becoming very sad because the price of everything is going up and Mama is sick and I haven't been able to find work. Cashing the check you sent was easy because one of my friends who works in the bank helped me. The tape recorder you gave me has given me many problems because many people are envious of me and they say that I robbed it from you and for that reason please write a paper that says that you gave it to me because there is a complaint filed against me. Another friend of mine, a policeman, will help me and another thing, because my mother is sick and I am sick and my money is all used up and I can't buy the roof for my house, it costs 45,000 pesos, I want the plastic containers that you bought to go with us to the river and thank you very much for this gift that helps me. Diego is very sad because you are a good friend of his and now the river is very sad it is drying up and the lake is drying up and the women are very sad because the river is drying up and now they have no place to do their wash. The women are crying and they know you as the Gringo Who Washes At The River and the drunkards drink mescal with water and the cows and the burros and the horses. That is all and I want a watch, thank you very much, signed,

Nano

subject to fines and immediate banishment north of the border.

The Great White Plague, carrying with it all our desires, our malaise of our form of love, our fantasy of "civilization." We bring it along with us like a curse, to ruin the innocents of this dry and dusty and wounded earth.

MARCH 1

The long day wanes: the slow moon climbs: the deep
Moans round with many voices. Come my friends,
'Tis not too late to seek a newer world.
Push off, and sitting well in order smite
The sounding furrows; for my purpose holds
To sail beyond the sunset, and the baths
Of all the western stars, until I die.
It may be that the gulfs will wash us down:
It may be we shall touch the Happy Isles.

— "ULYSSES"
ALFRED, LORD TENNYSON

I am to leave the day Emma reappears from Sweden. And it will not be a moment too soon. The school is a shambles. The kitchen folk are being accused of trying to poison the staff and, perhaps as a result, the meals are getting worse and worse. Franz the mad acid-dropping Austrian is looming about, trying to steal away what he thinks of as *his* three children who, he claims, are being poisoned by the staff with overdoses of vitamins. School volunteers know some of the men at the nearby Mexican Naval operation, and they've called on them for help, so a contingent of the Mexican Navy is lurking about, trying to prevent any kidnapings. The whole comic opera could be called *The Abduction from La Escuela.*

The women volunteers are saying that stoned hippies have been sneaking onto the campus at night to help themselves to whatever may be lying about. One of the female volunteers reports that she awakes to find a man hovering over, shining a flashlight in her eyes. No one knows if it is Franz or some bearded stranger from the beach. Even the children have started going feral. The older boys — ranging in age from seven to eleven — have formed a wild marauding band, terrorizing all, pulling down clothes-lines, turning mad and hungry, eating the trees. Diego and Antonio and Lalo, the employees who are supposed to clean up the grounds, have gone on strike because Babbette (who Emma left in charge of all financial matters) refuses to pay them, saying that Emma didn't leave enough money behind. They swear they will not work a lick until they are paid.

Emma is the angel who will arrive in the nick of time and save us all from these forces of entropy. When she is here, there are never any problems; or, if there are, she dispatches them with simple Zen-like gestures and words. It was thought that Babbette was going to be the surrogate Emma, but it hasn't worked. I go out to the school to make a last-minute appeal for the grounds crew. When I get out there, I find Babbette dancing in the kitchen. The radio is turned up, with its half-speaker (the other half has been eaten by roaches and geckoes), blaring away with "Cielito Lindo."

I ask Juana the head cook when Emma will return.

"Está aquí ya." (She's already here.)

"¿Adónde?" (Where? I ask, looking around).

"Cerca." (Nearby).

Juana has a lovely round Zapotec face. She walks barefooted, and when she talks to me, she rears back her head. Despite being only five feet tall, it makes her appear regal and queen-like as she looks up at me.

"¿Como sabes?" I ask. (How do you know?)

"Sé." (I know).

"¿Está al aeropuerto?" (Is she at the airport?)

"Está cerca." (She's near).

And no matter how I push and pry, she will tell me no more; only that Emma is nearby, and will be here "ahorita."

We fall silent, Juana and I and the kitchen help, watching Babbette dance her dance. She is zonked out of her gourd on some special herb that is copiously grown (and smoked) in this area. She wears the briefest of all veils wrapped about her rotund old body, and is dancing to a music coming distorted and loud out of the ruined soundbox. In her yellow teeth she carries a great wilted flower, a flower the exact color of her large, vague, gentle eyes. As she moves hips and hands, the forget-me-not petals begin to drop off, one by one. The kitchen-girls are bubbling up with laughter, watching the now passé voice of authority dancing about so gently, so harmlessly.

I essay to ask Babbette if she knows the whereabouts of Emma, who is, apparently, lost somewhere there in hyper-space — but there is no way my voice will penetrate that envelope of dreams about our slow-dancing Babbette. She has been transformed into a half-mad Ophelia of the jungle, her bare feet ranging over the earthen floor, eyes lost somewhere in the vicinity of the moons of Jupiter.

We are the geezers of the school, Babbette and I. No one is older — perhaps no-one in all of Puerto Jesús, perhaps in all the known universe. We were both born before the last war of the worlds. We are historical artifacts. Our story could only be told in Babbette's slow and ancient dance. We are out of the mirror of archeology, she and I: the ruins of past and ancient settlers. We are direct descendants of the gods with great carved features, eyes as large and old as the monoliths from the Golden Isles. Like them, we once emerged from the dark moraine at the site of huge-footed beasts who moved among the fronds. We are thus of the pale, sent by the wild-faced gods, who we imitate and worship as carved stone of centuries past. We were created by vagabond artisans who come here looking for the God of the Sun. They set up camp, made a place of worship, a ceremonial center, a resting place for the blind and crippled spawn of the earth. Then, just as mysteriously, they disappeared, leaving behind nothing but rags and ruins and the dark, foot-beaten earth. They move on to another land, far from the river of the sun, at which time we are forced to try to be the gods themselves.

"I want my skin to be as dark and fine as your own," I once told Nano, putting my arm against his dark, fine arm. "Hablas español tan bueno," he says. You speak Spanish so well. "When I first worked for you," he told me, "I couldn't understand anything you said. Now, I understand it all." We speak with tongues of the gods, and soon, the words flow more easily. But, in the final main, it can be nothing but a rich fantasy. Babbette's dance is perhaps divine — but it will never be the dance of the gods. The words of this *colonía* will never be my words. We'll use their vocabulary, their motions, their intonations — but this divinity is not born to our tongues, nor our bodies. We try to be at one with the divinities, try to be their *Doppelgängers*. But we must fail. Only the gods can worship the gods.

MARCH 7

I am not suggesting there are dragons in central Borneo, because their physical existence is unimportant ... [Still], it would have been grossly arrogant of me to disregard those beliefs or to trivialize the people's fears. What did I know anyway? I had been in the area two days; these people had lived there for generations. I soon came to realize how foolish it was for me to try to prove or disprove the existence of the dragon ... And, anyway, I liked the idea of giant dragons copulating for missionary pilots. And if I had to walk miles out of my way to avoid being eaten by a dragon, so much the better. I marked the appropriate spot on my map with an X and penciled a notation in the margin: "Caution: valley closed — dragon cave ahead."

— *STRANGER IN THE FOREST*

SHE: What was the first thing you did when you got back?
ME: I ate supper.

SHE: What did you eat?

ME: Butter.

SHE: And? ...

ME: That's it. Butter.

SHE: Nothing else?

ME: Well, I *did* put a little salt and parsley on it.

SHE: You ate butter?

ME: A whole stick of it. I peeled the foil off, sprinkled parsley and salt on it, and took my knife and fork and cut it into squares — and chomped down on it. It was delicious.

SHE: ¡ !

ME: They just don't have butter in Southern Mexico. I thought about it all the time I was there.

Of course, there are other ways to celebrate a return home. Like opening the mail. Is there a feeling more wonderful than pulling open the cardboard box jammed to overflowing — months of mail, waiting for you to tear into it? Letters, bills, flyers, the works. I divide it in three parts. The personal letters are first, to be opened, to be sure that all is well out there, that a friend or family isn't sad or sick or dying or dead. Handwritten letters which will be read, then lingered over later.

Then come the bills and junk mail. The junk mail! What a pleasure to dump it out all at once. The luxury of receiving mail; the extra luxury of dumping it out without even bothering to look at it, letters I might well have savored so far to the south. Especially the ones that look like checks (you can just see part of it there at the top of the window, barely read the words "five thousand dollars ..." and then you open it up and it says "You may have won five thousand dollars ..." But you haven't.)

And, then, last, the business stuff. By now it's two a.m. — dawn, Puerto Jesús time. The old eyes are beginning to dance the tango. I yawn, tears of animal fatigue in my eyes. I am now worth $56,072,147.08, says the statement from Dean Witter.

"Your Active Assets Money Market Funds Plus Cash: $87.17." That $87.17 has been around for quite some time now.

Then, just below:

Your Portfolio Market Value: $56,072,147.08.

❧ ❧ ❧

It's a long story, how I made all that money. I won't bore you with it. Or should I? I don't even want to think about those years of $$$ obsession that led to this. Suffice it to say that tonight, after my long journey, I have at last, and not a moment too soon, come into the fortune I have deserved after all these many years of hard and grueling work. It couldn't have happened to a better and more deserving fellow.

I lay abed for awhile thinking about me and my life and the New Fortune. The journey is over. And no matter how weary I am, I can't sleep, not for a moment, thinking about all that money — where it came from; how to enjoy it thoroughly. I have been waiting thirty years for this, right? Or maybe a lifetime.

"It will take a lot of work to spend that much money," I tell myself. How much is it, anyway? If you take fifty-six million bones, and stretch them out end to end, you'd have a mess. Clogging up the streets, gumming up the sewers and the freeways. My new-found fortune is already making me very tired at the same time that it's keeping me awake.

❧ ❧ ❧

It's probably Rich's fault, if we can blame anyone. My ex-friend Rich was a promoter; no — a promoter squared. Once upon a time he invented this scheme to make a million dollars. "I have this idea for making a million dollars," he told me. "What we do is apply to the government for a whole stack of television stations," he said. This was back in 1978, when we were all more innocent. It was summer, at the beach, and we had drunk several of my beers. "We'll sell the idea of building these stations to the public, in a public offering. We'll call it 'Low Power Technology.' It'll be the nuts."

Well, I'm a hard man to convince, so it took me at least five minutes to figure out a way to borrow the necessary money to finance this scheme. And we did it just like he said. We applied to the government for a boat-load of television stations. Then we went with these applications to Denver, to the original dog-and-cat market. We got the Securities and Exchange Commission to give us permission to take these applications public. We issued 100,000,000 shares of stock, or was it 1,000,000,000,000? Anyway, it was enough to float the Queen Mary, enough paper to last us two lifetimes. It was the nuts!

I was appointed Chairman of the Board. Rich was the President. Another friend of ours (he put up money too — Rich didn't have any assets) became Secretary, even though he couldn't spell. The lawyers handled all the spelling, anyway. They did all that, and something called the "red herring." That was the prospectus issued for all the would-be stockholders.

Rich was right. That turkey *flew*. Each of us got paid in stock. The three of us shared almost twenty million shares. It was divine proof of the Law of Adam Smith (The Younger). He said that the way to make a fortune in America is not to buy or sell stock on the open market but to create it out of whole cloth.

In the first heady days after going public, the stock went from ten cents to eighteen cents a share. Between the three of us, we were worth over $4,000,000. My portfolio became so valuable I figured I should keep it someplace instead of the ratty Kamchatka Vodka cardboard box on the floor behind the desk. I sent the shares off to Dean Witter, had them put them in my account, the one that usually showed nothing more than a few Old Blue Chips that had been given me years ago by Deargrandmother. My bucket-shop Customer's Man couldn't figure it out. Here I was, the Blue Chip Kid, and one day I send him six million shares of this *hokey* penny stock.

"What's this shit?" he says. Customer's Man is very direct.

"It's my next fortune," I tell him.

"I can't believe it," he says. "What the hell is it?"

"You'll see," I tell him. "You might think of picking up some yourself. It opened at ten cents, and now, as you can see, it's almost doubled in value."

"We'd better sell," he says. "At once."

"Nonsense," I tell him. "You should climb on board. Rich says it's going to the sky."

"Who is this Rich?"

"Trust me. He's an old friend of mine. From Texas."

"What part of Texas?"

"Trust me. It's going through the ceiling."

"Do you want to sell any of it?"

"I'm not supposed to. How much could I get for it today?"

"Oh. You're right. You can't. Sorry. It's what they call 'restricted stock.' "

"I can't sell even a little bit of it?"

"They won't let you do squat with it."

"Really?"

"Except paper your walls with it."

"Stop it."

"Here, on the back: it says you can sell in 1992."

"That's a long time from now."

"June 16, 1992."

"That's a very long time from now. Are you sure you don't want to buy a bit for your own account?"

"Listen, do you know how much of this crap is floating around?"

"I think I don't want to know. What should I do?"

"You might consider getting a job." Customer's Man always did have a droll sense of humor.

❧ ❧ ❧

Well, you already know about gods and fate and fleeting fortunes, right? I don't have to tell you the whole sordid story, do I? Rich was a genius at finding the assets to get LoPo (its official ticker name) off and flying. He was a genius at getting low price stock gurus in Colorado fighting with each other to buy into this geckoberry. He had a dream, and who's to say if his dream was any more terrible or wonderful than that of the Golden Fleece, or Martin Luther's vision in the outhouse, or Freud's royal road to the unconscious.

Rich had the ability to bring us chickens deep into the chicken-hut for our necessary feathering. He was so good that the first thing you reached for was not the gun but the checkbook. He had some other talents too. He had tastes that could best be called regal. Thus, he was an all-out champion not only at garnering money, but in spending it. How in hell he got rid of almost three million dollars in less than fourteen months beat the hell out of all of us who were supposed to be part of the operation. It was no less than spectacular. "What the hell are you doing?" I asked him once, "investing in porkbellies?" "Not a bad idea," he said, after thinking a moment.

"The start-up costs are unbelievable," he told me, early on, after LoPo had become the Darling of the Denver Exchange. "I had to hire a lot more employees just to process the FCC applications," he said.

"Revenues aren't quite living up to our projections," he said, somewhat later. "We might have to cut back on expenses."

"Do whatever you think is right," I said.

"We might even have to cut back on your salary as Chairman of the Board," he said.

"Oh..." I said. "Do whatever you think is..."

"Have you heard of Chapter 11?" his attorney said, not long afterwards.

"It's my favorite chapter in *The Money Game*," I said. He didn't laugh.

"Does that mean...?" I asked.

"You got it," he said. He was a man of few words, just like Customer's Man.

"How did you take it when they told you about the bankruptcy?" my friends wanted to know, later.

"No prob," I said, "I heard about it on a Tuesday. That night, I slept like a baby."

"Really?" they said, "Like a baby?"

"Right." I said, "Every hour on the hour I woke up and cried."

"Do you have a quote on it?" I ask Customer's Man, not long after.

"Are we grasping...?" he says.

"... at the moon," I say. "What's the quote?"

"Do you want one from Shakespeare or Milton?" Customer's Man and I went to college together. He flunked the English courses, I flunked the math.

"This is not a time to be funny," I say. "This is a time that tries men's souls."

"Let me see what I can pull up the screen." He sighs. "There seems to be a problem with the computer," he says.

"What sort of problem?" I ask, pulling at the frayed cuff of my Brooks Brothers shirt, the old one. The oldest one.

"The computer gives a figure for *Ask*. It's a half a cent."

"One-half a cent?" I say. "That means I can sell for a half-a-penny a share?" It's better than going to work.

"No," Customer's Man says. "What you want is something we call *Bid*." It appears that he's still being arrogant about passing Math 25 while I merely excelled at Browning.

"What's the *Bid*," I ask, my voice a bit softer now.

"There seems to be a problem with the computer." When he calls for a bid on LoPo, the computer lifts its shoulders, rolls its eyes, and says *SYSTEM MALFUNCTION*. "We have a phrase for it in the trade," he says.

"What's that?" I ask.

"It's called 'Falling out of bed,' " he says. Although we are not by nature religious — neither of us — at this moment, I believe, we both fall out of bed onto our knees, to say a silent prayer. Praying for the ghost of LoPo, and, as well, sending brief notice to the Gods of the Marketplace, the Divine Force of Chance and Fortune, telling them we would appreciate any help they care to send our way.

❧ ❧ ❧

I didn't have the heart to ask Dean Witter to send back the 6,596,712 shares of LoPo. I didn't want to bother them. They had troubles enough of their own, what with being bought up by Sears, becoming what the brokers call "Socks 'n' Stocks." Besides, what was I going to do with all those certificates? And don't tell me I could paper my walls with them. Sometimes those old wheezes just aren't very funny. Besides, I wasn't interested in looking at them anymore, if you want to know the truth. Let Dean Witter paper *their* bloody walls with them. They have more experience in such things. And probably more wall space.

What I did mostly was to try to be done with it. There were a few 3 A.M. wake-up calls, for the next year or so, where I cooked Rich over slow and hot and painful fires. But, on the whole, I think I took it very well. I put him and the Denver Stock Exchange and Going Public and what I was now calling Low Pooh out of my brain, even though the Dean Witter statement kept coming in to remind me of its existence. There it was, right below General Foods and General Motors and General Dynamics and General Despair, followed by our old friend *NO BID*. It stayed there long after I sold off all the Generals to pay a few lawyer's bills, the ones paid out trying to recoup something — anything at all — from those heady days in Denver.

❧ ❧ ❧

And that's where it stood until I arrived home from Puerto Jesús and opened the mail. Letters from old friends, letters from old forgotten unfriends and old unforgotten friends. Letters from The Penguin Conservancy and Tomorrow's Whales Today and Save The Naders. Statements from the electric company and the telephone company and the company company and my friendly S&L, teetering on the edge. And Dean Witter. A formal statement from Mr. Dean Witter, of stock and bond fame. A definitive statement.

Name (mine), address (mine), account executive (ours) credits to the account (none) charges against the account (none) the closing account balances are, the closing account balances are...*the closing account balances are...*

It takes a while for these things to sink in, n'est-çe-pas? They say things, and you don't even listen. You are so used to not listening that you don't even listen anymore. "Dad, I'm going to marry my roommate," your youngest says. You're in there watching Dan Rather, and you didn't even know that he had a roommate, and even worse, you don't know if it was a boy or a girl. "I can't take this anymore," your companion-for-life says. You're muddling through the quotes for the Jacksonville (Fla.) Thruway District 2222 A.D. Sinking Fund 8-1/2% Debentures, and your companion-for-life is practically out the door, going off — forever — in your car. "They've declared war," the man on television says. You're about to step in the shower, a hot shower, your first for the day, and they decide at that very moment to declare World War III, *glasnost* or no *glasnost*. Do you go ahead and shower? Is it time to fall to your knees yet again?

"You're now worth fifty-six million dollars," says Mr. Witter. "That crazy goddamn Rich," you say. "He always told me that he would pull this dog out of the fire. I *knew* he was a genius. Why in the hell was I so hard on him?

❧ ❧ ❧

"Has he really done it?" I say early the next morning to Customer's Man. It's not that I was eager, but I knew he got in at 6 A.M., and I was on the horn by 6:02.

"Last time I heard, you were in Oaxaca doing naughty things on the beach." he says, being quite chummy — too chummy for me at such an ungodly hour.

"This is no time for idle chit-chat," I tell him. "My fortune's at stake. What's the quote on LoPo?"

"*Jesus Christ*," he says. "I'll get right back to you," he says.

❧ ❧ ❧

Fifty-six million tusheronies burning a hole in my pocket. "What am I going to do with it all?" I ask myself. "If it's for real," I say to myself. *If it's for real.*

Your former ne'er-do-well Brooks Brothers hippie transcendentalist flake capitalist, long-time Master of the Money-Lose, now transformed into a gentleman of substantial means. Butter wouldn't melt in my mouth.

It's morning. It's nice outside. It's always nice in the morning in this area in mid-March. In fact, mid-March is probably the best time to be home. (Will the neighbors stop being so piggy to me, for a change?) The sun has made a particularly nice entrance this morning — coming up over the dark grey-green Fortuna Mountains to the east. There's a wisp of cloud, shaped like a finger, or maybe like a fish, or possibly a silver platter, loaded with silver. It's floating over there in the morning Turquoise Blue sky. "What a nice time to be alive," I tell myself. Will they stop sending their dogs over to relieve themselves on my lawn? How will they treat me when they discover that they are dealing with a man of means?

Someone on the radio is playing the *Dances from Terpsichore*, the version put out thirty years ago by Deutsche Grammaphone — the one with the funny musicians playing flüglehorns and tubas, dancing around like they were crazy. And rich. "What the hell am I going to do with all those *clams*?" I wonder.

I fall to thinking of me a few days before, back when I had been ... well ... not quite so flush. I think of the Tonameca River, me and Nano and Diego, floating, belly-down in the river, rising up to squirt water at each other, eyeing the ladies doing their wash down river. "Maybe I'll get a four-wheeler — so we won't have to panic everytime we try to back up out of the river, after our swim," I think.

And it would be nice for the Escuela Palma Real to have a few real buildings, wouldn't it? Not those dorky palm huts anymore. A couple of white-washed, nicely decorated buildings with air conditioning, real tile-work — a place where the kids could be comfortable, not sweating all the time, flies always bothering their eyes.

Professional teachers, and physical therapists, too. "We'll bring in some of the best. We'll get them nice places to stay, with a real sleeping area," I think. Not those hammocks hung on fall-down poles, open to the mosquitoes and all the weirdos from the beach. There'll be fans, and window-screens — a proper eating place, too — not the heap next to the school garbage dump, where you have to hold your nose while you're trying to eat your beans.

We'll get them a place to eat, on the bluff, near the port. They'll be able to see the ocean. And we'll get them some good food, too. We'll set up a trust fund so they can have something besides old chicken — how well I remember those chicken-feet in my stew — something more interesting than bones and beans and potatoes.

Therapists and nurses for the kids. "We'll find the star therapists of Mexico," I'll tell Emma. "We'll fly you to Mexico City, and you can hire the best in the Spanish-speaking world." They'll love it at the new Escuela, what with the exercise rooms, the modern equipment, hot pools with warm, filtered, clean, sparkling water — water you can bathe in, and drink, feel safe with. "Not the mud you had to use in the past," I'll tell her.

Doctors? Hellfire — we'll hire a dozen doctors, if that's what she wants. "There'll be applications from all over the world, now that you've got the facilities," I'll tell her. It'll be the most famous rehabilitation center in this part of the world. We'll make it a learning center for the entire Third World. It will be *the* place to go to learn about rehabilitation for kids. "They'll be begging to get in, to work with the patients," I'll tell her. "The kids will be the teachers. Just like now. It'll be a learning center for all of Mexico, and Central and South America ... " No more dust, the geese making such a racket, dogs peeing in the beds, chickens flying up on the dining-room tables.

"You're not forgetting you?" they'll ask. The new 4x4, which we'll bring down on the boat. The boat won't be too show-off, but it'll be nice. Wood paneling, and showers. Hot showers right there in Puerto Jesús. A couple of decks. Twin screws. Stabilizers. We'll use it to transport all the doctors and nurses and therapists and supplies from up north. That's what it'll be for — to bring down all the things we need for the school; it won't be just for us.

Nano will love it. Dressed up in his white uniform, with his new cap, and the gold braid. "Dáme cerveza," I'll call from my bed next to the chartroom, calling him up on the speaking tube. "Get me a beer." "Sí, ¡ya!" he'll call back, and in an instant, he'll be there, his Mayan eyes merry, him in his snappy white uniform, the gold braid on his cap, the uniform in such sharp contrast to his lovely dark face, his eyes so very merry. In his hands, his dark hands, he'll be carrying the silver tray, with the silver mug, filled to the brim with ice cold beer. "No hay cerveza," he'll say. There's no beer, he'll say. "You'll have to drink this," he'll say. And he'll hand me a big silver mug of ice cold Corona, and then he'll be off, to climb into the cat's cradle, so he can hang out there, looking at the

Puerto Jesús harbor, all around us — Nano hanging there, he and the boat and all of us moving back and forth in the swells. He will feel so merry as he looks out at Puerto Jesús, his former home, the little shack on the hill where he grew up, the one with the pigs and the dogs running through all the time. There he'll be, rolling with the great warm blue-green waters, there at the omphaloskepsis of the earth, the vortex at Puerto Jesús, with its dark and lovely people, and its grackles, and the mysterious Kissy-Kissy bird, the strange phoenix, the one that comes so strangely in the night to make the sounds out of the night, the creature that might well be responsible for all this ...

❧ ❧ ❧

"Computer," says Customer's Man.

"Computer?" I say.

"Yeah, computer," he says. "It was something wrong with the computer."

I can hear people yelling and talking behind him, telephones ringing, people making money, people losing money, life going on, like it always does. Life going on.

"Goddamn computer," I say.

"Yeah," he says.

I'll say this for him — he went to bat for me. He took it all the way to the top, right up to Mr. Dean or Mr. Witter or perhaps even Mr. Roebuck, if Mr. Roebuck still exists; if he ever existed. If any of us ever existed.

They all said the same thing. They always say the same thing. Despite the fact that I am an old and faithful customer who kept a small, neat account that never attracted flies, didn't bother them too much — despite that, they still have the gall to do these heart-robbing things with their goddamn computers.

"Sorry," he says. "I really tried." He sounds sorry, too. I mean, beyond the commissions and all.

"I couldn't ...?" I ask.

"No..." he says.

"Not even..." I have several old blank Dean Witter checks — numbered 103, 104, 105, etc., at the back of the drawer, next to the old passports and the gnarled spiders.

"I wouldn't ... you'd better not ..." he says.

"Ah ..." I say. "Qué lastima."

"What did you say?" he says.

"Nothing," I say. "I'll talk to you later. Qué lástima." I say.

[1989]

THE BLOB THAT ATE OAXACA

NOVEMBER 29 [SANTA ROSA, TEXAS]

"You are old, Father William," the young man said,
"And your hair has become very white;
And yet you incessantly stand on your head —
Do you think, at your age, it is right?"

"In my youth," Father William replied to his son,
"I feared it might injure the brain;
But now that I'm perfectly sure I have none,
Why, I do it again and again."

— *ALICE IN WONDERLAND*

Ernest has created yet another scheme for being fabulously wealthy. He is going to syndicate something called "Geri-Gyms." These are places where we will send the old geezers (like ourselves) when time has converted our bones to jelly — when age has frozen our juices and our smiles.

In the Geri-Gyms, we'll be floated about the room attached to helium balloons. Those of us unable to move on our own because of stroke, varicose veins, heart attack, arthritis or sheer fatigue at longevity will, in Ernest's Gym, be raised above the floor on warm floaty cushions. These pillows will bounce about from here to there, to the walls and ceilings and back again. A hundred gummers, coasting about in this vast chamber, rolling off the skylights, brushing against walls, ramming gently into each other, giggling, bounced about on air currents, a lighter-than-air gas for all who had thought that life had no more thrills, nor secrets.

"I'm writing a chapter in my book about Geri-Gyms," Ernest tells me. He's always talking about the book he is writing, and the various chapters the book. "I'm putting one in about 'Om-ming in the Shower,'" he'll say. Or: "I'm writing a book about Pol Pot, President Bush, and the deBeer's diamond cartel." We'll be driving up this hilly road, outside Cruz Blanco, and he'll say, "I'm thinking about a chapter on W. Y. Evans-Wentz. (Pause). You know who Evans-Wentz is, don't you? (Pause). He wrote *The Tibetan Book of the Dead*. He lived in the next valley over from us. One time he asked me to find a young lady to give him a massage. (Silence. General disbelief.) So I did it. But I guess he was too old by then to enjoy it. (Pause). He wanted to buy a mountain. He had a vision when he was climbing a mountain in East County, so he decided to buy it, and wanted me to help him. (Pause. Disbelief. Despair.) I'm going to get that into the book, too."

I often wonder who Ernest takes me for. He thinks it's a big deal to be writing a book. I am sure that when he stops talking about it and actually tries it, he'll find out it's more like being trepanned. I want to tell him about this novel I've been writing but he won't give me a chance. He'd like the plot-line — even though I've grown to loathe it. The novel, *For Love of Torquemada*, is set in an unnamed Central American country, in throes of revolution, with an ersatz-Buddha federal policeman named El Jefe who befriends this puddin'-headed ninny named Ignacio.

It's a bit of a sore subject with me right now, if you want to know the truth. And although I'm thoroughly sick of it, it's not about to stop writing itself. I've been dragging this monkey around with me for over five years now. Writing, and rewriting, and rewriting (and rewriting) *Torquemada*. The sequence gets pulled from the box in my brain and bears an uncanny resemblance to dental floss, continuously getting knotted up in itself, breaking off at all the wrong places, driving me to distraction at 3 A.M. It's the original alcoholic grandfather in the attic, barging around, screaming, barfing out the window. The characters won't sit still long enough to jell: all they want to do is talk. I've had a belly-full of their talk.

I almost confess the whole dreadful stool to Ernest right then and there. Like a night of heavy drink or psychoactive drugs, being on the road with someone will lead a man to wild confession. However I decide against it in the nick of time. I've been around Ernest long enough to know what will come of it. First he'll be hurt that I am actually doing something that he's been talking about doing for twenty years or so. He'll start right in abusing me. He'll ask me to explain the plot-line to him in ugly detail. He'll ask me all sorts of embarrassing questions about the characters. He'll ask me who I think I am, involved in such a dumb project — and what I think it is going to do for my karma. Although Ernest pretends to be under the spell of a Master by the name of Vivekananda, chanting love and peace for all mankind, once you get on his turf the son-of-a-bitch turns into a regular dog. I'm having problems enough with the plot-line (and sub-plot, structure, sub-structure) without getting him in there to gum it up. If he thinks I am going to let him in on this Laocoön, he has another think coming.

❧ ❧ ❧

The day after I tried to murder myself, I go to visit El Jefe. I wear a black turtle-neck sweater that I find in the bottom of my bag. It has long sleeves that come all the way down past my wrists. It is very hot.

El Jefe is sitting, as usual, rocking back and forth. Today, he is drinking a reddish alcoholic brew called "Sangre." He offers me a glass. He sips it, then sits, blowing bubbles with his saliva, thick bubbles popping from his lips. He blows one or two spit bubbles, then sucks them in, then rolls the saliva about on his lips. "Lickety-spit," I think. I turn my chair half-away, looking out at the cathedral, with its dusty louvres, the angel atop the spire, with the thin, once-shiny trumpet that's bent and twisted, so the bell of it points at the ground.

"I read once that we all have someone inside of us," El Jefe says.

"Someone inside of us?" I think. "It's a madhouse around here," I think.

"Right. A person who is, well, like us, and..."

"...And not like us." I say. It's not just that it's a madhouse. It's that we're so culturally and emotionally deprived here in El Vapor that when somebody says something interesting, we start thinking that we (or they) are mad.

I pick at the end of the surgical thread underneath my sleeve, rub it back and forth, twisting the coarse hardness of it. From the mountains comes the rattling of guns, the low "thunk" of mortars.

"It's like Señor Pedo," he says.

"Yeah," I say.

Señor Pedo. He's a joke in the village. "Pedo" means "fart," so there's this old man they call "Mister Fart." He doesn't care about anyone or anything. His sandstone face is passive, his lumpy body is passive, he moves slowly, watching everything, saying little, farting regularly. He lives with his sister in a shack that looks over the dump. She has warts on her face, warts she seems to be counting with her fingers, constantly. She'll mutter numbers, picking at the "flags." "One, two, nine..." She always stops at nine.

"I think there is someone like Señor Pedo inside of me," El Jefe says.

"Ah, so," I say. I would like some coñac. Sometimes El Jefe serves coñac in glasses that show a picture of a man drowsing on the ground, hidden behind a large sombrero, his head on his knees. The man is sitting in front of an agave plant, and the sun is shown overhead with a dozen or so thick red rays sprouting out of it.

"There is this man inside of me who doesn't react to anything," he says. "He's inside of me, watching everything, like Pedo does — not reacting, not moving, not being changed."

El Jefe gets up and goes into the kitchen. I can hear the refrigerator door slam, and the metal caps falling to the tile floor. He comes back with two bottles. He is absently-mindedly blowing another thick bubble. He puts a bottle of Sangre down in front of me, and sets the other on his table. He sucks in the bubble. "When they shoot people in the stomach," I think, "it's said that they blow bubbles of blood."

"He just stays there inside of me, watching, watching," says El Jefe. "Sometimes I go downtown, get a bowl of kidney soup — kidney soup is what I like most in the world. When I die and go to sweet Paradise — I want Marta to be there, and I want to be eating kidney soup for breakfast, lunch, and dinner, with cilantro on top of it."

There is a single-engine rebel-spotting airplane buzzing overhead. He watches it for awhile, then says: "So I go to Marta's, and she scratches herself and spits behind the butano tank and serves me kidney soup, and I cover it with cut-up squares of *pan frances,* the ones that have been fried in garlic and olive oil. I take one of her scratched wooden spoons, one I've used a thousand times before, and I dip it in the soup, getting two or three pieces of kidney, and then I bring it up to my mouth and blow on it, and I am about to put it in my mouth, and I am thinking about how much I love kidney soup, how it tastes so good, and Señor Pedo is sitting there inside of me, not doing anything, sitting there inside of me, and he nods his head a little bit, just as I am about to suck up this spoonful of kidney soup with cilantro and onions, and he says 'Eating some more soup.' That's all. While I am having my favorite lunch, he sits there inside of me and says: 'Eating another bowl of soup.' "

A mockingbird flies down, lands on the clothes line, wobbles back and forth, its long grey and white tail springing up in the air with each move. It unlimbers a song, eight or ten distinct warbles, repeated once or twice or three times, then flies off.

"You know what happened last night?" I ask him.

"I never know what to do with this man inside of me," says El Jefe. "I don't know whether to be glad or angry or what. It bothers me to have him sitting there and nodding his head, and saying 'Eating another bowl of soup,' or 'Fighting with your wife again,' or 'Fucking another whore.' No anger, no love — not even pleasure."

We sit quietly for a few more minutes. I can hear the mockingbird, over in the next yard next over, singing "Cadbury, Cadbury." I wonder if it is singing for love, for me, for itself. I wonder who Cadbury is.

"You know what happened last night," I say again.

"Have you ever felt there was someone inside of you?"

"Yes," I think. There is this boy inside of me, this boy-in-a-box inside of me. And I sometimes try to cut through so he can escape. Only he doesn't. I try to set him free, but he refuses to come out. That's how scared he is. He stays huddled down inside, and no matter how I cut and slice, I can't make a hole big enough for him to get out.

"I know exactly what you mean," I tell El Jefe. He blows another thick pink bubble for us and nods, looking at me over his glasses and nodding. Overhead the single-engine airplane circles endlessly, its rasping motor mixing with the sound of the cicadas sawing away in El Jefe's gold-yellow jacaranda.

NOVEMBER 30 [UVALE, TEXAS]

The greatest men in the world have passed away unknown. The Buddhas and the Christs that we know are but second-rate heroes in comparison with the greatest men of whom the world knows nothing. Hundreds of these unknown heroes have lived in every country — working silently. Silently they live and silently they pass away...They are the pure Sattvikas, who can never make any stir, but only melt down in love...

— VIVEKANANDA

I would like to take a moment to introduce Ernest to you more properly. Ernest is a deranged hippie, a friendly fossil of the 60s. He manages to hide his many summers behind a devastating smile and a lean and agile — if talky — way. He is a bit of a mystic, sporting a guru to whom he refers on occasion, a plump and gentle master called Vivekananda. As we drive, he places the master's picture over the sun visor. It stays there for most of the journey, beaming down at us, with the single exception of five minutes, on our fourth day, when Vivekananda decides to take a mystic journery to a far hill, at the East side of Texas Highway 181. The master is swept out the window by a freak breeze (or divine intervention) half-way between Beesville and George's Knee. Always respectful of other men's gods, I stop long enough for Ernest to chase and retrieve him from the jackweed that grows at the side of the road. Returned to his rightful place, still smiling, still sage, Vivekananda is none the worse for wear from his flight, in that hot mistral, fifty miles from the border. He had merely moved, as masters will, to another resting place, ending up in the lotus position (Ernest swore to it), beaming out at us from atop a clump of ragged rag-weed, smiling pacifically in the Texas boil.

Little do the folk of Jackson County know how close they came to having one of the major eastern gurus permanently established in their neighborhood to protect them from whatever doleful karma the people of Jackson County need to be protected from. Like their own non-existence.

It is Ernest who points out that there's no one in south Texas. I hadn't noticed — but now that he mentions it, there does seem to be a paucity of people walking, laughing, talking, taking their dogs for a stroll, children running to catch the school bus (there are no busses). We drive and drive (and drive and drive) down from Junction to Telegraph, from Cherry Spring to Luckenbach, from Seven Sisters through Jim Hogg County, down into Pharr — and at all times, the streets are empty, the lawns deserted, the fields soulless. "Perhaps they do need a Vivekananda to minister to their nothingness," I think. The only signs of life are cars, pickups, Ford 250s, Chevy Vans, Dodge Trucks, and the Texas Highway Patrol. Even then one can't be too sure if the cars and trucks are being driven by men or women or whatnot — because the windows are heavily tinted, presumably to prevent any of the occupants from being seen breaking the law by going outside their homes or anywhere but a shopping mall. The eeriest part of it is that there is, as well, not a child in sight — no schools, no kids playing basketball, riding bicycles together down the edge of the road, running through the fields.

"This myth of a huge Texas (with its equally huge population) is another Texas yarn," I think. Papalote and Uvalde and Yoakum and Runge are ghost towns (although the houses look inhabited, the fronts well scrubbed, the lawns weeded, the windows clean, the porches swept, the rockers waiting silently.) "Texas doesn't exist," I think, "except as a location for shooting westerns." Behind the facades of these houses there isn't a soul. South Central Texas is a front invented by Shell Oil, H. Ross Perot, Houston Industries, Texas Monolith, Inc., and the Hunt Brothers to own all the land and all the votes. They keep this elaborate deception going so they won't have to bother with the messy processes of democracy: registration of voters, polling-booths, elections, people.

The population of this area — an area as large as the entire state of California — is nothing but fantasy; a few thousand highly paid front men and women going to the K-Mart or 7-11, pretending that the whole vast area is populated with millions of people and not just dogies and hoot-owls.

It becomes so obvious what has been missing, what we have been missing, the moment we cross over into Mexico at Nuevo Progresso: dogs flea-biting in the unpaved streets, men with their bottles of beer, laughing, talking, gesticulating; mothers with babies in arms, going down the middle of the street — old ladies with canes; boys kicking at the soccer balls, the thousand children watching us with their lovely dark all-pupil eyes. We have found humanity at last.

DECEMBER 1 [TAMPICO, MEXICO]

The history of such a people promised to be turbulent and disorderly. Peace, with its attendant economic benefits, would be less prized than elsewhere. Personal ties, the ties of friendship and blood relationship, and the love for extravagant display would be more valued than political integrity. The Mexican would be easily attracted by rhetoric, by fine words without substance. Delighted by a beautiful appearance, he would be apt to ignore the greed and the brutality which it cloaked. If he could be witty at the expense of a tyrant or an invader, he would sometimes feel himself absolved from action. Unable to be parsimonious, he would leave economic development to foreigners. He would prefer circuses to bread, and pageantry to thrift. Yet life in Mexico would have a vividness of color, a freedom from routine, an aesthetic charm, unknown among more utilitarian races; and occasionally, in its stormy and often sordid history, there would appear from mestizo stock a figure who, combining a Spanish devotion to ideals with an Indian self-abnegation, would display a nobility, often tinged with melancholy, such as few other races in the world could equal...

— *A HISTORY OF MEXICO*
HENRY BAMFORD PARKES

Ernest and I are both free not to travel. We have nice simple homes with friendly dogs, friendly relatives, friendly friends. We have bathrooms that work, cars to take us to the store and the post office and home again, roads without benefit of smudgepots and potholes and donkeys. We have supermarkets nearby, and water — real water, not badly-treated sewage — flowing through the water pipes. Yet we choose, time and again, to take ourselves out of our respective paradises and into the dust and confusion they call Mexico. Ernest says it is the hourglass of our lives. "Every six months or so," he says, "I have to turn my whole life over, stir it up. If I don't do that, I'm dead."

We move down the Gulf Coast of Mexico, telling stories: two geezers, who have seen too much, who don't care as much, who certainly don't want to know that they've done so much, so long. We have reached the time where we are being given discounts on busses, always have cold feet, and get special bank accounts. It's the age when kids yawn when we fumble with their names (or our own), when we receive a "Swinging Seniors" pass to the Pussy Cat Theatre, and the gang members on the streets of L.A. feel free to push us over to steal our wallets, hearing aids, and walkers. It's the time when we scorn the AARP, find ourselves breathing too hard on the steps — instead of in bed — and are damn sure we've heard almost everything before.

Ernest and I find that in our dotage we have several things in common that are beginning to drive us crazy. We begin to enmumerate them, and then on our second evening in Mexico, we set them down, the Tampico Manifesto.

AS CHARTER MEMBERS OF THE OLD GUMMY CLUB
WE HEREBY ANNOUNCE
THAT WE WILL NO LONGER TOLERATE:

- being told how young we look;
- worrying about zipping up our flies;
- or closing our mouths;

- being told what's good (and bad) for us by doctors, nurses, and "experts" who were in diapers when we were having our first marriage, or our first extra-marital affair, or our first nervous breakdown;
- having the doctor ask "is there anything else you want to talk about?" and we say, "Oh, no — nothing," because we don't want to take up another hour of his time (at $200 a shot);
- waking up in the middle of the night, then waking up some more, then waking up yet again;
- waking up cold, cold, and thinking that our circulation has finally gone out on us, and then finding out it was the dratted cat sleeping on the thermostat of the electric blanket;
- having a friend complain about his first grey hair;
- having our hearts go hell-for-leather, inexplicably; then quit, for a moment, equally inexplicably;[1]
- walking fifty feet at night to pee (fifteen times);
- looking down and not being able to see our private parts;
- finding yet another grey hair — or worse, a bald spot — in the pubic area;
- squinching up our faces when we're trying to see — or hear, or understand:
- living with a knife-edge pain-in-the-knee or back or shoulder that doesn't go away (and probably never will);
- getting the government check a week late; finding out that we spent it all last month;
- getting a half-assed hard-on, one that puts in a brief, ghostly appearance, like Hamlet's Father, then disappears without a whimper for the rest of the night (or the rest of the year);
- jerking off, and thinking, "Are people at my age supposed to jerk off, anyway?" — and then not being able to come;
- listening to some old Brontosaurus telling about his or her aches and pains — and then realizing that we were talking about some of the same aches and pains the week before;

1. The doctors call it "arrhythmia." They tell us it is not life-threatening. Sometimes, though, we suspect we are going to have a heart-attack worrying about whether we're having a heart-attack.

- finding three new saphenous veins;
- having our glasses fall off our noses, and then, when we lean over to reach for them, being barely able to get back into the upright position again;
- getting stuck while going upstairs, or going downstairs, or getting out of a chair, or getting out of the car, or getting off the john;
- having one of the top pop hits of 1945 running through our brains again and again (and again);[2]
- hearing the kids tell a joke that we first heard (and told) in 1948;[3]
- watching kids waste their energy on self-pity, dumb pursuits, and their dorks;
- watching old geezers wasting what is left of their days on self-pity, dumb pursuits, and their dorks;
- waking up alone (again) and not knowing, for a moment, where we are, or how we got there, and thinking, "I really do have Alzheimer's, don't I?"

Growing old, we decide, is like a fire in the rag-bin. It creeps up on you. We can vaguely smell something going on, we know it's around here somewhere, but we don't want to acknowledge it. We scarcely look at it, certainly don't change

---

2. STUPID SONG — CIRCA 1945

"Chicory-chick, cha-lah, cha-lah,
Checka-la broma, in a bannanical,
Bahlica-wahlicka, can't you see,
Chicory-chick is me?"

3. FUNNY JOKE — CIRCA 1948

See, there was this woman who was never satisfied, so she went to the doctor, and he gave her an Automatic Penis. "Anytime you want to be satisfied, say 'Penis — my pussy,' and it will take care of you," he tells her.

So, she went home, and she took the Automatic Penis out of the box, and she said "Penis — my pussy," and it went right to work. Oh man was she satisfied! But came the time when she wanted to stop, and she couldn't stop it, so she had to go back to the doctor's office to get him to turn it off. She got on the bus, and was going downtown, with this thing still going at her, and there were two drunks sitting across the aisle, and one of them said,

"Do you see what I see?"

"Whas' that?"

"That woman has an Automatic Penis pumping away in her pussy. Look!"

The other drunk looks, blinks his eyes, and says,

"Penis, my ass! OW!"

our ways — in fact, we do nothing to honor its presence. "You could have fooled me" is the way we think about aging. Like smoke it curls around the ankles, the knees, coming up, slowly, to the brain.

Every now and again we look in the mirror, but it is merely to tell ourselves how young we look. We find excuses to tell people "Oh, I'm fifty-five," because invariably they say "Well, you don't look fifty-five." And then we can say thank you, and figure the time machine has been fooled some more.

It hasn't. We go to the post office, or a party, wait for the elevator, and we look around, and realize that we are the oldest — by far — in the room.

Compensations? Well...There can now be a leisure in what we do, and the way we do it — not giving a damn. Counting out money at the bank, standing at the head of the line. We used to be the one that stood behind, sighed, scraped our feet noisily. Now we are the ones holding up progress, and we delight in so doing.

Then there's reading the paper, or hearing on television, about some new or continuing rape that humanity has done to the land, to the ocean, to the ozone, to each other. And we remember that we are now so far down the line that it makes no difference: when they finally have to pay the piper, we'll be long gone in the grave, far away from the consequences of what people have been doing, for so long, to hurt themselves, and their surroundings.

And yes, there is also that fragile confidence that comes from five or six or seven decades of accumulated knowledge, of having learned something. It's the confidence in looking for, or finding, a new companion, or a new love (if we are brave enough to make such a search).

Some of us thought that love would be out of the question after the half-century mark. But here we are, pursuing it as vigorously, and probably as foolishly, as we ever did. We don't get less passionate; we just become more astute in the manifestation of our desire, and in our search. We become especially careful in the act of loving someone new, because there are now two wild cards: our partners (how will he or she react to me without my clothes?) and our own bodies (how will this body I've been renting so long react to being called into service yet again, for the thousandth time?) Both can become unimportant after awhile.

The loves of Now can be as riveting as the loves of Then. Our insane rutting passion that ran us so hard and so long, so long ago, wasn't able to teach us much about others — we didn't have time. Now we have something that may be worth offering to someone we love, and it might be important for us too. Our passion from Now is not more nor less beautiful than the passion from back Then, but it has more of what one might call grace. With that, we can teach others a warmth that we never thought possible in this lifetime.

Ernest and I realize that of the old people around us as we were growing up, there were always two or three who stood out from the others. They usually showed a calm, a peace, a gentleness. It was as if out of their lives — no matter how difficult, hurtful, or brutal — they had drawn nourishment and hope: they refused the opportunity to chew on the bone of despair for the rest of their days.

It may have been blind courage in the face of "the dying of the light," but I'd rather think of it as power that was pulled from a reservoir of hope and goodwill — out of themselves, for all of us. They had the singular ability to forgive all, to scorn few, and to hate none.

DECEMBER 2 [VERA CRUZ]

"You're the only person I know who's given up your subscription to *The New Yorker* for *Trailer Life* my friend Laura said recently, when I told her I was going to go to southern Mexico with Ernest, a travel-trailer, and a truck. "You are embarrassing all your friends." And it's true. We used to call each other long distance to discuss the latest "Reporter at Large" article. Now it's hitch weight, sway-bars, and the virtues of Destroy-lets over chemical black water tanks. It's the relative merits of travel trailers, tent trailers, 5th wheels, camper shells, "toy houses" and RV's. "I'm not getting an RV because I don't want steering wheels and brake pedals in my living room," I tell her. "Tent trailers don't have bathrooms, and 5th wheels make you sleep in an overhang. It's a travel trailer for me. I don't want to take my house with me when I go grocery shopping."

Subscriptions to the *Arizona Mobile Citizen, Van Life, Trailer Daze, The Good Sam Noosenotes* and the *Newsletter of the Airstream Good Time Charleys* fill up my mail box and my waning days. And if you think old geezers high up in their Winnebagos, or hauling Laytons or Shastas behind their Dodge Caravans, are frail, white-haired retirees — you got another think coming. Ladies who look like they just got out of the Orange County Garden Society Meeting (blue hair, heart glasses, tiny, bird-like waists) lever themselves into their Ford 450 SuperHaul diesels, complete with seven forward gears and a pulling capacity of an International Harvester tractor — and using a triple bypass hitch attached to a forty-foot King-of-the-Road with a gross tonnage of twenty thousand foot-pounds, race about the continent on double-action Wambler axles with a braking stop-weight of a half-a-million ergs.

And they aren't content to drive their rigs through the forty-eight contiguous states on four-lane highways. Oh no — you'll find them in tiny rutted winding up-and-down-hill roads forging through the forests of Canada, the bear country of Alaska, the wild parks of Montana, the fall landscape in Vermont — down even into the narrow roads of Mexico, Guatemala and Nicaragua (racing ahead of the Contras and their seek-and-destroy missiles to get to Tipitapa in time to pop a Swanson's frozen turkey dinner into the Trav-L-All microwave.) They drive hell-for-leather on a schedule that would cause your common truck driver to O.D. on meth. And when they arrive at their destination, after a fourteen day run from the far ends of the earth, they descend from the driver's seat, brush off their bottoms, and head to the washroom to do to a load of laundry that would fell a Dutch maid.

After a few days of wrestling with a Cheverolet Suburban hooked to a 4,500 pound Airstream, I come to respect these simple folk, the unsung heroes of the highways. I'm here to tell you that driving a rig is not just a matter of hitching 'em up and moving 'em out. The Ox is twenty feet long, the Silver Pill twenty-seven. The hinge is in the middle. The two of them, when so conjoined, never ever want to go where you want them to go: never. In reverse, something strange happens to the focus, or the locus, or bofus. An analogue is created that has befuddled the brains of top scientists for decades, and given trailer owners heart-failure. It is as if The Theory of Relativity had gotten entangled with Newton's Third Law to create a special new corollary called the Airstream Law of Perverse (and Reverse) Directionality.

There is, for example, that gas station just outside of Truth-or-Consequences, New Mexico — the one with the moving guard poles. Second day behind the wheel, second day of travelling with the Airstream, I pull in close to the pumps so that they can fill the Ox's Endless Maw with its preferred and expensive drink. Somehow in the process, the trailer gets entangled in one of the uprights. And no matter how I push and pull, no matter how I pray and cry, the freeboard of the trailer stays rammed up against the guard pole. Each time I back and fill, I scrape another three-foot swath on the starboard side of my lovely silver pristine baby.

"How does this goddamn thing work?" I yell to Ernest.

"You want to get the trailer away from the pole," he yells back, "not closer to it." This has a novel effect: despite my travails, I am ready to put the Chevrolet in reverse and get enough backwards motion to run over Ernest's ass. However, I restrain myself and put The Ox into gear once more, mashing in another section of the shiny aluminum of my lovely winter home, and Ernest comes over, leans on the windowsill, smiles with that devastating smile, and says, softly: "You're doing it backwards. What you want to do is the opposite of what you want to do. Think of the famous talk on calmness delivered by the Master DoughJoe." At least it sounded like DoughJoe, although I wasn't listening too carefully. I mutter a few thoughts about his Master DoughJoe, put it in reverse, close my eyes, go backwards, just as instructed, exactly opposite to my instincts — that is, turning the wheel so that the trailer, by all right logic, should moosh even more against the upright — and dang my boots if it don't move away from the poles, getting us disentangled and on our way once more, left with only the smarting memory of two pimple-faced, rude gas station attendants laughing up their sleeves.

❧ ❧ ❧

Carrying a twenty-seven foot trailer behind you is not unlike having diagnosed AIDS. No one wants to be with you, no one wants you parking near them, no one wants to eat with you and certainly not to sleep with you — and after awhile, you don't even want to be with yourself. Today, we drive all day and most of the evening, looking for a place to park, looking for a place that will have us and our twenty seven foot tapeworm. Then it starts to rain, and we think we'll never find a place, anywhere; that we'll have to continue forever, two wandering hippies, our great backpack filled as it is with whatever it is we are carrying south with us.

I always thought trailer-pulling was like being a turtle — but a turtle, at least, can stop at convenient places, pull in his wheels and motor, and take a nap, free from all intrusions. It's not that easy for those of us with The Silver Pill.

So we go on and on, on this dark Mexican highway, far into the night. It is difficult to remember that we are on the main east coast Mexican highway. Often it has no markings whatsoever, so that by eleven, we want to haul in the flag and park anywhere, even in the noisy Pemex station at La Ribiera, next to a dozen muttering trucks. I see a quiet paved road, running off to the west, so on a whim, I drive down it. After a kilometer or so, it narrows from two lanes to one, and then in the next kilometer, from one to a mere paved path, no turn-around whatsoever, not even a country road going off to left or right where we could pull in and turn around to escape this awful, never-ceasing FORWARD.

All the while, Mr. Cool next to me is getting more and more nervous, muttering that the road will peter out into a mud-filled slough, and I'll have to take full responsibility for whatever happens to him. He suggests that the captain is not doing an adequate job of navigating, suggests that it might be a time to stop, dead on the road, for the remainder of the night. "There is no rest for the weary," I sigh to myself, as I contemplate the muddy roadside (no shoulders, even — just wet and mud and grass down there, falling down into unknown chasms on each side). I know if I get off the pavement for a moment, we'll be stuck: we'll be forced to spend our winter here, among the tree frogs and ferns, because we could never ever in a hundred years pull The Silver Pill back onto the pavement, even with the great hulking power of The Ox. All the while, I am thinking of the single Law of All Good Sams, which is — never ever get into a place that you can't turn around in, from, or off. Backing truck and trailer down and out from a place like this would not only be ludicrous, it would be — if my experience in Truth-or-Consequences is any example — impossible.

This is, I think, sadly, our end as sentient beings on earth. All is now beyond my capacities. I resign my fate to the great Trailering Divine. We're doomed to an endless trail from which we'll never be allowed to escape. Even tomorrow, in the full day's light, our way will be shown to be ever forward; we'll be forever stuck here, driving along into the dark future with our Silver Space Machine (is it moving closer to us?).

Night monsters begin to rise out of the mud swamp around us, but ahead, up there through the black, I see a sign — the universal sign of Mexican salvation: the omnipresent mercury vapor light. It stands at the edge of a tiny lake, complete with boats, houses, fish, fishing wharf, warehouse, and Oh Blessings of St. Good Sam — a full wide road circle turn-around, perfectly designed for overlong trailer-rigs and their nervous occupants.

We pull over by the lake to sleep for the night, assured by two very drunken fishermen that it is perfectly fine with them if we do so. They are delighted with our appearance; so much so that they offer to crawl right in with us for the night, falling over each other in their attempt to be hospitable, waving the taditional Mexican long-lost-friend symbol before us — two smudged and half-eaten bottles of Corona Clara. As they argue and gibber, Ernest goes off to bed in the trailer. I choose to sleep in the Ox, which does not deter our two new friends from standing a foot or so away from my bed, laughing and singing and pissing on the tires. I rest on the dusty floor, and do my best to shut them out. The merry Mexicans (one, thin, singing and falling down; the other fat, cursing and falling down,) have failed in their attempt to get us to come home with them, to eat with them, to move in with them, to live with them, to take over their houses, wives, family, children, dogs and birds, but this does not deter them from talking long into the night about our magical appearance.

After a few hours or so, through the misty window of the car I can hear the two of them, Juan and Jose, or Jules and Jim, or Quixote and Sancho Panza, supporting each other in their long, hard journey back up the street, pushing against the night and each other into the darkness of the drunken night, going towards home.

DECEMBER 4 [LA RIBIERA]

Like all the writers of my generation, I had been struck by the passage in The Brothers Karamazov *where Ivan says, "If the divine will implies the torture of an innocent child by a brute, I'm handing back my ticket." I had lent Karamazov to the chaplain of Glìeres, and he had written to me on returning the book, "It's first rate, but it's the eternal problem of evil; and for me evil is not a problem, it's a mystery."*

— *ANTI-MEMOIRS*
ANDRÉ MALRAUX

In the misty morning, when we rise, we find five children sitting on the ledge of the nearby fish shed, wide-eyed, watching our rising. I will never know, until I die, what they do to these children, what they say to them, with their incantations, and the magic. Perhaps it is the mountain air of La Ribiera, filled, as Ernest later claims, with sacred and important ions. Perhaps it is something greater — perhaps one of the gods himself came down to this tiny lakeside village of Encantada, leaving behind his divine spawn in the loins of wives of drunken fishermen. Have we found, in our magic globe of silver, the enchanted lake of Iona, where the children of the gods play and sing their way through their lives, their gentle fawn faces, faces set with the mysterious eyes of the divine, mysterious as the mist which even yet wraps the lake, and from which appears, from time to time, a launch, to deliver another boatload of magic children to watch us. Where they come from, from what Olympian heights, we will never know. Only the godlets, with their dusky skin, their impenetrable eyes, only the incarnations know the answer to that, and they aren't talking.

They watch our rise, accept our offerings of pomegranates and apples and candy. They speak in a musical tongue, and move with a regal languor. The bread man arrives in his truck. Perhaps he has a divine mission too: he brings out hot freshly-made anise-seed buns which threaten, in their very lightness, to pull us up into the stratosphere. Our two frumpy gringos — escaped from last night's nightmare — make their breakfast beside the lake, smiled upon by the bedimpled children of the enchanted isles, and I know, and I promise you (if I didn't make the whole thing up), by my troth, and Ernest corroborates this, and he doesn't lie, at least, no more than I do: I promise you that some day we will return to Lake Godlet to watch the pearl of the morning emerge from the far enbankments, and the dark-eyed children of the cosmos come to join us at our morning ablutions.

DECEMBER 5

Driving with Ernest is like having All Talk Radio going throughout the day and much of the night. He rambles on endlessly about the surroundings, the thoughts that wamble through his brain, his ideas, his history, his experiences. He is enraptured by a half sunken fishing boat in the lagoon near Alvarado. He wants to make a movie there with the boat as the central character; or he has already made a movie there; or he has already scripted such a movie there, or has merely been thinking about making a movie there — one can never be too sure.

While this monologue is going on, there are the accompanying commercial breaks. Women are Ernest's soul and life and heart. It makes no difference — age, race, distinguishing marks, social rank, dimensions, or redeeming natural features: there are women he danced with, in the moonlight, "moonbeam" dancing; those with waist-length hair, hair he has loved (and combed)(and kissed); there are those who have those special breasts — very very special, of a special luscious quality, great black casaba melons (one was black: Ernest is not only omnivorous but omniracial in his loves). There was the girl that wanted to marry him, everything was set, mother, father, all at the ready: then Ernest disappeared. With another woman.

The women the women the women: the ones from Russia, from France, from California. The woman who reads, the one who sews, the eighty-year old woman who plays the sax and dances the Twist; the one who sang all day, the one who cried all night — all of them passing like tea (Constant Comment) with us in our march through Central Mexico, all of them described in all too tender awe. He loves the way they walk, the

way they move, the way they grow, they way they think, are, see, grow old, love, laugh, die. They are to be taken to the beach, buried in the sand, then pulled from their warm graves and plunged into colorful warm oceans — nixies in the sweet soft waters of the sweet soft sea.

Ernest is a Don Juan in the best sense — he loves women because they are there to be loved. I regret that I did not fit The Ox with microphone and cassette, for our conversations, suitably transcribed, would go down as the Boswell-Johnson dialogues of the 18th, or the Miller-Durrell exchanges of the 20th, Century.

❧ ❧ ❧

The next time I come to see El Jefe, he is sitting out on the same patio, under the scraggly grape vines. He has taken off his dark glasses. The weekly *Hoja* newspaper lies limply on the table. He goes over to the jacaranda, picks a dying blossom, once virulent purple, now yellowed and coarse. He throws it over the wooden fence.

"Jefe," I say. "I want to ask you something very important." I pause. "Is someone following me?"

He comes back to the bowed metal chair, with rust stains running down the leg. He sits down so heavily it bends back as if to fall. He looks out at the dusty colonia, then down at the street. The town is quiet. The sun is hot, and I can hear myself panting.

I sit at the table, with its three legs, and a hole in the middle for an umbrella "C-i-n-z-a-n-o" above the faded tassels. A festive beach at Nice, tan bodies under the sun, glistening bodies, the breeze puttering in from off the sea, trembling waves, dark moist hair, the sand. Here in El Vapor there are no tan bodies, no sea, no waves, no moist hair, no beach. When the wind comes, it comes up dusty and acrid.

"I was sitting out here last night looking at the stars," says El Jefe. "It was very clear last night. I stayed here for a couple of hours, sipping coñac, letting the stars move about me." It is perhaps the first time I have seen him without his glasses. He has an intricate system of *canaliculi* about the eyes, a tiny fretwork of lines on the purplish skin across the bridge, down his sides of his soft rounded nose.

"If you look at the stars long enough, you can see them move," he says. "They don't always go forward. Sometimes they go backwards, too. They go into...what's the word?...yes, they go into retrograde." He pauses. "It's very strange. I was looking at one, a very bright one, right above the steeple over there." He points over La Sagrada Familia on the other edge of the village. When the wind is from the west, sometimes you can smell a trace of incense, hear the lowing of the choir.

"It was probably one of the Gemini. It was poised over the steeple for a half-an-hour, then suddenly it lurched west, maybe a half a degree. I watched it for the next fifteen minutes. It didn't move."

I can see the man standing, waiting for me, on the pathway leading up to El Jefe's house. In the waning light, I can see his hawk's beak, the pimples clustered on the upper cheek, his thin and sullen mouth. He leans against a lightpost wrapped in the tendrils of a vine they call "the suffocator."

"When I looked again, it had moved back to its original position," he says. "It stayed there for a long time." He sighs, moves his commodious belly about under the huge belt, with its buckle, silver, etched in the figure of an ox. "I am not sure, I went to bed not long after, but the last time I looked at it, it had moved more to the west and — see that *Cercis* over there?..." He points at the squat tree over near the cantina. I can hear the jukebox playing, a song about Matamoros, and the border. What is it about a language, a people, that would name a city after the death of those of a different culture? "Matamoros"— "Kill Moors."

"It was right over that manzanita. And do you know what I thought?" Here he leans forward, and looks at me. I can see the tiny red lightning strokes running down his nose. "I got the idea that if I wanted, wanted it badly enough, I could make the stars move. I could make them go backwards, or forwards, or stand still: whatever I wanted." He looks at me intently. "And more than that, if I was patient enough, soon enough I could learn to control the sun, could make it go backwards, or forwards —make it stand still, frozen in the sky. Perpetual day, or perpetual night. Can you imagine? The shadows never moving?" "He's going totally batty," I think. "Why would anyone want to be following you?" he asks.

He finishes off the coñac in his glass, then pours himself another, and one for me. On this side of the glass is a picture of Minnie Mouse, too-spacious high-heels, those long wiry eyebrows. "She's looking at me too," I think.

DECEMBER 6 [PUERTO PERDIDO]

Who cares for freedom...
I do not want wealth or even health;
I do not want beauty
I do not want intellect:
Let me be born again and again,
Amid all the evils of the world;
I will not complain, but let me love thee,
And that for love's sake.

— HINDU LOVE SONG

We arrive at our destination, at eleven, after a marathon drive through the coastal lowlands of Oaxaca. We back the trailer into spot number 6A of the Playa Cula Trailer Park. We

are home — our winter home — and life becomes instantly simpler. No longer on the road, no longer looking for a place to stop, or to eat, no longer haunted by the Silver Pill always nagging at our buttocks — we now can live in it, our self-sufficient trailer, along with some new and inquisitive visitors from the area who join us: 6,000 - 8,000 mosquitoes, ants, squash bugs, lace bugs, crickets, midges, dung flies, snipe flies, march flies, and do flies. Throughout the invasion, Ernest is a comfort. "At least we don't have roaches," he says. He says that if you have roaches, you don't have ants, but if you have ants — there are no roaches. After waking up being tickled to death by the red fire ants of Puerto Perdido, all too willing to sink their little fangs in my bum when I roll over on them, I'm about to send home for some German roaches for protection.

Ernest makes cheese quesadillas for lunch while he tells me about another of the books he is writing. I count twenty books in the oven as of today, on subjects as wide-ranging as Eastern love, right wing politics, and (what else?) women. "I'm going to put that bit about ants and roaches in my book on War and Tantra," he tells me. "Or maybe it'll be part of my book on Sex and Kali." I have this vision of Ernest's house (another trailer, on fifty acres near the central California coast) filled with half-eaten manuscripts in various stages of decay. He tells me about his various how-to-do-it books, essays, novels, screen plays, Broadway shows, and a modern opera — in the mode of Gian Carlo-Menotti. It's about crossing the border, and is called *Exposito*. The hero (Manual Labor) with his lady (Rachael Prejudice) confounds a bunch of villainous coyotes — border smugglers — then saves a village of migrant laborers from the depredations of certain Sheriff Raul Diehl.

Ernest also claims he is working on a movie about three surfers — dope smugglers all — abandoned by an evil connection, in the middle of the Pacific, on their surfboards, thousands of miles from land. At the moment of ultimate despair, Jesus comes down to them on a Boogie Board, turns the waves magenta and gold and silver, and saves them from certain doom.

Ernest, when he isn't making movies and operas (and quesadillas), is into something called Ouroboros Breathing. He doesn't spell the word for me, to write in here, because (1) he can't spell; and (2) he suspects I will describe it all wrong, fucking up his karma. "You always twist my words around to say what you want them to say," he says. "It's called New Journalism," I tell him. "I take people's old-hat ideas and turn them into high art. You should be honored. Look at Tom Wolfe."

Ouroboros Breathing, which he learned from Oscar Ichazo, when he was making a movie about him, or thinking about making a movie about him, or refusing to make a movie about him, he finally explains, calls for one to put the tongue up against the back palate (or uterus.) You then force air in and out of the nose — going "snew, snew" (or "snee, snee"); from thence, you send energy jolts (or joules) up into and through the brain, down to and around the coccyx, and at the same time visualize a pair of snakes winding about the spinal column, through each of the chakras. "You're safe," I tell him. "I couldn't write about Ouroboros Breathing because I can't make head nor tail of your description of it. Besides, it makes me sick to my stomach chakra to even think about it."

Ernest collects plants, such as the purple palm, the suffocating fig, the white ocotillo, and various exotic ferns (which if you but inhale the perfume of their lovely flowers, he says, will put you into psychedelic heaven for hours). Searching out these exotic seeds has taken him across Mexico and Guatemala on foot, boat, bus, trolly, ox-cart, motorcycle, donkey, wagon, DC3, and bicycle. While searching out seeds, he claims to have come across, and loved, many women of many ages, at various times and places, staying but one step ahead of irate fathers, policemen, mercenaries, revolutionaries, sons, uncles, brothers, and husbands, all with revenge in their hearts and murder in their eyes. He claims, however, another great lie, to love trees and botony far more than he does the ladies.

DECEMBER 7

One of the time-honored rituals of Mexico is "The Changing of the Gelt." In every other pursuit, Mexicans are pleasant and fun and conversational. Only in the money-changers tent do they turn sullen and impatient. The line at the Puerto Perdido Bancomer moves along slowly until the cashier runs out of pesos. Then it stops for an hour or so, and one finds oneself trapped in this a steel holding tank, with no windows, where the sunlight is captured and magnified for the benefit of two dozen sweaty gringos who came to Mexico because it's nice and warm, so the bank figures it might as well give us heat in spades.

We melt and wither, our complaints muted by the oppressiveness of it all. As we inch closer to the front of the line, all travellers checks and passports are examined minutely for forgery, mutililation and illegal modifications. If the signature varies in any way from any of the documents, one is sent away destitute. When, finally, the money is changed — it is handed out slowly and deliberately, counted and recounted. Even then one isn't necessarily free: one may find oneself with a shopping bag full of smelly five-thousand peso notes, if that is what the bank is touting at the moment (5,000 pesos equals approx $2.00 U.S.). To change $200 U.S. into Mexican money is to command a wad of three or four inches of wrinkled pesos. Try walking down a dark street in Puerto Perdido — or anywhere, for that matter — with a gummy wad like that leaking out of the back of your slacks.

If one happens to be in the part of the line that stretches beyond the bank's door at closing time, you've had it: they shut you out. In contrast to the closing time of every other institution in Mexico, which is purposefully vague, when the banks say they close at 11:30, they mean 11:30, and not 11:31, or 11:30 and three seconds.

As we are waiting in line, sourpuss me is standing behind charming Ernest, who, for an hour-and-a-half, diverts a gaggle of retired Texans, an alcoholic from New Zealand, and two young ladies from New York City who are wearing — in a bank! — skimpy black bikinis designed so we can see skulls tattooed about their various private parts. Ernest is talking about everything under the sun (botany, Mexico, the beach, the sun, Bush — his all-time favorite) and charms the pants off the entire flock. I can see him right now: 6' 4", tanned, bright of eye, with a great toothsome smile, in his pink "Vivekananda Loves" tee-shirt, telling tales for all to hear. My sullen response may well have something to do with the ease with which he eases into his relationships (and out of them just as easily). To be with Ernest is to remember me as a juvenile always hiding in the kitchen while everyone else was in the playroom laughing and talking and necking; I was the one at the library when everyone else was making out at the Spring Prom; when my friends were getting laid for the first time, it was dutiful me who drove them to and from the rendezvous; and when their love affairs fell apart, it was Mr. Lonely-But-Loyal who drove them home drunk and insensate.

Maybe that's why I hang around people like Ernest. Even now, at this late date, forty years later, I want some of his charming ways to rub off on me. When they ask him what business he is in, he says "Oh, I'm in oil." That's a kick. What he means is that he has a tiny company that sells coconut oil. His real business is massage, which is his favorite form of communication. "Let me demonstrate my cocoa oil," he'll say, his huge hands twitching, as he sizes up some lady he encounters on the beach. He claims that he will rub many, many naked bodies of the world before he dies — and at the rate he's going, and with his sheer chutzpa — it might add up to the tens of thousands.

DECEMBER 9

[The dictator] Santa Anna's amputated leg was disinterred from its grave at Manga de Clavo and solemly reburied in the cathedral. His statue was erected in the plaza, with one hand pointing towards Texas, which he was still promising to reconquer — though it was remarked that it also appeared to be pointing towards the mint.

— *A HISTORY OF MEXICO*
HENRY BAMFORD PARKES

Friend Sam'l, fresh from Ecuador, blond, healthy, rugged, filled with life, arrived today. For the next few days, for hours on end, especially at dinner time, Ernest, Sam'l and I regale each other — later with Chuy and Diego, my two Oaxacan workers — in telling fearless lies out of our common, and not so common, history.

For instance, Sam'l tells us that the biggest crop in Ecuador is coffee — and that the farmers who grow hectares of coffee beans near Quito, where he lives, adjourn every day to a bar adjacent his apartment where they drink coffee and brandy, the coffee being imported Nescafé instant, out of a jar.

Sam'l has a job with a Canadian international development organization that is working with the Ecuadorian government to provide water and sewage treatment to the villages. In the four-block area where he lives, there are hawkers, runners, children, prostitutes, electricians, iron mongers, bicycle shops, food salesmen, beer shops, gas shops, and cassette shops (two burnt out speakers and music tape.) He lives with, talks with, drinks with, visits with dozens of friends, workers and peasants in his adopted home, far away from the country of his birth. Sam'l admits to us he has an addiction, a drug he has been using for the last three years, which he sticks directly in his heart eighteen hours a day. It's called love-of-Ecuador, and it lights up his eyes and delights his days. It also makes him nervous and irritable when he has to go through withdrawal.

He tells us of the goat man who brings five or six nannies to the door in the morning, in case you want milk straight from the udder. He tells us of the twenty-five-cent-a-pound fresh shrimp, the great mountain cheeses. He tells of the political candidate from his area who claimed, in the last election, to have "the highest sperm count." He tells of the seventeen political parties, and the fifteen-year-old girls who eye him as he goes, blonde gringo that he is, down the street. A year later they are married and pregnant and turn their eyes away from him as they pass him.

He tells of the bugs that, when you try to brush them away, shit on your skin, causing it to burn. He tells of the flies that gather on his light-bulb at night, fill up his beer glass with their little fly bodies. He tells of the streets filled with burros and pigs; he tells of five kinds of bananas, the fruit everywhere; he tells of the man who travels on his bicycle and sells bananas, one at a time, for two cents. He tells of travelling the length and breadth of Ecuador, drinking with the village mayors, doing his reports on water resources, sharing caña and rumors and political tales with them all. He tells of the music of Julio Jaramillo, the politics of oil, and the black tepid water in which he bathes every morning. In all, Sam'l is deeply and dangerously in love: not with any woman — at least not any to speak of; certainly not with any ideology; but, rather — with an entire Latin American way of life that, it seems, is very fortunate to have such a loving fan.

DECEMBER 10

I had a dream last night. Or was it a delusion spawned by the randy anis we drink. Anyway, it was of the Reverse Society. The fifty- or sixty-year-old children come to their parents' graveside, and disinter mom and dad with appropriate ceremony. The old folks stir in their ancient beds, brush away the cobwebs, rise — make their way home with their children. Slowly, they become more vigorous. At the same time, the children begin to "youthen": they grow in strength, their faces smooth over, they develop pimples and acne, and grow down into their new smooth skin and rosy cheeks. The parents, now filled with a strength and confidence, watch their children's faces turning softer. The kids run about, filled with a powerful energy, getting chubby, and smaller; they begin to lose the ability of speech, mouthing their words, crying. With their smiling, youthful parents hovering over them, they lie down on their backs, gurgling, wearing their new diapers. At the appropriate time, with great ceremony, the doctors come to jam the resisting babes back to their rightful place in the womb; it is a terrible squeeze. It is about this time that mom and dad go to the graveyard, and with suitable ceremony, disinter their own parents, wrinkled and aged, who stretch and yawn, rise up slowly, take their lives back, reclaim their days (backwards) like all those who've gone before, and after.

DECEMBER 11

Today, the five of us find the river of our dreams, the *real* Rio Tonameca. We had heard vague stories about it, so we started searching through the town of the same name. A hollow-eyed farmer directs us up-river — not to the river that runs through the town, but to one beyond; a secret stream, hidden among the hills. We drive over dusty roads in our 4X4 (all Ox have four legs) and we find the Rio Secreto, where a great granite wall towers over a natural pool, where naked boys swim, where barebreasted women wash their clothes, where blue egrets and sand dabbers and boat-tailed grackles congregate. In the fields around, there are burros and grey flap-eared Brahma cattle. Great willows shade the stream. The ambience is sweet and sustaining, and the waters flow fresh out of the Oaxacan mountains.

We drink beer, and cavort in the water — Diego and Chuy splash each other, Sam'l reclines on the bank at the side of the river, Ernest looks for exotic plants, Carlos bubbles and babbles in the cool waters. We have found the river of our dreams.

Later, after we return to Puerto Perdido, Ernest invites us to come to worship with him. Each evening, he pays homage to his god, a great red ball that sinks to its death in the nearby sea. I explain to him that I will have nothing to do with his ceremony. "Sunsets are very provincial," I tell him. "What you are watching is nothing more than the revolution of a minor planet about a third-class dying star, located in the weaker reaches of an indifferent nebula, which is, in turn, a minor part of a lesser arm of an all-too uninspired galaxy."

"Futhermore," I say, watching his object of adoration slide further and further down into the great sea, "the sun you worship isn't 'sinking in the west.' It is, in reality, sinking nowhere. What you are viewing is not the movement of an orb, but, rather, the twisting of a planet about its own eccentric axis. You are not worshiping the sun, nor what you so provincially called 'the sunset;' you are honoring time — you are paying homage to the clock."

"And — I ask you," warming to my subject, "Who cares about time? If you want to worship time (or space, for that matter — it's all the same thing) you can do it anywhere. Big Ben, the cuckoo clock on the wall, the selenium timepiece at the Bureau of Standards, the governmental clocks at Greenwich, a Mickey Mouse watch, Rocky Mountain Spotted Fever Time, the Spiro Agnew Watch (whatever happened to Spiro Agnew?). If you worship time, you can worship any of these."

Later, over dinner, the three of us — with the occasional shy contributions of Diego and Chuy — discuss: peasant women, peasant women as lovers; peasant women as wives; peasant women as art; Ecuadorian politics, Canadian politics, Mexican politics, American politics; growing up in California; growing up in Vermont; growing up in Georgia (U.S.A. vs. Soviet Socialist Republic); music (native and classical); dope; sex; love; booze; property rights and ownership rights in the US, Mexico, Ecuador, and on the Isle of Lesbos; food; art; beauty; "boning"; international water policy; water use; water rights; the bourgeoisie vs. the upper class; upper, middle, and lower class morality; sense (and sensibility); birth control; abortion; active vs. passive love; art; writing; Torquemada; the love of Torquemada; artists' egos; egos; universal law; universal love; universal mean time.

It is a typical evening of typical table talk over wine, beans, rice, quesadilla, and hot sauce. Of the insights provided — few are new, none are profound, all are greeted by all with much warmth, scepticism, amusement, and — ultimately — fearless laughter and applause.

DECEMBER 13

Tracking thoughts is like watching light patterns on the surface of a pond, but even more paradoxical than that: when you want to see them, they stop. When you forget your purpose of watching, they begin again. Eventually it occurs to you that the watcher is thought. The watching happens in the gap between thoughts, when the watcher momentarily disappears and there is nothing to watch anymore.

CELEBRATING THE CHARNEL GROUND,
STEPHEN T. BUTTERFIELD

We drive The Ox up the river past cows and egrets and willows and lovely pools, past the people of Tonameca, crossing the river not once but six times, past the natural pool, going as far up as we can go, to a place (which will become our favorite place) with rocks and sand and a natural waterfall. We bathe in the moving waters, the mountains green and verdurous around us. When it is time to leave, I crank up The Ox, put him in reverse, and he up and groans and gets stuck in the soft sand at the side of the pool. "O no," I say. What will become of us? We're five miles up a semi-deserted road, up to our axles in sand and water. What Sam'l and Ernest and I do (we're such nice people) is, first, each of us takes full responsibility for the tragedy. Sam'l says it is his fault because he told me to turn the steering-wheel when I was trying to pull out; Ernest says no it was his fault because he forgot to change the treadless spare tire yesterday; and I say, no, no, blame me because I'm the driver, or at least was, until I could drive no more.

Sam'l volunteers himself (and Diego and Chuy) for Tractor Duty, and they set off downstream. I sit, expecting a hoarde of Army Ants, my bleached bones lying here unrecognized long after I have been consumed by the unfeeling creatures. To comfort me, Ernest gives me honey nougat candy and beer, things I would never consume — at least, not at the same time — if I were not facing certain death from exposure.

"We were a fine team," I think, later. Each of us did our own bit to get us out. Sam'l, Diego and Chuy went off for the tractor, Ernest fed me and then lay down on the sand on a towel and went to sleep, and I leaned on the hood of The Ox, contemplating the mountains around us. I studied the possibility of becoming at one with the trees and the horses and the clear, nacreous sky. In the distance, on the side of the sheerest mountain, two white horses turn into large mountain boulders. When I look away from them, they frolic and cavort again on the hillside; then, when I face towards them, they freeze in an attitude of stone, alone on the shadow of a falling sun. Only by concentrating on them as hard as I can (they command a powerful magic) will I be able to free The Ox from its grave of sand and mud.

I am well prepared for a week of prayer, fasting and meditation — once I finish my candy and beer — but in record time our three friends appear around the bend, in the cockpit of a large puffing green and yellow Massey-Ferguson. They aren't alone up there: it's loaded with a dozen or so Mexicans, heavy under the witchery of mescal. In a trice, the tractor is backed up to the butt end of The Ox, a tow cord the size of a watch chain attached, and they yank the groaning beast (and me) from our joint burial site. We wobble down the road behind this merry bunch of mescalanias, plunging into the sunset, past the valley of heavenly delights — a drunken band of rescuees and rescuers. They make us imbibe again and again the magic potion which, they insist, was what actually set us free.

DECEMBER 14

"I've heard a great deal of nonsense about suicide," my father used to say, "but for a man who kills himself resolutely I've never come across any other feeling but respect. Whether suicide is an act of bravery or not is a question that can only concern those who haven't killed themselves."

— *ANTI-MEMOIRS*
ANDRÈ MALRAUX

Before I came to the tropics, I lived in one of the few non-air-conditioned houses in Phoenix. It was a house in the old part of town, filled with a half-a-dozen sullen neo-mystics. I lived in the room just below Dennis. When he wasn't otherwise occupied, he sucked on this thumb and never spoke to any of us. He carried a ragged, stained teddy bear around with him, and he and his bear worked all night at the typewriter. He was doing something called Fisher-Hoffman, where you wrote the 500 worst characteristics of your mother and father, and then beat them — in the form of a pillow — with a stick, and then finally forgive them. The sounds of the two (or four) of them working this out through the night would be amplified into my room by the old wooden floor.

The other housemates ate wheatstraw and honey, went to Arica training sessions all day and much of the night, and either spoke monosyllables (to each other) or at philosophical length (to themselves.)

My bed was in the one room downstairs, next to the kitchen. There was a barred window that looked out over the Sunshine Market parking lot where winos and other derelicts hovered about the dumpster and laughed and coughed and coupled far into the night. In the morning, they would occasionally limp over to the window to ask me for spare change. I would sit up in my cot and shoo the flies out the window and shake my head. "He has risen to save the common fly," I would write in my journal. "He gives nothing to the poor of the earth, but he is the Savior of Flies." When I wrote in my journal, I always put myself in the third person. Terror had no name, no known origin, no root, no resolution, no beginning, no nexus. The first person did not exist. My mind would fiddle, constantly, with incomplete questions that I could never answer. "When is it not...?" I would think. "Is there any reason for your...?" Wheel of the mind. "Have you ever...?" It would not leave me alone, wouldn't leave me alone, would not, would not...

❧ ❧ ❧

It is one of those evenings, there in the trailer park, on the Playa Cula, overlooking the Sea of Mexico, during our time of freedom — one of those evenings, in which, I tell you, I haven't heard so many lies since I was back in high school. "I had forgotten how much work love and seduction and lying were — until you all began recounting these stories," I tell Sam'l and Ernest.

Ernest has just finished speaking of his latest love, a young black lady friend, a friend of his nineteen-year-old son, if you will. "You are stealing a girlfriend from your son?" I say, shaking my head. I am shocked and saddened by his duplicitous behavior.

"I'm writing a book about her," he says, by way of excuse. This particular piece will be included in the one on the DeBeers diamond consortium, the Kennedy Assassination, Pol Pot, the contamination of the national milk supply, and his first grey pubic hair.

Ernest had sent his son into town, forty miles away, for some nuts and this *honey* took him aside and told him that her life "had been too boring" so far (eighteen!), and that she wanted to experience Real Love. "She was sweet," he said, "she was little, her tiny body, this huge vulva." He actually uses the word, which tells me that he got his sex education the same place I did. From those books behind the bottles in his father's liquor closet.

He goes on at some length, rather too graphically, I think, with a list of his comings and goings with her, none of which are particularly germane to our present discussion. One detail I do remember, however, and in the interest of honorable journalism, in fairness to the salaciousness that noodles about inside all of us — I report it to you forthwith. It was his description of "what they always love the most" (his eyes mist over at the memory). "They love to look down," he says, "and see your eyes, shining, peering up at them through the thick, dark bush," he says, a catch in his voice.

After he and Sam'l have exchanged a few further empurpled stories like this, I explain to them that my youth was a dam site different than theirs. I spent the first six years of puberty in study of not so much the day-to-day, but rather the applied theory of love. I was very bookish, and because I never got laid, I read everything I could get my hands on, which, in those days, hundreds of years ago, wasn't much.

The best literary source was my dad's liquor closet, right under the attic stairs, smelling of cedar and straw and gun oil. Because the door was an old fashioned one with hinges, we could pull out the pins and get inside in five minutes. If we heard a car in the driveway, we would get the books back in place, the door back on its hinges, all of us innocent as before, long before he and my mother got even near the stairs.

Inside the sanctum sanctorum, behind the cases of Wild Turkey, under the forty-ought-sevens and the rods and reels — were the dozen or so books. I would guess that I studied these tomes more thoroughly than those of Shakespeare and Dickens and Wordsworth and Hardy they were trying so to shove down my throat in school. After so much time with *The Perfumed Garden*, *Lady Chatterly's Lover*, and *The Complete Memoirs of Jacques Casanova*, I knew everything that they could teach one about eighteenth century French courtyards, nighteenth century Persian castles, twentieth century English gardens, flowers in naked gardens. I was quite accomplished on the nibbling of earlobes like lettuce, the licking of inner thighs like ice cream. I was a purblind master of literary sex, and my first unpublished bit of prose — the hoary grandmother of what you have in your hands this very moment — was a story ripe with those dandified words out of 19th century erotology — "member," "vulva," "she gasped out her passionate consent."

And what did it get me? A woman, much later, perhaps too much later, who thought I was a stunning wonderful lover. And all the while I was courting (and winning) her, I was peeping longingly through the keyhole at my roommates. Now, so much later, now that I know what I know, I figure in all likelihood my roomies probably would have welcomed a few ice-cream nibbles of their own from their nibbly friend, me. But you must remember: we weren't allowed, in those astringent times, to think about such things, and so we wasted our seed, futilely, on the already encrusted dormitory sheets.

❧ ❧ ❧

"If there were no existence in any form," I think, "would birth reproduce itself." I am lying abed, in the heat, staring at the walls, nursing memories of that summer I went crazy. It was a summer when I thought, practically endlessly, about birth and death. Was there really a twin with me, in the womb; a twin who, at birth-time, was so exhausted in competing with me for the nutrients coursing through the double umbilical cords that he lasted barely twenty minutes outside the *matrix*? Can I in all good conscience love myself after that tiny, post-foetal murder? Does he still exist outside of memory (not my own)?

Are there — as the philosopher has said — two suns, one hidden behind the other, the hot and the brilliant covering up the black and the cold, one swimming invisibly in the dark, always just behind our familiar, brightly burning eye? Can we ever bring them together, alive or dead?

When I went mad, I thought about that robbing of life, the stealing of the very breath from a younger, perhaps less innocent, brother (I made him push first into the void outside.) Sometimes the sadness of my unidentifiable crimes so overwhelmed me, in that summer of 1977, that I couldn't decide whether to get up or die. If I did get up — if I chose not to die — I had to decide whether to make coffee or tea and put on my clothes; or perhaps decide to decide to stay in my old, dirty, three-week-old-worn underpants, yellow (as they were) with the stains of my past indiscretions. It was a hot summer there to the north, in the desert, and the heat went at us as if with a club, and there were a great number of flies.

❧ ❧ ❧

My father came to see me there the next day, there in the trailer park, on the Playa Cula, overlooking the Sea of Mexico. It was quite a surprise. I certainly didn't expect him to turn up here: my aloof, proud, patrician father, in his seersucker suit (1940s style), his straw boater with the white band, his Phi Beta Kappa key joining the vest wings, his white shoes and black socks. He flew in so suddenly, and unexpectedly; and the news he had was not all bad.

He turned up in the bathroom, of all places. He didn't care to go out to the public market, or the beach, certainly not to the Tonameca river. He did all his business with me in the bathroom, peering at me over the sink — that fifty-five year old face, with the heavy lines down each side, between cheek and nose, the downturned mouth, the dimple in the chin, the dewlaps, the high forehead, the heavy upper lids (beginning to fold down with the weight of the ages). Even the glasses.

This was the first time I had seen him since 1950, the week before the doctor said, primly, drying his hands, "He is expired." For the first time in almost four decades my father has left his hiding place and come to stay with us in our trailer there at the edge of the sea. A strange experience (I little expected it) but, if you think about it, his arrival was certainly no queerer than his sudden disappearance, so long ago.

He isn't grim. Far from it. He smiles at me from behind the pane, and I catch myself thinking that it's nice to have him back because, after all, while we were growing up together, he and I didn't have much of a chance to talk. He went off to work in his crisp blue-and-white seersucker suit, heading off for the office just as I was getting up. In the evening, long after I had come home, he would appear and just as quickly disappear, on his way to a business meeting, or a dinner party. By the time he returned, I was asleep.

On weekends, when I woke up at eleven or so, he would have already gone to the office "to clean up a few odds and ends." Later that night, he would be in his room, deeply involved in Ellery Queen. I slipped by the door of his bedroom as quietly as possible. Two men, or a man and an almost man, in the same house, scarcely exchanging a word, except when he came to my room, as he did from time to time, to tell me I had stayed out too late at night, or that he had heard I was driving too fast, or that I was being sullen, not communicating. "My children never talk to me," he once complained to a friend. He meant that we didn't know what to say to him that hadn't already been said.

When they buried him I was a stranger at a stranger's funeral. The church was filled with hundreds of people. I remember the stifling cathedral, and me in my new dark suit— sweating, wondering if anyone knew that I didn't really belong there, at the front of the chapel, with the grieving family. I should have been somewhere else, perhaps outside, or on the streets, racing about with my friends. When I got home that night, I remember being relieved that he wouldn't be there, calling me to some task (build the fire; get me a fifth of Wild Turkey out of the liquor closet; fetch my slippers). From now on, I was free: no longer would I have to polish his boots, work in his "Victory" Garden, trying to hide from his sharp, never deceived eyes ("you missed that whole row over there"), the hundred tasks assigned to me by him, tasks that never represented love nor affection nor something shared but a job that he wanted done because he paid my bills and couldn't think of any other way to charge me. To avoid these tasks, I turned myself into a house-ghost, staying out of his way, running down the back stairs when he came in the front, running to freedom before he found out that I wasn't there at all ("Where's that boy? I swear, he slips out of here and I never even see him!")

So when he disappeared, so suddenly, four decades ago, I thought I would never hear from him again. Yet here I wake up thousands of miles from where he last walked this earth, and there he is, peering back at me, not unkindly, over the sink — as I am shaving, brushing my teeth, washing my armpits. I contemplate his visage in the glass and wonder, why, indeed, this sudden appearance?

It might be that I was given the chance to see another side of my father last night. I didn't see the drudge attorney in a tall building downtown, the lonely man waiting impatiently for his lonely supper, a man alone in the bed upstairs, reading about murder. Rather, I get to see him at his weekend camp, on the Fernandina River, roughing it with his friends, in the small, drafty, clapboard cottage, wobbling as it does, on brick legs, the place verboten to womenfolk and children. I was allowed there once, and I watched and wondered (is this my father?) as he and his buddies Gus Lowenstein and Lou Fletcher and Tom Bilbo cooked up shrimp perloo, told stories, drank morning coffee laced with sour mash, got up at four to hunt deer and quail in that rich North Florida pine tar country with the morning mist and the tiny fishing boats huffing by on the Fernandina river outside.

I remember best when they came back to the cabin after a morning in the wet blind, raucous, laughing, "God, did you see that eight-pointer..." "Well, Herb told me that with a Double Ought Four you could...from fifty yards away..." "Jesus, where did that buck come from..." And later, making a potato rich fish chowder, piled with the scrappie and croaker we had pulled from the river in the late afternoon, eating with such gusto, telling stories, telling stories: "Tell them about the Navy wife — Bob...you know, when you were working in the garden."

"You mean where I was in my old jersey and she drove up..."

"Yeah, that's it..."

"...and she thought I was the yardman, tried to hire me away. It was wartime, and help was hard to get, so I said to her, 'Waaallll, I'd do it lady, I reckon, but the family, they let me live here.' And she says, 'Well, we can do that too, we have a servant's room in our house, and you're welcome to it.' "

And he pauses, and they are already starting to grin, and he says,

" 'Lady — I shud tell you: they let me eat with them, too.' And she gulped, and thought for a minute — help was awful hard to come by — and so she said, a little nervous, 'Well, I guess we could...'

" 'But the missus here,' " he said — and Gus and Tom and Lou are starting in to laugh, they've heard it, but they want to hear it again, and he wants to tell it again — " 'The missus in the house here. I shud tell you she lets me sleep with her, too.' " Great gouts of laughter, the cigar smoke rolling up on the Coleman lantern, its two hot nuts of fire, hanging down, the men weak with laughter, slapping their knees, and "Omigawd" and "Haw-haw," and then,

"Gus — tell the one about you and Mary, when that lady from the church, came to your door...you remember..." And I am watching them there (I have never seen my father laugh so hard before — and those stories!), the four of them talking far into the night, exercising their need, as men, to be alone, with their man's talk, and their freedom, to be alone with each other, and...

...We become them, for a week or two, there at the trailer park, on the Playa Cula, next to the great Sea of Mexico: telling stories late into the night, getting up the next morning, putting on the coffee (is there any greater life-smell than the aroma of fresh coffee of a morning?) We lived the lives of men, and the men before us, who lived (for awhile) a Man's world, a world from a half a century ago.

❧ ❧❧

I would spend the mornings trying to decide whether to take a bath, or to pull on the clothes I had worn so many days without washing, or to kill myself. My hair was crusted with dirt, flakes out of the brain — the brain extruding itself through the scalp. The decision to do nothing was probably the best one available, but even that was filled with self-argument. "Should I really do nothing?" I would wonder. "Why is there something rather than nothing...?" But I could never finish the thought, even if there was a conclusion. Can birth reproduce itself — even if there is nothing to reproduce?

I was thinking a great deal about death, puzzling over what it was going to be like at the moment, 25,000 years (light or no) into space. "When one begins the last flight, the stars surround one on all sides," I wrote in my journal. "There is no up nor down. There's no brightness within or without. The only lights are clusters of galaxies so numerous they might well constitute the haze of eternity.

"If I were an eye, a single eye, an eye as large as Jupiter," I wrote, "could I close huge lids around a Jupiter-size space?" Great Jupiter lids — large, stately valves, moving in a circle, golden valves coming round, closing down on the last of the light, reducing it from a jetting gusher down to a tiny vaporish spume of white, then to a trickle of bright turned dark in glow. The last of the valves gliding past, the trickle of nothing reduced to nothing. Could I close them, eliminate the solar system, the stars in all directions, the meteors, comets, asteroids, space? Eliminate them all, and myself, shut them out with a wink? Can birth reproduce itself?

DECEMBER 17

Even in the midst of the most remarkable experiences...we fabricate the greater part of the experience, and can hardly be made to contemplate any event, except as inventors thereof. All this goes to prove that from our fundamental nature and from remote ages we have been accustomed to lying.

— *BEYOND GOOD AND EVIL*
FREDERICH NIETZSCHE

I lie in my trailer bunk. Out the window, I can see the sky, and the neighboring plane tree. There is a peculiar center of the brain, they say, that serves no other purpose than to recognize faces and patterns, and patterns-in-faces. With this part of the brain, ill-used by most, we quasi-neo-schizophrenics see features everywhere: in clouds, woodwork, carpets, walls, and the leaves of plane trees outside our trailer windows. Blighted spots become eyes, irregularities in grain turn to mouths, old water marks are noses, bug-eaten edges form the ears.

I study this plant outside my window each morning, searching for a clue, an indication of the meaning (me, my friends, Mexico, the furtherest galaxy of them all which, they say, is some twenty billion light years beyond me and this portative room.)

Every morning two large leaves on a single stem resolve themselves to square off for debate. The one on the left is Nancy Drew, girl detective. Her blonde hair, the seared upper part of the leaf, is cut short. The frazzled edge of one side is a snubbed nose and a downturned, unremitting girl's mouth. The decay at the bottom forms a Buster Brown bow tie. Directly across from her is the one-eyed Green Blob monster. The circumference of his face runs along warped edges of the leaf; there is the single squinting eye and a round brown sore for the mouth. Each time a breeze comes by, Nancy Drew and the Green Blob bounce up and down before each other, arguing endlessly, she angry about something he's said or done, he responding with his angry insults.

As I watch them, I see that they are strong together — much stronger than they would be apart (despite the chasm in appearance and age). The two of them are endlessly querulous with each other; they never get beyond each other. "Get out of my face," the Green Blob might say, harshly. "You're not listening," she'll retort (hers is an upper-class voice, not grating and harsh like his). They'll bounce back and forth, held to each other by a bond from above that neither of them wants, but that neither of them can sever.

This vision, more than anything else, tells much about my past, and how I will weave it into my present and future, here in Puerto Perdido, far from friends and family and homeland. It is a clue to my father's sudden appearance; it tells me something about the bonds I have formed with Ernest and Sam'l; it foreshadows the growing importance of Diego and Chuy in my life here; and, perhaps, above all, explains the peculiar hold that the novel about Torquemada has on me.

Nancy Drew and the Blob, in their endless dialogue, reflect the *why* of my journey to this alien land — my loves and my thoughts, both fictive and real. Because of them — the inseparable two of them — my secrets will be revealed to me, as they will be — if they have not already — have been for you. (I trust you to treat all these revelations with appropriate discretion.)

I should point out that in the past, in these writings, I have often appeared to be baring my soul — but all that is the Möbius Literary Strip of deception. For the first time, and unless I am again prevaricating, shamelessly — I shall be laying out for you this time the true heart of me. And because of our separate experiences, it is entirely possible that you will be able to understand the beauty, the ugliness, and the consequence of these revelations far more easily than I.

❧ ❧ ❧

I suspect that the mark of change is that time becomes irrelevant — and, at the same time — worthy of comment itself. We awaken at seven, I read and go on a couple of uneasy rounds with Ignacio and Torquemada. All the while, I am wondering what is passing in the world, in my morning *Times*, 3000 miles to the north. Sam'l and Chuy, not at all concerned about the events of the restless world somewhere out there, start work together on Project #1 of the day: breakfast. After that, while Sam'l goes into town for lumber, Chuy washes the great silver skin of our trailer. When Sam'l returns, the two of them go to work on a platform that is to get me in and out of the car when we are at the river. The two of them are always watching out for me. While they are hammering away, one of them will yell at me, ask how I am doing. Sam'l will say, "Have you taken your birth control pills yet?" What he means is have I taken my daily blood pressure pills. "No," I yell back: "And anyway, you've got it all wrong. They're my death control pills."

They finish at one or so, at the heat of the day, and we drive to the river. Once there, I use the new platform to let myself down into the cool waters. I am constructing Presa Los Dioses — a dam across the narrow stream. In such a reverie (sun, water, stones, water striders, boulders lifted from here to there) I am also working on my theory of life, the stone dams that we humans have constructed to survive in a world of 5,000,000,000 people.

After a few minutes of work worthy of the Hoover, the Engineer-in-Charge lies down in the gathered waters behind Los Dioses dam. I eye the traffic on the nearby dirt road: donkeys, pigs, a tractor, a family on burro, a small truck filled with rocks. The water passes. All is passing; it may or may not mean something. Later, we return home, and rest in the late afternoon sun while Chuy washes The Ox. I watch him, my dark Zapotec worker, face passive, the symphony of his moves singing strange songs to me, every part of his visible dark and lustrous skin, vibrating, in the declining light.

Ernest joins us, and we go to our favorite restaurant, Doña Meche's ("Meche" is the nickname of the lady who owns it: we dub it "Don Ameche's"). Sam'l turns to the next table to talk politics with a local, and Ernest and I discuss, vigorously if not wisely: genetics, childbirth, palenotology, ageology, baileology, and flaileology. I start out with one of my usual operative question-statements:

ME: I was thinking about genetics today.

HE: I know what you mean.

ME: Do you know what Whitehead said about genetics?

HE: Coming from you, it's probably a lie.

ME: No, I'm serious. What do you know about genetics?

HE: What do *you* know about genetics?

ME: Well, there are these two trees, and they grow — and then they die. That's it.

HE: (Not hearing) We all have genetic coding. I know that. It's called Karma. We hold in our DNA our pasts and our future.

ME: Do you know that when a girl is born, she contains in her ovum not only the seeds of all the children she will have — but the seeds of her children's seeds, and the seeds of those, ad infinitum. That's karma squared.

Ernest (not listening) points at the floor of Don Ameche's where some wag (or wagger) has put doggy-prints in the cement, to be preserved forever. I tell him about that branch of geological research that specializes in coprology — where dinosaur turds that have been turned to rock by the ages are studied for dietary habits, form and substance, dimension, and insight into the tastes, virtues, vices, and dancing patterns of dinosaurs.

"There is also a branch," he says, "and I forget the name of it, but it exists, I know, where they take petroglyphs of the places, formerly mud, where the dinosaurs have sat, leaving impressions of their assholes, preserved forever. I can't remember what it is called."

"Retrograde fittings? Holistic Studies? Sphinctology?" I offer. I am still trying to catch up on Sam'l's conversation at the next table over, with the fat old man from Oaxaca — but his Spanish, sharpened by two years in Ecuador, is lost to me. I refuse to argue with Ernest any more. He makes up facts right and left, bigger lies than my own. I eat my favorite dish, freshwater shrimp, boiled, all the while eyeing my friend Chuy, that dark astonishing Zapotec, who says nothing, eats quickly and efficiently, leaves the red snapper, at the end of the meal, a neat pile of polished bonelets on his shining plate.

Three weeks ago, I was answering the telephone, writing at the computer, going to the mailbox, cooking, fearing the unknown, the disruption out of tomorrow. Tonight, I have no telephone, nor computer, nor mailbox. The loneliness that accompanied my last few trips outside the United States is not here, at this moment (it might well not return). Perhaps I have changed; perhaps the world has. Perhaps I am no longer dying. When we cease to cast the spotlight in the darkened chambers, we are free to find what we were searching for all along.

I am no longer travelling to travel. I am not venturing here and there for a night or two, a wandering damselfly (one rested on my moveless hand for a moment this afternoon, huge-eying me, at the Tonameca), moving on, every day, meeting only hotel clerks and waiters. I have chosen to live apart from the road, and my countrymen. Except for these two; and, when they depart, two Zapotec gods who will be here to change my life irrecoverably.

❧ ❧ ❧

The Hare-Lip Aldeo doesn't talk too much, but good soldier that he is, during dinner he marches through eight pieces of chicken, two helpings of rice, and more zucchini than I can count. He's from Los Heroes, at the edge of the mountain range. The sewer in Los Heroes runs down the middle of the main street, right out there in the open so you can see what the neighbors (those few who have inside bathrooms) do with their time to themselves. I have been there before, and I remember the sharp sickly odor of the refuse mixing with the scent of the honeysuckle. It is an unnerving combination. Sometimes they have to shutter the windows to be rid of the smells from outside.

I ask Aldeo what he does.

"Nada." Figures. There aren't many jobs for young harelips, even with big shoulders and nice eyes.

"What does your father do."

"Estuvo fallecido," he says. That means he's dead. It's a pretty way of saying it. Literally, it means "He had fallen." The pole has fallen.

"What does your mother do?" He shrugs his shoulders.

"How many brothers and sisters do you have?"

"Eight," he says. That explains what his mother does.

"Are you the oldest."

"Second oldest." Aldeo favors the shadows, even in the dim candlelight we normally eat by. He turns his head so that the darkness has charge of his upper lip.

"What do you want to do?"

He shrugs his shoulders again. "Mechanico. Soldado. Licensiado." Mechanic, soldier. Attorney? Is he making fun of me? His eyes keep flicking towards the window, and back again. I wonder if my "guard" is outside there, watching us. I get up, go casually over to the window, look out the bars. There is still the smell of hot wetness in the air, the rich smell of decay. The lights of the town of El Vapor reflect on the thin clouds. I think I see the shadowy figure of Paco under the naked bulb of the street light, but I can't be sure.

Aldeo tells me he is still a student. What else is there for him to do — although it's a wonder that he can come up with the 5,000 reales a month for the school fee, him and his poor widowed mother with a half a dozen children.

"¿Tienes trabajo?" I ask Aldeo (Do you work?). I offer him a tepid beer, "El Claro." He sips at it.

"En sitios," he says (Here and there).

"¿Qué tipo de trabajo?" (What kind of work?)

"Oh — como sabe Ud. — lo que haya." (You know, whatever there is.)

While we're talking, Aldeo gets up, stands near the window, in the shadows. Funny — he's so young, and yet he carries such a power, the emanation of one much older, the heat from a kiln. I can feel it — a self-possession that is unusual coming from one in a culture that makes no provision for physical differentness.

"Tiene un hermano más mayor. ¿Qué hace él?" You have an older brother. What does he do?

"O, pues..." he looks at the burning nightsky for a minute: "Se lucha." (He fights).

"Oh, sí," I say — "un boxer."

"De un modo" (so to speak). His eyes look through me. He seems something of a fighter, too. He has a stance that is in no way that of a poor, underprivileged student. He looks out the window again. I come up to stand next to him. The light of the city burns brightly on the undersides of the clouds from the west. It is like the brain, I think. Those clouds are the grey-white Dura Mater, with its complex fillibrations. A brain filled with the darkness of thoughts. But that's just a cover, a disguise. The real darkness comes from below, where the soul lies. If there can be said to be something as evanescent as a soul.

Later, as Aldeo is taking off his clothes, I forget about his brothers and sisters and mother and fighting and wars. I forget about his lip, too. Aldeo's body is out of Greece. The hair atop his head like steel; the hair below flaming black cotton. He burns me: he burns my flesh my soul in a way I have never been burned before. He must have been sent to me from some other world — with otherworldly experiences that belie his age. "Quizás eres un díos," I whisper to him at one point (maybe you're some kind of a god). He is silent. Where did he learn such tenderness? It is as if he didn't want me — and yet, he showed a kindness, made to me a special gift of his god's body.

His upper lip shines. How strange it is when I put my lips to it — how strangely complete it feels (despite the thin moustache he affects to hide it); and how, after a moment, he pushes me away, protecting the only part of him that is truly virginal. I wonder about the inversion of passion that makes such ugliness beautiful. Aldeo has power, inside and out: he could crush me to death with his arms — and yet the only part of himself he wants to defend is his poor ragged nether lip (that I have come to love, giving my own lips a scar that will stay with me to my dying day.)

As he sleeps, I study this strange mouth. "It is, perhaps, right," I think. It fits, it is at one with him, the young and scarred face. As he sleeps, later, I pull back the covers, put my cheek close to the dark upper-half-hourglass. My hand comes to touch its own point of love. I venture to the edge of suns, then back, come upon the suns again, again, and again — until I can sustain nothingness no longer. About me there are explosions, lightings through sky, roarings and tremblings, a room filled with white and blue and green and yellow, a trembling of bed and room, bombs bursting the air, blasts through night and the air, filling all with huge shaking flashes, the tearing of explosions.

Aldeo rises on one elbow, smiles through his tortured lip at me, rests his powerful hand on the top of my head for a moment, sighs, closes his eyes, falls back, and is fast asleep again.

In the morning, he is up before me, drawing on his cheap white shirt, his torn jeans, breaking my heart — my god disappearing. He goes to the window, pulls back the curtain, stares a moment, turns to me for a moment with his half smile — eyes shrewd and careful. He brushes past my outstretched hand and is gone. "How good that he is cautious," I think. "He is not out to advertise his liasons. It is good that he will protect me." He is careful; quiet; very knowing for one so young.

Later, El Jefe tells me the government ammunition depot in El Vapor was destroyed. They were sure it was the work of the mountain rebels. Someone had placed a charge within the heart of the dump — a charge that was large enough, and set in such a professional way, that it blew the top of it a hundred meters in the sky. The authorities are searching everywhere, but they still have no clues.

Long afterwards, the sight of that explosion bathing the undersides of the night clouds, bathing my love, stayed with me. "It is like something from below," I think. "The clouds are just reflections. The reality lies far below."

DECEMBER 21

We are in a cosmic realm, a realm older than religion. The idea of the creation of the world has probably not yet been conceived. They kill in the eternal. The gods have not yet been born...

ANTI-MEMOIRS

Diego's favorite ice cream is pistachio, but sometimes he likes the *nuez*, vanilla swirls with little bits of nut. He orders it for us, and then we sit and eat it and watch the people go by on the street of Puerto Perdido. We watch the pale Americans, the drunken Americans, the loud Americans, the unlovely Americans. Intermixed with them are the beetlenut-brown Mixtecs and Zapotecs — boys with buckets full of fish, women carrying brown-eyed babies, children running and laughing, old men dressed, still, in traditional white shirts and *huaraches*.

"Gringo watching," I call it, but I'm also watching the Mexicans, because of my prejudice. I've been living in Mexico on and off for twenty years, and slowly I'm developing this prejudice, this terrible prejudice, against pale skin. "They're so pale and wan — in such a hurry," I think, trying to forget that I'm one of them. Diego isn't prejudiced. He watches the young ladies, watches them all. Those from north of the border are as interesting to him as those from his own home town. He wants them all.

This morning we had our first rain in almost six months. This is a drought area, and the hills have turned sere. I often wonder that the whole area doesn't come down with some great fever from the sky: a grand conflagration that will burn up the fields, take the city of Puerto Perdido and the tourists, take them up in one smoky mass. The rain changes all that, turns the fields dark, filling the air with the smell of whetted ashes.

"What's it like being here, in Mexico, in a wheel-chair?" The lady asking this question is thirty, thirty-five years old. Her chin is sharp and pointed, her face pale, eyes hidden behind large dark glasses. I am watching the balloon-man across the plaza. He has balloons in all sizes and shapes, floating a bunch above his head, on strings. I favor the "monstro," the monster head, a funny face with squiggly balloons sprouting over the top of it. I wonder how he makes it look so — well — human.

"I have a brother in a wheel-chair," she says. "He's a quad. That's why I'm asking." Throaty voice, no accent. She must be from the west. A brother who's a quad. "I've got a brother who's a quad." They always say that. Or: "My mother has diabetes, they took off her leg right here," (slicing motion across the thigh). We hear that a lot. "My uncle's in a wheelchair. Viet-Nam." The non-specific description. Or the very specific: "My dad is a stroke victim and his whole side is useless — he uses a cane and we have to feed him." All these cripples. A world full of cripples. And we get to hear about all of them. As if we wanted to know, as if we really cared.

I always wonder why absolute strangers come up to me to tell me these stories about people I don't know, will never know, can never care about. "I have enough troubles without this," I think. "They are just trying to reach out, the only way they know how," I tell myself. "You're not alone," they are saying, sure that I feel alone. "I know someone who's just as bad off as you," they're saying. "Don't you feel better now?" they think.

Maybe I am softening. I don't pretend I'm a deaf-mute anymore, when they start in on their relatives. I don't — as I did, the last time I was here — pretend that I speak no English. "*Lo siento — no entiendo los gabachos,*" I said. ("Sorry, I don't understand Americans.") There were times, I have to admit, when I just looked them at them, and said "Oh?" or, nodding my head, "Mmm." Then I let it die.

Thirty-five years have probably softened me, made me more willing to listen: People hurting, everywhere people hurting. This lady hurting, with whatever it is that our families feel: angst, maybe; fear, possibly; guilt, certainly. "Anytime anyone talks to you, it is God talking to you, telling you something you need to hear right now," Stephen Gaskin used to say — but sometimes I wonder if the words are garbled, the messenger a little befuddled. What to respond? I know, in 1952 or 1966 or 1974 you couldn't get a whisper out of me on this "my brother's a quad" business. Now, it's different. *The idea of the creation of the world has probably not yet been conceived...*

"It's the same," I say. "No: that's not exactly right. It's complicated and it can be frustrating. But there are things to compensate for it," I tell her. "Like my two employess. Diego's been working for me for a couple of winters now, Chuy started a few weeks ago. They take me about Puerto Perdido, to the river, or to the beach, to swim. They get me out of the car and down to the water — and then back out again, rinsed off, into the car, home again.

"They buy my food for me at the public market (inaccessible), help me cook it (I'm learning to cook black beans and rice), even help me eat it," I tell her. "They help me a great deal," I tell her. Two employees. What does that mean? Two young people who are becoming part of my life here, so far from home. Chuy with his dark polished skin, his careful walk, his straight Mayan nose, his serene face. Diego with the rounded god's head, right out of the Yucatan, the great slow eyes, the eyes he rolls about so when I ask him to do something he doesn't especially want to do.

"They're fun to be with," I tell her. They are filled with that strange mixture of Mexican manhood and sentiment that fascinates me. "They might be the best part of my stay here," I say. "They're very good workers. They're with me every day. Nights, too. I pay them $35. That's more than the minimum wage here." Diego, who makes me laugh when I am feeling blue. "¿Qué pasa, gabacho?" What's going on, he asks me, at those times when I don't feel like going out. The two of them manage, somehow, to get me out the door. I don't protest, not too much. At the ocean's edge, I can't be thinking those thoughts anymore, can I?

"They teach me Spanish," I tell her. "I'd have to pay Berlitz a fortune for the lessons they give me for free." I tell her about the frustrations. Mexico isn't set up for wheelchairs. Not many ramps, almost no curb-cuts. There are very few hotels that have rooms for the disabled. I had to scout out the five restaurants (out of twenty) in Puerto Perdido that we can get to without having to go up or down steep stairs. I have yet to get over my unwillingness to be carried in and out of restaurants, bathrooms, banks.

"It's a concession to being in a Third World Country," I tell her. "With my helpers, it doesn't have to be a big deal." They like showing off their strength, and they can be very funny about it. *"Pinche Gringo,"* Diego will say. *"Pesa 400 kilos."* That means he thinks I weigh 850 pounds. It is his way of telling me he likes me: when he calls me *"Pinche Gringo."*

"There's no special parking, or special placards," I tell her. "But when I park my car on the beach, so I'm near the water, the police never bother me." I think of how they would do it in California, or Florida, or Texas. It's against the law, just like it is here, so the police there would probably give me a $250 ticket, and apologize for doing it.

"Sometimes, I feel like a mountain climber here," I say. Quite suddenly the sky turns iridescent, then a brilliant magenta. The usual spectacular tropical sunset that happens so quickly. Even when you're expecting it, it's a surprise — the sudden end of the searing heat and too-bright sunlight. "How'd he get to be a quad?" I ask her. The street turns dim and dusty. I can no longer see her face, only the outline of her head, the tiny round gold metal around her neck. She is still wearing her dark glasses. She tells me about the drinking, and the general helling around when he was twenty. The drugs, the accident. "They didn't know whether he was going to live," she says. "He made it." She pauses. "I think he's a much better person for it," she says.

I look at the balloon man. He's standing under the one streetlight of Puerto Perdido. The light has just come on, so the balloons cast a dark cloud over him. There are many of them straining up on their strings — and he is such a tiny fellow that I half expect to see him take off, floating away into the starry sky, rising up into the stratosphere. Our balloon-man which art in heaven.

"A much better person," I say, nodding. "That's an awful thing to say."

"I'm sorry?" She's not apologizing — she just doesn't understand.

"I can't stand hearing that sort of thing," I say. She turns her head to watch the balloon man. He creates his monsters right there, out of rubber and helium. He fills the balloons from the great bruised silver tank at his side, twists them into animal faces, or strange bodies, twisting and turning them this way and that. When he fills the balloons with the helium, it makes a raw, screeching sound. She sits down on the curb next to me.

"I don't understand," she says, "...but maybe I never will. I don't know. I just don't have your experience." She tells me that she is a professional nurse, living in Colorado. She says that even with her training, the hardest job was learning to deal with her brother's body. "I'm a nurse by training. I've done caths — lots of times. And yet, nothing is harder for me," she says. She stops. "He was the one that used to pick on me all the time, never had any time for me, called me 'stupid.' And now there he is, lying flat on his bed. Sometimes I have to give him his catheter in the morning. And he can't even cover himself up..."

A little girl, she can't be more than five years old, is trying to push two boys, probably her brothers, up the hill, in a tiny scratched red wooden wagon, with warped wheels. One of the boys, the older one, is yelling "*Recio, recio!*" (faster, faster!) The other one is just sitting there, at the front of the wagon, without a stitch on, just digging the hell out of his ride. The girl can barely get it to move, what with the hill and all: she's pushing with all her might. "I don't even know what I mean," I say. "About those words — 'maybe he's better for it.' I don't think it's up to us to say that sort of thing." What is it they say? *Only the gods can worship god.* Only the gods can pass judgement on those who are now so different.

Diego is behind me now. He is pushing back and forth on the wheel-chair, slowly, rhythmically. There's a fiesta in Pinotepla. He wants to get over there, to check on a young lady who he claims will be his next "novia." He wants to get me over there because he knows that by ten, when things are starting to happen, I'll be drunk, and insist on going home to bed. He doesn't want to miss a thing. I went to the Pinotepla Fiesta before, once last year. The ground is sandy, people will be pushing in on my wheel-chair from all sides. We'll get stuck, people will stare. From two feet away they'll stop dead and stare. They always do. I'm probably the only six-foot gringo they've ever seen in a wheel-chair in their town — possibly the only one they'll see in this part of Mexico.

Given all the bother, I probably wouldn't even go...if it weren't for the fact that when I'm there, I'm living. Going out in the world, seeing a different world. The lady wants to know if her brother in his wheel-chair would be happy here. "Sure," I want to tell her, "it'll be all right if he doesn't mind getting stuck, having people gaga staring at him, kids standing, just staring at him. It's all right, if you don't mind being a freak." I want to tell her that. But that sounds bitter — and it probably would be a lie. There aren't many of us around, and we're the object of curiosity; but it's a curiosity coming from some of the kindest, sweetest, most open, free people in the whole world. I think of my times here, the despair that occasionally comes from the inaccessible buildings, places I can't ever dream of getting up to, or down from: the times that my bladder is bursting, and there's no place to go, and I want to scream, or cry. And Diego, with his great wise serious eyes, understanding, somehow, always figuring out what is going on, figuring a way for me to make it, without going balmy.

"It's a whole different world down here," I tell her. "Your brother might like it, or, then again, he might despise it. You can never tell. It depends on him, and how much he likes Mexico, and Mexicans." I think about what happened this morning, after Sam'l and Ernest went off. I was feeling a bit blue, and then Diego started in pinching me, and then ducking away when I tried to grab him. He saw I was turning a bit sour, and he wanted to be sure I got my daily quota of tickles and pinches. I wonder if the attendants in the United States — what do they call them? "the personal care attendants" — I wonder if they are allowed to tickle their charges when they start to feel bad. Is that written in an attendant's job description? A good thorough tickling when the patient starts to feel bad?

"To me — they're all gods, so I forgive them everything," I say. I think of Diego, with his great round face, that monumental face out of the tombs of Quintana Roo — the lids so heavy, the lips so broad, so compassionate, the eyes so inexpressively expressive. Chuy with the elegant Mayan nose, his wry, gentle way with me. *The gods have not yet been born.*

"What do you mean by that?" she asks, moving her hands vaguely. I wonder if I can get it across. "To be here, to really enter the country, you have to be willing to leave a whole set behind. And not for a week or a month — but for a longer time," I tell her. "There's something special here. We might call it 'love' — but I think there are other better words."

"Mexicans learn to love so quickly and easily, no matter how unloveable we may be," I say. "Some of us learn to love them in return, without reserve. We gringos are so much slower, so much more fearful. We might call it love, but to us it's more like taking hostages. Especially for those of us..." I want to say "for those of us like your brother and me..." but I don't finish the sentence.

Over where the sun has died on the horizon, there is a bare smudge of rouge, a burning off, so far off. "It's god-love," I think. "The gods know it well." I look at her. She's brushing off her skirt. "It's hard for us to learn about them," I say. Sometimes we wonder what's left for us. She turns, smiles — is gone. I'm still talking, still formulating whatever it is I am supposed to be formulating, and she's gone. I think of that line from Beckett: *"The trouble with her was that she had never really been born."*

❧ ❧ ❧

An hour later, Diego and I are smack-dab in the middle of the Pinotepla Fair. Just like I thought: I get stuck in the sand twice, and at least 300 people give me a good going-over, not looking: *staring*. And, yes, Diego has talked me into eating several *tacos de cabeza*. Brain tacos. "It's all right if you don't mind eating all those thoughts," I tell my friends later. "It's supposed to make you smarter."

"¿Quién es esta mujer?" Diego asks me. Who's that woman? He thinks, naturally, that I should make her my *novia*, and eventually marry her. He thinks I should marry every woman I meet, settle down. He starts to look for his girlfriend in the crowd. I get a glimpse of her. She has long black hair, tied in a single long thick strand, interwoven with a length of bright red wool. Her eyes are as deep and as mysterious as his own, her skin the color of butter chocolate.

"*No sé*," I say. I don't know. "*Otra gringa*," I say. "*Poquita confusada*." A little confused. "*Como todo*." Another woman. A little confused. Just like the rest of us.

DECEMBER 23

Each time I see a crowd of people
Just like a fool I stop and stare;
It's really not the thing to do
But maybe you'll be there...

— POPULAR SONG, 1948

The Trailer Camp of Playa Cula is filling up with people from Mexico City. Before, we were spread out, fifteen or thirty feet from the next trailer. Now we are suddenly joined at the navel with a family that arrives one day in an old VW bus, complete with tent and dog, taking the space immediately west of us.

The first "zip" in the morning releases the ten or twelve of them — we're never exactly sure how many there are — from their tiny home. There tent is so small that we can only envision them lying, stacked like cord-wood, from eight at night to seven or so in the morning, not moving, barely breathing, like the dozens of circus people who erupt from a VW bug.

During the day, the Normals swim, talk quietly, and love up their mutt, a Ritalin-overdosed poodle named Molé (pron. "MOL-aigh.") He is one of those ratty (or moley) little numbers with sparse white hair, pink skin, and a venomous personality. The family, despite spending their nights *pied-a-terre*, seems quiet and serene. Molé makes up for it by yipping constantly at us, at our voices, at our footsteps — as well as any stray visitors, dogs, birds, and passing clouds. "Yip-yip-yip," he goes, two or three dozen times a day, in his piercing soprano voice. "Molé, O Molé," says the youngest daughter, a bit of a rachet-mouth herself. "O, shut up, Molé," I mutter. The family responds to Molé's disgusting personality by hugging, kissing, and sanctifying him. I think about making a true molé of him, poodle fricassee — with chocolate sauce and all the fixins'.

From the first zip in the morning until the last zip at night, we are conjoined to our unnamed family. And despite their lousy taste in animals — I'm quite in love with them. They are pleasant, kind, considerate, never raising their voices with each other, seemingly delighted with each other's company all hours of the day and night. The mother prepares gargantuan meals for a dozen or so folks with no effort — never demanding, never raising her voice. The father, looking slightly harrassed, never screaming or beating his charges, has his one period of retreat at eight in the morning when he adjourns to the front seat of the VW bus to read yesterday's newspaper and listen to a cassette recording of Schumann's "Spring" Symphony, in bits and pieces.

Sometimes I wonder what they think of our own musical tastes, over here to the east, ranging as it does from "Los Tigres del Norte" and "La Mujer" and Julio Jaramillo, Sublakshmi, the street music of Soweto, along with "The Thousand Faces of Lord Vishnu," and the entire B-Minor Mass (played ten times a week, less the middle part, which I lost somewhere outside of Cantamar) — and, finally, our triumph, the gutteral chants of the Bushmen of Burundi. If Sr. Normal and his Normal Brood find our musical selections strange, they never give indication of it — even resisting comment at those times when we let out yips in perfect imitation of Molé. I attribute it to Big City Living, where one learns discretion and that excellent Mexican trait of pretending that something funny going on is not going on at all and, if it is, is unworthy of attention or comment.

I am, as I say, in love with the whole family. I've always had this weakness for things normal. I suppose the family therapists would find that Sr. and Sra. Normal are so bound up in their children, and the children in each other, that the whole thing is emotional strangulation of the highest order — a massively neurotic family unit — but having never had the opportunity to live in such an world when I was young, I fall in love with those who go through their days with such apparent kindness and respect for each other.

I blush to think, however, what they may have overheard in the way of crude dinnertime conversation between Sam'l, Chuy, Diego and me:

SAM'L: There are some places in Oaxaca that you can't get a beer without getting a girl at the same time.

CHUY: Es muy bueno para salud. (It's very good for your health.)

SAM'L: Did I ever tell you about "Sopa Chepa de Vaca" (Cow Pussy Soup)?

ME: A hundred times — but let's hear it again.

SAM'L: That's the favorite morning soup in Quito. If you have a hangover, they order it for you. I was there with this girlfriend of mine from the States, the café where I usually have coffee, and the old man who runs the place found out that she had a hangover, and he said, "What you need is 'Chepa de Vaca' soup." And I had to translate.

CHUY: Chepa tu cula. (Untranslatable vulgarity in the command form.)

DIEGO: Estoy chepeando. (Untranslatable vulgarity in the gerundive).

CHUY: Me he chepado. (Untranslatable vulgarity in the past perfect tense).

DIEGO: Yo soy una pobre chepa. (Untranslatable vulgarity in the nominative case).

ME: Bastante, vergas — no quiero oir mas de este pinche chingadera. (Untranslatable vulgarity in the demand form.).

❧ ❧ ❧

This is the land of yesterday's newspapers. Sam'l goes to the newsstand to buy the Mexico City HOY from the day before. He's so cheap he reads it avidly for three or four days before he's willing to invest in a new one. Ernest, during our first weeks here, unwrapped all my pots and pans from the *Tribune* dated November 24, and read it faithfully and fully: first the news stories, outbreaks of leprosy in Madras, the lady in Tulsa who found Jesus in a tortilla, nuclear disasters in the Sea of Japan (he's big on nuclear disasters). Then, after a few days, tiring of these, he reads the want ads aloud. "Good opportunity for landscapers," he'll say. "And full term life insurance salesmen, EKG technicians. 'Retirees! Make $1,000 a week!' That's for you!" None of us bite, so he continues: "Here's another one: *FEMALE COLLEGE STUDENT, 40ish, still enjoys riding the merry-go-round and going for the brass ring.* Going for the brass ring — how's that for chutzpa? *I'll promise you a rose and a rose-garden! Need a wealthy companion-for-life. I'm waiting, Mr: Right. ARE YOU?* It's got her number here if you want to ring her up," he says, oblivious to me surreptitiously eyeing Chuy as he bends over with bucket and rags to clean the hubcaps of The Ox.

DECEMBER 24

Sam'l is always befuddled by our level of inactivity. I lie about for hours, scratching at my novel, or navel, or tuning in on Nancy Drew and The Blob. "The only work I care to do," I tell him, "is getting my mind to stop working." I watch the thousand thoughts going through the brain, and then turn over to watch another thousand. Rousing myself to go to the ice-house or the fruit market becomes a riot of activity. I can sit in my chair on the main street of Pt. Perdido, or lie in the Rio Tonameca, watching the water and the world go by, and I never feel the worse for wear.

"I'm bored," Sam'l says, and I feel a tinge of guilt that I am not keeping my good friend busy. "I'm sorry," I say. He waves his hand impatiently. "It's just that I don't like this town, with all its gringo tourists."

I look out the window at the coupling going on in the plane tree. "It's not your fault," he says. "I just need something to do." "I understand perfectly," I say. I toy with the notion of inviting him to join me in viewing the Nancy Drew Pageant for awhile, but Sam'l, as good a friend as he is, might not understand this most pregnant of my eccentricities, so I fall silent, peek at them out of the corner of my eye in case something new comes up (the petulant child's mouth, the Buster Brown bow tie, him bouncing up and down in rage). I think about how fitting it is that they are able, in their own perverse way, to reflect back to us the drama that we are acting out, ourselves, here — somewhere — below.

DECEMBER 25

The French Revolution, with a lot of pathos, really invented only three things: modern industry, which is extremely productive and extremely cruel; the nationwide war, in contrast to the cabinet wars of the 18th century — total war; and finally, the forms, the code of our sentiments. It's not simply emotion, but sentimentality. Which is just as cruel as industry and patriotic wars...

— ALEXANDER KLUGE

We wake up on the 25th of December without trees and holly, Silent Night and crèches, mounds of presents. I am thinking that those of us who have gone so far to escape American Christmas are the ultimate romantics. It is our memories of what it was that makes us go so far to avoid what it has become. We probably remember the simple family fest: carols on the doorstep, an exchange of a few presents, decorations (wreaths and candles) in the windows, a tall, freshly cut pine tree. It was the week-long end-of-the-year festivity with snow and lights and much color and heart. It had not yet become the sole province of Toys Я Us and Buffums and the electronic folks; had not been made the beacon of overcompensation for the wrongs of a civilization.

"Since I was the youngest in the family," I tell Sam'l, as he plods around the kitchen, stepping over the bob-tails of his dreams, setting up the coffee and whatnot — "my job was to awaken my sisters and my brothers at seven A.M., get them downstairs to open presents and not just lie about all day." It wasn't easy. Christmas vacation was the time for them to sleep. They were back from the schools where, presumably, they had been working hard. This was their vacation. They stayed up most of the night and slept most of the morning. I went from one room to another, begging them to come downstairs so we could open the presents, so I could open my presents. They snapped at me when I came in to wake them up, told me to stop being such a brat.

"They always called me 'brat' or 'shut up' or 'sissy,' " I tell him. Sam'l nurses the fire of the stove, fills the air with coffee pheromones. He may or may not be listening to me. Why do I still romanticise that time of my life? I wonder. Family love wasn't expressed in the no-nonsense society of the first half of this century. Whatever it was, whether it was love or not — we did it, but we didn't talk about it. "We were probably the last realists," I tell him. We consigned all our romantic notions to ceremony: Christmas, graduation, proms, funerals. The rest of the time, we lived our lives as a make-believe family unit in a fantasy world.

And it worked. Maybe that is why our lives were so straight-edge. We faked the whole process diligently and well. That's why I love Christmas so. That's why I have to get away from it.

❧ ❧ ❧

El Jefe is driving me back from the whorehouse in El Cerro. We go over there to drink, and watch the whores laugh and carry on, the men who visit who strut and get drunk and slam fists on the table. El Jefe is talking about his wife again.

"When she is nervous, she shakes her head back and forth, as if she is saying 'No' to everything," he tells me. "You want to ask her questions that can be answered with a shake of the head: 'Are you unhappy?' 'Don't you want to go to the store?' 'The world is in terrible shape, isn't it?' And there she is, shaking her head to all these questions. No, no, no.

"When her brother killed himself, she didn't go to the funeral, because she couldn't get hold of herself," he says. "She cried and talked to herself. Then she started saying that she was sure Antonio wasn't dead. 'I never saw his body,' she said. She repeated it over and over again. The thought went around in her head like a merry-go-round. She would wake me up at night, talking and crying. I couldn't shut her up. Nights were the worst. She'd get up with a wild look, and grab me, and say 'Are you sure he's dead?' I told her I had seen him in the coffin, with a purple carnation in his lapel, his arms at his sides, his eyes closed, his mouth straight for the first time. They had put powder on his face and rouge on his cheeks. He didn't look exactly like Tonio, because Tonio never wore rouge — but it was close enough for me.

"She wouldn't believe me. Tonio had been her favorite brother. He used to stand in front of her when her father would try to beat her. 'If you have to beat someone, beat me,' Tonio would say to the old man. He first did that when he was six years old, and she was four. 'If you have to do it, do it to me. I can take it,' he would tell the father, a wild-haired old man. Tonio would go and get a stick for the old man to beat him with.

"She paced around the bedroom for nights after Tonio killed himself, tripping on the same place on the carpet every time, picking at the sleeves of her nightgown, knotting and unknotting her waistband. She would ask me the same question a half-an-hour later, 'Are you sure that it was Tonio in the coffin? Are you sure they didn't put someone else in there by mistake?' You talk to me about crazy. I know what crazy is."

I am listening to El Jefe but, at the same time, I am thinking about the Arabs, and mathematics. Someone once said that the greatest discovery in the history of the world wasn't America, or how the earth revolves around the sun, or the cure for yellow fever. The greatest discovery was zero. "Whoever made that one up was a genius," I think. "Making up nothing." Astounding. Anyone can invent a 'one' or a 'seven' — but a *naught.* Like Bach's sonatas: The most important parts aren't the notes, nor even how the notes are played, but the silences between them. All these things, like zero, waiting to be discovered.

"They've been there since the first sun threw off its first rays of light and heat, waiting for us to figure them out," I think. What was it the master said? Newton didn't discover gravity. It was already there, waiting to be let out of its box. "There's no such thing as discovery," the master told me: "Just recovery."

El Jefe and I drive past the dump, close enough so I can see Lupe playing there. She's six years old, one of

Manuel's eight daughters. The people at the cantina always joke about Manuel and his wife. They say that he is just another daughter in the family. His wife will yell at him: "Get the frying pan!" Or she'll be washing in the sink: "Get the soap," she'll scream. The whole neighborhood can hear her, voice like a trumpet. At the Cantina El Vapor they'll be laughing at him, and he's just an old mill worker with a hump in his back and teeth so bad they look like ruined mountains.

And at the dump, his daughter Lupe is digging through a grey pile of trash. She has discovered a doll, its head crushed by the weight of stones. She picks it out from under the rocks, puts it to her breast. I see her swaying back and forth. She is thin, her cheeks famished, like a hungry cat. She looks around, as if to ward off anyone who might try to steal the doll from her. The streaks of dust in her hair make her look white-haired, prematurely old. I want to wave to her, but the window is closed to keep out the powerful smell of the dump of La Alma and El Vapor.

"Crazy," says El Jefe. "You want to know if I know crazy? We invented it." What is it they say: *Perhaps madness is the forgotten way. "Lupe, my mother, ay*— my mother. She used to go around the house, setting the clocks back. It would be noon, and she would decide she liked nine-thirty, so you'd come home for lunch, and the clocks would be telling you it was either time to get up or go to bed. I'd say, 'Mama. Why'd you do that, set all the clocks back?' And she'd look at me — right in my eyes — and say, 'Set the clocks back? I did nothing of the sort. What's wrong with you, boy? Do you think I'm *crazy?'* Have you ever had your own mother tell you that you're crazy for thinking she's crazy? I don't care if I'm fifty years old: I tell you, my family — we invented crazy. What's wrong?"

"I don't know, I don't know," I say. I turn my head away. "There's nothing to be done for these people. There's nothing to be done for them." I lean my head against the windshield, trying to blot out the memory of them. "There's nothing to be done," I say, sighing.

"For which are there?" he says.

DECEMBER 28 [OAXACA]

The mind, to be free, has to see itself as the result of time...

— KRISHNAMURTI

Chuy, Diego, Sam'l and I drive the winding mountain road to Oaxaca to take Sam'l to the airplane. From the moment it leaves Pochutla, until it passes through Miahuatlan, the road rises some 5,000 feet, from the tropical desert of Puerto Jesús, to the pine and oak forests of the Sierra Madres. It is one of those roads that would be marked with the "Scenic View" rays, "vaut le voyage" on the Michelin maps, but it would have, as well, those heavy intestinal curves to show its tortured path.

Sam'l is to leave tomorrow for Mexico City, and Quito. He is sad because he will be returning to his girlfriend Socorro. Most people would be happy to be returning to a girlfriend. Not Sam'l. She is only his friend. She is — as of yet — unwilling to be his girlfriend.

She is, he tells us, sweet and young, with long black eyelashes and two great, wide, loving, fawn-eyes. But when she says no, she means no. In his attempt to change her mind, he recently gave her an hour-long audio-visual presentation: pictures of men's and women's parts, culled from an old *Encyclopaedia Britannica* (1938 edition.) He also brought along, just in case, 100 condoms, borrowed from a friend of his who works in the Peace Corps. (The Peace Corps is very generous with condoms, of all shapes, sizes, and colors; they are not eager for rutting Americans to leave behind spawn, blonde-haired blue-eyed babes engendered in youthful American optimism and left behind in adult haste when the term of service is done.)

Sam'l lectures his girl friend on the function of the ovary, the pleasures of Labium (Majus and Minor), the hill-and-dale ride over the greatest mountain of them all, Mons Veneris — and the final plunge into the Valley of Fouchette. In the process, he introduces her to various types of contraceptive devices, proper positions, and the many accoutrements of love, labelled "*A*" "*B*" and "*C*."

I see him now, serious he is (for love is a serious business, not one to be taken sitting down). He is probably in front of the projector; he has a wooden pointer in hand, and with this, he follows the path of busy Mr. Sperm, past the armed guards at Fort Vestibule, up through the warm and friendly chambers of Ms. Uterus, into the hallways of the frivolous Fallopian Twins (avoiding the dead-end Pouch of Douglas, the trickster Organ of Rosenmüller), emerging at last into the large, rose-petaled bedroom where lives the great Madame Ovum: beaming, fresh-faced, open, warm, caring.

The lecture succeeds. Socorro is charmed beyond all good sense. She is a willing student, an avid listener. She also loves Sam'l for his diligence and persistence. But she still says no. She is not about to yield to the entreaties of her persistent American friend. She'll kiss and cuddle and fondle till the cows come home, but that's it. "Why in hell should she?" I ask him, one of a long line of Monday Morning Sex-Education Quarterbacks. "Her maidenhead, intact, is her life-time security and pension check," I say. "She'd be an *idiota* to give it up to some riverboat shark like you. When you leave (and you aren't going to stay around forever), all she'll have to show for her troubles will be a passel of memories, a faded and torn 1938 *Encyclopaedia Britannica*, a hundred used condoms, and a blonde and squalling Sam'l, Jr. You can't hide anything, even in a city the size of Quito (how is she to disguise this six-foot gringo creeping in the window each evening at nine, out again during the swing shift?) She will be saddled with a curse. No man in all of Ecuador will take her seriously after she has been ravished by this horny gabacho from the northlands."

I suggest he confine his devotions to a more noble project: the poverty-stricken countryside, the waterless poor, the needy and hunger-ridden of Ecuador.

ME: Just get rid of desire. That's where Paradise lies.

HE: In desire?

ME: No, in the getting rid of it. That's Paradise.

HE: I want to get rid of my shyness — and hers — so I can experience desire.

ME: You'll never do it. Take it from a master. You'll try and you'll try, and there'll always be something missing. When you capture the butterfly, you can either smother it, or set it free. Which would you prefer?

HE: Fuck the butterfly. Let me get rid of my shyness first. Then I can work on getting rid of desire.

ME: You're just like all other Americans. As the Master DoughJoe says, you are always becoming.

HE: How about you? Have you gotten rid of desire?

ME: The Master always has to follow a different path. That's why we're called Masters. It is very difficult. We're the carriers of the burning torch. We light the way for the innocents to follow.

HE: If I had to depend on a master like you, I'll still be a virgin at age seventy.

ME: If you keep on pursuing Socorro like this, you'll be one for at least the next twenty-five years. Take my advice: Take the pledge.

HE: I already did.

ME: What's that?

HE: To turn off my hearing aid when you start talking to me about women.

❧ ❧ ❧

Oaxaca is old and cheerful and lively. We fall in love with the cathedrals, the ruins at Monte Albán, the mercado. Some young men of Oaxaca are wearing tee-shirts that say,

New York
Bronx
Bad Boys Club.

They raise the shirts up over their bellies. I think it's because they don't want to be thought of as being from The Bronx, or the Bad Boys' Club, but Sam'l — a student of machoism as well as masochism — says a man in Mexico is a man with a sizeable belly. It's a badge of pride, these *panzas*. It shows that they aren't going hungry, that there's enough food at home, that they are good providers. "Maybe it has to do with empathetic pregnancy," I say: "What's more manly than a man that has made a woman look as fat as he is?"

We wander the city, eat at the 20th of November Mercado, visit the golden cathedral of St. Sebastian. When we die, we agree we would like the ceremonies to be held at the cathedral — then we'll spend eternity in the *viente de noviembre* market. What they have done is to gather a hundred or so eating establishments under one roof. All of them are simple, counter-and-stool deals, with a watch-the-cook set-up. Our favorite is "Lonchería La Pasionara," with three old crones who want to know where we are from, what our names are, how we got here, whether we like it here, and when we'll be coming back. They tell Diego he looks "just like his father" (Sam'l) and Chuy that he looks "just like his grandfather" (me). They feed us omelettes filled with cheese and chilies, or frijoles a la olla (black beans from the pot). The sound of two hands clapping brings the tortilla lady. Sam'l says that Oaxaca is a civilized heaven on earth, much like his favorite city (Madrid) with all its smells, the jam-packed Zócalo, the public everywhere sophisticated in the invigorating climate of the highlands.

Diego, Chuy and I stay in the Hotel Yaquil, while Sam'l — because he's such a cheapskate — stays at the Fleabag Arms

("Saquito de Pulgas") down the street. Diego and Chuy camp out in the bed next to mine, pushing and shoving and giggling before they finally close their eyes. When I waken at four, I find them asleep in each other's arms. Like most young men and women of this area, the two of them have grown up in a climate where people naturally come together for warmth and comfort during the night.

American (and English, and German) children are shipped off to their own beds as soon as possible. It is considered a sign of bad taste, bad judgement, and lousy economics if your children have to sleep together at night. Intimacy isn't countenanced, either in the young, nor in their elders. The earliest memories of my childhood are of me sleeping alone in the huge four-poster, waiting for the snakes to crawl up the posts and fall down on my face during the night. Additional beasts awaited me in the corners of the bedroom, along with the skeletons camped out on the stair landing. There was, too, much late-night slithering hither-and-yon in the bathroom, in case I presumed to visit it between sunset and sunrise. "Go to bed," my mother would say. "I don't want to," I would shout. That didn't mean that I wasn't sleepy. It meant that I didn't want to go alone into a room of shadows and darkness, to be alone, eyes squeezed shut, feeling the shudder as the creatures crept around above me to get me while I was at my most vulnerable.

We can learn to survive any disharmony in our lives — even come to enjoy it. American and German and English children grow up thinking they've accomplished something through their victory over loneliness-fear. Adult isolation becomes the extension of the acceptance of the dread of childhood; we pretend that the hollow feeling is all right. We live alone in our condos, drive alone to work, watch TV alone, sleep alone. If anything represents the tragedy of America's want in the midst of lack-of-want, it's the electric blanket.

From this grows our pushiness: Americans become pushers — pushing people around with our words, our cars, our needs, our wars. We grab at what we never had. The willful American child becomes a willful adult because we were taught that the most sacred of all rights (the right to cuddle) is dishonorable. American children spend a third of their lives alone and deprived — and it is called "affluence."

By contrast, in third world countries the kids don't know what it is to sleep alone. They can't afford to. As soon as a child is done with nursing, he (or she) joins brothers and sisters in the common bed. They sleep with living Teddy Bears and thus don't need the store-bought variety (Teddy Bears are unheard of on the other side of the world).

Chuy and Diego intertwined with each other are sharing their warmth and their dreams, breathing in accord — and will suffer no taunts from their family or friends (certainly none from me) for their intimacy. From time to time, I hear them stir, and whisper, and sigh in their dreams. Melville was right: bed is the best place in the world to be with your best friend.

The grace and peacefulness of their society flows directly from this. One of Sam'l's favorite stories of being in Ecuador occurred in his first week, when he was in the altaplana, staying over with a peasant family. It was getting wintry, and they offered him two of their children, in his bed, one for either side, to keep him from being cold. He is such a stolid (and deprived) American that he turned them down.

DECEMBER 30

I can relax about dying; I do it all the time. But a deeper discovery emerges through this experience that leads me to question whether anything happens at all —whether the very idea of dying may be just another illusion, which, beginning as insight, became incorrect the moment it turned into an idea.

— STEPHEN BUTTERFIELD

When we get back from Oaxaca, we find the trailer filled with mosquitoes. As we kill them off, another thousand take their place. I figure they got in the black water tank while we were gone, and pupated and spawned. Every time we step on the little flusher of the toilet, the door opens and a dirty cloud of mosquitoes fly up to bother us (and our asses). They sing relentlessly in our ears when we are trying to sleep.

"Scientists spend their lives and our tax-money inventing bombs and rockets to murder us," I think. "Why in hell don't they do something useful, like breeding a whineless mosquito." I don't care if they suck my blood — they can do that until they are drunk and bloated. It's their siren call that drives me to distraction. I start to drift off to sleep, and there she comes, buzzing my ear to let me know she's thirsty, that I am going to get eaten. I turn on the light to smash her between my palms — and she becomes invisible, is gone.

While we were away, Nancy Drew's bowtie has turned brown and sere, looks like it is going to fall off. Her nose has become pale and pinched. Her cheeks are lined and drawn. She seems older, perhaps has some tropical wasting fever. The Green Blob hasn't changed a bit. He still hangs there, a phantasm for her to argue with, into eternity. And no matter how I try, no matter how long I stare at them — I cannot turn them back to leaves again. No matter how I labor, to me they will always be Nancy Drew and the Green Blob.

We spend the day at the river. Diego washes his clothes, and I watch the butterflies. One of them lands nearby, on the sand, a carefully crafted creature with wings of silver blue and olive green, with thin brown separators. It's a Satyr, a flying Tiffany lamp, a fluttering window out of Notre Dame. It stops by my shadow. Is it dreaming that it is me at the same moment that I am knowing I am it: becoming, as we all must, what we see? Chuy runs by and nearly steps on it. I think on the difference between fly and butterfly. I wouldn't bother if he stepped on a fly, no matter how beautiful. Both flies and butterflies are exoskeletal, cold-blooded; both have colorful wings and big honeycomb eyes. Stephen Butterfield (or Butterfly) says you should never kill a fly because it may be one of your forebears, your great grandmother who "may have given me the breast in 1752. But who cares whether I kill them or not?" he says:

Do the flies care? If I kill them, will I be reborn as a spider? What about the struggle for existence? Did we get to be human by letting everything else near us, or by killing with more intelligence and efficiency than any other animal? What about fleas, cockroaches, and bedbugs? Maybe I should have a big party and feed them all? Maybe I could train them for circuses? If he was really serious, do I dare to eat from the kitchen of a Buddhist center? Who knows what kind of vermin might be tolerated there? How would a Buddhist deal with an epidemic of cholera? Would he or she kill flies then? If you don't kill, how can you live.

"The reason we don't like flies," I think, "is because of the juices: not necessarily the juices they possess, although those are bad enough, but the juices they love." Butterflies like the sap of flowers — the sweet liquids of buttercups, roses, and honeysuckle; sweet stuff, nectars. Not flies. What they crave are the juices of humanity — blood, shit, sweat, and snot. We are prejudiced in favor of flowerjuices, not in favor of humanity juices (we will stick our noses in the privates of a flower, but not a friend's). We obviously can't abide those who love smegmas.

In the *Tibetan Book of the Great Liberation,* W. Y. Evans-Wentz says it's all right to kill the little sons-of-bitches as long as you invite them to return to the earth in a somewhat more palatable form — like a wren or a sea otter. Because of this, I have swatted them with abandon, always saying, "Take that, you fool! And if you come back next time as a hummingbird or a porpoise, I'll be nicer to you."

JANUARY 4

As Plotinus also teaches, time is nothing more than the measure of movement.

— W. Y. EVANS-WENTZ

There are now thirty children at the Escuela Palma Real, ranging in age from six months to eleven years. The "School" was set up by my friend Emma Andressen to take care of the poor and homeless children of the coastal Oaxaca area. It is as well a meeting place for people in this area who want to do something more meaningful than lie about in the sun and smoke dope. It consists a dust-strewn collection of huts near the ocean at Cipolito. There are a hundred palm trees, thirty children, fifteen volunteers, two ducks, five dogs, three turkeys, a dozen chickens, forty-five lizards and several hundred thousand blue-bottle flies.

Emma is a Swedish Mother Teresa except that she doesn't have a big nose, is not given to lepers, doesn't wear habits, and doesn't presume to prescribe morals for the rest of us.

The only thing strange about her is this thing she has about children. She doesn't like to see them in the streets, or chained to their beds, as often happens to the crippled in this poor country. When she hears about a child prisoner somewhere, she heads right out to get the parents to entrust her with the babe, who she then places at La Escuela Palma Real.

Of the children, there are polios, muscular dystrophics, club-footed, mental and emotional retardees, and a collection of holders of the various other ailments that they lay on the children of the world. They come together, these children, during the day (and much of the night), to sing, aloud. You can hear it when you sit on the low wall of the main *palapa* of the school, the wall surrounding the central arena where all activities take place. If you are fortunate enough to sit near Paco, Juan, Lisa and José (they being the four Worst Cases), it's then you get to hear the School Song, a quartet — a cantata, really — that should be titled, if it isn't already, *Ich hab' genug*.

The Song may sound to the unitiated like a low keening wail, a drone, not unlike the drone of a bag-pipe, or the veena accompaniment of a *raga* that goes on, and on, in a very long Indian concert. It is important to assure you that it is not a song of despair, nor of grief, except the grief that lies inside all grief.

Rather, it is a regular musical accompaniment to whatever activities are taking place at the time: eating, sweeping, talking, taking or giving the school lessons, the rendering of directives from Emma, the preparations for bed.

The choral leader is José, the slim-faced, cross-eyed, fly-specked idiot who can neither walk nor talk nor do much else than lie there (Ernest claims that José is Adolph Hitler in the twelfth of his upcoming 589,969 incarnations). José directs the choir from the floor — and he renders his part of the cantata (he's the tenor) as Moan in d-minor, with excursions into F-sharp and E-flat.

Some might say these songs are songs from the breasts of the beasts of the night. I would rather believe that José's chorus sings to us neither of hope nor of hopelessness, but rather, a truth — the truth that The Fragile Four (all saved from certain death by Emma) are sentient beings, capable of transmitting into the void a powerful paean of existence and survival.

"Look at the poor kid," Ernest will say, motioning towards José. "He's been trying to die for years — and they won't let him. They keep on feeding him, taking care of him, forcing him to live." But Ernest doesn't hear the chorus master José performing, at regular intervals, with Paco, Juan and Lisa, in fine counterpoint. The most moving chorus of them all is drawn from the soul of all children and humanity — the crippled humanity in all children. The four of them, in alternating dithyrams, modulated as carefully as any Philip Glass study — intoning melodies that come without benefit of training, yet speak to the heart. This *Il Penseroso* tells the world out there that there is despair, but also compassion, and understanding, for the very young, and for the very helpless.

While the concert is going on, as it will for the next several hours, Emma and I carry on a conversation about this and that. She has to hear every scrap of information I have about her friends to the north, tells me of her summer (it rained; there is now water; the school wells no longer suffer from salt-water infusion). She has decided that the next thing for them to do (she runs the school for thirty kids with a staff of fifteen on $3,000 a month; she thinks she should do more) is to get a car, a jeep, or a four-wheeler, and start running medical aid to the children in the communities around Cipolete who can't get down to the school for help. She has envisioned the whole project, down to the medical kit that will be carried about in the 4X4 — the exact communities they will be serving.

I would guess that our affection for Emma grows out of the fact that she will not quit, despite the fact that she suffers from the gringo sickness — the sickness that comes to any and all of us who live in this land without surcease for more than a year. For the land of the desert tropics is not forgiving, and there are parasites, protozoa, inflammations, fevers, and strange miasmas that grow in the body of those of us who live here too long.

Emma is maintaining, despite her wretched health, and through some magic, this school of misfits and homeless. A word here, a gesture there — and the organization continues. We all bring her our stories and complaints while she runs this impossible institution — the White Witch of Oaxaca.

I complain to her about my blood pressure pills. It seems that my Beta Blockers are making me indifferent to sex and other entertainments. "Perhaps I have found a Nirvana Medicine," I tell her. "Without my Tenormin, I am my usual old grouchy self; but I'd be dead in two years. With it, I become sweet and unassuming, perhaps will live forever, and I have a sexual ennui worthy of the Pope.

"With the passing of desire, I'm being forced to turn into an angel," I complain. "What should I do?" She says it is like those anti-malaria pills, Atabrine, that you take that keep you from coming down with the symptoms, but they also destroy your night vision. Without them, you have Malarial fevers the rest of your life; with them, you go blind and run into walls. She says it's the perfect Zen choice.

We leave Diego in Puerto Jesús so he can spend the weekend with his girlfriend, and Chuy and I drive back to

Puerto Perdido. He doesn't speak all the way back, nor while we are preparing supper, nor as we are eating it. "Why don't you ever talk to me?" I ask. Nothing. "Your silence drives me crazy, you know that?" Silence. "Not speaking is like a weapon, a pistol. You are shooting me with your lack of words." Silence. "I'm taking you home tomorrow," I say. "I can't stand this. You're treating me like I don't exist."

Talk about Zen. Little did I know at the time that Chuy had been planted in my midst by the sprites, for they had seen that I was in need of instruction. They knew I had this problem with silence; they wanted me to have a chance to work with it. They sent Chuy along as my teacher. He was instructed to give me explicit lessons on the dark mirror that does not respond. They wanted to be sure I learned how to react to no reaction. Since my original reaction was anger, the first lesson has gone swimmingly. It is only later, much later, that I learn the best way to be around the very silent is by being very silent.

Besides, it's all a lie. That part about firing Chuy. I have come, through no fault of my own, to have a Divine in my midst. I also love — more than I should — being around the Divine. One doesn't fire the gods.

❧ ❧ ❧

"Who was here last night?" says Jesús.

I don't say anything.

"Who was here last night?"

"I don't know what you are talking about," I say. It's ten-thirty. "Get me some coffee," I say. Jesús barges in on me, without invitation, at least three mornings a week. I don't much care for this, but there's something about his arrogant ways that I can't stand to lose.

"Where is Aldeo?" he says.

"Who?" I don't open my eyes. It is very bright.

"Was it Aldeo?"

"I don't know who you are talking about. Get me some coffee."

"Who do these belong to?" he asks.

"What?"

"These." He holds up Aldeo's dirty underpants. I turn away. "Coffee." I say. I hear him rattling around in the kitchen, lighting the stove, filling the kettle.

"Did you tell him you love him?" he says from the kitchen.

I pull the pillow over my head. When he comes back with my coffee, he has taken off his shirt. He is wearing Aldeo's underpants on his head, like a snood.

"You should watch it," I say, sipping my coffee and wiping my eyes. "I don't *have* to keep you on here, you know."

"Lo siento. No entiendo inglés," he says, "I'm sorry, I don't understand English." "Did you tell him that it was going to hurt, 'but only a little bit?' " He imitates my voice, inflection, and accent to perfection. I try to stare him down.

"Do you think I can grow up to be a muscle builder?" he asks. He struts around the room, his little chest poofed out. He lifts up his arms, bunches up his biceps, just like he has seen in the muscle magazines I buy for him. "Don't you think I am handsome?" he says.

"I think you are a jerk," I say. Next thing he'll have his pants off to tempt me. He takes off his pants, struts around in his shorts. Underpants on his head, and down below, across the sacred zone. He stands in front of the mirror. I can see the tight and rousing configuration of his buttocks. Damn fucking passion. His legs are strong and menacing, have grown since I have known him. He bunches up his pectoral muscles in the mirror.

"Do you love me, Ignacio?" he says.

"O shut up," I say. I watch his body, watching, watching. He comes over to me, smiling, his eyes squinted, searching my eyes for clues. A lock of his hair falls across his forehead. He leans his face close to mine. I can see the black Fu-Manchu at the corners of his lips, smell the bubble-gum. He stares into my eyes, his pupils perfect round brown moons.

"What do you want?" he says, as glibly as any Paris whore.

"I want you to stop bedeviling me," I say.

He leans over on top of me. I rub my hand up and down that muscular back, once so thin, now a backbone buried in new-starting muscles, overlaid with dusky skin that has turned so shiny with the food I give him. I smell the musk of him. The passionate need. Again. Again and again. The need, the need. I run my hands under the elastic band, down to the great longitudinal incurving that separates right from left.

"Do you love me, Ignacio?" he says.

"Shut up, Jesús," I say.

"I am much better for you than Aldeo. He's one crazy hare-lip."

"He's very nice. And he doesn't try to rattle me."

"You like him?"

I don't respond. My mind fills with the memory of Aldeo asleep. I watched his face as he slept. At one point I ran my index finger along the raw upper edge of his mouth, back and forth, lightly. The waves of passion and compassion intermixed. My frail, pale, god, love.

"They say his uncle is one of the leaders out of Sacramonte," Jesús says, his face buried in the covers.

I stop rubbing his back.

"What did you say?"

"They say that Aldeo is the connection between the mountain people and the *guerrillas.*"

I push him away from me. He rolls his head around to look at me, smiles brightly, blinking his eyes rapidly. "Do you love me, darlink?" he says in his maddeningly bad English.

"You should have told me," I say.

"You never asked," he says, pulling back the covers, and crawling into the bed, next to me. He doesn't even bother to take off his ratty shoes. We could write a book, I think. *Love With Your Sneakers On.* Or, for today's meeting, *Impotent Love With Your Sneakers On.* I rest my cheek against his shoulder, but otherwise, leave him alone. I am thinking, thinking. Aldeo seemed so special — even needy. Christ. Why didn't they tell me? And while I worry, noodle with my deepest fears, Jesús falls asleep, walnut brown against my own pale chest, his sassy expression melting into innocence.

JANUARY 28 [PUERTO PERDIDO]

Words don't change anything — they just fill up the space between thoughts.

— DREAM, 1980

We go snorkelling at Angellito Beach. Chuy and Diego swim up behind me in the water, grab at my feet, then race away. Later, I tell them that there was a monster in the water. "It was big, with a huge snout, stubby yellow teeth, a huge white stomach," I tell them. "It's very dangerous. You should beware of it." The two of them grew up next to the sea. They don't swim in the water — they are of the water. One moment, they will be close at hand; a few moments later, they are on the far side of the cove, two porpoises, conjoined to the sea.

Later, they go to sit on the rocks overlooking the cove, Chuy and Diego in their dark swim suits, their glistening bodies, their powerful legs, their calm, expressionless faces. The sun is behind them, and I see the outlines, see them looking out at the sea, or down at me. "They are the gods," I think. "How lucky I am," I think. It is very dangerous to love the gods — or their representatives. They find it hard to forgive such trespass.

The two of them let me know that it is not an easy journey, not to be taken lightly — this adoration. The masters have advised against such love. They warn us that since all is delusion, god-love is a double delusion. Those who indulge in such can have no freedom. It's a love that creates more pain than pleasure. It is, they say, even painful to the gods. It might well consume us. This is, of course, as it should be.

1,000 years ago, Diego and Chuy were peasants, tilling the dry fields, raising maize, living from sunrise to sunset, sleeping in a simple hut with wife and dust and dogs. Then the foreigners came. They were forced into serfdom, where they learned to walk like panthers and meld with the land and the sea. 150 years ago, they freed themselves from the *conquistadores*, but kept on with their marriage to land and sea — fishing and hunting, planting maize in the dust, sniffing rain out of the wind.

A few years ago a new series of *conquistadores* appeared on the scene. Always tolerant, the people consented to pretend to work for us; in reality, they were here to teach us another language, another way of living, freedom from the chains we took so much trouble to bring with us.

These gods live and move and act with such an economy of motion that when we are with them, we must see ourselves as heavy and old. They are minimalists. They waste few words, suffer fools lightly, frown or smile only when absolutely necessary, and can sit motionless, for hours, watching the sea, or the traffic around them, or us.

Their clothing is simple: a daytime outfit (dark bathing suit), swimwear (dark bathing suit), evening clothes (the same), bedtime jammies (the same). Underneath the bathing suit they wear the briefest of briefs, called, here, for some inexplicable reason, "bikinis."

These are my gods, except for the part of them I can't describe, which has to do with a certain wisdom they carry so lightly. This must have grown from lessons out of the local version of Gurdjieff. As you recall, the Georgian master said that one could only hope to develop the Holy Truth by participating in hard work, at least once a day, every day of the week. Starting at age seven, Chuy and Diego have done so, carrying great buckets of water up the steep steps to their houses, fifteen to twenty times a day. While their peers in America are watching MTV or complaining about supper, or trying to score another lid of dope, or figuring out how to play hookey from school — my friends are toting, with singular goodwill, hundreds of pounds of fresh water up the steep sides of the steep hills so their mothers will have enough to clean the dishes, wash the clothes, and wet down the dirt floor.

When, over the remaining pages, you encounter, with me, Chuy and Diego — try to envision them as dark gods with a certain oriental wisdom. In the pursuit of anyone — divine or no — there must be the matching of fancy to dreams, so I will worship these two good shepherds in the same way that they will learn how to be worshipped. It is not easy for them — they would much rather be out playing — rather than being some divine.

The gulf between the seraphim floating up there and the old tiger down here might be, to most, a chasm beyond reason. Yet the greater the division between us, the greater my desire to find a permanent home in their dark and mysterious folds of wisdom.

JANUARY 29

She lives in a big white house,
The room's alive and she's devoted to life;
Keeping this house just right, keeping it perfectly nice,
She doesn't talk when he comes home at night.
Twenty-five years, she's just the same —
She's a lonely woman, quiet in her way;
He comes home at night, she kills him with her knife
Shes the one who's a-living in paradise.
Sister of mercy, O sister of mercy,
O don't cry for me
Sister of mercy, O sister of mercy,
It's all right for me.
Now she sits in a big white chair

— THE THOMPSON TWINS

Everyone pretends not to notice as my ninety-two year old mother shuffles across the street, holding her head down, using her aluminum walker, her hands bent about the aluminum bars, hurrying as best she is able, feet scraping the curb and the pavement, hurrying to be with the neighbor lady. Her silver hair bobs about as she moves along. This will be her last lover, and she doesn't want to waste a moment away from her and her love.

Sometimes I wonder what makes her tick, this mother of mine — *mama mia*! Did I make her up wholecloth? What planet did she come from? Did I, as the Buddhists say, pick her out specifically in order to rework the wrongs of my other lives?

She lives in the house on the river, the house that has not changed in any way since she bought it in 1940. "It never was your father's house," she says shortly; "I bought it with my money, in my own name..." We grew up, orphans, in the house of this woman. Our father — too — was orphan.

The house is cold, eternally cold, something not to be expected in Florida. The furnace is tiny, built a half a century ago. The water heater, installed during WWII, and never replaced, pumps two or three cups of tepid water every hour or so. I remember the coldest of winters, when a shallow layer of lukewarm water would be spread over the bottom of the tub for my bath. The old red-coil wire electric heater in the corner would sputter and smell of hot rust, and I would be all goose-bumps drying off in front of it. One sister said that all she could remember of those winters was blue hands and blue feet. "But it was Florida," our friends say: "How could you be cold?" They don't know the house was built to invite the airs of the Arctic, and Mum didn't cotton to the wasting of any energy to dissipate it.

She was born in 1898, my mother was, so that now, when she moves about, she and her walker move quite slowly. She lives in two rooms in the old Georgian house: the dining room, and the downstairs bedroom — the same one where my two sisters died. The other fifteen rooms, plus the attic, the basement, the maid's room — are dark and unpeopled, except for the spooks of the children that grew up and away from her and her world to the south.

Each day she moves from bedroom to dining room, and back to bedroom again, trailing my sisters behind her, muttering to them, telling them to mind their manners, wipe their noses, stop being so noisy. They hop along in front or behind her, jumping up and down with impatience at her impossible slowness. She can hear them telling her to hurry, and she tells them to be quiet. "You girls hush now," she will say. She always encouraged independence, and discouraged the word "Mother" or "Mum" — or, so common in our area — "Mammie." They call her Rachel. "Rachel, will you tie my shoe laces?" one of them asks. She mulls on the difficulty of bending down, trying to find the laces in the fog, taking laces in twisted fingers, twisting the laces together, make everything right again. She won't do it unless they persist.

The dining room has been converted to a war room: business reports are stacked tall on the table, and the morning sun stretches in through the windows, marking them with the shadows of the bars. The light is not enough. To favor her one good eye she has a spotlight mounted in the ceiling so she can pore over the reports with their small print: profit-and-loss, debt-to-asset ratio, cash flow, annual business expenses: a new set of babes — ones who cry less, wet their diapers less often, never leave home, don't come down with the measles.

"I didn't know anything about the stock market when your father died," she tells us; "I knew nothing about investments, or money. I had to teach myself. Your father never taught me what he knew, but that's all right — I'm strong. He was one of the kindest men in the world," she will say. During a seance she once asked him why he left her — and he said, loudly and clearly enough for her to hear without her hearing aid, "Rachel, I didn't want to." No one else heard it. A decade after his death, I dream of him. He has been forced by her to come back from the grave for some unfinished business. He is very reluctant to do so, but she insists, so he drives around the city with her in the old grey Cadillac. She does the driving. He wants to go back, but she won't let him — it took a lot of work to get him here, and he's going to finish what she has in mind, even though he's tired, even though he'd much rather be dead.

She trades a million dollars worth of stock a year, my ninety-two year old mother does. Carefully, slowly, she takes in the checks, folds them to her, and then carefully, slowly, with her bent fingers, disburses them. Not to herself, not to her children — certainly not to charity. But to The Children's Trust. The Trust is her new spouse, a friend who constantly speaks to her during the long nights. She lies alone in the single bed with the old scarred oaken posts, there in the seventeen-room house, there on the Savannah River — and the Trust speaks to her, of capitalization, long term debt, price-to-earnings ratios.

Once there were other sounds in her house. The river would speak to her out of the night, she'd hear the wind in the camphor tree and the soughing of the long-leaf pine. Now she's deaf, so she no longers hears the windsong of the river. Instead, she listens to the threnody of assets-to-liabilities ratio, earnings for the past three, and five and ten years, net worth, fixed charge coverage, growth in real and apparent income. The music comes to her in cantata form, sung by her favorite choirs: Boeing, General Motors, General Mills, Lucky Stores, Winn-Dixie, American Home Products, Columbia Gas, Northwest Airlines. The choir sings to her of security and stability and sanctity. The lyrics of open-high-low-last swinging through the ages, rocking in time, the eternal up and down, a rhythmical flow: the flood of "open," the waves of "high," the depths of "low," the sweet flattened notes of "last" — my dear old deaf and near-blind mother rocked in the bosom of Abraham, the evensong of the marketplace.

My mother is locked to her table and her bed and its ghosts, a prisoner in her house. The house she has lived in this half-century now has bars on the windows and bars on the doors, an eight-foot electrified fence outside. I once counted eleven doors and fifteen windows on the ground floor, and when we were young we never turned a lock, never secured a window, never passed a gate, never had keys. Our lives were free, at such ease in that southern city. The light came rippled in through oak and camphor and orange and fig trees — a light through the leaves, making this a great wide open green emerald garden of a palace. When we left for the summers, we never locked doors and windows because in our neighborhood there came no wrong.

Several years ago, one of my sisters appropriated the rapine and murder and manglings from television and newspapers and decided it was dangerous for the house to be open. At great effort and expense she put in bars and locks on windows and doors, inside and out: call-boxes and alarms throughout; a tall fence encompassing the large yard. And now this house we once called home is a prison for this woman of nine decades, my mother — renting, still, a body that now curves down on itself with the weight of ages. They have hidden her behind bars and locks and alarms, chained her to charts and graphs and figures, the prisoner-counter of monies, ten thousand memories barred in with her, scuttling movements under the piano — the great instrument unused for twenty-eight years, since the last wedding in the hallway, the day now gone, the people all gone, the children all gone, the marriage itself now gone.

There are bars to darken her world as she sits at the table, the table where once, evening after evening, people were dined so graciously, with green and gold edge plates, silverware — the heavy Lockheart pattern — and candles, always candles with dinner: great meals, filled with laughter, candles, a dozen or more candles, in the curve Regis candle-holder, with its fluted edges and the scalloped base. It would take Belora the maid all morning and most of the afternoon to polish the silverware, the candle-holders, the napkin rings.

Now there's a tuna sandwich and part of a baked potato spread out on yesterday's *Wall Street Journal.* To drink, not Poilly-Fuisse, but a glass of water (my sister doesn't favor drinking anymore). And no candles — her milk-white eyes could sense no candle: the spot-light in the ceiling will have to do.

As she eats, she bends to the figures from The Standard Revised Edition of Standard & Poors. She is hungry for numbers, as she never was for food. "If they could just line up pills for me," she says, has said a thousand thousand times, "one-two-three" — she counts them on bent fingers — "so I would never have to eat again, just line up the pills for me — that would be fine with me."

She is silent, now. She stopped talking to the girls an hour ago because they were so bad. When the girls are bad she applies a cure-all silence. When they scraped themselves on the pavement outside, she applied Epsom Salts. When they were naughty, she applied silence — no words at all. The children are wrong, and with a silence we'll break them of their badness: no words, no looks, nothing — mother turned to a ghost because of what the children have done — the club of silence. The girls have been bad, so she isn't to speak to them until they are good again. And the house is filled with silence.

❧ ❧ ❧

How should we approach her, stretched as she is against the late afternoon of her days (soon to be stretched to nothing)? Is not her dying the dying of all of us? Is not the bending of her back all backs bent double by the years? Is her mind so filled with memories that her neck must bend with them? She conjoined so stiffly with the man who was, she will always say, the gentlest man in the world. He was, too, as were the rest of us, an orphan child in a cold, wintry house, he was never able to teach her much about love, the hot and somewhat disorderly magic of love. There was no time nor inclination for such — there was too much to be done, there were too many silences to keep.

Sometimes he was bad too, a child, too, in this house of winter's children, so she wouldn't talk to him because he, too, was bad — sometimes there were whole weeks in which no words were exchanged, great gaps of silence into which all our hopes would fall. It was very quiet at times in the great seventeen-room house, until one day my Dad turned silent too, the ultimate silent treatment, where he took his presence (which had never been there anyway) and he went dead silent, left her with nothing but a stack of heavy papers with pictures. My dad left her in the company of pictures of stout figures in helmets and staffs, standing on words like "1,000 shares" and "debenture" and "security" and "common stock" and "sinking fund" — her own sinking fund of faith in self that grew out of his surprise departure, the husband of thirty years, bound, silently, for another exchange. "He never taught me about stocks, and money," she says. "I had to teach myself everything. I did. It took awhile, but I did it. You have to be a bulldog."

She wants no pity, my mother. If you reach out to her to help her with the weight of her years she will tell you that she needs nothing, thank you. Help her? She can do very well on her own, thank you. The eyes? They're getting better now. The hip? That too is much better now. No — she needs no assistance at all getting up from her chair. And there are always the maids. Doris comes in the morning, Lily during the afternoon. At night — she can take care of herself. Isn't that what all people do when they are ninety something, in their prison of bars and silences? The memories, trailing her to her bed, and she lies wrapped in them, in a vague sleep which is really no sleep at all, where she dreams (faint dreams) of the great white house in which she grew up, a great white house on Riverside Avenue; the white house with panelled rooms, dark wooden halls, bright hallways and porches upstairs, stairs with curving bannisters — the large white house where, so many ages ago, she grew up (she was always dressed in white) and lived so in the heart of her father, *nee* "Daddy."

Mother's Daddy was a man so omnipotent that he was not only father, but brother, confidante, good fairy, travelling companion, joke-teller, man-to-be-scolded, dear friend, a dear dear man in a large house where for the first and last time she was happy, wed as she was to this man in a linen suit who gave non-stop love for his lone, hungry child. "Daddy always told me..." she says, when asked about her being young. For her, being a child was always being with Daddy, who always told her things. "Daddy always told me never to go into debt," she says. "Daddy always told me never to buy bonds." "Daddy always told me never to be afraid." A Daddy who told her *always*: always sit at the head of the table. Always have candles with dinner. Always have a Daddy Our Daddy which art is in heaven. Never leave me, Daddy always said, and she promised over and over again never to leave him and when this other man came to the white house and said he wanted to marry her, she said, "Yes, I will marry you. But you must come and live with me and Daddy." And he did. They slept right next door, next to Daddy's room.

Now they are gone from the great white house where they lived. Daddy lay down and died one day and he left her bereft. She missed, still misses — a half-century after his departure — the Daddy of the white moustache and white linen suits and white shoes, now gone, dark shoes now, dark suit somewhere in the ground, dark in the ground now, gone from the house leaving her bereft, with only a husband. And soon enough, not even a husband but the ghostly girls who come to her to laugh and play, who hide in the corner of her bedroom and giggle softly to each other as she is falling asleep, giggle so much that she has to call out to them, telling them to hush so she can sleep.

❧ ❧ ❧

Sometimes I wonder what makes her tick, this mother of mine — *dios mio*. Did I make her up whole cloth? What planet did she come from? Did I, as the Buddhists say, pick her out specifically in order to rework wrongs out of my other lives?

I have one last dream of her, as vivid as the one of her crossing the street to be with her love. I dream that I am visiting her house — the same house I grew up in. She is sitting upright in a frilly, silk-lined casket — mounted on carpenter's horses in the big hallway. She chats, asks questions — is lively, watches me with bright-eyed attention. She wants to know who I am. I try, but I can't seem to get the word out of my mouth. The word my name is stuck like some gum I can never pull out of my mouth, although I try and try again.

JANUARY 30

We are fighting over the basket — and the fruits have fallen into the ditch.

— VIVEKANANDA

After today's ritual of the changing of the money at the bank, we plan to go over to the Tonameca River to swim. Ernest stands behind me in the line, talking to a thin and energetic lady, so I invite her to go along with us. She's from the southwest, studies "Spanish Culture" at the University of New Mexico, smokes Marlboroughs, talks through her nose, and has a vague, wandering gaze. "I did it as a favor to you," I say to Ernest, later. I am trying to set him up so he won't have to abuse himself any more, or — at worse — feel bad about it.

As we drive over to the river, Lila, or Lily, or Lola tells us she wants to be a writer. She says she understands I am working on a novel. She wants to know how it is going. She asks if she can look at it. She asks me how to start writing, where to mail off things, whether she should get an agent. She asks me how long short stories should be, and how short long novels should be — where they should start, where they should end.

"The best way to start it is don't," I tell her. "Forget it, just forget it. The only people who become professional writers are people who cannot communicate their lousy childhoods to anyone except themselves, the computer, or their shrinks — if they are fortunate enough to be able to afford one.

"All writers are cripples," I tell her. "If you have a wretched childhood, you go into pushing drugs, mass murder, child abuse, or writing. Writing is probably the worst of the bunch, because it perpetuates our emotional and social crippledom. Writers take pride in their lack of humanity, their lack of balance, their inability to communicate with other humans in a human way (touch, silence, interchange of a spoken and loving word). Writers are so enmeshed in the mirror that they cannot see the trees, much less the forest of real people around them." It's the myth of Narcissus all over again, I think. Like Narcissus, we don't know who or what it is staring at us out of the deep pool. We think we're having another vision, and we don't realize that we are seeing but a reflection of ourselves, a lost face in the lost bend.

"We believe that we're god's gift to the world, but the truth of the matter is when we're around people, we start sulking, getting drunk and anti-social," I tell her. "Then we go home and write insults in our novels or poems or essays about the people we've just met. Writing is one of the most selfish pursuits you can take up. Forget it." These goddam kids. They all want to be Stephen King or Joyce Carol Oates or J. D. Salinger. "Of all the career fixations, this has to be the worst," I tell her. "If you want to know what it's like to be a writer, read the biographies of Faulkner, Hemingway, Isak Dinesen, or John Cheever, Eudora Welty, William Saroyan, Willa Cather. Find any glory in their lives, and then you can tell me you want to be a writer.

"Be a rock star," I say. "Go into term-life sales, fixed annuities, funeral directing, frog farming. Sell sex toys imported from Hong Kong, stay in college and major in late Urdu, or Bio-Medical Research; become an expert in the Nōh drama,

Medieval midwifery or Courtship Rituals in The Sudan. Take up the Shan'ai and Pi'pa or the harmonium. *Anything* but being a writer. You will never forgive yourself if you get caught up in it, because once you jump into the pot — and I am talking about the real thing, not laboratory writing — once you get in there, you'll never get out. You become a word addict, a plot-twister, a master character manipulator — and you are done for. Spend an hour, just one hour, wrestling with all the fools that turn up in your novel, then tell me you want to preside over the Laocoön they call writing." Nuts — that's what it is.

As I watch Lola (or Lila, or Lala) with Ernest, and their frail courtship (Ernest a flower child of fifty, she a cigarette-smoking, would-be Joan Didion of thirty) I think how many barriers like "I'd like to be a writer" we set in the path to intimacy. What can they be thinking of? Ernest is probably mesmerized by her breasts. She, in turn, sees nothing more than a lovely, bemused, bronzed hippy — a slightly ding-ey mystic, one that she thinks she will enjoy cavorting with.

And I see in the two of them my own lack of love. Outside of my sage advice, I have nothing to give this lady — nothing at all. I reserve myself only for people who entertain, or delight, or confound me — sweet Emma of the school, Ernest with his Moonbeam Dancing, Diego who loves to bedevil me, Sam'l in love (or worried about love), Chuy who never talks to me. These are my preferred companions. Spare me would-be novelists from New Mexico. It is an *en passant* offered and rejected. I will probably have to return to the earth a thousand thousand times to repair this slight, and the awful truth: that I am indifferent to the middle-aged, aspiring, uninspired (and uninspiring) bulk of humanity. When they hove into view, I have to bow my head and bow out.

❧ ❧ ❧

It's not the pale moon that delights me
That thrills or excites me;
O no — it's just the nearness of you...

— POPULAR SONG, 1947

Not to make this a sad parting — but as this will be practically our last meeting with Ernest, I want to dictate his obituary to you. Surely he is not dead, nor dying — at least, no more than the rest of us. It's just that for the purposes of this narrative, we won't be seeing much of him (or his like) again. For this reason, I want to leave you with a last picture of him as I drive him and all his worldly possessions to Puerto Jesús, where he will stay for the rest of the winter. On the road, he speaks of the denuding of the Oaxacan mountains, the paradise nature here, the endless sun, the lovely people, the ions, the bare-breasted Oaxacan women (who started putting on brassieres "when the road-builders arrived"), the beaches, the tranquil rivers, the books he wants to write (and will never write), the films he wants to make (and will never shoot) — including one with images of 1,000 women, like the thousand names of Lord Vishnu, but made up of faces, thighs, arms, feet, hair, backsides. A thousand images shot in fast sequence: women aged six to eighty, brought together in visions that will flow one after the next, images that will dazzle the audience, be seen all over the world, a small and private paean he has created in his love for the 2,500,000,000 or so ladies of the world.

I suspect that Earnest is a butterfly, perhaps a lesbian butterfly — floating over the hot fields of his days, filled with pollen and juices, seeking out sweet blossoms from which to sup. He is of the generation of Alan Watts, Allen Ginsburg, Jack Kerouac, Jay Landisman, Les Blank — those who grew up as rebels in America, when it was still easy to rebel. It was an America of safe (if boring) high schools, Rotary Club meetings, bridge parties, debutante parties, rowdy drinking parties where we smoked cigarettes and debated loudly about Joseph McCarthy, Charlie Byrd, or e. e. cummings.

The most daring thing we'd do was to drink ourselves blind and drive the Plymouth or Oldsmobile 88 too fast, looking for fast ladies (which we never found). All was stultifying, but it was so stultifying that we didn't even know that it was thick and oppressive, blinding us to our reality.

For Ernest, escape was escaping from one Juvenile Facility after another. In those days, one could easily escape (JD's weren't taken too seriously; they weren't killed for trying to run away.) He evolved early on into a doper: he first smoked pot thirty years ago, when it was called "Berkeley Boo" and it was a felony (to smoke, or have any quantity — a lid or a joint — in one's possession). He continued to smoke it non-stop until sometime last year when, bathing in an outdoor spring in Tulare County, he toked on an especially potent pipefull and found he could not escape from the hot mineral bath. The sun was blaring down, and the truth of his years and mortality got to him at last. He had resigned himself to slipping under the surface, bubbling away his soul with memories of that hoary *mot* out of James Dean: "Live fast, die young, and have a good-looking corpse."

At the very last moment, when he was preparing for the final breath, a good faerie stole out of the pepper trees at the side of the pond (he swears by this) and asked if he needed help. He bubbled his assent, so she pulled him gently — ever so gently, his steaming body — into the shade, where she wrapped him in a towel, kissed him cooly, and disappeared. "Yes," the mountain people told him later, "we know all about her. They call her the 'Magic Lady.' " Ernest, a confirmed romantic, continues, to this day, to think of her, his savior. The blood of the Pre-Raphaelites, as thin as it is, flows ever in his veins.

Ernest married several times, once to the ex-step-mother of one of my best friends, reconfirming that old wheeze about there being only 600 great people on earth, and we all know each other. He sired four children (two "normal" — at least by his lights; one not so; one mad — at least by his mad lights).

He drifted in and out of the pleasures and pursuits that we late-blooming hippies have sought out over the last quarter-century: book publishing, living in Mexico, doing the Haight, experimenting with video, dope and est; communes, Arica, love, horticulture, love, writing — love-making, love — all this, despite the strong possibility that all means nothing, and, at the same time, everything. At fifty, he looks to be thirty-five. He is tall, regal, smiling, arch, wry, composed, hides his fears and angers exquisitely well — which, as we know, is the sign of a sentient being in 20th Century America.

He, like most of us from that time (variously characterized as Beats, Bohemians, Fringies, or Hippies), was (and is) militantly opposed to war, the killing of women, men, children and living creatures (excepting mosquitoes, gnats, and roaches — who, we agree, are just too small to have room for souls). He believes in the holy power of peyote, acid, and pot, loathes the addictive powers of cocaine, crack, smack, PCP, and the other preferred poisons of the 80s and 90s. He is tolerant of all fashions of love, as long as they don't incorporate the usual American corporate control.

Although not rich, he's managed to tap into a small portion of the incredible wealth of our country to live simply but well seven months of the year to the north, five to the south. He gives himself over to sunsets and moonrises, dances nude on the beach at night, masturbates at five in the morning (listening to the sad subaudible whisper of the sea outside his bedroom window) and, before his first morning cup of tea, contemplates with a paralyzing fear his coming blindness (he's lost most of his night vision; they tell him his daytime vision will be gone soon, too).

He believes in the infinite power of karma to reward and punish all of us. He floats through his days as a furry butterfly, who — I suspect — is one of the more gentle and novel moonstruck creatures to be produced by the Western World.

❧ ❧ ❧

Jesús comes in the next morning and demands that I go with him. I am sipping my coffee and brandy and I don't want to be bothered, but he is frenetic, so we go out to the far *arroyo* behind my house. It's hot and dusty. Scraps of plastic and bits of cloth hang in the bare trees, christmas decorations. The plastic milk cartons form crèches around the base of the trunks.

We go around the deep gully and towards the next hill. He pulls aside the thick candytuft bushes. There's a man lying there. Jesús tugs me by the shirttail, pulls me closer. There's something about the way the man's head is turned, something about his back, and the torn yellow shirt. The man...

Aldeo. He isn't sleeping. Nor is he passed out. At least, not temporarily passed out. Ah, Aldeo.

Jesús and I pull him up to the lip of the arroyo. There's just a single O, in the middle of the forehead. There's scarcely any blood. I shut your lids, Aldeo, because I don't want you to look at me, not with those eyes, brown, now very dry. You look at me with the certainty of one who has no more questions left. No more fears, no more anxiety, no more worry, about love, or youth, or me, my love for you, even with your poor tortured upper lip that you carried about with such shame for so long. No more fears, nor troubles —nothing but the round neat O, the spot of wisdom graved above the bridge of your nose, up between the eyebrows.

Your body can still be moved: arms can be opened and closed, legs raised and lowered. What is it they say, one stiffens in six hours, and in eighteen, turns human again. I suspect that Aldeo has been here only a short while, for his hands are still pliant. Was he coming to see me again? Was he just passing by? Was he waiting — afraid to come in, his feelings so mixed — about this gabacho who wanted to be with him?

"Jesús!" I call out: "Where are you going."

"I have to go to school, it's late," he says, his voice shrill. "Come back," I yell — "Jesús, come back!" But he is around the house and gone, I can hear him coughing as he goes down the drive. I don't want to call too loudly. There's still time, before we're seen. I grab Aldeo under the arms, drag him towards the back door of the cottage. His heavy feet leave two dog-trails behind, and a dust ghost rises up as one shoe begins to slip off. I drop him just inside the doorway, go out, pick up the shoe, look around to see if anyone has been watching. There's a blue gecko under the plane tree, moveless. Señora Cremora from next door has her fat buttocks turned to me — she's leaning over the laundry. There are two pigs nuzzling at the garbage pile up the hill, pulling at the bags, ripping them open, spilling the guts of rancid food out onto the mound. There are no other witnesses save what looks to be a pair of black hawks overhead. I can hear a helicopter in the distance.

I erase the tracks as best I can with the heel of my shoe. I drag Aldeo across the room, listening to my own panting as I pull him up onto the bed. I must be groaning as I lay him on it, put my hands together under those still boyish buttocks, heave him around, begin to take off his shirt and pants. I took them off before, I take them off now — but now he (and they) are colder. His eyes have popped open again with the effort of our journey. He watches the flies circling, circling him and the rumpled bed. I close the eyes, trying to remember some benediction from my childhood, white against black, the censers, Father Brautigan sweating and red-faced, his head riding above his plump body like a red-on-black double pumpkin, the risen moon of his face grown out of a black chasuble. Agnes Dei. Is that it? *Sunt lacrimae rerum: similia similibus curantur.* Why can't I remember?

I pull off his pants and get his blue jeans tangled in the dirty brown plastic shoes. I pull at them impatiently, almost pulling him off the bed. While I boil up some hot water to wash off the dirt, I listen to my own panting. "Why am I'm panting like a dog?" I wonder. I clean his face, rub off the little dried blood that has leaked into his left eye. I wash his ears, and behind the ears; always wash behind your ears, Aldeo; then the face — being careful with the lip, the life-time wound, the scar so painful to everyone but me. Wash the neck, and arms, and armpits (with those very few hairs) and the torso. Can they hear me panting outside? I have washed him before. Washed in the blood.

A seventeen-year-old body — no body's body now. "Ah, Aldeo," I say: "You had so much left in you, for me, for the world. This body was a fine home for you for as long as you were there." We don't own them: we just rent them for a while. Then the landlord comes along with the quit-claim deed and takes possession. We may have scarred the walls, broken the lights, flooded the subasement. We're evicted, and they repossess it all, not even issuing a court order.

Aldeo had much life left in him. His term was far from over, and the fact that his body has been vacated is a sin. "Someone with a pistol has committed a major sin," I think, angrily. No matter how they speak to their gods after they violate the young, they sin. Whoever their divines may be (white cloths, scepters, jewels, censers of perfume, crosses) — whichever masters they call on for forgiveness — those who murder the young are sinning mightily against all humankind. They murder the young and the innocent, and whatsoever name they choose to do it in — *"Dei," "Dios," "El Grande" "Allah"*— they have the vile blood of evil on their hands.

I turn him over, wash his back, all the way down around, in between (lovingly between) and past the buttocks. I squeeze out the brown-white cloth, soap it, scrub down to the thin, highly arched feet, those feet so strangely white. "You never gave me time to love your feet properly, Aldeo," I tell him. I clean them carefully, eight tiny arroyos between the ten still unblemished toes. Piggly, Wiggly. The white cloth is now streaked with black. I kiss the left second toe, the long one, warm it a bit in my mouth. It is a fine cold toe, Aldeo. I had so much more to learn about you, Aldeo. I hear someone outside the house, kicking at the door. I cover the body quickly with the quilts and sheets and pillows, a cocoon, so that it looks like my bed is merely fat and ruffled — but when I get to the window, there's no one there.

I spread the covers, turn him over again, fold his hands across his chest, still a boy's chest, no hair to be seen up here, except the tiny black hairs about the hummingbirds' nests. The back was broad and strong, with its two down curves. But it was at the front, ah, Aldeo, that you were such a wonder. I muse on how our bodies are divided against us. Front and back, in and out, quick and dead. I lean my cheek against his cheek, his dry high cheek bones against my old man's scraggly ones, touch the sweet and sad half-a-lip with the tip of my finger. He never had a chance to know how much we could love him for something he thought so wrong: the honorably brutish lip of the hare. We can be so crippled by our differences; and in the process, we scarcely know that these differences don't exist for much of the world. We can be so crippled by the way we think people see us that we scarcely hane a chance to realize that we are beautiful.

"We only had one night to know each other," I tell him. "You wouldn't begrudge me this time with you now, would you?" We had so many more things to do, so many places to go. I take his love, hold it cold in my warm hand, put palms about it, nuzzle with my old man's cheek — the two round worlds of a thousand thousand babes that will now not come into the world. "If I had a way," I think, "I could take some of you, Aldeo. Find a girl, perhaps

Angela, ply her with the seed of you, perpetuate another god like you, Aldeo (we would name him Aldeo Amantea Dios) and, in enough years, I could hold him warm as I am holding you cold now." I run my fingers through the sparse hair around the scarcely fallen moons.

Can I bring you back to life, Aldeo? I take the still cold joining in my mouth, the last round of our giving. I pull back with my tongue the dark cap of it, wait to feel it (as it did so recently) begin to start, the involuntary part of him starting to move involuntarily. "Can this revive you, my old friend?" I rub my wet cheeks against the grand thighs, the lower belly, the inset where legs meet torso.

No one will ever be able to love you this way ever again, Aldeo. You will never respond ever again, this part of you, the part that you could never control — no matter how much you tried. No matter how distant and manly we want to be, it moves and it tells us we are ultimately and finally alive to all loves.

I pull away, but it is too late, as Don Iglesia, the judicial investigator for the El Cero District, comes into the room. His eyebrows are raised, and even behind his almost black glasses, I can see a certain wild light. Not in his dreams could he expect to find me and Aldeo come together like this, in death as in life.

"Ah, mi amigo," I say, standing up, moving to the head of the bed, my head slightly canted, as if I were praying, or involved in some holy ritual. I am more calm than I ever would have thought possible. "My friend. ¡Qué bueno de verte! Quisieras busca nuestro amigo Aldeo." How good to see you. I expect you were searching for our friend Aldeo. "Aquí está. Somos a su servicio." Here he is. We're at your service." I hold one hand out to Don Iglesia, the other to my cold love on the bed.

❧ ❧ ❧

FEBRUARY 7

A man is walking in a dark, dangerous forest, filled with wild beasts. The forest is surrounded by a vast net. The man is afraid, he runs to escape from the beasts, he falls into a pitch black hole. By a miracle, he is caught in some twisted roots. He feels the hot breath of an enormous snake, its jaws wide open, lying at the bottom of the pit. He is about to fall into these jaws. On the edge of the hole, a huge elephant is about to crush him. Black and white mice gnaw the roots from which the man is hanging. Dangerous bees fly over the hole, letting fall drops of honey....Then the man holds out his finger — slowly, cautiously — he holds out his finger to catch the drops of honey. Threatened by so many dangers, with hardly a breath between him and so many deaths, he still can't throw off his chains. The thought of honey holds him to life.

— *THE MAHABHARATA*

Max comes to visit, and — being gringo — he immediately makes a long distance call back to the States. In Mexico, one doesn't pick up the telephone and dial a number. One goes to the telephone shop, where there are three pay telephones strung up next to each other on the wall, with haphazard wiring and receivers that smell richly of Faros cigarettes. You go to the lady, tell her who you want to call, and where. She, with telephone receivers on both shoulders, one ringing at her elbow, places the call for you.

"She was a girl, with a blank face — a blank Indian face," he tells us that night. "She took the number I wanted, dialed it, and I waited a long time. We waited a long time. She looked at me with her blank telephone face, receiver on her left shoulder. There was no one else in the shop at the time, and I waited, and finally she said the call had gone through, and I picked it up, and I looked at her and thought, *'Time isn't even an illusion here.'* "

We sit on that one for awhile, our gin rickeys crackling in our glasses, the waves crushing out their lives on the sands below. I think, "That's how Sherwood Anderson and Henry James and Chekov and Beckett would do it. They would take some simple commonplace scene — having tea and toast, going to the train station, walking through the park, making a long-distance telephone call — and as they write about it, it becomes a great (and puzzling) statement about the cosmos."

I have been rereading *Mrs. Dalloway*. It's the story of a woman in London, some seventy years ago, organizing a party. An old friend comes back to town from India, and the party is a success. Not much on narrative excitement, but we readers get caught up in Woolf's universe, full of the paradox of being human, and at the same time, surrounded by death (a man named Septimus kills himself by falling out a window onto a picket fence). What does death mean: or rather, what *doesn't* death mean, at a 1924's London party, with the prime minister in attendance?

"*Time isn't even an illusion here*," I mutter. "That's too much." I remind Max of the words of Chang Tzu, even though he has fallen silent. Perhaps he is asleep. It's hard to tell, with him — especially in the moonlight. His face is pale, except in the shadowy places where his beard is struggling to get born. I can't see his eyes — only the shadows where eyes should be. "Chang Tzu's words," I say, "were, and you can correct me if I am wrong, *There is nothing in the world bigger than the tip of an autumn hair, and Mount T'ai is tiny. No one has lived longer than a dead child, and P'eng-tsu died young. Heaven and earth were born at the same time I was, and the ten thousand things are one with me.*"

I pause to let the words sink in. There's the smell of skunk in the air. "Dana Lewis claims that Chang Tzu is entirely tongue-in-cheek with these words, 'that only quibblers and the myopic make such distinctions.' I'm not so sure..."

Max is silent. Like Chuy (and Chang Tzu) he is not given to talking. I can barely hear him breathing. Perhaps he has expired on the words of Tzu, to whom ten thousand things are as one. Perhaps he is struck dumb because the moonlight has drenched all the trees about us in its rich white stock of light. Maybe he is is allergic to the smell of skunk.

"Korzybski said 'The Word is not the thing,' " I continue. "Maybe the word is the source of all our troubles," I say. We write books, strange books, about people, and revolutions, and gods, and pain, and truth, and love, and beauty, and horror. Gods and words. "What is the most common, most beloved phrase in Western letters?" I ask. *"In the beginning was the Word,"* I say, *"And the Word was with God, and the Word was God."* What a grand, linear, western, lock-down, hard-on thought. Anyone with bat-brains knows that the Word was not the beginning, nor will it be the end. It's just another cross, one of those absurd crosses that we in the literate West have to tote about with us on the streets, in the market, to bed. "It must mean something," we think; and yet, it is possible it means nothing.

"In the beginning was the Word..." I repeat. They have it all wrong. Better:

"In the beginning was Nothing, then there was Something. After there was Something for awhile, then there was Nothing again."

All those words, jammed into letters and sounds, smeared on the page. Wonder, hate, joy, happiness, tears, love are all reduced to nothing by our gutteral need to stick feelings into words. *The Word was not God.* God was and is outside of words or thoughts. Creating the very word *God* is arrogant. We may believe that merely by saying it, we represent the divine, but we are merely being propagandized by language — especially by those folk who think that reading The Book is important — that it can carry something as sacred or as important as the notion of the divine into, and out of, words.

Overhead, the stars twiddle their thumbs. And here I am, using words to speak the uselessness of words. Max may be alive or passed out or dead; I refuse to give him the satisfaction of my asking. So I go to bed. "That'll teach him to not talk words to me," I say to myself, using the very words to talk to myself.

It's too bad about Max, I think, sometime later. I had grown rather fond of him. He is — or was — a secret Harpo Marx. It might have been the telephone operator that did it, or the moonlight, or the singularity of my thoughts. Evan's-Wentz once wrote: "At the moment immediately preceding death...there shines a white light like moonlight, then a red light like sunlight, then darkness comes. In the reverse order of their appearing, the *yogin* must mentally dispel one after the other — darkness, the red light, and the white light." Maybe when the moon goes down and the sun comes up, Max will have floated off the earth, like those balloons they sell on the streets of Pt. Perdido.

When I rise the next morning, he's gone. He probably revived, I think. They always do. His landlord's daughter had taken an interest in him, had insisted he feel her belly. "Am I fat?" she asked. "My boyfriend says I'm fat, but I'm not fat, am I?" And she took Max's plaint, willing hand, placed it on her honied belly, ran it up and down. Perhaps that is why he didn't die, outside there, in the thin white joy of the moonlight. He revived enough to return home and pass the remaining darkness with hand pressed to his landlord's daughter's firm, dark, and impatient belly.

FEBRUARY 19

I believe that much of early Freudian theory was upside down. At that time many thinkers regarded conscious reason as normal and self-explanatory while the unconscious was regarded as mysterious, needing proof, and needing explanation. Repression was the explanation, and the unconscious was filled with thoughts which could have been conscious but which repression and dream work had distorted. Today we think of consciousness as the mysterious, and the computa-

tional methods of the unconscious, eg., primary process, as continually active, necessary, and all-embracing...
GREGORY BATESON

Denver is the Playa Cula Trailer Park hot-water heater expert. Belying his name, he's from Arkansas. His face and hands are well lined by his seventy years. As he leans over my expired Onan heater I mull on these great lines writ across the back of his neck, great crevasses hatched across skin, elephant skin.

Denver wears thick bifocals that make his watery orbs larger than life, slit through the middle like the cloud-crossed eye in *Un Chien Andulou.* His finest traits, outside his willingness to fix my plumbing, are his legs. They're strong and tan, blonde hairs bleached by the sun — the legs of a man twenty years his junior. He sits in my captain's chair, modelling his pretty legs for me as he conducts the devolution of my hot-water heater while dealing out a selection of highly opinionated and doubtful judgements about Mexico, Mexicans, the world, humanity. Yes Siree-Bob (he actually says "Yes Siree-Bob"), the owner of the trailer park is an old friend, but sometimes gets hot-headed, and Denver has to lead him to wiser pastures. Yes, the Mexican manager, Alberto, is sullen because he has an "inferiority complex" (he actually says "inferiority complex") because he is around all these Americans, and can't deal with the modern world (like hot-water heaters) and is sullen because of his inferiority complex.

As he is saying this, Denver lights a match, pushes the red button on the heater, and is engulfed in a blast of flame which erupts from the lower half of the Silver Pill and threatens to put all of us — Denver, me, trailer — into orbit. "See," he says, "ya ruint it." He is referring to my attempt to light the heater with a candle. "How cum yer laughing?" he says, beaming at me, shorn of eyebrows and eyelashes. I explain that I thought we were both doomed in this Hiroshima of Playa Cula Trailer Park.

"That far t'wern't nothin'," he says. "One time I lit a boiler and went plumb through the wall." I move back some more while he returns to fiddling with the gas pipe. He talks on about a friend of his who's bald as a hoot owl. "Bald folks operate on solar power for increased sex drive," he says. He likes this *mot* so much that he repeats it for me no less than six times in the next twenty minutes — just in case I missed it the first go-round.

His wife arrives in timely fashion to rescue him from the Playa Cula camp hippy, the one that always has "Mescans" going in and out of his trailer. She has big glasses too, and the two of them remind me of those great blue-black Jewfish in the windows of the acquarium (they always block two or three windows). They float there and eye you with such deep indifference that you think you might be looking into the very soul of the universe. Mrs. Denver looks through me for a moment or two and then tells Mr. Denver to get the hell home for lunch which, I gather, is frozen fishsticks (they brought a freezer-full in from the U.S.) She tromps off, and he shrugs his shoulders, and says, "These wimmen!" He works on the heater some more (unsuccessfully), but before he goes, gives me a piece of advice: "You oughta let us know when yer goin' out of town. You never talk to us," he says. "We din't know what had happened to you for a week there. You mighta been dead for all we knew. We take care of each other here." Softly, as in a morning sunrise, I feel the noose tightening.

"I told Alberto, the manager," I say. "I'm surprised he didn't tell you."

" 'Berto don't tell anyone anythin'," says Denver. "I taught him everythin' he knows. I spent one winter coachin' him on English so he could handle the Americans, and he don't even talk to me now." I thought of plump, 100% Mexican Alberto with his silver teeth, speaking English with an Arkansas accent, talking about going to the "haw-tell" when you're "tarred" or "plumb wore out." The thought gave me — and, I hope, Alberto — some pause.

Ernest comes in later to bitch at me for awhile. He had just looked up my article about Puerto Jesús from last year. He claims that I take his speeches, as good as they were, and twist them about so he can scarcely recognize them anymore. "Just think of me as a bonsai master," I say. "I take your ideas — shape and move them, wire them up with artful phrases, make them more perfect: distinctive and beautiful. Perhaps they are somewhat bent out of shape — but that doesn't stop them from being art. That is what The Muse is all about." He stomps off to puff on another joint and think about me being such a lousy amanuensis.

Max went back home yesterday. I'll probably follow him soon. I'll certainly miss him. He's the product of the American way of thinking at its best: books, word-hungry, reading, always reading, thinking, always thinking. He once told me that he and his family had a fairly heated argument, over breakfast, at 6 A.M., on the highest and best use of the subjunctive in written and spoken English.

When he talks, it isn't making words, he's making ideas. His mind is fecund, impatient with simple solutions. "He's always thinking, always thinking," I tell Chuy and Diego. "His mind is always going." The girl at the Piedra Oscura Hotel probably fell in love with him, and why not? He's silent, thoughtful, loyal and true — and she saw that something in him that the people of Oaxaca are so good at seeing.

"As I get older, I find I am more fearful of trying anything new," I told him once. "So many things we tried over the years don't work, so we grow quills about us, like a porkipine, and we refuse to explore and experiment."

MAX: It's spelled porkypine. Besides, you've said that before.

ME: Just because I've said it before doesn't make it any less true.

HE: Just because you say it over and over again doesn't make it any *more* true.

❧ ❧ ❧

When I get back to the cell, El Jefe is there.

"Jefe," I say. "They're trying to kill me. What's going to happen if they kill me." My jaw muscles are in dreadful pain. I have trouble opening my mouth to get the words out.

He looks at me and nods. "If you could just stop thinking," he says.

"Do you have any coñac, Jefe?" I lay my head down on the cold cell floor. The cold feels good to my forehead. "These people hurt me terribly. They don't even understand the word 'stop.' What should I do?"

"I don't know what to say, Ignacio."

"If you don't have any coñac, get me a glass of water, Jefe. I'm dying of thirst. They never give me anything to drink. They put that bag on my head, and they beat me and they beat me, and they won't listen to me, and they won't stop. I wonder if I can get it down."

"Remember where the pain comes from," he says. He takes off his dark glasses and looks down at me. He smiles, and his smile is as radiant as the sun. He rubs his forefinger at a point just above my nose. At first I think he is making fun of me, but when I see the kindness in his eyes, I know he is trying to help me.

"Is there anything I can do for you, Ignacio?" he says.

"I don't want them to hurt me anymore," I tell him. "That's what I want the most." The grey stone floor turns darker. "See," I say, "I'm watering the stones. What do you mean 'Remember where the pain comes from?' " I try to lift my head to look at him. He smiles, as if to say "You're doing all right, Ignacio; you'll make it — one way or another." I wonder that I never noticed his gentleness before.

"The pain," he says. "Remember where it comes from, remember where the nerves are. It doesn't come from your legs or your stomach or your arms. It comes from somewhere else."

"Does that mean that I can do something to stop it."

"It's up here, Don Ignacio," he says, rubbing his forefinger on that point on my brow. "It doesn't exist in the world, or in the place of the gods. It's all here."

I lie there thinking on that for awhile.

"What happens if I die, Jefe?"

"All you have to know is that your thoughts will go along with you," he says. "You die, and your thoughts will accompany you, no matter where you go."

"O no," I say. I look at him, shake my head, shaking, shaking. "No. That's terrible." I start to cough. "That can't be true. I don't want that. I want to leave all of my thoughts behind, here. I've got to be free; I can't stand them." I pause, catch my breath. "Even in Blanco's office, when they're...when they're...doing those things to me, when they are through, my thoughts start back in. I think about the one they call Panzito, how he grunts as he hits me, and Blanco, what he wants from me — even the smell of the wild roses that he keeps on top of his desk." I stop, and breathe deeply. My chest knifes in pain. "I don't want to take it with me, Jefe. I can't. That would be as bad as dying itself." I water the stones some more.

"You can't get away from your thoughts," he says gently, sitting down next to me. He puts an arm about my shoulders. I seem to draw some strength from him. "No matter where you go, your thoughts will go along, too. What do they call it? It's *the eternal present.* All those things in your head that bother you, and all the things that you know — they go right along with you. Lust. Love. Anger. Hurt. In space you can think on those things as long and as hard as you want."

"Stop scaring me, Jefe," I say. "It's bad enough with Blanco trying to beat me to death. I tell you — I'll just refuse to die if they're going to make me keep on thinking. I won't hear of it, do you hear me?" I can feel my voice rising — hoarse and quavery as it is. "What do you think I want to get out of here for? It's bad enough thinking, and *thinking* that I'm thinking. Now you tell me I have to go on thinking forever. I won't put up with it. I'm not going to do it..." I sit up to emphasize my point, groan, lie back down, quickly. "I can't. I won't. Listen to me."

El Jefe is looking at the gecko on the far wall of the cell, up near the bars. It is a stunningly beautiful creature, with scales of burnished gold. It moves about on golden legs. It stops, freezes, turns to stare at me. The eyes are jewels, a pale roseate color lit from inside, the glow of a fire from within.

"I won't take it, Jefe. If they think they can kill me..."

"Hst," says El Jefe. "Listen!"

The gecko opens its mouth, emits a sweet pure vibration that touches the walls, the ceiling, the air — a low, fine, fluting timbrel of music.

"It's the sound of the universe," says El Jefe. "The universe, you know, turns on golden hinges. It makes this music as it goes. Listen."

As I listen, my eyes fill with tears. "O god, why can't I stop weeping?" I say. "I'm so ashamed. It's so beautiful." Through the blur I watch the golden gecko turn quickly away, then back again to watch me. In its mouth rests a tiny diamond bird, a minute hummingbird with wings of pure isinglass, wings moving so quickly I can barely see them. I want to thank El Jefe for bringing me this vision, a vision filled with such a powerful music — but he is gone. The cell is empty, and the golden gecko disappears through the far window.

Between the bars I can see into the night, see the dim configurations of the Southern Cross. I wonder if the tiny bird, with its isinglass wings, is flying towards the Southern Cross, flying through space, away from this cold dark cell we call living.

FEBRUARY 21

Thought does not itself think.
— *THE TIBETAN BOOK OF GREAT LIBERATION*

You had plenty money 1922,
But you let other women make a fool of you,
Why don't you do right, like some other men do;
Get outta here, and get me some money too.
I fell for your jivin' and I took you in,
Now all you got to offer me is a drink of gin,
Why don't you do right, like some other men do;
Get outta here, and get me some money too.

They were playing Peggy Lee on the Voice of America this morning. It was what we used to call a Torch Song, sexy cynicism blended with lovely disgust. In our palmy, innocent youth, "*Why Don't You Do Right?*" represented what sex and love and women were all about. It was the lament of the world-wise, jilted, fagged-out woman — the split command of "get out of here" aligned with the contrary, "and get me some money too." Nowadays, they call that a Double Bind.

It made me pensive. When I was young, I liked to believe that I was somewhat cynical, like Peggy Lee. Cynicism — like sarcasm, boredom, non-involvement — were heavy burdens, and we juveniles didn't assume them lightly. Her song was at the top of my personal Hit Parade, along with "Nature Boy," "They Tried To Tell Us We're Too Young," and "The Four Winds and the Seven Seas:"

A train came to town,
A stranger stepped down,
A-smilin' for my love to see.
She answered his smile,
And after awhile,
The only stranger there was me.
And that is why
My heart and I,
Follow every breeze.
You ask where I liiiiiiive,
Here's the answer I giiiiiiive, [pause]
The Four Winds and the Seven Seas.

When I first heard those words — in 1947 or so — I thought of all my lost loves, even though I had neither loved nor lost a thing up to that time besides my beautiful complexion. These songs were part of my uncritical fifteen-year-old nature, a lack of taste coupled with a generous lack of judgement with regards to people, places, and things. How open we were to all people (except our own families) — openly giving of our energy, spare time, and friendship.

Being young forces us to suspend all critical facilities. We yield solely to the judgement of the gang. Our peers are without fault — although they may be heavy with pimples, incipient with alcoholism, and in love with the trivial and dumb. Our all-pervading catholicity was represented in our clothes (white bucks and chinos, shirts with a pack of Raleighs rolled up in the sleeve), cars (big Chryslers and Plymouth coupes preferred), food (peanut butter and guava jelly on Wonder Bread) and songs like "The Four Winds and the Seven Seas."

That must be why I like being around Chuy and Diego. They remind me of that time when I could so easily be cynical, wise, wisecracking; when I could accept as gospel a tawdry song by a heavy-voiced, heavy-eyed singer — thinking that it made me more sophisticated. I was permitted to act out a pretend scorn for my friends — all the while loving them deeply.

I know why Denver's wife was so eager to get him away from our end of the trailer park. To the average gringo (like Denver, like her) Mexicans are dirty, probably thieving, certainly unreliable — they can be stuffed in the easy category of "lazy Mescans." Mr. & Ms. Denver don't even try to understand these people that live, work, talk, play, laugh, and love around them. They might as well be living in a tent on the Arctic tundra. They exist in a foreign country — the country they've brought with them in their trailer. Instead of celebrating their difference, they scorn the people of whom they are guests. It's said that when the Americans first arrived in Japan, in 1857, the Japanese were non-threatening, even polite, but commented later to each other, at length, on the rank smell of their new visitors. We were known as the "unwashed barbarians." And they say that despite their continuing courteous treatment of us as visitors (and conquerers) — they still reflect on our barbarity — and on our unwholesome stink.

FEBRUARY 25

The German occupation was beautiful. Beautiful because it was my youth, my one and only youth. There won't be any other.

— TADEUSZ KONWICKI

There's a poignancy to the last few days of my stay in the land of the gods. Even the worst things appeal to me now: the crackers that are always stale (they are tightly packed in plastic so I assume they stale them up at the factory); the tumblebugs and furniture beetles that insist on sharing my bed at night; the unnameable creature of carapace and wings that snuggles in my hair and doesn't want to let go until I wake up and pluck it out.

I am even smitten with piss. All the men piss here, piss openly, in public. I saw one ten-year-old turn away from his soccer game to take a leak. There were no comments or finger-pointing or laughter. It's a fact of life to which I subscribe, and often join. I well remember last year a young man on the rooftop of a house on the road between Puerto Jesús and here, pissing into the sunset as we drive by, pissing proudly into the wind. I'll miss the Urinary Life of this region.

I wake up on the last good Friday and the light turns the field outside into a Van Gogh painting — dusty gold and magenta, painted just for us. Diego growls and grumbles and snuffles and makes my tea. I put the middle third of Purcell's "*Fairy Queen*" on the cassette. I ask Diego why Chuy isn't here. "He'll be late," he tells me. "I just talked to him on the telephone and he told me he would be late." This is rich, since Chuy lives in a hut fifty miles away with no running water, much less a telephone, while the nearest phone for us is two miles down the winding dirt road, at the telephone stall that gave Max a chance to understand the meaning of time and the dimensions of timeless Mexico.

We go to the river to say our farewells, to get cool in the late day, and to pick up a case of Giardia. Giardia, a particularly nasty protozoa, inhabits the human duodenum, eats your food for you, and dumps its disgusting wastes in your own intestinal wastebasket. It breeds in unsanitary waters (like the Tonameca) and looks under the microscope — as one doctor told me — like a tennis racket with eyes. It's a particulary pushy, invasive, and persistent visitor. Because it's related to malaria, Giardia requires ten days of bitter, bitter gall, three times a day, yellow stink-pills called atabrine, to force him out the door. Sometimes he doesn't want to leave, the original man who came to dinner, with his bad habits, fouling up the air and one's goodwill.

At the river, Chuy and I indulge in one of our Abbot and Costello dialogues:

CHUY: ¿Cuándo vas? (When are you leaving).

ME: ¿Cuántas veces hay que contestar este? (How many times are you going to ask that question?)

HE: Como cien veces. (About a hundred times.) ¿Cuándo sale? (When are you leaving?)

ME: En dos dias. (In two days).

HE: ¿Cuándo vengas? (When are you coming back).

ME: ¿Hace quanto años que habla español? (How many years have you been speaking Spanish.)

HE: Diez y seis años. (Sixteen years.)

ME: Debe de ser "¿Y cuándo volverías?" ¿Eres pendejo? (You should be using the conditional future tense. Are you some kinda nit-wit?)

HE: Si. ¿Y cuándo vengas? (Yes. And when are you returning?)

ME: Quisiera noviembre. (Probably November).

HE: ¿Y cuándo sale? (And when are you leaving?)

ME: [Resigns.]

After this exchange, he goes off to join Diego in the river. In their skivvies, they run past me, their black hair streaming with water, their great classic Indian statue bodies, their wonderfully muscled legs, the feet — like the feet of so many Oaxacans — rooted to the earth. If I were Michaelangelo, I would be sculpting these dark, horny feet instead of pale marble heads, shoulders and arms. I'd be putting feet all over the cities of Mexico, models of great paired feet: the most powerful symbol of a powerful culture. Feet of stone, planted firmly on the earth, on the riversides, on the village square, in the traffic circles, along the highways, in front of the President's house. Oaxacan peasant feet: the symbol of the past, the hope of the future of the Republic.

I watch my two friends in the water, running, chasing each other with that grace of young men who have used their bodies since childhood for honorable work. As I watch them, I am reminded of poor Mrs. Dalloway:

The strange thing, on looking back, was the purity, the integrity of her feeling. It was completely disinterested. It was protective; sprang from a sense of being in league together, a presentiment of something that was bound to part them...

She seemed all light, glowing, like some bird or air ball that has flown in, attached itself for a moment to a bramble. But nothing is so strange when one is in love (and what was this except being in love?) as the complete indifference of other people.

The camera of my eye has registered memories that will never be developed, but will never leave me. As I write this I can see Diego and Chuy jumping from rock to rock, calling out, laughing, calling to me. "*Stephaneforos...Pinche gringo — míra*," the two cry out from atop their pedestal of granite. "*Pinche 'migo, ¿qué pasa contigo?*" What's going on? The gods call to me. "*Pinche, qué pasa?*" they call, run by me, stop, return. "*¿Qué pasa, amigo?*" Chuy says suddenly kneeling beside me. Great dark moons fill with wonder. "You should be more careful," I say, looking away. "You splashed water all over me," I say. "You have to be more careful," I say. "Hurry," I say, getting up, getting in the car, "we have to be home soon."

Si alguien habla de mi mi nieta,

they sing, as we drive home:

Si alguien habla en tu presencia,
Díles que yo soy tú negro santo:
Yo soy un feo
Un feo que sabe amar
Con todo su corazón
Y que quiere deber dar.

("If anyone speaks of me, my little one; if anyone speaks of me in your presence; tell them that I am your black saint; the ugly one, the ugly one who knows how to love with all his heart, who wants to give you anything you want.")

"*Yo soy un feo...*" they sing. "Tell them I'm your black saint." Chuy calls out to me, wants to know where I got the cold. I don't know, I don't know, I say. Don't bother me, I say. I don't know where I possibly could have gotten a cold in such a warm and loving climate.

❧ ❧ ❧

"They won't leave me alone," I tell Jesús. I am not sure if I will ever move again. I can feel a burning inside of me. He smiles, leans over to me, his face close to my face. "If my jaws didn't hurt so much, the top of my mouth so raw," I think, "I would..."

"Go ahead — kiss me," he says, moving a little closer. He is watching me from inches away.

"I can't Jesús," I say. "I can't even move. If I tried to touch you, it would hurt too much. They've been using electric shocks on me." I let out a deep huge sigh. It makes my jaw and body ache more. "I can't believe what they're doing to me." The words seem to take more time now, as if they were more precious. "You know, I used to be so careful, of my body. I would never hurt it, would never let others hurt it." I sigh again. It seems to help when I sigh loudly, without restraint. He understands. "I didn't want anything to happen to my body, Jesús. I was so proud of it..."

Jesús smiles at me. I can see every detail of his mouth and face and eyes. He burns with a rich light. His mahogany skin is lit up as if there were a fire inside. My boy young and so fresh, so filled with joy, a life just starting, a life pure and simple, full of promise. I'm overwhelmed with a tender love for him, a remorse that I haven't been better to him — the bittersweet joy at his coming to see me here in this dark cell.

"I'm sorry I'm in such a state, Jesús," I say. "This is a bad time for me." I stop, and sigh again. "O God, I should have been kinder to you. I should have given you everything you wanted. When you were hungry — I knew you were hungry — I should have given you what you wanted without demanding anything in return. Your clothes, when they were torn...I should have bought you some new ones, and not made you...made you..." I stop. I am exhausted with my speech. My eyes are watering again.

"Touch me, Ignacio," he says. "I want you to."

I reach out to his face, gingerly, then pull my fingers away from it. His skin is burning, like the hot wall of a furnace.

"I can't do it, Jesús," I say. "I'd burn up. I can't do that. They've already..."

"Don Ignacio." he says. He leans down and kisses my cheek. His lips are cool and gentle.

"I don't want you to be so kind to me," I say, my voice hoarse. "After what I've forced you through." There's the dark scent of vanilla drifting up from his skin, a fragrant steam, a full cloud of dark aroma.

"We've got to make them leave me alone, Jesús," I say. "They tried to destroy me today. I mean...before this, they hurt me. But today, they tried to destroy me. I couldn't breathe when they were doing...what they were doing, with the shocks...down there. I couldn't breathe. It's funny what happens when you can't breathe, when you have these spasms from the jolts and you can't breathe and they've got you tied down so you can't move or stop it." I sigh, and sigh again. "I thought my joints were going to come apart, and when they..." I look at him, his smile so grand and encompassing and loving, so filled with love for me. "Can't you make them stop?"

"When they get done with you, it won't hurt anymore," he says.

"Is that true, Jesús?" I feel my eyes stinging again. "I hope so. I don't know what to believe anymore." He sits down next to me, cross-legged on the floor. "It makes you sad, doesn't it, Don Ignacio?" He puts his arms around my shoulders, holds me, despite the bruises and cuts, despite all the aches and hurt.

"El Jefe told me yesterday...or...whenever he told me: isn't that funny, I don't even remember the days anymore. Anyway...what was I saying?..."

"El Jefe..."

"Right. He told me that if I die, my thoughts won't go away — that they'll go with me, where ever I go. If I die...*IF* I die! What am I talking about? *IF* I die! That doesn't make sense. Anyway, he said...he said..."

"He said that when you die..."

"Right...that when I die, my thoughts will go along with me, that they won't be left behind here, but will go wherever I go. I couldn't stand that. The thought of my thoughts going with me drives me crazy. I want to be thoughtless...is that the right word?"

"You can't be thoughtless, Don Ignacio."

"I didn't know you spoke English, Jesús. You speak English so beautifully. You understand everything."

"I always have, Don Ignacio."

"I wasn't completely cruel to you, was I, Jesús? I didn't want to be. I wanted to be loving." My heart is beating so hard I feel like it is going to jump from my body. I breathe — what is it they say? — I breathe the strength in, concentrate it in on the heart. How strange it is when they won't let you breathe. Nothing becomes as important as breathing. It becomes more important than anything in the world. I read once that we can live forty days without food, four days without water, but only four minutes without air.

"Most of the time I can shut up my thoughts, except late at night, when I am alone," I say. "That's why I don't like being alone at night. Do you know what I mean, Jesús? Does any of this make any sense? Please tell me it does?" I try to look at him through my double vision.

"What sense, Don Ignacio?" he says. "Of course you make sense. You've always made sense to me..."

"When I get out of here, when I go out there," I say... I pause. "When I go out there, my thoughts will go along with me. I won't be able to get away from them. I'll be like a comet, going from sun to sun, and from universe to universe. There'll be a white trail of thoughts burning after me, going with me across the night sky.'' I shiver. Jesús takes off his soft golden jacket, drapes it around my shoulders.

"What's wrong with your thoughts?'' he asks.

"Oh god, Jesús. I'd go crazy. I would, wouldn't I?''

"So?''

"I'd probably wander around, from one sun to another, from galaxy to galaxy, all by myself, crazy as a bedbug. There wouldn't be a bit of sense left in me. I wouldn't be able to think straight, I wouldn't be able to talk to anyone, even though no one would be there. I wouldn't have anyone to talk to, if I was alone. Do you see?'' I go into a spasm of coughing. Jesús takes the white linen handkerchief from his jacket pocket, wipes off the spot of red on my mouth.

"I wouldn't have anyone out there with me in space? Except, maybe... Would you come with me out there Jesús, into...'' Far down the hall, there's the sound of the heavy metal door being opened, held open for a moment, then banged shut.

"I hope they're not coming for me again, Jesús. Oh, God. I don't think I can take any more. I know I can't take any more what they're doing to me.'' I listen to the footsteps. "I'm scared,'' I say. "What does that mean, do you think? 'Can't take any more.' That doesn't make any sense. There's not much left for me to give them except... what's left. They can have that...'' The footsteps come closer, pause. I whisper: "Jesús, it's that...that...I'm worried that my body won't let me die. Bodies make up their own minds on these things.'' I try to smile. "Can you imagine a body making up its own mind?'' I almost laugh, but then I remember my ribs. "Think of that,'' I whisper. "My body has a mind of its own. Do you see how silly that sounds?'' I smile. "You know, there might not be anyone out there in space for me to talk to.'' The footsteps start up again, go past the cell.

"It is possible, isn't it, Don Ignacio?" he says.

"If there's no one at all out there at all," I say, "If I am out there in space, with no friends, with no one to communicate with...it will be very...very hard to concentrate..."

"Maybe you won't want to concentrate," he says. He stops a moment to think. "Or maybe...maybe there'll be a multitude of Ignacios out there, great white and orange flowers, blooming, turning, turning about, there in space, reflected in a million suns."

"I want you out there with me, Jesús. Please say you'll come," I say. "If you're not there, I'll be alone. I don't think I can take being lonely anymore."

"It might be the same thing," he says. "Being alone and being with a thousand thousand Ignacios." He smiles, rests his hand on my shoulder a minute, looks out the window, and then turns to watch me. "Look at you. Weeping again. At a time like this. You've got to be brave."

"I'm not brave, Jesús — I never have been. I don't want to be brave. When I was a kid, they'd hit me. And I would try to run home, and they'd hold me and hit me again. I'd say, 'You don't have to do that. You know you don't have to do that to me.' What I was doing was asking them to stop, to be nicer to me, to be my friends. But they didn't hear me. They'd laugh and chase me home.

"Now I have all these bullies around me — and I can't run home anymore. They won't let me be a sissy. How can you be a sissy when they keep you locked up, then drag you down there with a big bag on your head, and they beat you silly, then try to drown you — run water up your nose, or tie you down and shock you in the most hurtful places — and there is nowhere to run. That's the worst of it all. They won't even let me be a sissy. I'm tired of being brave. I want to be a sissy again."

I look out the cell window. The sky has turned steel and blue. The Southern Cross has faded. There is a single branch of lilac growing across the sky, the bit of sky I can see. Thin blue flowers etched against a greying sky. How sacred that plant, that tiny portion of the heavens. It's a holy church, this arch of sky. "I'm tired of them hurting me, Jesús, making me sad. Do know what Blanco the Chief does when I start in feeling bad?"

Jesús's puts his head on my chest. His face feels cool to my chest. I feel the life coursing through his body. My lips are torn, yet I bring his face to my own, touch his lips — just for a moment. "Here I am, being murdered, slowly," I tell him. "Sometimes when it hurts too much, I start to...to...I can't hear very well now, I have this ringing in my ears all the time now where they've been banging me on the head — and I can't see anything with the bag over my eyes. I know Blanco is disgusted with me, because he can hear me sniffling under the burlap, just like when I was a kid. I can hear him stop for a moment and then yawn — I can hear him yawn! He's probably looking at his fingernails, or going to his desk, checking off something on a paper. *Prisoner cries, prisoner screams, prisoner begs us to stop,* he'll write in his fine hand. He probably has this *Torturer's Checklist* that he consults every few minutes, to see if I am doing what I am supposed to do, to see if he is doing what *he* is supposed to. He's keeping tabs on me, I know he is, trying to figure out how far he can push me. Can I really go any place I want to?"

Jesús smiles. His face is getting dimmer. Something must be wrong with my eyes. There's a haze, as if a cloud had dipped down from the sky to envelop him in pearl.

"You'll go with me, won't you, Jesús?"

"Maybe you won't want me, Don Ignacio. Or maybe you'll go too far, out to the edge, so far out that there won't be anyone who can reach you — there beyond the edges. Some people do that. They want to go as far away as they can. They go out so far that there isn't anywhere left to go.'' He nods. ''They say you can stay there as long as you want. And after awhile, once you are there, you'll find that you can do anything you want with your thoughts. If you want to create another you, you can do it. If you want to create love, you can do that, too. Some people go there and start whole new worlds, whole new universes.'' Jesús isn't smiling now. He's serious. He is speaking like people do when they're thinking hard. He's getting fainter and fainter. He stops for a minute, and I can see him smiling again. His smile fills up the misty cell, filling it with a thin blue light. I can barely seen him now.

''Wait a minute, wait a minute, Jesús...Are you saying I can create a world, just like this one, with trees and oceans and...and people? And prisons?...''

''If you want. You can create whatever you want, Ignacio. No dying, if you want — no pain. You can do anything you want. There are no limits.''

His arm is very light on my shoulder now; at the same time, my body is coming to be so hot that I am afraid it will turn to ashes. I want him to stay, to cool me. But he is going.

''If you want, you can create a world that has no hurt in it at all. If you want...'' his voice is now so faint that I am not sure I am hearing it at all. His hand on my shoulder feels like nothing. There's just the whisper of ''your own world...''

FEBRUARY 27

I wake up and look for Nancy Drew outside my window, but a fierce wind came along during the night (it rocked the trailer like a boat on the great sea) and tore her from her place outside. The Green Blob remains: oblivious, waggling his head back and forth — as if the controversy were continuing, as if

his confere were still there, scolding him, calling him "obtuse" and "insensitive." The Blob is arguing with the wind, treating the past as if it were the present. There is only a stem to remind us of the girl that once lived across from him, a torn stem to remind us of the battle that went on for so long, the battle that was never resolved, could never be resolved.

MARCH 1 [ON THE ROAD]
We are hurrying to get to Ciudad Industrial by nightfall. We pass a striated mass just outside Nacimiento, a chart of a hundred or so world epochs. There are shiny layers of hard grey-white igneous rock, intersticed with scree and breccia — a geologic baklava. A recent upthrust has turned the whole formation vertical. Before us, like a book, are 100,000 years alternating with another 100,000 years alternating with another 100,000 years, and on and on. We are able to read dozens of pre-human epochs, with earthquakes and lava, sedimentary evaporites and cumulates. Before us are civilizations that have come and gone — life and death, great (and strange) creatures who walked the earth —fed, slept, fought, aged, and died. The filaments of their bones lie frozen in the rock face before us. And here I am, hurrying to get to Ciudad Industrial to eat some tacos and find a place to sleep for the night...

— JOURNAL

Mexico is filled with people — the eighteen million of Mexico City, the forty-five million in the seaside cities and towns, the border and the industrial workplaces. At the same time there is the other Mexico, the stark, barren countryside. For six lonely hours before reaching Acapulco, we scarcely see another car on our coastal route: villages like Guagua and Colola consist of a few palapa huts, a dozen pigs and chickens; nothing more — not even a Pemex station. And the mind twists about like the road, a snake, everything turned about itself. Up we go, up the sides of the foothills of Sierra Madre del Sur, and then, turnabout, down the other side, into the valley of the Toscano, past the Aguilillo River basin.

There are moments when the road emerges hundreds of feet above a river-mouth. Below us is a delta, three palapa fishing huts that face the ocean, spare land barren of people. "If I don't like gringos," I think, "I could spend the rest of my life here." The loudest noise is the sound of ocean and the rattling of palms, the barking of a lone dog. Why not? Fresh breezes stream in from Punta Tehupan. It's an isolation so grand that it makes the mind timorous. "If one of the mountains sneezed," I think, "it would push the road and us and the village into the sea and no one would ever know that we were here."

No houses, nor restaurants, nor trucks, nor cars — not even sheep or goats. I am very glad that Diego decided to come with me. (Chuy elected to stay behind. Our last vision of him was him reflected for us in the dusty rear-view mirror of The Ox. We had just pulled the Silver Pill over to the far side of the Playa de Cula Trailer Park — its summer home. We left him standing there before its shimmering, he dark, his shadow washed out against the brightness of it. I see his face: the high cheekbones, his cheap shirt and torn shorts, his bare feet resting against the earth his home. Despite his great, noble, passive face, he looks tiny against our home of the last four months. We wave, he waves, we wave and wave, and he is gone.)

Diego slipped away without telling his girl-friend. "It's better this way," he says. The truth is, like many young men in love, or half in love, he chafes under the idea that his love may own him, that she may one day appear with his "alma pequeña" — his little one — in the *matrix*. Diego, with the lust of a rutting goat, gets a little antsy with his lovely Marcellina. It is time for him to take a vacation from her, he says: from her and the little village of Pinotepla, where you can't walk down the dusty road with another girl without everyone humming on about it, laughing behind their hands. It is time to move on, perhaps for a month, perhaps for a year.

So we set out on our journey. He is ready to go, as countless others before him, to the next city or the next state or the next country, to make a fortune, or taste another world. The well-known Itchy Foot Syndrome, the heritage of the life in the towns and villages of Mexico, of Central and South America, the world. It makes for a tide of people swarming up the coast, running up against — sometimes squeezing through — the dark wall that separates Mexico from the United States. Last year, the U.S. Customs and Immigration Service captured, and returned, at approximate count, a million people from Mexico, and Central America. No one has records of how many flowed through the many holes in the barrier.

We meet several other kinds of barriers — ones set up by the American drug police to harrass innocent tourists and Mexican truckers. One especially hard-eyed number, looking like Marlon Brando trying to look like Emilio Zapata, holds us up for an hour in the blazing sun just outside Ciudad Pitiquito while he sifts through our belongings, bangs on the insides of the car, looks down the window slots, removes panels, opens all the doors, and the hood — and asks me (imperiously) what I do for a living. He takes Diego aside and asks him if I smoke dope or shoot heroin. "While this pinhead has us baking here at the side of the road," I think, "twenty-five Piper Cubs have flown overhead to drop enough raw cocaine into the wastelands of Arizona, the deserts of Texas, the swamps of Louisiana, the scrub palm savannahs of Florida, enough to turn the entire city of New York into a solid stoned mass a dozen times over."

"What kind of books do you write," Sr. Brandito asks me.

"Oh," I say, thinking briefly on the *Love of Torquemada*, its hero stuck in the revolutionary wilds of Central America, arrested and tortured as a card-carrying radical (as if he gave a toot about anything except buns and *pitas*) — "Oh," I say, "You know — novels, travel books, technical." "What kind of technical books?" he leers, and for that brief suicidal moment I hear myself saying, "You know, mostly chemical — simple chemical reactions one can perform with benzene, and ether, to make lysergic acid." "Books on zoology," I tell him. (The word I use is *zoológico*, which means Zoo — so I may have told him that I write about bears and tigers behind bars). Whatever I said seemed to satisfy what was left of his conscience, so he set us free, with only two more snarls and a growl.

❧ ❧ ❧

Diego is a fine travelling companion, but he is lost. His world is back there somewhere near the sea. He is a country boy who has lived barefoot most of his life on the coast of Oaxaca. When he's hungry there and has no money, he puts on his scuba mask and, in an hour, plucks three or four lobsters, or a bushel of oysters from the water, cooks them over the open fire with his friends, eats them straight — along with tortillas and hot sauce, imbibing a bottle of Corona. He is a creature of the sea and the earth. (His huge muscular feet can hardly be squeezed into the Reeboks I have bought him.)

If this is a life journey, his possessions are pitifully small: a couple of white shirts, two tee-shirts (one saying "Stolen from Folsom Prison"), two pairs of pants, three "bikinis," and six pair of socks. And, of course, the Sony Walkman, with earphones: earphones that have become a permanent fixture atop his head, as if he had sprouted a message center leading up from the black box on his belt to the two tiny saucers about his ears. A geezer couldn't be as faithful to his hearing aid as Diego to his beloved "Son-ee," except he is not using it for listening to the world about him; he is listening to a sweeter world far, far away. He's plays his three tapes of "Los Tigres del Norte" over and over again, with their tales of the police of Tijuana, songs of working as waiters in Chicago, trying to hide from *La Migra* — the American Immigration Service police. One of my favorites tells of the plight of a first-generation Mexican living (illegally) in Los Angeles, trying to get his second-generation American high school son to travel back to Guadalajara with him, and the son says, halfway through the song, in perfect English, "You want me to go back to Mexico. *No way, dad.*"

Diego, I learn, as we travel, has never seen a freeway before, never seen a grain elevator or a field filled with reapers, the sky filled with crop-dusters. In the hotel room, I hand him the telephone to dial room service. He holds the receiver upside down to his face, wonders what it's for. He has never been in an elevator, never seen a tollbooth, never crossed a high bridge span, never seen a showroom full of new cars.

It isn't an easy trip for him — being on the road with a gringo with a vocabulary of a six-year old child. Sometimes our words get crossed; sometimes we talk at cross-purposes. I learn, too, the real pain of his illiteracy. Like most non-readers, he hides it expertly. His eyes slip past the road signs, never focussing, while he casually asks me where we are. I begin to read the signs to him, pretending that I am reading them aloud to myself. We carry the lie forward: I protect my good friend from the hurt of knowing that so much of the world is cut off from him.

They always use the words "illiterate" and "tragic" in the same sentence. Rather, I think, it's a lifetime spent in a not very exciting shut-off room, a jail filled with a fog about how the outside world functions. The courts and libraries and universities — books, newspapers, magazines — have been, are, and always will be a secret fraternity, ones they can never enter. Those of us who have travelled to Russia or Japan or the Arabic countries know the feeling. The script, Cyrillic, Arabic, the ideograms, are so different from our own beloved Roman alphabet, and thus do not permit us to grasp content. The medium is not the message. A sign that says "No Tire Basura" is as mysterious to Diego as it is to most Americans (what are they saying about tires? Does it mean "No Bald Tires?") It is as confusing as the signs that once almost led me off the roadway through the Atlas Mountains in Morocco, took me close to plummeting down into an olivine valley far below (there were no barriers). There are pitfalls that never can be anticipated. Those who cannot read have to rely on friends and good sense to protect them from their special kind of blindness.

There always are compensations, at least to those who live in the second half of the 20th century. Compared to an illiterate of his father's time (his father could never read, only work in the caña fields) or his mother's (his mother could never read, only cook and wash and bear children) — now, what with movies, radio, television, cassettes, his life is that much brighter. He is allowed to see and hear direct — instead of indirect — fantasy. Much of the culture, at least the culture of popular music and talk and "novelas," is given him. The Walkman connects him to his contemporaries, and to the cultures of his friends.

At the same time, I bring along my own cassette of Amparo Ochoa's "La Mujer" — a long, funny, sad, existential cry of the urban Hispanic mother:

Abrío los ojos,
Se hechó un vestido,
Se fue despacio para la cocina.
Estaba oscuro.
Sin hacer ruido,
prendio la estufa,
y ya a la rutina.
Sintió el silencio
come un apuro.
Todo empezaba en el desayuno.
Dobló su espalda
vozó un suspiro.
Sintió ridicula la esperanza.
Al mas pequeño le ardió la panza...

[She opened her eyes, threw on a dress, went slowly into the kitchen. It was dark. Making no noise, she lit the stove and — now — the same old routine. She felt the silence like a goad. Everything began with breakfast. She stooped down, she sighed. Hope remained ridiculous. The littlest one burned in her belly. She waited on her husband; dressed the kids; changed diapers; served bread; took the kids to school; thought about what they were going to eat; checked her change; bought vegetables; felt the greyness of her poverty. She stood in the line for tortillas; carried Francisco; looked around the street. Everywhere there were women. They were all buying and they moved carrying out their errands. They reminded her of ants — and suddenly she felt they were slaves: she felt that they were all friends.]

And the chorus, repeated over and over again:

Se va la vida, se va al agujero,
Como la mugre en el lavadero.
Se va la vida, se va al agujero,
Como la mugre en el lavadero.

[So goes life, so it goes down the drain — like the dirty water in a washing machine, like the dirty water in the washing machine.]

How strange it is, I think, to be listening to these Hispanic Urban Blues as we are winding up and down this stunning, uninhabited coastline. "Maybe I should write to La Mujer," I think, "tell her to get the hell out of that rented house in Mexico City, or wherever she is, come down here to Sierra Madre del Sur where her husband can fish all day, and she could let the kids run naked; the sea at her doorstep, the night free of the sounds (and dangers) of trucks and busses racing up and down in front of her door. The waves falling, falling, then falling some more."

❧ ❧ ❧

El Jefe meets me in the courtyard. He throws his head back, looks at me between narrowed lids. The sun leaks through the boxwood tree, dappling the ground around us, lacing us with yellow and golden spangles. It is the first time I have been out in the sun for a long time. The brilliance of it draws my skin, makes me feel alive.

"They've arranged it so you can have your own cell," he says, "so you can have visitors, and better food."

"I don't know if it makes much difference, Jefe," I say. He sits down next to me. "I don't seem to eat anything any more. I don't seem to have the appetite. I think they did something to my...my hunger."

"You should eat — before...when you can..." he says. His words are broken up by his sharp little cough, like a the cry of a child.

I shrug my shoulders. I breathe in deeply, taking in the air. It is cooler today, cooler than I remember from before. I let the air out slowly. "What a privilege it is to breathe," I think.

"You've gotten to be a hero to the folk, you know," he says. "The mountain people are all talking about Ignacio *Gringissimo.* That's what they call you. They love you as a father." He thinks for a minute. "The people here don't like Gringos — but you, Ignacio: it's as if they've decided you are a god, even though they don't even know you. They think you are being tortured because of what you did for Aldeo."

I nod. How fresh the air. And the sun on the dark red flowers, the lilies, near the base of the tree — how dark their flowers! Resurrection Lilies: is that what they call them? Flowers moving slowly in the breeze, waving, waving...

"His family has organized a special mass to be said for you," he says. "They say that you tried to protect him — and then after they murdered him, you protected his body from being defiled by them."

I look at the lilies. If you watch them closely, sometimes they turn, turn towards you, even if there is no breeze. The sun will make them darker, later, like blood — but now they are light and full of life.

"The mountain people talk of you all the time now. It is very strange...as if you struck a chord with them." He pauses, smiles. "They're very suspicious, but when they come to trust a person, they never quit."

"It might be..." I stop and think for a minute. "I wasn't sure at first what Don Blanco wanted of me...I mean, when he started, what he did... He never came right out and told me. He had to be patient. He had to let me find out my own way. Now I think I know." I pause again. "I signed everything he put before me. By then, it didn't seem to be all that important."

He looks at me — and then up at the tree. There is a mockingbird perched above us. "Cadbury," it says. "When I was young," I say, "I always thought mockingbirds were singing 'Cadbury, Cadbury, Cadbury.' There was a milk chocolate called Cadbury. Since it was sweet, and since I like chocolate, I could never get enough. I always liked hearing mockingbirds sing about it." The sunlight dapples over us, back and forth, coins thrown from above. "Children are so easily touched," I think. "I loved Cadbury's chocolate. And the mockingbirds...and their song." "We children are so easily touched," I tell El Jefe.

"Cadbury, Cadbury," says the mockingbird, jumping up into the air, then coming back down on the branch.

"They'll take you to your new cell this afternoon," El Jefe says. "You'll be much more comfortable there."

"Jefe. I signed everything they put before me. I'm not a hero. I'm a coward. Don Blanco knows that...and his assistant, Panzito..." I stop. "Everyone here knows I'm no hero. You should tell the people that. I was scared, Jefe. Scared of being hurt. I think for a while there I was even scared of dying." What is it they say? *Timor mortis conterbat me.* Scared to death of dying.

He rubs his cheek. Then he says, "It doesn't make any difference, Ignacio. The people know you are a hero.

It probably has to do with the boys. Jesús, the street kids — Aldeo. Most of all, Aldeo, and his parents. They're the most important. His father is a leader up there in the Monte Esperanza area. He says you were very good to Aldeo, gave him something he had never had before — even though he was just a poor harelip. He says you helped him before the Army got to him and murdered him. He said that you cared for his body until they could retrieve it. The mountain people feel very strongly about caring for the dead. They think of the dead as if they were holy. They say you protected Aldeo from being defiled."

I watch the tree for a minute, watch the leaves, and then I say: "You know what you were telling me the other... the other...how long have I been here?" I stop, and breathe sharply, the breath knifing into my side. "O God, Jefe — I can't remember anything!" I pause again. "Anyway, remember what you were telling me...about our thoughts; how they go with us, will always be with us."

El Jefe looks at me, and then back up at the mockingbird. He lifts his dark glasses, rubs his eyes slowly and methodically. "He's an old man now," I think. "He won't be around much longer." I feel a spasm of grief that we come, and rest here for such a short time, and then must be gone. "It doesn't make any sense, does it?" I say.

El Jefe replaces his glasses, then looks at me. A single ray of sunlight plays along the edge of his glasses. I can see myself reflected in them. They make my head huge, my body tiny. "It's just like being born," I think. When we're born, the head comes out so slowly. The exit is very, very difficult. After that, the body just slips out, as if it were nothing.

"At first I was scared," I tell him. "I didn't want my thoughts to go along with me when I died. I believed it would drive me crazy to have them following me across the universe." Some other prisoners come out of the building, and start kicking a soccer ball about. "I wanted to be able to do what I did before — to sleep and drink and make my thoughts leave me alone." One of the *futbol* players bounces the ball along the top of his shoe, dribbling it in reverse, balancing it there as he runs around the yard. El Jefe and I watch, fascinated by this ability to hold onto a round orb like that.

"But then I realized that once I get out into space, it will be a perfect time to be alone with my...with my...with these parts of me: pure, no distractions. I'll have eons out there, and nothing to distract me." El Jefe watches the futbol players as they run back and forth across the narrow courtyard. One of them runs into the wall, falls down laughing. El Jefe's shoulders are bent. "It is as if he was the one beaten, and not me," I think.

"What I think I will think — can I say that? — *'what I think I will think when I am out there'* (it sounds so strange)...Anyway, I will finally know if my thoughts have power — whether they can change and affect me, and the world, even temporarily." I look at El Jefe. He doesn't seem to be hearing me. "Still, sometimes I think thoughts are no more important than this," I say, and I try to snap my fingers, so he'll understand, but my fingertips are still swollen, so the sound comes out as a thud.

"They are nothing at all. A cloud, a flower, a mist — then they're gone, and we're still here, as we should be: thoughtless." Can that be the right word? I stop and look down at him, my heart so filled with pity for him, for all mankind — but suddenly I feel strange, have to sit down. I hold my breath for a moment, try to catch my breath. "What I'm telling you about thoughts," I say, after a moment: "It may be the most important thing I've ever...thought about." I start to laugh, despite my broken ribs. "To get rid of all thoughts. It would be, it would be..." I pause because I don't want to use the wrong phrase. "If I could finally get rid of my thoughts, it would be *a most sacred act...*"

With a sudden motion, he stands up, turns to me, takes hold of my hand. "It is time for me to leave," he says. "Is there anything you need?"

"No, no, no..." I say. "I have more than everything I want. I can't think of anything else..."

He nods, takes my hand again, drops it, starts to go off, then stops, turns, and says: "I asked one of the boys to come over tonight to your new cell. He will bring you a little gift." I can no longer see his eyes.

"He'll be smuggling poison to me," I think. That is the way they do it. A piece of paper, with a little white powder folded inside it, smelling of burnt almond. I can swallow it, if I wish — be free to rise above all this...If I wish. As if it would make a difference.

The golden spangles of the sun rain down on El Jefe's back, coins tossed on my friend as he disappears down the tunnel. "As if it would..." I say aloud. He stops for a moment, waves, hurries on.

MARCH 7

Tecoman, Manzanillo, Malaque. The memories of long trips are always meshed with hours and hours of driving which is, at first, boring; then, at some point, you don't even notice — it becomes a meditation, time against, then time eaten by — space. Space becomes a flattened galaxy, spinning inexorably towards other galaxies, or the Black Hole. Hour after hour the great black swath reaches before us, white comets blurring down the center of it. I drift off — then catch myself. It was that noisy barking dog, going at it last night all night behind the Las Puchas Hotel. That was what robbed us of our sleep. I dreamed of dogs, little barkers, pee-wees, black and lusty Great Danes, snippy Pekinese. Next to my house to the North a barking relative of last night's songster holds forth most of the day, and much of the night. "Pumpkin" is the obnoxious name of the obnoxious, pumpkin-headed beast. I once wrote a note to her owner. I said,

"Dear Paul:

"You own the dog when you're home. We get her when you're away.

"Pumpkin goes:
bark bark bark bark bark bark bark bark bark bark bark bark bark bark bark bark bark bark bark bark bark bark bark bark bark bark bark bark bark bark bark bark bark bark bark bark bark bark bark bark bark bark bark bark bark bark bark bark bark bark bark bark bark bark bark bark bark bark bark bark bark bark bark bark bark bark bark bark bark bark bark bark bark bark bark bark bark bark bark bark bark bark bark bark bark bark bark bark day and night. Please do something about it."

My elegant letter was met with stony silence from the owner, and oft-repeated performances of "bark bark bark" etc. from Pumpkin.

When the Acapulco Pumpkin woke us up for the fifth time, I said the hell with it, roused Diego out of his dreams, and we got out of Las Puchas before the sun came up. On a causeway north of the city, our right front tire starts saying "bark bark bark" etc. It is, in the language of the country — *descompuesto*: "uncomposed;" flat. All we have is a cranky jack, a tremulous spare, a grey pearl fog, and ten or so thousand hungry mosquitos. They bite through our shirts and pants and socks, needling our necks and hands, trying to suck us dry, but I am more worried about being squashed by a truck hurtling along in the predawn along the causeway, for the highway has no shoulders or pull-outs. While Diego struggles with the jack, I sit in my wheelchair behind The Ox, swatting little nippers and cursing my fate ("and the wet Saturday afternoon of my conception" — Samuel Beckett). And sure enough, a huge Pemex truck comes bearing straight down on us. I say my farewells to Diego, make my peace with whatever gods I have floating about there above the swamp at sunup, think on the wet afternoon of my wild wet conception, and the truck swerves around us and lurches to a stop. The driver gets out and — in three minutes — removes our flat, throws on the spare, cinches it in, and is off, on his way, barely accepting the kisses (and the 20,000 pesos) that we press on him.

❧ ❧ ❧

Tecoman, Manzanillo — Peñita de Jaltemba, Barra de Navidad, El Salado ("The Salad?") The oceans and the hills and the cities and the plains come and go. Cars and trucks and busses pass us at high speed, shaking us in our primordial journey. Diego goes to sleep with his Sony full blast in his ears. Piloto, Puerto Vallarta, Zacalpan, Ciudad Guzmán. Ciudad Guzmán? Good God. Where did that one come from? It would not be unlike naming a street in Palestine "Eichmann Way," an Austrian village named "Atilla." It would be rechristening Beijing in honor of Tojo, the Japanese minister of war, responsible for bombing China in 1937. It would be as if Ethiopia decided to create Mussolini City, and Kabul honored Brezhnev Pass. Georgia would change "Atlanta" to "Shermanville," Viet-Nam erect the Pol Pot Memorial Dam, and Chile would dedicate a Harold S. Geneen Memorial Plaza in downtown Santiago. Guzmán! The name that so terrorized Mexico so long ago:

A number of friars were busy among the Tarascans, performing baptisms and building convents; and their kindly labors had almost caused the Tarascans to forget what they had suffered from the soldiers of Olid and to believe that the Spaniards had come to America to bring them a higher civilization. Nuño de Guzmán showed them their mistake. After seizing several thousand Indians to act as porters, he asked the chieftain of the Tarascans for gold. The efforts of the chieftain were not sufficiently munificent, so he was tied to the tail of a horse and dragged across a plain, and subsequently burnt....From Michoacán he marched into Jalisco, burning villages and building crosses. When the Indians received him peacefully, they were goaded into rebellion in order that the

Spaniards might have a pretext for enslaving them...In Tepic his Indian allies were decimated by floods and pestilences; a number tried to escape, but they were captured and hanged or driven to suicide...

— *A HISTORY OF MEXICO*

Those of us who have travelled far off to Spain in the past half-century think of it as a country of noble if poor toilers, many close to the soil, the peasants showing a warmth and a welcome for strangers, the hearty city-folk laughing and drinking *tinto* with us. We forget that Spain conducted a pogram in the New World that matched in time span and in ferocity a similar pogram by the Germans four centuries later. The Iberians decimated whole cultures — stole, robbed, murdered, raped, burned, pillaged — and did it all for the greater glory of god. And here we have the Mexicans, in their kind blindness, naming a city after their own personal Hitler.

MARCH 8

"Always remember," she said, "your journey is different than the others. I don't mean a little different: what you want and feel and do are far out of what most people consider to be normal. You'll do things, and they'll start to feel like the norm. You'll get swept away by your actions; you'll start thinking your actions are right and proper. 'Maybe it's OK,' you'll find yourself thinking.

"You'll be wrong. Your world view is skewed: what you want will always be contrary to the wants of 99% of humanity. Your needs are so vastly different from those of the rest of the world that if you ever forget how different they (and you) are, and how dangerously explosive that difference to the general public — then you are done for."

— *THE DANGEROUS LOVER*
EMILE D'AVIGNON

We travel on, through Caponeta, Escuinapa de Hidalgo, Villa Union, Culiacan, Guachil, Navajoa, Çiudad Obregon — the Pittsburgh of Mexico. Diego and I travel on our stomachs, and so we both have a warm (and special) spot in our heart for Ciudad Obregon because of the wonderful public market, and the torta stand next door, where the homemade rolls are filled to brimming with moist white chicken meat, savory with a special bitter mustard. We feel bound to Ciudad Obregon. More than the fact that it the home of our favorite beer, Corona, there's the anti-drunken driver campaign we see while we are eating our *Tortas de Pollo*. To the great roaring of motorcycles and the shriek of sirens, wrecked automobiles are dragged through the streets, filled with real live people, acting like corpses, painted vigorously if not well with geniune imitation blood. It's no — I almost wrote "it's no accident" — It's no accident that we found ourselves face-to-face with a real live corpse lying beside a real live upturned car no more than twenty kilometers west of Ciudad Obregon.

Vicam, Empalme, Hermosillo ("little beautiful one") — where the Pemex man overcharges us six dollars, and has the temerity to laugh at us when we ask for change. El Oasis, Altar, Querobabi — where we buy a package of delicious tortillas. "A good tortilla is just like human flesh," I note in my journal, "which is probably part of its attraction. Soft yet firm, slightly moist, a chill warmth that is uncannily like the flesh of my ninety-year-old Aunt Beulah, when I leaned over, dutifully, to kiss her. But she certainly didn't smell as good as a tortilla," I wrote. Sam'l once told me that while he was in the off-the-beaten track town of Tenango, the mother of his family there used tortillas not only for filling stomachs, and sopping up gravy, but for potholders, polishing, and general clean-up as well.

Estacion Llano, Santa Ana and Benjamin Hill. Benjamin *Who* Hill? Or *Who* Benjamin Hill? One time my friend Glenn Thompson climbed a California peak, and after breaking his ass to get to the summit, found out it had no name. "How can I tell people I braved the heights with the name No Name?" he wanted to know. I told him we should get it named after our favorite radical, so we dutifully made application to the California Board of Orthography and Place Names asking that the unnamed peak be christened *Joe Hill.* The CBOPN, in full seriousness, studied our proposal for a full year, had the bad humor to change the application to "Joe Hill Peak," forcing us — as gracelessly as possible — to bow out. I would like to meet (and congratulate) that member of the Sonoran Associación de Ortografía who had the wit and good sense to pass on Benjamin Hill — a noisy, sand-blown railroad switching area of no interest and with nary a Hill, Benjamin or otherwise, in sight.

Caborca, where the real desert begins. San Emeterio (Saint Emetic?), Sonoyta. Driving over the hill coming into Sonoyta, we can see the border, America hazy and bleak in the distance. I point it out to Diego, but he won't see it. He has already refused to move the hands back on his watch, even though we have passed through two time zones ("I can't see them," he says.) His Oaxacan disbelief system won't permit him to accept a concept as silly as space = time.)

Los Vidrios — as dry and as barren as any town in the Americas, deserted homes, dusty, dry, deathly — many with broken windows ("vidrio" means "glass.") Near Cerro Prieto, the sun dies magnificiently, split at the waist, a brilliant orange-yellow hourglass, carefully leaving us in its own best symbol, the Ouroboros. We plunge down-hill and into San Luis, a shady little border town on the edge of the dry and silty Colorado, the river reduced to nothing by the depredations of American "flood control," a once grand river now a combination weedy dust bed and junkyard ("yonke," in the parlance of Tex-Mex.)

At nine, we locate the one remaining room in town at the Motel Verga Azul. Since the next rest stop is four hours distant, we reluctantly take it. Our room combines the charm (and smell) of a local whorehouse with the peeling interiors and dank corners of early 1950s Porno Moderne. There are two television sets (neither of them work) and a dead (or dying) mouselet, circling lazily in the leaking toilet. We dub him Mighty Micro Mouse — after the nearby town's "microwave" tower, and I release him from this painful wheel of life with a brief prayer and a pull on the flush-box handle.

After dinner we fall to our beds. Diego asks me what I imagine to be a stupid question, I snarl back a cruel answer, he turns on the pillow, is silent, then weeps. I ask my pardon of him; I lie close — beg the eternal pardon of my good and kindly friend. Words are useless: wooden words. I lie there, side-of-face to his bare back, until he falls asleep. I know, he will soon know (it might be a comfort) that he is weeping not only at my harsh words but at the whole new mysterious spin of his life: 3,000 miles from where he has grown up; going to a city he does not know; the possibility of living alone in a place where he has no friends. He is weeping for Diego the young-man-now-gone running along Angelito beach, kicking at the emerald waves, filled with the joy of being alive, racing the hot sands. His soul tells him to mourn Diego past. He does so until his grief turns to the quiet of a quiet, soulful night.

❧ ❧ ❧

We leave before dawn, and as we speed towards Tijuana the sun nudges the mountains behind us, frames the desert hills in shadows curled from sable to chiaroscuro to dark pearl, then indigo. The hills on each side of us rise pyramids sharp in the heliotrope that is the desert sky. Round cacti stud the sides of the hills, green drops on dry conicals. The colors around us are such that we are no longer driving the desert — but, rather, floating a few meters above the endless face of it, winding between great sharp grey hills born out of the universe. Past Mexicali, we ascend in hairpin between coralline boulders, giants' heads poised at the edge, rounded against the skies. "One of these boulders could swoop down and squash us flat and roll on to its ultimate destination, none the worse for wear," I think. Round beasts, as tall as a two-story house, edged along the side of the road, the road a black strip that squirms to get us above them, into the flat highlands of El Cóndor. At certain twists in the road, we can not only see where we will be, but where we think we have been. The road bands narrowly in the face of a brightening sun.

This is Highway Two, the escape route of Mexico, Central and South America. I think of the thousands of people who have passed this lordly beauty which is the Sonoran Desert and the Rumorosa Mountains. I see them, streaming along this road, day and night, year in, year out: the hopeful young of Michoacan or Sonora; the *abuelitas* of San Salvador and Guatemala; the men of Tuxtla, Gutierrez; the mothers, nursing their babes, coming from Las Toronjas, Nueva Palestina, Libertad el Panajal. They all pass this way, have done so, will do so for many years. This is the path to freedom, no less than for those who came through Ellis Island, journeying to escape poverty, to come into a world free of past hopelessness and bondage — escaping dictatorships, persecution, the deadend autocracies of Central Europe, the militarists. Crowded busses passing through the Mexican panhandle are making a similar pilgrimage, a pilgrimage no more nor less hopeful.

It is estimated that 3,000 people journey through here every day: northwards from the mountains and valleys of the altaplano. They come to the jumping-off point, the last miles towards the border: beyond to the great golden grid known, merely, as "Los." 20,000 people a week, 80,000 a month, filling the rooms and streets and alleys of the upper western Baja borderlands, waiting for the nightly jump through the San Ysidro Hills, into Chula Vista, National City, San Diego — and from there into the whirlpool which is Our Lady of the Angels.

They come from all points south, and the destination, the last one before the dangers of the border, is Tijuana. Tijuana — the city long known to all the Americas as the passion-pit of the west — known internationally for lewd ladies on the boards of the gin-mills, bevys of whores plying Avenida Revolucion, the place, as Ernest had it, "where you could get anything you wanted — if you were willing to pay. In dollars." (Until recently, the Mexican peso did not exist in Tijuana: it was strictly on the American plan.)

Like most truths, the titillating tales of Tijuana had a life of their own, somewhat at variance with reality. The tourist areas, after all, had been hacked out of the city not through the built-in moral depravity of Mexicans, but because the Mexican conscience never did stir as fearsomely to the evils of lust as in Puritan America across the border.

Tijuana was but the negative plate of the condensor, responding to the power grid looming in from the North. It was another "landmark for hungry Americans" through no especial fault of those who lived there. It was geography, and the endless need of gringos to get their rocks off, that made Tijuana "Sin City." It was born of a need of the dry moralists to the north to hide their passions in a place more open and accepting. It was no accident that the word for the red light districts south of the border was always "Boystown."

There was and is another Tijuana, the one that few Americans see. It is rumored to be dangerous, lawless, wild — a place where Americans can get mugged and beaten. That too is a myth. To those who know it, the streets of Houston, Miami, Washington, Los Angeles are far more perilous to life and limb than Tijuana. I once asked some friends who live in one of the poorest *barrios* south of the border — they survive in windowless shacks with no electricity, no water, no sewage — about crime, guns, robberies. They shook their heads. What were we talking about? The only crimes they were familiar with were those they had seen on the television programs coming in from the north.

The city Tijuana I speak of is the New York of a century ago: Hell's Kitchen, Brooklyn, the Lower East Side. It is a place filled with bounteous multicultures, as rich a mix as those that ever existed in the time and place of Tammany. In the valleys, up the sides of its dusty hills, toenailed into sharp declines, are whole cultures drawn from the Southern isthmus and the subcontinent. In Canyon Verde, the neighborhood is inhabited by people from Chichen Itza, and each block represents its own village. In Laureles, the people of Chiapas predominate. In Mira Mesa, it's the Oaxaquenos. In La Paloma, the towns of Sinaloa have their own cluster of shacks. Las Brisas is filled with those from the hills of Veracruz — people who have brought with them their lives, customs, belongings, music, ways, and special language. The foods of Campeche, the vegetables of Guatemala, the sweet dishes of the hills of Costa Rica, the woven baskets from the mountains of Nicaragua: all have a home here in this most singular melting pot at the unnatural confluence of the Pacific and the Tijuana River, the only wild card — the big draw — being the border between two great countries.

Melting pot! That's what they always called San Francisco and New York. Like those two, Tijuna has become the product of the thousand variables of a thousand cultures that have settled there. It has the cosmopolitan air of a city that is willing — as its predecessors were — to accept all peoples and races and languages, to leave them to their own individual stamp. Like the great Yankee ports at the cusp of the 20th Century, Tijuana can be corrupt and vicious, a place of hardship and cruelty and greed. At the same time, it shares with its heirs to the north that noisy blend of separate accents, rich habits, diverse customs, distinctive lifestyles — the meld of a million different natives of hundreds of different Latino worlds.

I have spent years exploring the canyons and river floors and hillsides of Tijuana — hillsides where plywood and rebar combine with vigorous colors (called, variously, Tijuana Pink, Tijuana Green, and Tijuana Blue), to make *colonias* filled with the most original housing. Rather than being confusing and depressing, this do-it-yourself building encompasses variety and originality in design and execution which gives it a warmth and humanness so far beyond any of America's rigorously zoned corpseyards called "suburbs." The streets are filled with life; each tiny house can be a store or place to take in laundry, to do repair, to clean, mend, cook, fix. Automobile tires are used for steps, crates for outhouses, hard beaten earth for floors, any available material for ceiling or wall. I once saw a dozen fine blue-and-white Coldwell-Banker signs — a large real estate combine north of the border — making up the sides and roof of a shack in Rosarito.

Most of these homes have no water, no electricity, no sewage. "The Calcutta of the Americas," some have called it; but like Calcutta, amidst the poverty and garbage are children everywhere, and dogs and chickens and people, people of every possible hue, every culture, people grappling with an inhospitable land but, in all the poverty, a ceremony, an individuality, a life — a rich life of the streets and interaction of neighbors that is so alien in those prim and sanitary cities to the north.

Tijuana, scorned by so many for so long, yet a place filled with a life that was once the sole province of other, grander cities with their great oceans and bays. In its barren, gullied, tiny plots of hillside — a parody of those individual housing tracts to the north — live people who are a blend of the conquistadores, and the Indians, and even, they say, the patient ones that came from the furtherest lands, far across the ocean, making their way across the straits, then down: a flow of humanity as great as has ever been seen on the face of the earth.

Tijuana, the center of mock-passion, the butt-end of jokes of countless sailors and military folk, the sexual training ground for so many pale-faces from across the border, the *situs* where bordello and saloon and seamy street life were mixed into high camp, is now the unlikely capital of a different kind of passion. Tijuana — corrupt, scheming, dirty, vulgar and obscene is, as well, an *olla podrida* of the engaging, energetic, raucous, exuberant, hopeful, diligent, mostly kind, open, willing and alive peoples from far to the south. It is right that

Tijuana be seen merely for its vulgar past, for after all, the owl of Minerva flies only at dusk. When some wise historian writes the history of the two countries, Tijuana will loom large, a rich conglomerate of blending cultures, a history that has lived in the underground for the last hundred years.

FINAL DAY [EL CÓNDOR]

Harke! the ravenne flaps hys wynge,
In the briered delle belowe;
Harke! the dethe-owle loude do the synge,
To the nyght-mares as theie goe;
Mie love ys dedde
Gone to hys dethe-bedde,
al under the wyllowe tree.

— ALEXANDER POPE

As we drive the last miles, I think on the pilgrims who have preceded us, and those who will follow. Some of them will look out, as we have, to see the great mysterious peaks of the Sonoran Desert at sunrise. They might be moved, as we were, by the boulders of the Rumoroso; like us, they may wonder at the singular violence of geology that extruded a rich crop of stones which, in a million years of rains, have turned rounded and golden.

All of those who come on this journey may be passing through the *Via Doloroso*, the highway paved with hope and fear. It is, as well, one rich with timelessness, born of these golden boulders cast out of time. With the countless tiny crosses at the side of the road, we know, too, that some of the wayfarers have left part of their beings among the stones.

❧ ❧ ❧

Father Zeta is a favorite in the village. He never smiles. He is a very serious drunken priest. He is also heavy with the weight of his office. Fortunately his priest's cassock is large and hides the pain of his body. They say he likes taking confession from the women because they talk about their husbands, and the secrets of the village. He doesn't like the confessions of the husbands, because they only talk about their jobs and their fights with their wives. One of the most interesting women, Doña Hortensia of the long face and sad eyes, is said to be so specific about the physical sins of her and her randy husband that Fr. Zeta spends an hour in the confessional with her every Saturday morning — from which he exits heavy with sweat, his eyes dark and baleful. That's when he goes to the parish house for the first *vino* of the day. At the biennial fiesta in La Alma, he is known for helping with the drinks. But he never carouses: he just falls asleep.

He mutters to me in Latin, waving the pudgy fingers over my head, then sits down heavily next to me. His eyes are phlegmatic behind the thick rimless glasses. He is strong with the incense of sweat and fatigue.

"Don Ignacio," he says, loudly, "I understand that you were born of the faith so I am here to ask if you would like to confess and take the Body of Christ." I want to tell him that in my family the Kaddish and the Missa Domine fought constantly, and neither won, but I bow my head and permit him to work his miracles on me. I read somewhere, "Don't mock any man's god, if it leads him to humility, love, or peace."

Father Zeda adjusts his dress — then starts to intone, his mouth scarcely moving, *Asperges me, Domine, hyssopo, et nundabor.* He makes the sign of the cross over me and leans forward, stuffing a wafer between my lips so quickly that I am sputtering — so unexpected it is — and whispers, without moving his lips, "Eat it. It has an analgesic in it. When they tie you up, the horsemen will save you. You'll not see them until they are before you. They'll take you off. Do everything you are told to do.'' I look away, feeling nausea in the smell of his breath. I hide the wafer, barely chewed, in my hand. He rises, makes the sign of the cross over me, and says loudly, *Ut turpiter atrum Desinat in piscem mulier formosa superne*, and bangs his way out the door. And thus my rites are at an end.

❧ ❧ ❧

When the sun of La Alma rises, it pauses at the edge — then suddenly throws itself up over the escarpment. All goes from black to grey, then to arsenical green. Mourning doves in the cells above turn quiet as the blood tumor spills out of the corners of the mountain into the cell. There is a sullen alien brightness that burns the sky to light.

''Can the sun compose a minuet?'' That was a question I read, once, long ago. At the time, I thought it an arrogant question. Now, I am more willing to entertain such a thought. ''Of course,'' was the response I read: ''the sun has already composed a minuet — thousands, perhaps millions of them. It is just that we haven't invented the machinery to hear them, so we can dance to them.''

''When we look into the heart of the sun,'' I think, ''we are looking into the most private — perhaps the most private — part of ourselves.'' One must always look indirectly, so as not to ruin the vision. We learn to reflect its brightness onto something else — a piece of paper, a canvas, a score — so that we can spy on the flames without being harmed ourselves.

''Since we grew from the sun, it contains all the elements of all of us,'' I think. ''It is alive, filled with thoughts, angers, rages, hopes, dreams — just like us. It is capable of being sad, maybe thoughtful, perhaps artistic and funny, even silly — like all mankind. No wonder so many of our forebears worshipped it as god. It is the *deus*, just as we are."

As I watch, it moves past the obscuring edge of the horizon and the heat begins to vaporize the dew, dispel the coolness. The globe turns familiar, and thoughts, knowledge — the fatal wisdom — begin a circular journey across the sky. "How strange that it is there above us, all of our lives, and we never even think about it. The single most salient part of our being, burning brightly, searingly — the highest part of ourselves — and we pretend it is a mere commonplace."

I had once read that the sun is isolated by 6,000,000,000,000 miles of black and cold space from its nearest neighbor, Alpha Centuri. Because of its isolation, it is impossible for it to reflect on itself. If it is indeed a sentient being (and I believe it with all my heart), it still impossible for the sun to recognize any other but itself. "The sun is not like the rest of us," I think. "If it were not so isolated, it could (at the very least) love the shadows. But isolation has delivered it from such a fate." I wonder if it could do the same for us.

❧ ❧ ❧

They sit me on a grey donkey that takes me down the rocky path from the prison and up the bare stone trail of La Montaña de los Siete Heridos. I sit uneasily on the beast, hands tied behind my back, blasted by the sun now brilliant and cruel. The shadows limn the dust — my own, those of the soldiers on either side of the road; soldiers in uniforms, their belts heavy with bullets, their thin rifles awkward on their shoulders. My shade bounds over the dusty rocks and pebbles. There is a smell of burning garbage in the air. There are flattened and twisted Cercis trees along the side of the road.

Ahead of us rides Don Blanco, and the military adjutant for this region, Captain Amado — pale, fat, sweating. Señor Iglesia is there, as is the thin, angular mayor, Placido. Soldiers line the road as far as the eye can see. Our journey takes us over the saddleback, the narrow bone ridge of roadway between prison and parade ground. Behind the soldiers stand a mass of dark-faced, dark-eyed, black-haired Chinatecs from the mountains. They intone prayers in a soft language I can scarcely hear and do not understand. The muttering of their holy words are like waves come up to the beach, rising up to expire, then falling back for the next rising.

In front of the power station, several of the women try to push through the line of soldiers, but the men force them back with their rifles. Further on, near the *Panteon*, a crowd of boys breaks through, several of them grabbing at my feet, trying to kiss them. They retreat as the soldiers hit at them with the hard wooden butts. Their crying out seems distant to me but still makes me grieve that I should be causing pain to those who may not yet know the sanctifying power of pain. The soldiers twist their mouths with the effort of beating back the crowd. One of the boys has his hands raised, and he's calling out, *"Pobre mi dios."* It is Mundo. They drive him down into the dust with their blows.

"The purest act of all," I think, "is to convince the world that we are all divines — not just any one of us." *The gods have not yet been born.* I remember the twelve just men who pursued their lives as quietly as they were able, denying their holiness at every turn, protecting themselves from anyone who might make such an accusation. "Who me? A holy being?" they would say. "Me? Are you mad? Please don't say that. It's a terrible blasphemy." They know that humans will tear, murder, and brutalize each other in the name of god.

As we get closer to the cathedral, the crowds get larger. They surge back and forth, ramming into the line of soldiers, then being hurled back. People are tearing at each other, shoving, calling out. Their tramping feet raise clouds of dust that obscure the sun. At times, a mass of dark faces surges towards us—then falls back in waves, pushed back by the sweating soldiers. The battle takes place in silence. I hear their voices, but it is as if it were a distant river. The dark eyes of the people glisten in the sunlight, birds who have been trapped and are about to die.

I want to send a message forward to Don Blanco to stop the parade. I want him to permit me to address the crowd, so I can explain to them that I am not who they think I am. I will tell them everything — that all I have done I have done for me, for my blind vision of what I thought was love. I will announce that if they are looking for the works of gods, they are looking in the wrong place: that they would be better off to look into the souls of their neighbors — to pray with the woman next door whose drunken husband beats her ferociously every night, and yet she forgives him; to pay homage to the wide-eyed child who sells his body because he has lost both father and mother; to kneel down before the old crone who lives down the street and — on her miserly pension — feeds the beggars despite everyone's complaints of the noise and smell. They should ask forgiveness of the old soldier who was driven from the army because he refused, time and again, to shoot at the boys who came at him during the wars. "That's where real divinity lies," I will tell them. "I am just a miscreant, one who has finally come to honor the pain we bring each other in the name of love, sacred or profane. I may be going to my ultimate reward," I will say, "but even so, do not trust me. There are no gods in the world except the secret gods. Besides (and here, I will raise my voice, because I want them all to hear — the alcalde, the police, the Chief, even the soldiers guarding me), you must remember, if you learn nothing else here today, remember that life is but a dream of death."

At one point near the crest, Jesús breaks out under the police lines and runs up beside me, the waters of forgiveness running down his face. *"No te olvidaremos..."* he calls out. The curse of the ages for the world of men. "We won't forget you..." Before I can beg him not to say that, three of the soldiers corner him near the security building and hit him with their rifles. I can hear the crushing sound of wood against bone. The last vision I have is he trying to get his arms over his head, crying out for them to stop, please to stop, that he meant no harm by running to me. They are leaning over him, the butts of their guns rising and falling, as if they were threshing wheat.

❧ ❧ ❧

The guards have formed themselves into a rough circle before the wall at the edge of the square. Thousands of people stand in the porticos, on the balconies and the roofs of the dusty yellow buildings around us. They fill all the windows with their dark faces, peering at us from above the ramparts of their dun-colored cathedral. Even Saint Cecilia, whose visage is carved above the cathedral doorway, watches us.

At the edge of the square, there is a small platform. The donkey stops before it, and three soldiers pull me down to the ground. I can hear what I first thought to be the wind, but I realize is a sigh, coming from the crowd: a sigh of wonder and despair. The soldiers kick at me as I struggle to rise. One of them, a light-faced corporal with an aristocratic Iberian nose, calls me "*puto*" and "*malrincón*." "*Pinche puto, levántate*," he says. "Get up, you fucking queer." I roll about in the dust, trying to regain my balance, stagger up into the upright position.

At one point, the crowd surges forward near the platform where the alcalde and the chief justice and the military governor are sitting. The soldiers force them back. The voice of the crowd becomes the voice of the mistrals. It never stops, dying down to a moan, then rising in pitch and volume until it turns to a harmony of "O's" all about us. "Go away," I want to beg them. "I am not not what you think I am." But they give me no chance to speak.

Near the top of the wall, jutting out from it, are the statues of two birds. One is what appears to be a loon, with a long pointed beak and twisted neck. The other is a hawk, its eyes of hollowed gold. Both are frozen, beaks turned from each other, wings half-extended. Their bodies are covered with the droppings of pigeons that even now are perched on heads and shoulders, moving about, pacing back and forth, worrying the hot air. Three of the soldiers back me up to the wall, tie ropes about my wrists, and from there to the feet of the bird statues, stretching my arms out into a Vee. My body sags with the weight of it; my knees buckle and split apart, like those of a drunken old man.

Father Zeta breaks through the line, appears before me a moment. He whispers to me in Latin, makes the sign of the cross, and says *"No tienes miedo. Fernando venga dentro de un momento."* Don't be afraid. Fernando will arrive in a moment. *"Recuerda — seran trece caballos negros. Haces lo que se dicen."* There will be thirteen black horses; do whatever you're told.

I find myself panting like an eagle in the zoo, the sun burning straight down on me. "I hope they come," I tell myself, and then think, "No, no, they musn't, they musn't." The Chief taught me to ignore my body — and I am starting to worry it again. I think of the story of the

Chinese farmer of long ago who finally understood, after so long, why he was, what his life was. "Yesterday I watered the crops, fed the cows, watched the setting sun," he is reported to have said. "Last night I came to understand the reason for all existence. Today I water the crops, feed the cows, watched the setting sun."

Chief Blanco has given me a lesson in understanding, but it doesn't mean that I can obliviate the past. It is here with me, still sending the old messages of fear and loneliness. I treasure it working its original task of trying to protect me against something from which I need no protection.

I treasure even more what has come in its place. Father Zeta said that Fernando would be here soon enough to save me. I know it is not so. Fernando was invented by him to make it so I wouldn't suffer.

It is at this moment that I remember my dream from the previous night, the dream that came to me just before I rose for the last time. As I think on it, I can hear the guns being loaded, the bolts being driven home. The Master of the Fire Guard is looking around, all ready to say *"Ya,"* and *"Fuego." "Fuego!"* he will cry, and I will think of fire, the fires of suns — but it will be too late, for just as he is mouthing the sacred words, the dream will be washing over me again:

The gods have risen from the sea. The waters have subsided so the great ones can come up out of the darkness. Jesus and I are there. We have grown. We are huge figures, statues from the ancient times. Tears the size of whole lakes could cascade from our eyes.

Jesus is riding on my back, and as we start up the mountains, roots and branches catch at our legs and feet. A blackberry vine crosses me, leaves a dozen black-cherry drops frozen on my chest.

The beasts follow us, and Jesus begs me to hurry. He clutches at me, grasping me about the neck with his legs.

I hold on to his knees, the ankles riding in my ribs. I am laughing — laughing with my fears, laughing because he is with me, riding on my shoulders above the dark and twisted mountain, with its twisted plants.

When we reach the crest of the mountain, we can hear the beasts behind us, yelling for us to stop. Jesus begs me to hurry and so, for love of him, I unfold the great white wings, the ones I have never used before. At the edge of the cliff, I can feel them begin to beat, swirling dust around our feet. In the distance, I can see the twisted plants along the line that divides us from our fate.

I push from the cliff and we start to fall towards the water below. Suddenly, I am afraid, afraid of falling, afraid of dying. "I will die," I think. "I am afraid of dying," I blurt out. It is at that moment I remember the words I once read, the whispered message given before the battle, a god whispering to the frightened soldier, there in the campo, both armies massed — a message from so long ago, a message still as powerful now, a message that said, "If there is anything in the world that can be called sin — it has the name 'fear.' "

I pound at the air with my wings, and at the last moment we become a pure instrument of ascension, rising like flame, rising into the sky, leaving the water and the cursing monsters below us, the monsters screaming imprecations at us from the edge of the cliff.

"*Ay, qué bueno, Ignacio,*" Jesus whispers in my ear, arms around my neck. *"Qué bueno, mi amigo,"* he says. I feel the power surging in my shoulders, the wind full on our faces as I take us higher, away from those who came to destroy us. We can now feel the wind in our hair. *"Ten prisa, Ignacio,"* he whispers; "Hurry, Ignacio." We rise pure ascension far above the earth, into a sky that now turns more golden, the great full fields of clouds all about us, the fields and mountains below us more faint now.

Over at the edge of the horizon the sun, a great circle, rises with us, and it turns: peers at us with its huge, fat lids. It grows out of the turquoise sea, and, as it does so, it turns full on us. As it sees us, it stops. In a frozen moment, in its pause, it winks at us. A great big cool wink, just like it knew us — just like we were all old friends, rising together into the skies — the three of us, together, on fire, en fuego, *fuego.*

❧ ❧ ❧

Tecate is the last town between Tijuana and the border. Our passage is almost done. Before us there is a truck — one of the many noisy, overloaded, about-to-tip-over trucks, so ubiquitious to Mexico. It is heavy with flowers, thousands of carnations of a particularly delicate mauve. With each lurch of the truck, a few dozen of them sprinkle down before us onto the highway, circle about in its wake. Many trucks must have gone before us because the roadway and its edges are littered with hundreds of these mauve carnations. They roll merrily across the asphalt, come to rest in the center, and atop the weeds and trash at the side of the highway.

A floral highway. They are greeting us, aren't they? Those who have gone before are laying a carpet of flowers for those of us to follow. In the pearl light of the Cóndor Mesa, the golden mountains behind us, the fresh landscape: we're being glorified with blossoms out of our days.

"La vida es simple." That is what Chuy used to mutter to himself, stomping around the trailer on his great Oaxacan feet, him in his ragged blue bathing suit and dirty tee-shirt, shaking the trailer as he goes about, cleaning the windows, banging the doors, scrubbing the floor. Kind Chuy, with his high cheekbones, eyes filled with no visible delineation between pupil and iris. Chuy with his thin Mayan nose, a cranky gentleness that never permits real anger or violence. He stops and eyes me out of the blackness. "Carlos," he says, scratching his navel: "¿porque la vida es simple?" Why is life so simple.

I think for a minute. I'm not so sure. "La vida no es simple," I tell him, after a bit. "La vida es sueño." Life isn't simple. Life is a dream. "Ah," he says, his great expressionless face, peering at me from out the centuries. His black hair catches the sunlight; his head turns enflamed in gold. "¿Es la verdad?" he asks, "¿La vida es puro sueño?" Is it true, that life is but a dream? "Es cierto," I tell him. For sure.

He watches me a minute more, then stomps outside, down the stairs, out to water the Cercis plant growing there just beyond the door — the strange plant with its strange purple flowers hanging down almost to the ground, as if in mourning. "La vida is simple," I can hear him muttering, "No, no — la vida no es simple; la vida es sueño." My Oaxacan friend, scarcely the age of reason, already talking to himself about life, about the life of dreams, and the dream of life.

[1991]

The late Carlos Amantea was born in Savannah, Georgia and was educated at Harvard and at the Sorbonne. He lived most of his life in San Lorenzo, Honduras. His other work of fiction, *The Lourdes of Arizona,* is published in English by Mho & Mho Works, and, in Spanish, by Cuatros Vientos of Santiago, Chile.